Books by
CLIFFORD DOWDEY

BUGLES BLOW NO MORE
EXPERIMENT IN REBELLION
THE LAND THEY FOUGHT FOR
DEATH OF A NATION
LEE'S LAST CAMPAIGN
THE SEVEN DAYS
LEE
THE VIRGINIA DYNASTIES

Editor with Louis H. Manarin
THE WARTIME PAPERS OF R. E. LEE

The Virginia Dynasties

CLIFFORD DOWDEY

THE VIRGINIA DYNASTIES

The Emergence of "King" Carter and the Golden Age

Illustrated with photographs

LITTLE, BROWN AND COMPANY

Boston · Toronto

Published simultaneously in Canada
by Little, Brown & Company (Canada) Limited

PRINTED IN THE UNITED STATES OF AMERICA

Contents

Illustrations

x ILLUSTRATIONS

The Virginia Dynasties

Murder on Sunday Morning

THAT YEAR THE people were made uneasy by three ominous portents. First, every evening for a week a large comet appeared out of the southwest, streaming like a horse's tail across the sky until it nearly reached the horizon before settling into the northwest.

Then came pigeons in flights a quarter of a mile in breadth and "of their length was no visible end." At night when they settled in the forests, their weight broke great branches with a crashing, rending sound. The old planters said the like was seen the year of the last great Indian massacre, in 1644, and Thomas Mathew, the merchant-planter, said they were put under "Portentous Apprehensions." Despite the uneasiness, colonists with fowling pieces ran out in the darkness to shoot into the masses of pigeons, for hard times lay upon the land and food was scarce.

The third phenomenon was the appearance of swarms of flies about an inch long, as big as the tip of a man's little finger. They rose out of spigot holes in the earth and devoured the new leaves sprouting from the tops of the trees. Doing no other harm, in a month the flies disappeared. By then the settlers did not know what next to expect, as before the three "Prodigies" the countryside had been turned into a

swamp by the most torrential rains ever to flood the Colony and hail-
storms had pelted the people with pellets the size of small eggs. From
the frontiers at the head of tidewater in the big rivers came rumors of
Indian depredations, of restless movement among those tribes who had
not come in as dependents of the English.

Suddenly in the summer of 1675 the rumors became a reality,
arousing the settlers out of their brief respite from troubles with the
heathens.

Thomas Mathew was developing a second plantation in Stafford
County, the farthest from the settlement at Jamestown — a hundred
miles by the trails through the primeval forests and uncountable miles
by water. On a Sunday Mathew's overseer rode to the house of a
freedman named Robert Hen to talk to him about taking a job as
herdsman. The summer air was scented with the fragrance that rose
from the forest — the humus of fallen leaves and pine needles min-
gling with the freshness of leaves in full flowering, with the scents of
mushrooms and toadstools and the wild grapes that hung from heavy
vines encircling the trees.

As the overseer neared Hen's house, on the edge of a clearing
around a country church, families on their way to church were beginning to converge from all directions on woods paths and the crude
road. When the overseer rode into the clearing he noticed that some of
the churchgoers were gathered in front of a small dwelling, which he
took to be Hen's house. On reaching the doorway, the overseer saw
Hen lying across his threshold. He was bleeding to death from cuts on
his head that looked like hatchet blows. Several men were bending
over, asking him questions. With his last breath Hen murmured,
"Doegs."

An anger, born of all their apprehensions, rose in the Sunday-
dressed men and women who watched the white man die. Since the
settlers had begun to hack out their isolated clearings farther to the
west, there had been occasional collisions with the Doegs, whose
habitat covered that area of north-central Virginia. But the Doegs did
not have the fearsome reputation of some of the tribes and had never
taken part in the large-scale massacres aimed at extermination of the
English. Up until that Sunday morning, their menace lay chiefly in
their position in the chain of Indian communities which, reaching
from New England to Florida, populated the uncharted wilderness
beyond the fringe of settlements along the Atlantic coast.

In Virginia, the white intruders were scattered east of the "fall
line" — the head of tidal waters, navigable by oceangoing vessels —

on the four great rivers emptying into Chesapeake Bay. From the Potomac, near the site of the present city of Washington, south to the James at the present site of Richmond, the fall line would measure on a straight course one hundred miles. The Rappahannock flowed midway between these two rivers, the York between the Rappahannock and the James; and the longest land distance from the bay to the head of tidewater was less than a hundred miles. Criss-crossed by smaller rivers and creeks, and by bays and inlets near the coast, this was a semimaritime wilderness in which about forty thousand settlers lived on clearings so isolated that a European visitor said Virginia looked uninhabited.

By 1675 the Indians in this tidewater area had spent their powers for making war, largely in the great massacres of 1622 and 1644. Most of them existed as "tributary" tribes — under the protection of the English. Like tribes west of the fall line, the tidewater Indians lived in settled communities, with their own villages and forts and fortified towns. Their wigwams were built of wood; though crude affairs, they were actually houses, not tents. The Indians made use of window space, which could be covered by mats; they had louvres as smoke exits for their central fires; and the larger houses were partitioned by mats. The house of a "werewance" — either a chief or an emperor, ruler over chiefs — was a large affair with winding interior passages. The Indian temples, where the important dead were prepared for burial, could be more than 150 feet long, and contained hand-carved and hand-painted images of idols.

As with white nations, the tribes varied in their stages of civilization and power for war. The Doegs, who were not among the great tribes, had been having their troubles with the Susquehannocks. The Susquehannocks, of fierce reputation, were a very warlike people. Although they were not a large tribe numerically, the Susquehannock warriors were powerfully built and skillful fighters. Under a working agreement with the Maryland colony, the Susquehannocks had for some years acted as a buffer against approaches of the Senecas from the north. It was the custom of Indians in the middle states to roam up and down across the backcountry trading among themselves, and frequently a tribe killed a few white families in passing. By 1674, Maryland had so expanded that the colony, no longer needing the Susquehannocks, made a separate peace with the Senecas. The abandoned Susquehannocks, heavily outnumbered by the Senecas, retreated to the northern banks of the Potomac. There, sullen and restless, they began to disturb the Doegs.

Evidently in reaction the Doegs had turned their hostilities to the whites — although the churchgoers at Hen's simple home did not give any thought to such causes. Confirming their worst apprehensions, a war party had been bold enough to swoop out of the forest into a public clearing and murder a settler without provocation, even while his distant neighbors were approaching the church. In a group response, the men decided to go after the Indians right then.

The county militia was quickly mustered around its lieutenant colonel, John Washington. These county units were the only forces for maintaining law and order, including protection against Indian uprisings and attacks from England's enemies. When Colonel Washington's militia marched out of the clearing, the force was joined by frontier people carrying muskets, their powderhorns hung over their shoulders.

Following the Doegs, Colonel Washington ignored the treaty which forbade armed bodies to enter another colony's territory, and led the aroused settlers across the Potomac into Maryland. The Doegs had by then retired to the neighborhood of the Susquehannocks. In anticipation of the later aphorism "the only good Indian is a dead Indian," the Virginia force opened fire on Susquehannock and Doeg indiscriminately.

When the fighting grew general, the Maryland authorities, overlooking the violation of their border, hurried off militia to join the Virginians. Against that combined force, the Susquehannocks fell back to the west. It is not clear whether the Doegs gradually slipped away or stayed with the Susquehannocks during the flight. The pursuers referred to "Susquehannocks" when the Indians made a stand in a rude fort.

The earthen walls of the fort were enclosed by a ditch, outside of which trees were stuck in the ground and wattled together, leaving six-inch spaces as firing holes. While it would have been worthless against artillery, the fort was effective against the short-range fowling pieces of the militia. The white men laid an informal siege. When food ran low in the fort, the Susquehannocks sent out six chiefs to parley under a flag of truce. But in some kind of misunderstanding, the Indians were shot.

The Virginians blamed the Marylanders, and the Marylanders blamed the Virginians, especially Colonel John Washington. Militia Colonel Washington was the son of an English clergyman who had experienced difficulties with the Cromwellian Puritans, and at the age of about twenty-six, John had come to Virginia in 1657 as partner in a small trading ship. His first marriage to Anne Pope gave him a good start in the Colony through his father-in-law, and Washington had the education, vigor and shrewdness to advance his fortunes rapidly in the Northern Neck — the land between the Potomac and the Rappahannock rivers. Acquiring land and buildings, growing and shipping tobacco, by 1666 he was a justice of the county court, member of the vestry, representative in the House of Burgesses and lieutenant colonel of the militia. There was no color about this prudent, businesslike entrepreneur. But when he went after the Indians, he left at home a sixteen-year-old son, Lawrence, who was to be the grandfather of George Washington.

It was never established who was guilty of killing the Susquehannock chiefs. With this act of the white man's treachery, the Indians stole out of their fort at night and dispersed into small parties. The two militia forces began to lose their ardor as each day's tracking through the tangled green woods took them farther from their homes. Growing apprehensive about their families, with hostile savages on the loose, the men abandoned the pursuit and returned to their homes.

When winter settled on the countryside, making the isolation of the settlers' clearings complete, the Susquehannocks began ravaging the frontier. Bands swooped down on lonely dwellings and murdered the families. The settlers began to petition the royal governor for protection.

Most of these settlers were not such successful plantation operators as Colonel Washington or Thomas Mathew, who employed an overseer to direct other workers. Having come without education or money, the men hacked clearings out of the primeval forests on fifty-acre tracts and threw up crude one-and-a-half-room houses, the half-room upstairs for the children to come. They petitioned through their successful neighbors, representing them in the Burgesses, for the right to form armed bodies to take the war to the Indians.

Governor Sir William Berkeley, for an amalgam of complicated reasons, wished to avoid a war between the white men and the red men. By March of the following year, 1676, Berkeley admitted that at least thirty-six murders had been authenticated. Finally aroused, he ordered an expeditionary force to form. The Susquehannocks had their own ways of getting news and immediately made a peace offer. Since this was what the governor wanted, he called off the expedition and returned to planning more of the forts which had proved to be no help at all to the frontier settlers. By spring, only eleven of seventy-odd holdings along the north-central border were still occupied, and the settlers throughout the region began to ignore the prominent citizens who represented them at Jamestown. They began to talk of marching against the Indians without the governor's authority.

At this stage the repercussions from Hen's murder had aroused the settlers into a potential mob without a leader. When they found a leader in young Nathaniel Bacon, a patrician idler newly arrived from England, the mob swelled into a force composed of a cross section of colonists from all over Virginia and, with no one planning it, brought on the first revolution on the American continent. It was a curious rebellion, in which the leaders were transplanted English aristocrats. And that fight to the death on a colonial frontier had a curious result: from it grew, with other factors, a new ruling class in the New World — a native-born Virginia aristocracy.

2

No facet of American history has been the subject of more myths and countermyths than the *native* Virginia aristocracy. The colonial ruling class which developed in Virginia first became an aristocracy in the formal meaning of the word: "government . . . by a relatively privileged class or order . . . any form of government in which the ruling power is vested in a minority consisting, presumably, of those best qualified to rule." Extending from these, the definitions include "the ruling body of such a government."

In common usage the word "aristocrat" carries the implication of noble heritage, of a patrician way of life — of attitudes and manners, of values and privileges, even of physical appearance. An essential element for the aristocrat in the broader social sense is the leisure and the means by which tastes and sensibilities can be cultivated, and sometimes are. In this general definition the aristocrat is the product of time. Succeeding generations habituate themselves to the privileges secured by wealth, the influence based upon wealth, and the prestige produced by privilege and influence.

All aristocracies began with wealth and its concomitant powers, and the warrior knights who founded the early aristocratic families in England were pretty crude articles. They were the robber barons who formed an alliance in 1215 (Magna Carta) to assure their role of authority in government. There was nothing continuous about the original families of that aristocracy. The generic aristocracy was almost wiped out by the Wars of the Roses, and recruitment from among the commoners was constant and necessary for the nobility to maintain its vitality as a class. It was the class which, with steady infusions of fresh blood, was sustained, and families regarded as "distinguished" when Jamestown was settled had been simple yeomen three generations before.

By 1607 sufficient generations had passed for many English families to have undergone the transmutation from new wealth into aristocracy in both meanings of the word — power in the government and hereditary social prestige — along with the arrogance of position. It would be nonsense to imagine that the offspring of such families would journey three months on a scurvy-ridden ship to set up life in a wilderness infested by savage Indians and wild animals.

The myths of the Virginia "aristocrat" began when the personal attributes of the established English aristocracy were imputed to the men and women who ventured to Virginia and, in building a colonial ruling class, founded an aristocracy of their own. In time the social attributes associated with an aristocracy would be developed, along with a graceful and elegant style of life which characterized the society. But this was the evolution of a colonial order founded by ambitious emigrants whose traits are not usually associated with the "aristocrat" in the social meaning: tight-fistedly acquisitive, ruthless and resourceful, they were driven by an exhaustive energy which left no long-livers among them. They came to better their fortunes in a new land and, by circumstance and coalescence, at first formed an aristocracy only in the formal meaning of government by a few.

The myths which imputed socially aristocratic backgrounds to these successful builders of private empires were based largely upon another myth, that of "the younger sons." The younger-son myth implied descent from a noble house. In England, at all social levels above the landless working classes, the majority of the male population was composed of younger sons — younger sons of younger sons, extending back for generations beyond recollection or record. In the English laws of primogeniture, the land was entailed intact in each generation to the firstborn son, whether the land was a small parcel held by a yeoman family doing its own work, a large tract held by a country gentleman who engaged others to work, or one of the vast manors whose tenants provided a nobleman with his splendid luxuries. Statistically, for every male whose family owned any amount of land whatsoever — and England was a rural country — it was hard not to be a younger son or of a branch of younger sons.

Younger sons — in the sense of men without land in an agricultural society — increasingly went into the army, the clergy, and law;

they went into trade in streams, becoming merchants in the city; some earned the money to acquire land of their own and begin primogeniture all over again. Governor Sir William Berkeley was of a younger-son line that long in the past had branched off from the Berkeleys of Berkeley Castle, outside Bristol. By his father's generation this line had risen: Sir William was knighted and his brother ascended into the peerage as a lord.

Among the ambitious men who succeeded in Virginia, there was no record of connection with the nobility. Richard Lee I, one of the first of the empire-builders, came of a younger line which had branched off from modest landholders and was now established in London as merchants. Dispelling all questions about his status, Lee identified himself as a "merchant trading in Virginia." John Carter, one of the greatest dynasty-founders on the continent, most probably came from a family of London vintners, also a younger branch earlier uprooted from the land.

The myth associating noble connections with younger sons was buttressed by the ever present coat of arms which, like some magical tribal token, was assumed to imply patrician ancestors. Every first-generation founder of an aristocratic line in Virginia prominently displayed a coat of arms, as authentication of his English status prior to his colonial position. In point of fact, in the eighty years before 1640 the College of Heralds granted upward of four thousand new claims for coats of arms. They went to almost any person who possessed or had acquired enough land to substantiate a claim. William Shakespeare, the son of a yeoman, was granted a coat of arms after he acquired land with money earned in play-acting. What a coat of arms chiefly established — if it was not spurious, as countless were — was that a family possessed or had once possessed land in a nation where the "land," "the county," "the country," was associated with the peculiar mystique of England. Except for the nobility, themselves of the land, no status had the aura of "county family."

However, county families, whether small or large in the scale of things, were constantly coming and going. Some grew richer and some of these ascended into the nobility. In only forty years before 1641 there were nearly one hundred new creations in the peerage, as newly invented titles transformed commoners into aristocrats. Other county families drifted into obscurity, disappearing from their known haunts, and new families with substantial holdings surged forward to take their place in the gentry.

As the myths fail to suggest, the England from which emigrants came to Virginia was anything but static. It was a time of restless mobility. Vestigial elements of the Middle Ages, with feudal practices which had carried over into the early Tudor periods, had begun to pass in Elizabeth's time. Her great reign saw the rise of the country gentry in the late sixteenth century as the coming power in England. Simultaneously with the settling period of Virginia, industries began to grow and there came the rush in the expansion of trade that was to push England into the forefront as a mercantile nation.

The fall of old fortunes, the rise of new fortunes coming in on the tides of change, and the continual shifting of families' positions produced a yeasty ferment within the existing order. In the fluidity within the stratification, the goal was to climb up the hierarchical ladder.

Outside the cities, the first rung on the ladder was the yeomanry. There is today no equivalent of the English yeomanry. In ancient times the backbone of England's famed infantry, the yeomanry, by the seventeenth century, formed what then seemed a permanent segment in the traditional agricultural life. They were holders of land, usually small holdings, under various complicated legal systems which had extended with modifications from the Middle Ages. Some owned their land outright by purchase, as land is owned today, and others occupied land by a system of leases (usually long-term and often hereditary) which made the holdings, in effect, theirs by tenure. Sometimes only a token rent was paid. Except for his defined status in the legal stratifications in English society, the average yeoman would be most nearly like the independent small farmer of the old America.

In England, however, identification by status was an integral element in the social structure. The law required men to identify themselves by "degree, estate, and mystery" — as type of artisan, as yeoman, as gentleman, and so on. Shakespeare, terming degree "the ladder to all high designs," wrote: "Take but degree away, untune that string, and, hark, what discord follows." By degree, the yeoman stood above the landless agricultural worker and below the gentry. He would not be addressed as "Mr." nor his wife as "Mrs."

Within this degree, yeoman families varied in condition from those barely hanging on by doing their own work to those of modest wealth who, like farmers in the old America, hired helpers. But essentially they were workers of their own land. When a resourcefully enterprising yeoman continued to expand his holdings and to bring shrewdness to trading, he could earn the means to build a good house, establish a system of tenant-workers and, by his new estate, change his degree to "gentleman."

While everybody differed on what a gentleman was, everybody knew what a gentleman was not: he did not work with his hands. One of the ancient definitions was that one "who can live idly and without manual labor, and will bear the port [deportment], charge and countenance of a gentleman, he shall be . . . taken for a gentleman." An old saying ran that "gentility is nothing but ancient riches." This could not apply strictly to the minor gentry, into which a yeoman ascended when he had the means to live like the gentry. Usually he then acquired a coat of arms, as something like a certificate of his new degree. When merchants and professional men in London acquired estates with the money earned in the city, they passed into or returned to the landed gentry.

During the first decades of Virginia's colonization, the yeomanry and gentry were shifting with almost revolutionary change. Rising prices since Elizabeth's reign, with the growth in industry and dynamic expansion of trade, sent land prices up, and the ancient rhythms were broken by speculators moving into the land market and operators bringing in new methods of large-scale farming. Those landlords stuck with ancient leases felt the pinch in cash, while those landlords whose tenants held no tenure bore down hard to get higher returns on their land. Men of the land became also men of business. In the trend toward combining holdings, the shrewd entrepreneurs grew larger and the unadaptive became dispossessed.

While some distinguished families, descended from the warrior knights, fell from position through extravagance and lack of adaptiveness to the changing England, the casualties were heaviest among those with little. Yeomen of small holdings were displaced by "modern" methods, and agricultural workers were uprooted from their hovel-like "cottages." Some of the dispossessed drifted into the cities, others swelled the ranks of vagrants roaming the countryside. Outlawry became common and so did hangings (a rough expedient for decreasing unemployment), and heavy punishments were meted out for minor offenses.

In this dislocation, the gentry was the class to be continually strengthened. While some of the country gentry ascended into the peerage and others vanished, the class as a whole grew in numbers, in wealth and in influence. The core of the successful businesslike farming gentry among the country families benefited from the accretion of energetic, practical-minded former yeomen and eminent merchants and educated professional men. The newly wealthy farmers might be wanting in the graces, but tone was sustained in the surgent class by those successful men from the city who themselves derived from landed county families or had received similar educations and moved with the same society. In this interchange, the younger son of the younger son of a duke and the newly tailored son of a shrewdly acquisitive farmer could meet at the home of a prosperous, old-line county gentleman — the "squire," who was privileged in his degree to sign himself "Esq."

With a minor gentry and a larger gentry, the gentry as a whole formed a political power that was to dominate the House of Commons. With their rise it could be said, "Spain was ruled by priests, France by kings, and England by gentlemen." Henry Peacham's *The Complete Gentleman* (1622) and Richard Braithwaite's *The English Gentleman* (1633) became standards among the books published to confirm the gentry's sense of importance and to offer guidance to the newcomers.

This country gentry, not the nobility, was the class which formed the model for the emigrants who succeeded in the Virginia Colony. They came with dual drives: to rise in the Colony along the commercial patterns dominant in England, and to attain the desirable estate of country gentry.

Those who founded the biggest fortunes and established the most famous dynasties were distinctly not country gentlemen when they came, nor were their immediate families established as county families. On the other hand, this should not imply — as the antimyths have — that the successful emigrants were disadvantaged people "of the meaner sort." All who rose swiftly to high place came with some money, some education, and some connections. These advantages would not have been sufficient for the individual to make a spectacular advance in England. In a frontier community, they gave an incalculable advantage among settlers of whom most had neither money nor connections, and few had any education.

3

While the adventure to Virginia offered those with some advantages the opportunities to partake of the upward thrust of the age, the Colony provided even the landless casuals an escape from the desperate conditions at home and an opportunity to create a better life than could be expected in England. To this extent, the majority of the colonists came to the New World wilderness with fundamentally the same motivation.

They came under the impact of the Renaissance, with its awakening sense of the individual, of personal responsibility for self in this world and the next. They were the "restless, pushing material" who took the hazard of looking after their own destinies by adventuring to a New World. When those who made the big successes rose in this community — within the social order brought from England — there was no fixed class in the Colony. As on any new frontier, the first to win riches and influence arrived within one generation at the top of the ladder. The difference from any frontier was that in Virginia the first families to win position laid the framework of a ruling *order*, which the second and third generations evolved into a ruling class, or aristocracy.

The colonial aristocracy in Virginia was able to emerge so suddenly, as if full-blown, because of the completeness with which Virginia society functioned as an extension of the England of the Establishment. There were no dissenters among Virginia's colonial leaders — political, social or religious. The Church of England itself served not only as a foundation of the Establishment but as a line of continuity of the aristocratic concept in the New World.

The English aristocracy, as a truly *ruling* class, was different from the Continental aristocracies, where the members of the nobility were often disassociated from government. In France, adorned by the most elegant of aristocracies, the nobility gyrated around the court in total separation from the *canaille*. Since the English aristocracy, the most powerful in the world, was associated with government rather than court life, the Virginians graduated into a colonial version of the existing aristocratic order with which they were familiar. They were not required to adapt themselves to personal modes of life foreign to their backgrounds; nor did anything in the home models require the individuals to cultivate an unfamiliar style of living.

The English country gentry was neither small nor select — it numbered approximately fifteen thousand heads of families, of whom three thousand carried the honorary title of "esquire" — and was not generally distingushed by refinements of the sensibilities, fastidiousness or cultivation of the mind. A rural people centered at the manor, the country gentry (like, indeed, the peers) were distinguished by hearty eating and drinking, boisterousness, lewdness and rough humor. Their chief pleasures were those the colonists found among the Indians — chasing and killing animals. While many enjoyed pleasures of the mind, by their natures they were not set apart from the run of humanity. Essentially they were active people. They were active in politics and were strengthening their traditional control of local affairs. By and large, they did hold one ideal — the Renaissance ideal of the whole man, "the *complete* gentleman."

In following this model, the successful emigrants in Virginia naturally adapted the details to their environment and condition. The scarcity of women, the absence of urban centers and the distances between holdings gave little opportunity for lewdness. The hard work and unremitting effort necessary to carve a personal domain out of the wilderness allowed little time for any pleasure. For a certainty this scanty leisure time was not spent in chasing animals in a country where men had to go armed because of wolves and bears and poisonous snakes. In the loneliness of their isolated holdings, the planters found their greatest pleasure in visiting distant friends and exchanging gossip over a mug. To those in government the semiannual trips to the capital at Jamestown were welcome changes. Since they were new to their position, most worked diligently at cultivating their minds, and books were important items in cargoes coming from England.

The big ones lived and worked with one fundamental difference from the typical English country gentry: they were merchants and traders as well as agriculturists. Their plantations, based upon the one money crop of tobacco, were all situated on tidal rivers, and their private wharves were shipping centers for their complicated trading operations. They shipped out tobacco and imported, along with their own needs, goods for the small settlers who paid in tobacco. They were clothiers, hardware merchants and sometimes slave dealers. In this fashion, they combined the new commercialism of their age with traditional agriculture: on the model of the country gentlemen as men of business, on the practicalities of handling the riches of tobacco on a dangerous frontier, they emerged as a new phenomenon in world trade — the merchant-planter, "the Virginia planter."

In their lives the fortune-founders combined forms of the traditional society they had brought to the Colony with adaptiveness to the New World as they found it. The traditionalism, not formalized or articulated, formed the framework of values, attitudes, institutions — especially in the English social hierarchy. In adapting to the geography and climate, to conditions and opportunities unique to the frontier, the emigrants neither consciously tried to preserve the traditional nor consciously introduced the new: by a day-to-day pragmatism they evolved a new type of man.

These men and women were not characterized by sensitivity. With little shading and nuance, the builders of personal empires were people of primary colors. While as individuals they had their own apparent contradictions, they were not complex. The successful rose above the average by the higher demands they made upon themselves in exploiting their initial advantages. In these higher demands — self-discipline and the management of energy in working through a complex of operations toward their large-scale aspirations — they achieved a different quality of individual, a different "class" of men, by personal attainment. When the individuals gravitated to a center of power, they became a "qualified minority," fitting the formal definition of aristocracy.

The rise of these fortune-founders into places of consequence has been steadfastly ignored in all myths. As, of all things, an aristocracy must appear to be hereditary, Virginians adopted the attitude prevailing in England, where, it was said, "arrangements existed which were intended to make it easier for the noble family to give the impression that it had always existed." The most beguiling myth to cover the obscure beginnings of the founders of the aristocracy was that of the "cavaliers." Pictured as elegant members of the nobility, during Cromwell's reign they supposedly sought sanctuary in Virginia in droves.

"Cavalier" was a derisive name for Royalist supporters in the civil wars (1642–1649) between the adherents of the Stuart king, Charles I, and the Parliamentary forces which came to be led by Oliver Cromwell — a conflict which was in no sense a class struggle. As in any civil war the causes were complex; alliances were formed across all class lines and arose from mixed motivations; and in the English civil wars politics were entangled with religion. Among the King's opponents were a strong strain of religious Dissenters, which included zealous Puritan elements.

Including the religious elements, the struggle was fundamentally between the absolute authority of the King and the assertive power in Parliament, particularly the House of Commons. In the showdown, 80 peers and 175 members of the House of Commons supported the King; 30 peers and 300 members of the House of Commons supported his enemies. Oliver Cromwell himself was of the country gentry and some of England's greatest families followed him. The merchants, lawyers and tradesmen in the City of London, then separated physically from the King's demesne at Westminster, heavily favored the Parliamentary forces and held the capital for Cromwell. On the other side, where the King's followers were defending the Establishment, Charles I drew heavily from the minor gentry and the decidedly nonaristocratic elements in the north and west of England.

Perhaps because the businessmen of the city were identified with the Cromwellian forces, while the majority of the landed peers and country squires followed the King, and because Cromwell's reign (1649–1659) was characterized by grim Puritan repressions in contrast to the color and bawdy gaiety that came with the restoration of Charles II — because of the aura inherent in a king — the Royalist forces became the romantic side. Having lost in the civil war, with their chivalrous Prince Ruperts, to the efficient organization of Cromwell's modern-style army, the Royalists emerged in the prodigality of the Stuart Restoration as the men of gallantry.

Some of the gallants among the Royalists — the "cavaliers" of the legend — did come to Virginia. They came in clothes that seemed rakishly elegant on the frontier. Their large hats with curling brims were sometimes decorated with plumes, they wore deep ruffled collars and flowing sleeves, and there was a truly lordly carelessness in their boots with the wide tops flopping below the knees.

Their numbers are not known. Colonel Henry Norwood, a Royalist officer, visited Ralph Wormeley's hospitable Virginia home, where he found several of his intimate acquaintances "that had lately come from England . . . feasting and carousing." Francis Nicholson, a colonial governor in the latter part of the century, complained that all the young heiresses had been married either to natives or to "men of parts" among the gentleman-Royalist refugees, who had been welcomed by the Virginia planters for their style and position. William Byrd I, among others, was considered to have taken a giant social step upward when he married the daughter of a Royalist officer, exiled in Virginia, who unmistakably belonged in the "cavalier" tradition of the wellborn.

Later, the antimythists denied that the "cavaliers" of the legend had come in sufficient numbers to have exerted any social influence among the families of the newly weálthy merchant-planters. Whatever the unmeasurable extent of the influence of the Royalist gallants in Virginia, their effect was considerable in the development of later attitudes which grew from acceptance of the legend. The coming of the "cavaliers" in a formative stage of the Colony gave color to Virginia's unquestionably Royalist sympathies and made it dramatically fitting to attribute a "cavalier" background to the early fortune-founders who were in Virginia during the interregnum of Cromwell.

Even eminent historians fall back on the "probability" of Royalist exile when in doubt about the origins of the first aristocrats.

Unfortunately for romance, the records show that the first generation of the dynasty-founders were in Virginia before the civil wars. Richard Lee, Benjamin Harrison, the first Randolph, the Thomas Stegg (or Stegge) who founded the Byrd wealth at his store and trading post — all were established in Virginia by 1642, as was John Carter, whom recently uncovered records show to have purchased land while he was in Jamestown in 1642.

It was John Carter's younger son Robert, child of his father's old age, who became the archetype of the Virginia aristocrat in the complete meaning of that word. Both the biggest merchant and the biggest planter of his day, he was shipper and boatbuilder, stockman and store-owner, moneylender and investor, and the largest robber baron of his time in acquiring land. The richest man in Virginia, probably in the colonies, he was also the most powerful politically: as president of the appointive King's Council, for one period he served as acting governor.

Out of a strong love of learning and of the Anglican Church in Virginia (he built the magnificent Christ Church for his parish at his own expense), Robert Carter imparted to his sons and daughters his own deep convictions of the virtues necessary for the estate of Christian gentleman and gentlewoman. His children married into the most consequential families of their day, were among the first builders of manorial "seats," and — a rare occurrence among the families of dynasty-founders — his descendants still occupy two of the manor houses. Among his descendants were two signers of the Declaration of Independence, two Presidents of the United States, a Chief Justice, and a number of governors of Virginia, and Robert Edward Lee — in whom the strain of his great-great-grandfather was still dominant in the fourth generation.

This archetypal figure, who would be called "King," was a thirteen-year-old orphan with thin prospects when the revolution broke out in 1676. The fourteen years in which he grew to maturity coincided with the changes in Virginia which, following the revolution, opened the way for a homegrown ruling class, a native aristocracy. Robert ("King") Carter came into his estate simultaneously with the beginning of the new era, the era which emerged, during the next forty years of his life, into the "golden age."

Of a cross-generation, younger than the second generation of dynasty-founders and older than the third, crossing both in his span of nearly forty years as a colonial power, "King" Carter appeared at precisely the one moment in history suited to — as if waiting for — his particular amalgam of talents. As to the old question of whether the man produced the age or the age produced the man, Robert Carter definitely did not create the age. He personified the germinal era during which the solidification of the ruling class in power brought forth the emergence of the "golden age," — the age which produced the generation of the founders of the Republic — and as a personification he was of course reflected in the era.

In the meeting of the man and the hour, he was of his time and his place, with the qualification that his place involved a continuous interrelationship with England. An enlightened provincial, totally identified with his country (Virginia), he operated financially and culturally through the mercantile and cultural centers of England.

Ultimately, it was this oneness with their place, in that time, which distinguished all the masters of the new native aristocracy from the two transplanted English aristocrats who clashed in what was called "Bacon's Rebellion." Young Nathaniel Bacon was a creature of circumstance, who found his reality as a person only and briefly in the violence of the rebellion. Old Sir William Berkeley belonged heart and soul to the ancient order that was doomed to pass. He had brought to Virginia the Old World which had formed him, with which he was identified and to which he was committed. Seen often in the legends as a villain — and some of his deeds were indeed bloody — Berkeley was a tired old man who had outlived his age and brought savage violence to the Virginia he loved by trying to hold back a frontier.

· 2 ·

Genesis of a Despot

GOVERNOR BERKELEY WAS seventy years old when the unseemly petitions from the frontier settlers sounded the rumblings of a coming rebellion in 1676. Sir William did not interpret the mutterings as portents of things to come. Although he recognized the dangers inherent in "the wild beast multitude," he had imposed his will too long in Virginia even to consider the possibility of any disturbance to his existing order.

Sir William Berkeley had spent almost exactly half his life in the Colony, and this wild and sweet land, which he had come to love, was like his own principality. As the royal governor, sole representative of the King, he *was* the Crown to these English people, extending the rule of England along this fringe of coastal land on the unexplored continent. He had served well both his King and the Colony. He could write home in honest pride that the "younger brothers" who had prospered in Virginia during his administration — the John Carters and Richard Lees — had added "more strength, wealth and honor to [their] native country than thousands did before that died forgotten and unrewarded in an unjust war."

If he gloried in the rise of those emigrants with great talents for commercial conquests of the water-drained country, he was not unaware of the hardships that brought suffering to the multitude, nor of their peril from the Indians. Yet for a complex of reasons, some unknown to him, he rejected their assertiveness. He followed Archbishop Williams's warning to Parliament: when the multitude made the laws, "you will have so many masters to yourselves that we shall all be slaves." It was not that he was a political person in this attitude, not at all. The attitude represented his inborn convictions, and his intimates in government shared them.

None subscribed more passionately than his wife, a younger woman whom he had married only six years before. My Lady Frances, just past forty, was intense, high-spirited and willful. Her dark eyes glinted with malicious humor in a soft-skinned, high-bred face. Of one of the bona fide "cavalier" families, she was perhaps the most powerfully connected woman in Virginia in those lines of power interweaving between England and the Colony. Through intermarriages, she was related to those English personages who had wielded the authority in early Virginia, including Governor Sir Francis Wyatt, her husband's predecessor. Both her father and her grandfather had been subscribers in the London Company, which had underwritten the settlement at Jamestown.

Her father, Thomas Culpeper, who had studied law at the Middle Temple, had owned with her uncle a ship plying in the Virginia trade. One of the loyalists who, Berkeley said, "lost all his estate . . . and liberty in the King's service," he had been sufficiently regarded by Charles II to be included among the seven favorites to whom Charles issued the enormous Virginia land grant known as the Proprietary. Since this grant was issued (September 18, 1649) while Charles was in exile at St. Germain, Thomas Culpeper's inclusion would certainly establish him as one of the "cavaliers" of the legend who came to Virginia during the civil wars and Cromwell's interregnum.

My Lady Frances herself had started at the top of colonial society at the age of eighteen. Having come to Virginia with her father at an unknown date, in 1652 she married Samuel Stephens, later governor of the Albemarle colony in North Carolina. When, after Stephens's death in 1670, she married Sir William, her brother Alexander, who had either remained in or returned to England, was given the plum of surveyor general of customs (collector) without even coming to Virginia. The duties were collected by deputies on the scene, the brothers Ludwell, Lady Frances's cousins by marriage. A cousin by marriage on her mother's side was a young merchant-planter, William Byrd, who would in time receive the lucrative post of auditor and receiver general. Yet another cousin was young Nathaniel Bacon — the future "Bacon the Rebel" — who was appointed by the governor to the lordly King's Council almost upon arrival in the Colony.

With this background, soft-skinned Lady Frances assumed a position of royalty among the planters in the governor's coterie, whom she entertained in the mansion at Green Spring. Named for a spring on the property, Berkeley's spreading brick mansion was the first manor house built in Virginia and among the very first on the continent. At the end of a road running about three straight miles from Jamestown, the estate was sliced out of a forest of oak and poplar, chestnut and walnut, holly and sycamore. During the warm weather the trees were draped with vines and creepers, and sweet-smelling wild flowers blossomed along the borders of the clearing. Sprawled along a terrace of raised ground, the main house and its outbuildings were set among grape arbors and orchards. Beyond, cattle, horses and sheep grazed in meadows, and farther beyond workers moved slowly under the blinding white sun, pruning stalks in tobacco fields. For Berkeley was himself a considerable planter, and Green Spring served both as the model of a country gentleman's estate (the larger gentry) and as a colonial version of the royal demesne.

There in the candlelit salon the gentlemen of consequence and their ladies were received by the bright-eyed, imperious Lady Frances, glittering with a necklace and pearl earrings, turned out in the latest finery from London. Her tightly laced, long-waisted bodice bared her white throat, and her soft shoulders were revealed under the film of lace edging her chemise. From her narrow waist a silken skirt, pleated over her hips, billowed to the floor. She was wont to gather up the skirt with her left hand and allow it to hang, diagonally and suggestively, in studied carelessness. When the summer heat gathered even inside the thick brick walls of the mansion, she would languidly stir the air with a fan of plumes.

On Sundays when she went by carriage to the red-brick church on Jamestown Island, people outside the governor's coterie observed with lowered eyes the bejeweled and beribboned elegance of the English-born lady, and talk of her was whispered throughout the back regions of the Colony. Resentful talk was heard about her finery displayed in the desperate times, and she was linked with what seemed the governor's hardening of heart toward the people's desperation.

There were higher-placed persons, burgesses and not among the governor's detractors, who whispered that Berkeley's vigor and judgment were dissipated by his "passions" for his younger wife. In all truth, Sir William did appear to be more removed from the people since his marriage, as if My Lady Frances had accentuated his native imperiousness.

A theatrical strain ran through Berkeley. In London he had been an amateur dramatist. When the aging beau, with his high-tempered wife, struck gallant poses, his normal hauteur was emphasized and he gave an impression that seemed to reflect arrogance rather than an old man's vanity. The upward turn of his mustache and the upward tilt of his chin — lifted to tighten the slack flesh — seemed to give disdain to his expression. Above the discolored pouches under his eyes, his proud gaze seemed to hold the contemptuous assurance of a lord of the earth.

This physical appearance was relatively commonplace among the English aristocracy, one of whose distinctions would be to develop insolent arrogance into a blond animal magnificence. But, understandably, in a sparsely settled frontier community, whose borders were being eroded by Indian ravages, the old English courtier could be seen as the prototypal despot.

2

In the thirty-four years since Sir William Berkeley had landed at Jamestown, England had changed, Virginia was changing, and the governor himself had been changed by the mutations of time and events. But Sir William (along with many of his younger contemporaries in England and Virginia) showed no awareness of these changes, either external or within himself. To him everything remained as it was when, at thirty-six, he had first walked from the ship to the high-banked shores of Jamestown Island.

He had left behind him the great world of the court of Charles I, of the London theatre and the silken drawing rooms where women's red lips parted over silver cups of sweet wine. But he had left behind him also the mists and the fogs, the chill rains and the meager sun. He took to himself the land of golden sunshine, of early springs coming with an ever incredible burst of flowering, and of long autumns with the slowly changing colors that aroused a nameless nostalgia. The summers could be stiflingly hot for spells, but one learned to go with the engulfing heat, never fighting it but relaxing in the warm fragrance that rose from the earth, and at intervals experiencing the sudden contrast of quiet shade. Winters could be cold in spells, with snow turning the woods into a ghostly stillness and bitter winds lancing off the tidal river. But always the sun came through, bringing mellow days under the intense blue of the sky.

The times were happy when Berkeley arrived. Those colonists who had survived the eighty percent mortality toll to emigrants had not only made a hardy adaptation to the country but developed skills in bringing forth the golden leaf of tobacco for world trade. With Virginia's fortunes at the flood tide, the government was in a transitional state, ready to be stabilized into an uninterrupted personal reign by an adroit diplomat such as the court-trained Berkeley then was. Sir William had actually come to act as mediator between the factions of two former governors who were trying to continue vestigial practices from the days of the London Company.

During its period of colonizing Virginia (1607–1625), the London Company was essentially a commercial operation, similar to the East India Company. While "for God and for King" was the slogan of the company's first representatives, and of the doomed adventurers who at Jamestown staked England's claims in the New World, the real purpose was to promote England's first venture in a new design for nationalist expansion. Of course, the investors expected to make money and the first adventurers expected to find riches, but the enterprise was part of a new European concept of national wealth, in which the wealth of a nation depended upon the prosperity of its tax-paying citizens.

The discovery of the New World, allowing trade to break out of the ancient confines of the Mediterranean, had opened the era of this new concept to the countries facing the Atlantic. Spain had moved first in the development of transatlantic trade. This master of the seas established claims to all of South America (except Portugal's Brazil), the Caribbean islands, all of Central America, Mexico (extending into areas of the present states of Texas, Arizona, and California) and the Florida peninsula. Spain claimed colonization rights to all of North America and stressed its claim to land along the Atlantic coastline, as far north as the southern border of Virginia, embracing what would become Georgia and the Carolinas.

Despite Spain's claims, Elizabeth gave England's first support to North American colonization in 1578, and after the encouraging defeat of the Armada ten years later, active movements were started toward colonization. To England, colonial expansion offered a means of obtaining national wealth through a favorable "balance of trade." Along with supplying England with needed products, the Colony would produce raw materials cheaply for the English manufacturers to sell dearly. This practical purpose was emotionalized by the rampant pride in nationalism and colored by the romance of a new world.

To the newly influential mercantile class and to the rising power of the landed gentry, investment in England's experiment in empire held the appeal of an exciting financial adventure. When rights of colonization were given to the London Company, a cross section of English people subscribed, and a number of the subscribers, their kin, and their representatives came to the Colony themselves.

The leaders in the Colony during the 1607–1625 era, representing the interests of the company and the King, were not settlers. Some were career soldiers, some were highly placed persons who came to make a quick killing (and a few did), others were educated gentlemen who came for the adventure or with the idealistic purpose of advancing England as an empire. A few idealists even came with the missionary purpose of converting the Indians, who responded by murdering them. With all the mixture of personal motivations, the early leaders came from similar privileged backgrounds, and between them and the officers of the London Company ran the most entangled lines of kinship.

These men controlled the General Assembly, composed of the appointive King's Council and the elective House of Burgesses. When, on a hot summer day in 1619, the first Burgesses introduced representative government in the New World in the church at Jamestown, this elective body was only a supplement of the King's Council, and its leaders were indistinguishable from the councilors. The House of Burgesses' first speaker, John Pory, was an Oxford graduate, a protégé of Hakluyt and a former member of Parliament.

These powers at Jamestown were quite distinct from the average settlers, those lonely men cutting out clearings and growing tobacco on holdings at increasing distances from the capital. While the presence of these gentlemen in Jamestown contributed toward extending the English social-political order to Virginia, toward establishing the character of the controlling order in the colonial government, they did not represent a native government. This type of English gentleman did not abandon Jamestown in 1625, after the dissolution of the London Company, and those with stakes in the Colony, either financial or in careers, brought on the conflicts which Sir William Berkeley came to resolve. He was the first royal governor of the Colony to settle permanently among the people he was to govern.

3

At about the time when Berkeley was building the first unit (or apartment) of the house which would gradually expand into the Green Spring mansion, a new strain began to arrive in the general run of emigrants. From the early days at Jamestown, men of education and some substance (many privileged to affix "Gent." after their names) had come as permanent settlers to work holdings of their own. The first Benjamin Harrison in the Colony, settling about 1625, had sufficient education and connections to land the post of clerk of the House of Burgesses, and used his salary to develop a holding on the south side of the James River. But most of these early holdings, like Harrison's, were not extensive. Though much larger than the average clearing, these plantations were modest compared to those that would be developed by the large-visioned entrepreneurs — combining shipping and trade with planting — who came around the time of Berkeley's arrival in 1642. The first *generation* of Virginia's dynasty-builders ("FFV's") began to arrive in the 1640's.

Three of the more substantial of these new-type emigrants, coming from mercantile backgrounds, were loosely Berkeley's contemporaries. Thomas Stegg, Jr., had come to join his father who, after trading for some years from a ship plying the James River, had established a "store," a combination trading post and commercial warehouse. Richard Lee I was in Virginia, as clerk of the Quarter Court, when Berkeley arrived. Lee had come to represent the colonial interests of his cousin's London mercantile business and to speculate on his own. John Carter I most probably came to represent the Carter family of vintners in London and most certainly to speculate on his own. Neither he nor Richard Lee worked any land holdings during the first years after their arrival.

Each of these three young men possessed sufficient social presence, formed by habituation to polite society, to attract the new governor's interest. Sir William made them his social intimates, forming friendships which would last throughout their lives, and selected them to be among his political allies in a governing group which would hold allegiance to him. As vacancies arose on the King's Council of twelve, he appointed them to this select body which became the Colony's nearest equivalent to the House of Lords. With Richard Lee he went further. When Berkeley set up his own government six months after arriving, he appointed Lee (August, 1642) to the newly created colonial office of attorney general.

At that stage, twenty-nine-year-old Lee was more solidly entrenched in the Colony than Carter and Stegg. Having lived two and a half years at the seat of government in Jamestown, he had established his social position by marrying Miss Anne Constable, an eighteen-year-old "lady of quality" who had come to Virginia (for reasons unknown) with the family of Royal Governor Wyatt. This first Richard Lee was a formidable-looking man. In a full-cheeked oblong face, his features were strongly marked and massive, with a large, straight-lined nose that would characterize his descendants for generations. With its self-contained immobility, his face, from the level dark gaze to the knob of chin, looked as invulnerable as the face of a mountain.

Of all the English-born newcomers of the first generation of fortune-builders, Richard Lee ("The Emigrant") had come to Virginia with the most exact balance of the qualifications required for a rise to wealth and power in a new world. While his kinsmen remained obscurely well-to-do at home, he seemed fitted by nature to partake of the upward thrust in the ultimate mobility — the adventure to the Colony.

Governor Berkeley listed "a small sum of money" as a requisite for "a younger brother to erect a flourishing family" in the new country. His reference to younger brothers implied that they came of families sufficiently established, however modestly, to have some connections and to have provided the sons with some education. Since education beyond the rudiments was rare among the colonists and illiteracy commonplace, as "in the land of the blind the one-eyed man is king," the emigrants with some educational background — such as Berkeley's young friends — began their new life in superior positions.

It would seem likely that Lee had studied law before coming to Virginia (the records of the Inns of Court were destroyed during the civil wars). He was appointed clerk of the Quarter Court so soon (April, 1640) after his arrival as to suggest the possibility that he came to Virginia with the appointment, and Berkeley would scarcely have appointed as Virginia's first attorney general a man without at least some background in law.

Beginning his rise when Berkeley came, Lee possessed the three basic requirements — "a small sum of money," education, and connections — together with a combination of personal mechanisms unsurpassed in his generation for their fitness to the opportunities in Virginia: he combined acquisitiveness, ambition, commercial enter-

Richard Lee I (Courtesy of the Virginia Historical Society)

prise, broadly based resourcefulness, self-discipline, confidence, great boldness, and good health.

Richard Lee I was one of the few dynasty-founders whose English line was established beyond question. He had the right to use the generic arms of Lee of Shropshire, first borne by the Norman Reyner de Lega, or de Le', about the year 1200. His family lived on the estate, or manor, of Nordley Regis, though when Richard Lee was born the unpretentious house and modest holdings had passed to the older brother of Lee's father. Another of Lee's uncles had established himself as a prosperous merchant in London, trading overseas on a large scale. In 1621 John Lee, an older cousin of Richard's, succeeded to the business. As four of Richard Lee's younger cousins went into business with John Lee and as an association was known to exist between Richard and his cousin John, from the nature of his first trading enterprises in the Colony it has been accepted as a reasonable assumption that Richard learned the family business from his older cousin in London and was representing John Lee in the Indian trade when he first came to Virginia. After fifteen years in Virginia, Richard Lee still identified himself (in a petition) as an ''English merchant trading in Virginia.''

Mercantilism was then the admired, dynamic order of the day, associated as trade was with the central drive toward national wealth and the pride in national expansion. Descendants of Virginia's dynasty-founders (like other Americans) later developed a superior attitude toward ''trade,'' and some old-line English country families were wont to sniff at new peers who ascended by way of mercantile houses. But when the first Lee came to Virginia, the merchant generally occupied a position of prestige and influence similar to the great industrialists of a later century. When Lee took his time in appraising the opportunities before committing himself to planting, he was seeking openings for his advance in the prevailing commercial patterns of his day.

After he was assured of his position in Virginia by Berkeley's favor, he patented a comparatively large holding of one thousand acres north of the York River in the present county of Gloucester. Most of this land was acquired through the headrights on seventeen indentured workers (fifty acres per headright), but Lee did not import those indentures. A ship's captain named Florentine Paine traded in headrights on indentures (a complicated speculation skirting the border of illegality) and Richard Lee, who was continually associated with Paine during his early years in Virginia, acquired the headrights' land in a deal with him.

Beginning with his first holdings, Lee ventured into sparsely settled country where Indians were all around his family. During the 1644 massacre he got his wife and children to safety only by having a shallop, which he used to negotiate the creeks in his trading. He seemed to be one of those men who are fearless in the literal sense of "without fear." Berkeley could not have chosen a stouter associate for his new government.

With Lee, John Carter I and Thomas Stegg, Jr., Berkeley also brought into his governing group two kinsmen he had known at home — Thomas and Philip Ludwell, former neighbors in Somerset. (A number of the early colonists came from the west of England, leaving from the port of Bristol, and a natural bond existed at all levels between emigrants from the same regions.)

Sir William had formed a new governing group of English-born men who became permanent residents of Virginia. Although Richard Lee for some years entertained the notion of returning to England with his wealth, eventually all of Berkeley's personal appointees identified themselves with Virginia and established their families as Virginians. With their children's futures bound up with the Colony's future, Berkeley's political allies worked in harmonious efficiency with the governor to advance Virginia's interests without antagonizing those powers at home who regarded the Colony as existing for England's benefit.

While Sir William was adroit in handling this ticklish dual assignment, his tasks were simplified by the civil wars which broke out almost as soon as he became governor. The government of Charles I was too bedeviled at home to be occupied with a scattering of colonists on another continent; and the settlers, let alone, were doing well for themselves.

4

In those days, though quick wealth came only to a few large-scale planters, about ninety percent of the colonists had developed a sturdy self-sufficiency on small holdings of from fifty to a few hundred acres. Most of them did all their own work in developing tobacco-producing clearings out of the forests. Tobacco prices were good then, and because of the comparative ease with which a subsistence diet could be produced, the solitary planter could concentrate on his money crop (tobacco was legal tender in Virginia).

The great staple was Indian corn, simple to plant and easy to weed when the stalks were well separated. The corn was ground into a water-mixed meal from which corn bread — as batter bread or spoon bread — became more familiar to most settlers than flour bread and was enjoyed by all. When the meal was shaped into small cakes and cooked over hot coals, a thick crust formed to produce what became the famous corn pone. Served hot at breakfast, with butter or molasses, corn pone continued from generation to generation across three centuries.

Little attention needed to be given Irish and sweet potatoes and varieties of peas — of which the black-eyed pea became a permanently favored staple in Virginia cooking. Hogs ran wild, developing a uniquely fine flavor in hams, and chickens roamed in such profusion that they were not listed in the modest inventories of wills which included such items as "the heifer calf and the looking glass." Wild pigeons, ducks and geese, oysters, varieties of fish (including the delectable shad), and sometimes deer appeared on all tables in their seasons, and in the shadowed vines in forest thickets wild grapes waited for the picking. On most plantations of any size (a cut above the one-man, fifty-acre operation), cattle and sheep were raised — mutton was, of course, a delicacy — and many planters cultivated small or large orchards of apples, peaches, plums and figs.

The early adventurers' description of Virginia as an "Eden" was not too fanciful — for those willing to work — during the first years of Berkeley's administration.

In 1649 Berkeley's administration was interrupted by the interregnum, the eleven years when Cromwell ruled England after the beheading of Charles I. In this span, the colonists were not affected. Cromwell made no serious interference with their practices, and Berkeley's appointees retained their colonial offices. Though Berkeley was removed from office, he remained unmolested at Green Spring, cultivating his fields and flocks and filling the growing brick mansion with his friends.

All of Berkeley's intimates were loyal to the exiled Stuart king, representing the Established Order, and John Carter was so outspoken in his allegiance that for a time his political position was threatened. Richard Lee, who then held the Colony's highest office, Secretary, performed his duties in Jamestown with high competence while continuing his visits to Green Spring. Without flaunting it, Sir William made Green Spring a Royalist sanctuary, where heavy-booted planters and elegantly styled visitors from England drank toasts to the "King" and waited for the passing of this upheaval in the Divine

Order. Berkeley himself was something like a Royalist governor in exile.

When 1660 brought Charles II to the throne, amid a tumultuous outburst of gaiety after the Puritan repressions, Sir William enjoyed his own quieter "restoration" with a return to his apartment in the State House facing the river at Jamestown.

It was in another, earlier phase of his own journey when, taut-skinned and lithe, he had first glimpsed this little capital. Now Jamestown was the home where he expected to live out his days. Under a mellow sun, warm to the flesh that had begun to sag, the most dearly familiar sight was the roll of the grassy esplanade between the brick-basemented houses on Jamestown's front street and the tidal river lapping against the steep banks. England-bound ships rode at anchor where — just the year after he was born — those first hundred men had left their ships and, against a background of howling wolves and the rustling of unseen Indians, had planted the English flag on this shore of a continent and prayed to their God. Where the vivid green, tangled wilderness had then spread, where unmarked graves held the hundreds who had died of starvation and malaria, of Indian arrows and homesickness, now rose the two-story oblong State House, symbol of the order he intended to maintain in the New World as it was restored in the Old.

Berkeley's "subjects," not having been affected by the disruption in the old order, expected to go on as before. The better educated, those who exchanged letters with friends and kinspeople back home by way of the ships they saw upriver once a year, those with acquaintances in the government at Jamestown, could expect favor to the colony which had given the new king such unswerving loyalty.

Instead, the Restoration as it was reflected in Virginia brought a cruel, bewildering turn to the fortunes of the colonists and created a gap, ever widening, between them and their local government. To their governor the longed-for Restoration brought insoluble problems in the dual nature of his task of promoting the colonists' welfare while serving the interests of England. In his frustrations, Sir William Berkeley began to undergo changes within himself which led gradually to personality disorders and eventually to distortions in his judgment. Since in that nonintrospective era he never took recognition of these changes, he never faced the heart of his dilemma: believing in the old Stuart order which had formed him, Berkeley tried to govern for the colonists' welfare through blind allegiance to a monarch who showed only conscienceless indifference to the colonials as people.

5

Charles II always had the support of the English people, who knew him for his quick-witted personal charm, his love of pleasure and the notoriety of his mistresses. To the people he glamorously personified the "restoration" of personal liberty in their daily lives. Virginians, who had not suffered repressions under Cromwell and to whom Charles II was a distant personification of the Crown, knew the effects of other facets of his character.

Behind the facade of the easygoing good humor of a profligate, Charles II maneuvered with a cold and amoral craftiness in looking after his own interests. While invoking the philosophy of divine-right rule, with all its absolutism, he was under no illusions about the tenure of the Crown. The assertion in Parliament, chiefly through the formerly weak House of Commons, which had led to his father's overthrow, was by no means ended because reaction against Cromwell's despotism had returned a Stuart to the throne. Parliament's temporary quiescence only established an uneasy equilibrium between Charles II and Parliament, many of whose members never fully trusted him.

An ancient power of Parliament came through its control of taxation for revenues. Charles's father had tried to evade that power by not calling Parliament for eleven years. Charles II was more deviously clever than that, and his personal expenses ran exceedingly high: along with maintaining his extravagant court, he lavished rewards on his mistresses and spent a fortune on the Duke of Monmouth, the oldest of his ten (known) illegitimate children. Among his maneuvers to raise revenue, he got cash from young Louis XIV in exchange for trying to reestablish the position of Roman Catholics in England. To avoid antagonizing the Protestant majority, he relinquished outwardly any "popish" tendencies — if anything, he was a crypto-Catholic — and waited a decade to make any effort to improve the status of Roman Catholics.

One source of revenue which would not involve him with Parliament was Virginia, whose colonists were shipping to London cargoes of a product that could be turned quickly into cash. That those people had been loyal to him meant nothing at all. Already he had gouged out tracts of their land to be given, in lieu of cash, as rewards to favorites and supporters to whom he was indebted. Since the faraway colonists had no power with which to threaten him, he regarded them as no more than sheep to be fleeced.

With this attitude, Berkeley's beloved King put the governor in the position of executing policies ruinous to the welfare of the people among whom he lived. To exploit the colonists through the tobacco they shipped was to strike them where they were most vulnerable in a one-money-crop economy. The scheme itself, as evolved by Charles II and the London merchants, was a triumph of shortsighted greed over realities.

During the Cromwellian government, a Navigation Act had been passed which restricted colonial shipping to English vessels. As this law had been loosely enforced, private river wharves continued to load tobacco hogsheads onto Dutch ships bound for European markets. With Charles II not only would the original Navigation Act be rigidly enforced, but all shipping would be restricted to English *ports*.

At that time the Lords of Trade (a committee of the Privy Council, later to be reorganized as the Board of Trade) were generally in charge of colonial affairs, and a strong influence was exerted by a bloc of powerful London merchants. In approving the new Navigation Act, the London merchants expected to act as middlemen for Virginia tobacco which, with a markup in the form of a tax, they would sell to the European market. With this one act, the tobacco growers were cut off from the competitive world market of buyers.

The results were swift and, in wrecking the tobacco market for the planters, very costly to the London merchants. The European consumers refused to buy at the raised prices. Soon the planters' shipments gathered in merchants' warehouses and became a glut on the English market. In a few years prices dropped from fourpence a pound in Cromwell's interregnum to one penny (from eight cents to two cents).

Inevitably, the persons hardest hit were the small planters working their holdings alone — the "freeholders," who comprised two-thirds of all landowners.

A good man, without help, could by diligent attention to detail and hard work, the most toilsome done under the broiling sun, make about fifteen hundred pounds of tobacco in one year. He raised the plants in beds, like a cabbage patch, and during the "season" (when rains came in late winter and early spring) he transplanted and replanted. When the stalk began to grow and the leaves sprout, his weeding began, then the "topping" (cutting off the head) and the "succoring" (cutting off the ground leaves). Topping the stalk, to check the upward growth and produce a broader leaf, was a delicate operation requiring experience and skill.

The planter cut down the ripe plants with about six or eight leaves on the stalks, and after they had withered a little in the sun he carried the stalks into an airy tobacco shed, where he hung them on sticks to dry. When he judged the dried tobacco to be "in proper case," he "struck it" (took it down) in a spell of weather neither too moist nor too dry, and "stemmed it" (pulled the leaves from the stalks). Some of the smaller planters sold their tobacco loose to the larger planters with wharves. Others of the small planters, and all the shipping planters, "prized" (pressed) the leaves with a machine into hogsheads, which ran from six hundred to over one thousand pounds.

"Sweet-scented," the milder tobacco with a rounder leaf and finer fibers, grew best in the lower tidewater regions of the big rivers, where most of the land was owned by the large-scale planters. Upriver, where the later and usually less privileged arrivals settled in the backcountry, the planters mostly grew oronoco, a strong tobacco with a leaf shaped like a fox's ear.

On fifteen hundred pounds at fourpence a pound the average settler grossed about £25 a year, a sum impossible to calculate in terms of today's money values. Out of this total, nearly half went for customs fees and commissions to tobacco merchants. After shipping charges, which averaged eighteen percent, the tobacco grower realized something over thirty-five percent net of the selling price of his product. When the small planters shipped through the large merchant-planters, these figures became more complicated, especially where the big planter operated a store. At his store the planter-shipper imported goods ordered by the small planter whose tobacco he shipped, and the price for the goods was taken out of the small planter's tobacco credit. In this way, no cash was passed and many small planters seldom possessed a coin.

Under Charles II, when the average planter grossed only about £6 for his year's toil, and received purchasing credit for little more than one-third of that, a pittance was left for buying clothes and shoes, the powder and shot on which he depended for game, and nothing for replacing equipment, or for utensils and furniture.

While the majority of settlers struggled to keep body and soul together, few of them able even to dream of their original goal of "improving their lot," the big planters were able to survive precisely because they *were* big. They could grow tobacco in volume by using indentured servants — workers who gave their services for about five years in exchange for their passage and a start when free. Some larger planters began to use black people from Africa, whom traders brought up the rivers on ships and offered for outright sale as slaves.

In addition, the volume of hogsheads reduced the planters' shipping costs, and they also stood to gain a little by handling the tobacco of small planters. Sometimes a big merchant-planter underwrote an entire cargo or bought a partnership in a ship. As wealth makes wealth, profits were earned from handling the clothing and articles imported for the stores operated by Lee, Carter, Stegg and, among others, Benjamin Harrison II — then little known outside the county, south of the James, where he was rising in political influence. The very extensiveness of their operations made it possible for the big merchant-planters to grow other crops for market as well as for subsistence. Richard Lee sold heavily in wheat. Finally, under the inexorable natural law of "him who has, gets," some of the big planters also drew salaries and commissions from official posts under Governor Berkeley.

Because the very big merchant-planters were then few in number, and the biggest had (as the best qualified) been drawn into Berkeley's government, in the widening gap between them and the average hardused settler, the colonists in general — "the people" — began to view Berkeley's Green Spring coterie as a privileged circle of favorites. However, several of these men in the government, notably John Carter and Richard Lee, grew very concerned about the colonists' welfare. They collaborated with Sir William in drafting a petition to Charles II, which the governor would take to London. Up to this point, 1663, Berkeley appeared to believe that Charles II could be reached by a presentation of the realities of the conditions in which the colonists were struggling for life.

6

Berkeley and the members of the King's Council resorted to the petition, as the only action available to them, when Charles's rapacity turned him to new measures which bore no practical relationship to the conditions in Virginia. Supported by the London merchants, Berkeley's monarch ordered him to cease complaining about tobacco prices and squeeze more revenue from the Colony by producing products England needed — planks, silk, cordage, flax, hemp. Never mind that settlers in their isolated clearings had spent years learning to produce tobacco, many investing five years of their youth in labor as indentures on tobacco plantations before they hacked out fields on their own patches of land. Let them build mills for iron.

Then, though the English merchants viewed with distaste the idea of colonial towns — where local merchants could compete for trade — the King also prodded Berkeley to build urban centers for manufacturing and shipping. While trading and shipping centers would have been most helpful to the Colony, urban centers did not spring up on a king's demands. Centers grew from a coagulation of trade and manufacturing and, first of all, manufacturing required capital and skilled workmen.

Berkeley wrote in his petition: "There is with us a great scarcity of able workmen. At whose doors ought this defect to lie? Not ours, who would procure them. . . ." However, the artisans "will not be procured, but on great wages, to leave their country, and hazard (as they style it) their lives." With the low tobacco prices and the high duties, "great wages" could not be paid by "the poor planter . . . whose whole sweat and labours amount to no more than to clothe and provide for the ordinary necessities of his indigent family." The only indentured servants who came were such "as have been brought up to no art or trade . . ." and came ". . . from hunger and fear of prisons."

For the promotion of the specified manufacturing that would lead to urban centers, Berkeley advanced the Council's proposal for the addition of one penny on customs, to go to "the country." This revenue would come from "the poor planter, whose tobacco must sell for less the more is imposed on it." The Council could not suggest any other kind of general contribution, Berkeley wrote, and then he made a profound observation that was profoundly neglected: the Colony's leaders had "this axiom firmly fixed in them: that never any community of people had good done to them, but against their wills."

The governor gave a list of other recommendations, all circumspectly presented. In his desire to relieve the peoples' burdens, he actually told some half-truths in making out a good case for them. He entirely omitted one of the basic factors that contributed to the absence of a "working population" required for manufacturing. The fact was that most of the English people who made the adventure to Virginia did not come with the slightest intention of forming a "working population."

Outside the small percentage of those who arrived with some advantages, the largest proportion of the English emigrants seem to have been agricultural workers (either landless or displaced yeomanry) and their motivating desire was for land of their own. The artisans themselves wanted land. The scarcity of skilled workers, felt throughout the Colony, continued because of the numbers who ceased to work for others (or worked only irregularly) as soon as they acquired their own holdings. Even with the hard times, when none thought of abandoning tobacco-growing, demand was constant for the cheap and easily acquired land.

Every adventurer received a headright of fifty acres, and planters received fifty acres for each indentured worker or slave brought into the Colony. As this system proved to be too cumbersome for the spreading domains of the big planters, the clerks in the land-recording office connived in various devices for circumventing the law by which land could be, in effect, bought outright at from one to five shillings for fifty acres. Gradually the circumventing devices passed into general custom, and then into law, with the price fixed at five shillings. There was a proviso that all purchased land must be settled and planted. Though the provision was meant to discourage land specu-lators, the powerful planters (who either were councilors or had influence with the Council) managed to circumvent even this restric-tion. Something like ''land fever'' possessed the colonists, and the last thought in anybody's mind was an urban center.

Without plan, the big plantations began to become centers. This actually was not so different from the agricultural regions of England. In England, where agricultural families formed an economic unit, villages spread along the streams that furnished waterpower for manufacturing and, as county centers, these villages and towns pre-vented mass coagulation. In Virginia the plantation became the equivalent of the village.

To their riverside wharves the small planters rolled their hogs-heads by road or floated tobacco on bateaux down creeks; the planters built the commercial warehouses that served as stores through which the small planters could order goods from London; planters' mills ground the neighbors' corn and occasionally wheat. Importing and exporting from a few private wharves, scattered along more than fifty miles of winding rivers, was a wasteful shipping operation for all concerned — though the settlers delighted to meet the ships as they gathered and delivered their cargoes, and the ships' captains were important, colorful personages. But however inefficient the extempo-rized shipping centers, they had become fixed in custom and a basis of wealth for the big planters. Not every big plantation was a shipping center but, except for Jamestown, every shipping center was a plantation.

In making no mention of these extemporized centers in his peti-tion, Berkeley revealed his recognition of the power of ''the custom of

the country." To have imposed change — without a long-range program adapted to the country and supported by the home government
with assistance in developing the details — would only have brought
upheaval to such stability as endured under Charles II. In recognizing
the custom of the country, the governor also recognized the sources of
wealth evolved at the shipping centers by the merchant-planters —
and they were his friends, officials in his administration.

Even with the omissions, the petition was a fair and accurate
presentation of the problems besetting the settlers in Virginia, and Sir
William could reasonably expect the King to give it consideration. But
Berkeley underwent the three months' rigors of a trip to his native
land only to have the petition dismissed. Charles II showed no faintest
interest in being either fair or reasonable about colonial people who
existed, as far as he was concerned, only to yield revenues for the
Crown.

When Berkeley returned to report the failure of his mission,
Secretary Richard Lee grew so disturbed about the harmful effect of
Charles's policies on the Colony that, with his whole family, he took a
voyage to London to make a personal representation to his merchant
friends. His mission, in 1664, was also fruitless. While in London, the
fifty-three-year-old colonial empire-builder fell ill, and he died soon
after his return to his permanent home in Virginia.

The governor and his councilors were forced to accept the reality
that they administered a forsaken people, exploited by a sovereign
who denied any moral obligation to the governed. With this acceptance, Sir William Berkeley began to experience those internal
changes of which he seemed unaware. Simultaneously, as if in reflection of his changes, attitudes began subtly to alter among the councilors, and they appeared from the outside like a favored coterie
separated from the struggles of the people.

7

Berkeley's allegiance to the King, who ruled by divine right in
the natural order, was the foundation of his own sense of security in a
world that had been shaken by violent upheavals since he had come to
Virginia. When his monarch's wishes made him powerless to alleviate
the hardships of the people he governed, Sir William did not resent
Charles II: he resented the people who would put on him demands
which he could not meet.

Since their demands were just and reasonable, he avoided meet-

ing with their representatives who would present the demands. From
the time he returned from his bootless trip to London, Berkeley ceased
to convene the House of Burgesses, and for fourteen years the people's representatives did not gather on the second floor of the State
House.

As he could not explain the situation to the people's representatives — nor, probably, even to himself — Sir William did the obvious
thing: he assumed superiority to explanation. This, of course, made
him appear despotic and contemptuous of the people. Then, as the role
of despot more or less descended on him, the ex-dramatist began to
play it for all it was worth. In the following years he role-played himself into the part of the classic tyrant.

In the class structure of the Stuart England which had formed
Berkeley, there was implicit an attitude of looking down upon inferiors, and since the civil wars any Stuart adherent had reason to
fear representative government. By 1670 — when the governor
brought his patrician bride to Green Spring — the tenuous equilibrium between Parliament and Charles II was changing into a struggle
for supremacy. In this struggle in England the House of Commons,
with its vital political class of country gentry, was breaking the control of the nobility, with its traditional working agreement with the
Crown. In Virginia, the House of Burgesses represented both the
despised multitude and the distrusted representative government.

Before the troubles brought to the people by Berkeley's monarch,
the governor felt no need to assert his superiority to the House of
Burgesses. But when the people grew restless under their legitimate
complaints, their representatives became a threat to the order in which
Berkeley knew security. For their demands put in question the absolute authority of the King who existed as the capstone and symbol of
the hierarchical order. Sir William would seem to have grown determined to suppress in his domain any reflection of Parliament's renewed struggle to reduce the Crown's power. He shared the sentiments of the Old Order that were expressed in sermons, pamphlets and
poems, and summarized in the line ''When the beast did imagine it was
loose from the chains of monarchy and law, who would tie it up
again?''

In keeping the beast chained in Virginia, Sir William was uncon-
sciously protecting his own security by supporting the Divine Order.
In doing this — with the growing resentment of the people to whom he
had been forced to renounce his obligation — Berkeley withdrew not
only from the people's representatives but from the life of the people

themselves. Playing the autocrat more and more heavily, he seemed deliberately to blind himself to their acute needs and to reflect his monarch in callousness to their sufferings.

When he separated himself from the problems in the daily lives of the colonists as individuals, Sir William — in an ultimate extension of the reflection of Charles II — imposed upon the colonists a rule from without which both denied their rights as English subjects and ignored the conditions of life in Virginia. In representing His Majesty, he had ceased to represent the Virginia colonists.

Berkeley kept as treasurer of Virginia his cousin Sir Henry Norwood, who drew the salary in England. Norwood had been a very adventurous "cavalier." He fought in the first civil war, came to Virginia in 1649, and plotted against Cromwell. Berkeley had petitioned Charles II, during his exile, for a patent as treasurer for his cousin. The patent became effective in 1660, and the actual work was done by deputies in Virginia — including another cousin, Thomas Ludwell.

In the complexities of Berkeley's change from 1663 to 1676, the more the settlers became to him a "native population," the more he identified Virginia with himself. In embracing the divine-right doctrine which Charles II, a pragmatic realist, talked about, Berkeley was actually more like Louis XIV than the English king. The aging ex-courtier developed the conviction that he *was* the Dominion of Virginia.

What Berkeley had done, without conscious intent, was to turn back the clock: he had made the frontier a miniature England of a past age, when the nobility worked with the King in imposing rule on "the meaner sort of people." He had returned to a day before the restless mobility in English society brought forth the power of the country gentry, along with that of the London merchants, and forced the King to an amoral craftiness in maintaining his position. While there were plenty of people in England, especially among the nobility, trying to halt, to control, the changes, Sir William had actually recaptured a static, postfeudal England in a colony surging with the expansive individualism and potential violence inherent in any frontier. Without awareness of what he was doing, the old man was living triumphantly at the crossing of two ages: he imposed the most obsolete Old World aspects of a passing order on a New World whose own indigenous order was inarticulately struggling to emerge.

Berkeley was able to suppress the individualistic assertiveness of the colonial settlers, "the unruly base multitude," partly because they regarded themselves as English citizens subject to the authority of the King (through His Majesty's representative in Virginia) and partly because the successful, educated men among the colonists joined him.

These merchant-planters were not appointed to the Council, as the people believed, merely because they were Berkeley's favorites. They were appointed because, through the management of their own large-scale affairs — through the assumption of "giant responsibilities" — they had demonstrated their fitness for sharing the responsibilities of government. Along with their ability and their familiarity with large affairs, they were also personally compatible with the governor and contributed to the pleasures of social life in the uncivilized country.

However, since the governor refused to convene the House of Burgesses, the intimates of the Green Spring "court" became more of a coterie than a body of the General Assembly. They were similar to a king's advisory council, to the "cabal" (Clifford, Ashley, Buckingham, Arlington and Lauderdale) of Charles II. As an elite group, the councilors enjoyed a scale of privilege which separated them from the problems and hardships endured by most of the settlers. The councilors apportioned among themselves and their relatives and friends all the major and most of the moderate-size posts of collectors and auditors, and the important post of escheator of lands reclaimed by the government. Then, as judges of the General Court, to which were brought criminal and civil cases above the jurisdiction of county courts, the councilors passed upon their own accounts as collectors of fees, duties and taxes. Exempt from paying taxes themselves, and from arrest, the councilors stifled any opposition or investigation from county officials by their influence in the appointments to cash-paying county offices — clerk of the court, sheriff, minor collectors and such.

Councilors made their presence felt directly in their home districts by command of the county militia. Except for a few soldiers in the gun position, called a fort, on the Jamestown wharf, the militia provided the Colony's only armed force. The colonel of a county militia, though not appointed because of any knowledge of military affairs, assumed many responsible duties, including particularly that of maintaining law and order. By no means an empty title, "colonel" was a designation of high rank, and the proper title was as carefully used in addressing a colonel as in addressing a lord.

As individuals, the merchant-planters with their heady power were no more indifferent to the plight of their fellows than was the average rich man in a time when every person was required to look out for himself and the poor were taken for granted as a faceless multitude which would always be there. But as a governing group, by sharing Berkeley's regal separateness from the "natives," the Council in 1676 did not assume any real responsibility for the welfare of the Colony as a whole. As a group, while conscientiously maintaining law and an orderly operation of civil life, they assumed that their families would continue as a privileged elite and the rest of the settlers would continue their hazardous, borderline-subsistence struggle with the wilderness and the policies of Charles II. Like Berkeley, the councilors acted as if time stood still. They showed no awareness of the contradiction in maintaining a static order on an inevitably changing frontier.

Although the councilors varied in background and personality, all shared the one vital ingredient of allegiance to Berkeley, to the King he represented and to the order upheld by the King. When gathered in the Council's first-floor chamber in the State House, dignified in their wigs and wearing their colonel's swords swinging from belts buckled outside their wide-skirted coats, they represented the finest flower of Englishmen of the Establishment in the New World.

In Richard Lee II, Berkeley had a native-born Virginian as the first to assume a "hereditary" position on the Council. An austere scholar, not at all like his father, the prematurely old Lee brought a high sense of civic responsibility to the meetings and, as one of the councilors who had never sought any sinecures nor cut corners to increase his estate, brought also an inflexible personal integrity.

Ralph Wormeley II, another native-born Virginian and the first to be graduated from Oxford (Oriel College), had a flair for elegance of person and lived "bravely" — as the natives said for "gallantly." He was growing famous for his hospitality at Rosegill, the inherited mánor house where his father had entertained Colonel Norwood's "cavalier" friends. With all his extravagance of living, young Wormeley was an able man and progressive in the diversity of small manufacturing at his plantation.

His stepfather, Sir Henry Chicheley, who had married Wormeley's well-endowed widowed mother, came of an old-line English county family. Though he was getting along in years and was not too well, Sir Henry brought to the Council a gentle fair-mindedness.

John Carter had been lost by death in 1669, and his serious-minded son, John II, had not yet participated in government beyond the county level. (At the great maritime site of Corotoman, which he had inherited, John was looking after the small estate of his younger brother Robert, whom he was having educated in England.) But the governor regarded the son of his old friend as dependable.

Then there were the substantial men of prudence: Berkeley's own

Ludwell cousins, Philip and Thomas, the latter then secretary; Nathaniel Bacon the Senior and Thomas Ballard; and Colonel Edward Hill of Shirley plantation, whose father had planted land originally held by the sons of Lord de la Warr.

Lately they had been joined by Nathaniel Bacon the Younger, a brilliant and personable kinsman of Nathaniel Bacon the Senior. A little unstable yet, he was a man of parts and had settled down with his wife on a fine plantation on the James, obtained for him by Councilor Thomas Ballard.

From Berkeley's perceptual view, he had reason to be proud of the men of consequence he had selected in his government. Their pride of place seemed natural enough to him, and he was not treated with the overbearing haughtiness which some — noticeably Colonel Hill — showed to their less fortunate neighbors.

If he heard rumblings of the people's resentment of the Green Spring clique, that too was in the natural order of things. Charles I, the monarch who had appointed him governor of Virginia, had spoken of the implacable hatred "between the gentry and the commonalty of the kingdom." That Charles I had been beheaded indicated no tide of change to Sir William. The event of consequence was the restoration of the Stuarts, and nowhere did the Restoration so fully recapture the old order as in Berkeley's Virginia dominion.

8

The pinched-faced settlers had, by the nature of things, a different perceptual view of the Green Spring coterie. When a councilor's family swept into a pew at the parish church, when a sword-belted councilor addressed a militia muster, their pride and haughtiness were associated in the people's minds with their immunities — such as exemption from taxes — and the special privileges bestowed on them as the autocrat's favorites. Although, except for the Ludwell brothers (who brought shrewdness and energy to the opportunities given them by their cousin), the councilors had won their favored positions by success as merchant-planters, the men and women from the small backcountry holdings did not analyze the cause and effect of favoritism. They saw that the result of favoritism was to set the councilors apart, as superior beings, from those they supposedly governed. Without representation in the government since the House of Burgesses had been indefinitely prorogued, the tax-paying citizens saw the Council not as a responsible governing body but as a caste.

It was this caste attitude that aroused first the resentment and then the hatred of the majority of the colonists. For this *caste,* alien to all their experience and beliefs, violated the *class* structure with which the transplanted English people were familiar and in which they felt security.

In the English class structure, the State was woven into the fabric of all the people's daily pattern. Authority began in the neighborhood with their local squire, himself a familiar part of the routines of everyday life, and extended upward among men who belonged, as did the most humble, to the transcendent order in which all lives were controlled.

> *The heavens themselves, the planets, and this center,*
> *Observe degree, priority, and place . . .*

No such hierarchy of authority existed in Berkeley's autocracy. In England, where mobility brought recruits into the peerage, the new elite were absorbed into a continuity of the ancient lines of the Establishment. Berkeley's ruling clique, all new to immense power, did not extend upward out of the citizenry in a line of continuity. Nothing of a class, the Council acted more as a foreign rule imposed from without. It was neither English nor indigenous to the Colony.

In the new frontier community of Virginia, with the sparsity of its families of great privilege, the councilors could not immediately have formed a class. However, by divorcing themselves from the life of the Colony, when the House of Burgesses was for all practical purposes suspended, the Council deprived the people of any sense of representation, either as English citizens or as Virginia colonials. With no one concerned about their welfare as individuals, the voiceless settlers could only regard Berkeley's coterie as rich men acting in the exclusiveness of self-interest.

It was a narrow, short-sighted self-interest which, reflecting Sir William's recapture of an old order, refused to recognize the effects of the New World frontier on individuals. The self-reliance developed by carving out and working one's own holding, with the influence of the expansiveness of the illimitable, unbordered land, produced an assertive individualism in all the American colonists. The repressed assertiveness of the Virginians' individualism found its only outlet in growing hatred for Berkeley's coterie.

Though the settlers oversimplified the complex interweaving factors which permitted the big merchant-planters to import silver gob-

lets and casks of wine while the people were haunted by the specter of
destitution, it made their problems seem simpler to hold other colonists responsible for the poverty over the land. Charles II and the
Navigation Act were too distant and too vague. The settlers' bewildered frustrations were relieved by having visible, personal enemies
at whom they could direct their hostility.

Of the councilors, the overbearing Colonel Edward Hill of
Charles City County — west from Jamestown on the river — was
hated almost as much as Berkeley. Richard Lee II, the councilor most
innocent of exploiting his fellows or using his office for profit, was
probably the most alien as an individual to a frontier community.

On the Council this second Richard Lee was known as a man of
honor whom some likened to a Roman senator for his civic virtues.
This respect was not limited to the Green Spring coterie but was given
Lee long after Berkeley was no more. A later governor would describe
him as "a gentleman of as fair character as any in the country for his
exact justice, honesty . . . and loyalty in all the stations wherein he
has served." But Lee was a vinegary man with a shriveled response to
humanity, more at home in his library than among people. One of the
first English-speaking persons in the New World to be born into an
hereditary position, and the first native-born Virginian to be con-
spicuously a scholar, Lee presented to the world a personality of
austere seclusiveness that, outside his circle of intimates, could easily
be seen as coldly aloof superiority. The average settler would not
suspect that a twenty-eight-year-old gentleman of Lee's assured place
was shy and inward-turning. Then, with his expressionless dark eyes,
his sallow cheeks, and his mouth pinched between lines coursing down
from his large family nose, he did give the impression of suspecting
that something distasteful hung in the air.

Lee was not the only scholar in the Colony. His contemporary,
Ralph Wormeley, also had a good library. But young Wormeley liked
people, lusty pleasures and the style of high living the settlers could
understand. He kept a personal tailor and shoemaker, rode a prized
pacing horse with a crimson broadcloth saddlecloth and silken holsters,
caroused all night and served wine so strong that a visiting Frenchman had to dilute his.

Lee, shunning social gatherings, devoted his time to reading
Greek, Latin and Hebrew, even writing casual notes in those languages. His cargoes always brought books by classical authors and on
such scholarly subjects as ethics and conduct, history and biography,
science and geography; for guidance in his official capacities, he read

Richard Lee II (Courtesy of the Virginia Historical Society)

books on politics and government, and he had two dozen books on law
as guides in his legal duties. as a councilor. Responsible, like most
planters, for the physical well-being of those in his private community,
he doubled as doctor and had more than twenty books on medicine.
Also, as did most of the big merchant-planters, Richard Lee II had
more books on religion (fifty-eight) than on any other subject.

The framework that religion provided for the Lees and their
contemporaries (especially the Carters) was extremely significant in
their sense of values. In the new religious attitudes which appeared
with the Reformation, the impact of Calvinism was to make men attribute virtue to success in amassing worldly goods; proficiency in
one's "calling" was regarded as the performance of religious duty.
Removed from its trappings of piety and the embracing belief in a
Divine Providence, as a practical guide the religious attitude of the
Lees and other families anticipated what came to be called the "Protestant ethic." To them, to do well was to be good.

While lip service was given to such Christian axioms as "It is
easier for a camel to go through the eye of a needle than for a rich
man to enter the Kingdom of God," their practices adhered to those
teachings of the Old Testament which were inclined to regard the poor
and the ill as unfortunates who had not earned the blessings of God.
By this standard, the Lee family had been established among the
blessed by the emigrant Richard Lee I.

This first Lee had continued to acquire and sell land between the
York and the Rappahannock, established a store, and around 1655
began to concentrate on planting tobacco when he settled at a maritime site, Dividing Creek, on the eastern tip of the Northern Neck —
the strip of land between the Rappahannock and Potomac rivers,
both very wide where they emptied into Chesapeake Bay. Dividing
Creek itself was approximately one mile across at Lee's holdings. All
running waters in Virginia which rose near their mouths were called
"creeks," though Dividing Creek was more like a broad inlet where it
emptied into the bay. From the base of this ideal site for his shipping
and trading enterprises, Richard Lee engaged in the extensive planting of tobacco and general crops at the home plantation — and at
least one other plantation, Paradise — which built the colonial barony
for his descendants.

None of his eight children possessed his total excellence, his qualities of the Renaissance "whole man," and only one son followed the
career his father chose for him. Francis Lee, the third son, beginning
with a share in two ships left him by his father, established himself in

London as a merchant in the Virginia trade. (Successive generations of Richard Lee's descendants lived in London as merchants or agents to Virginia until the Revolution.)

The firstborn son, John, educated in medicine at Oxford, was untypical of Richard Lee's descendants in becoming a happy hedonist. John Lee established himself farther westward from his father's holdings, on the Potomac in Westmoreland County, in the region which was to become a Lee demesne. After John's early death at thirty-one, in 1673, this property came to Richard Lee II, who had been living at his own inherited plantation, Paradise.

Nothing was known of the education by which Richard Lee II cultivated his wintry scholarship, and little was known of his seclusive early years before his marriage to the desirable Miss Laetitia Corbin, which connected young Lee with a transatlantic English-Virginia family of merchants and planters. He moved to his late brother's Potomac holdings and, at Mount Pleasant, built a large, substantial brick house, enclosed by a wall and surrounded with outbuildings. In his father's generation, few of the fortune-founders had built elaborate houses as "seats" of the manor, and the first Richard Lee had built utilitarian dwellings with no eye for permanence. Although Richard Lee II did not design his own home as anything of a great manor house, it would have appeared a mansion in contrast to the average one-and-a-half-story house of one and a half rooms, sometimes with rude extensions.

On the inside, the Lee house was of a different world from the frontier. Carpets covered the floors, chairs were upholstered in stylish turkey work, the rooms were furnished with carved chests with locks, brass candlesticks, silver dishes engraved with the Lee coat of arms (Richard Lee I had been very careful about that) and, the ultimate vanity, bookcases to hold a "gentleman's library." Lee's collection was representative, in size and selection, of books that would have been found in the manor houses of educated country gentlemen in England.

With no acquisitiveness at all, and none of his father's zest for commerce, the second Richard Lee acted as a prudent, conscientious custodian of the inherited estate. At a time when his contemporaries were patenting thousands of choice acres for their heirs and laying foundations of future baronies, he took care merely to pass on his considerable portion of his father's empire, with its yield in revenues, as it had come to him. In his indifference to the fortunes burgeoning around him, Lee was guided by a sense of duty in which he assumed those obligations to the State he accepted as inherent in his position.

Yet, though Richard Lee II brought unassailable convictions to every act of his life — and in later years, when the Northern Neck became more thickly settled, was recognized as a community leader — in 1675 the people saw his forbiddingly unapproachable exterior. There was a rigidity in his convictions, a touch of self-righteousness, that would stir those starving people who glimpsed the private domain in which he pursued his books, aloof and remote from the illy rewarded toil and the anxiety which *his* government, the Council, permitted to be the lot of their fellows. By personality rather than by acts, he served as an *image* of the enemy of the colonial settlers.

9

As Richard Lee II, Edward Hill and other merchant-planters of the governor's clique became the personalized enemy, the Indians became the concrete issue. During the 1670's the settlers along the fringes of the frontier had reason to hold Berkeley directly responsible for the new Indian scourge that climaxed their troubles. Outwardly the haughty old man, unmenaced among his gardens and arbors, did appear at his most cruelly indifferent to the colonists. But inwardly the colonial governor faced problems for which he found no solution. As in executing the destructive policies of Charles II, when he knew of no remedies for the people's condition he hardened his heart to their dangers. As he grew personally more inflexible, more the defender of his autocratic order, Berkeley seemed to reject all petitions as manifestations of the people's right to petition.

Actually, Berkeley was concerned with maintaining some policy of justice to the Indians, and in this he was caught in a dilemma which Americans were destined never to solve — the need to develop a rational, humanistic policy which extended rights to the Indians in the face of the continuous advance of white settlements. This dilemma embraced another insoluble problem in the relationship of English people to nonwhites, a problem made murkier by the religious attitudes which caused the settlers to regard the nonwhites as "heathen," godless savages.

Sir William never ceased searching for some practical policy for the cohabitation of the two races in those more settled regions of tidewater where tributary Indian tribes had been established. While the colonists were indifferent to the disintegration of the tributaries as tribes and their deterioration as people, Berkeley's laws sought some realistic adjustment between the white men and the red men in their mutually alien ways.

The spread of white settlements inevitably reduced game in the forests. The settlers killed wolves, foxes, minks, polecats, bears and occasionally panthers, partly for safety and partly to protect their poultry and young pigs. For their eating "boards" — planks laid across two wooden horses — they killed deer and rabbits, and the possums and raccoons they hunted at night. When game grew scarce, and as the settlers allowed their hogs to run, Indians picked off strays and developed a taste for pork. But if an Indian chased a hog in sight of an Englishman, he could be arrested for stealing or even shot for trespassing. This was the sort of practice the governor tried to correct in the settled regions.

For the border clashes with the hostiles that occurred at each push of settlers farther from Jamestown, Berkeley stayed with the system of forts even after this method had proved futile. Bands of Indians naturally avoided the forts as they glided through the forests for a sudden swoop upon some little house set in its newly made clearing, with the stumps of felled trees still rising from the ground. To the men and women in these exposed border regions Berkeley's attempts at a broad policy were meaningless, and they saw only his indifference to their safety.

Realistically, short of extermination of the Indians, there was no practical way either to prevent ravages by the hostiles or to save the territory of the tributary tribes, except by containing the spread of the English colony. This, in effect, was what Berkeley tried to do in groping for some solution to the problems. He prohibited the sale of land on certain frontiers and established broad controls for protecting the individual rights of Indians.

Unaware that he was trying to halt time, unable to adapt to the changes that had come with the expansion of the Colony since he first started building Green Spring, Berkeley believed he could enclose the evolutionary movements of a new world within the structure which he controlled.

Berkeley's personal reactions to the threats of change, specifically to the Indian menace, were outside the concerns of the endangered settlers. In their need of the concrete, the specific, the colonists attributed Berkeley's apparent indifference solely to his interest in profits from the Indian trade. When men and women gathered to lament the times, they said the governor valued "pelts" over their lives.

Not all the colonists who had not won the big success were illiterate people of "the meaner sort" working isolated fifty-acre holdings. There were educated men of personal substance who themselves could boast of armigerous families — entitled to bear coats of arms — and were regarded by visitors as of ''good condition.'' They had developed holdings of several hundred acres, brought in indentured workers to help enlarge their tobacco-growing, and, by frugality and sound planning, managed to earn a measure of security for their families despite the ruinous tobacco prices. No safer from the Indians than the humblest settlers, these relatively substantial colonists were in a position to know what kernel of truth there was in the charges about Berkeley's regard for the Indian trade.

It was not, as the settlers believed, so much Sir William's personal avarice that dictated his handling of the Indian trade, as his concern over a systematic revenue from the trade, along with the effort to be fair to the Indians in his general policies. His laws were designed largely to protect the Indians from exploitation by rogues, and some of the fly-by-night traders were very scurvy characters. But his laws did operate in favor of the big established traders. Since two of these, Abraham Wood and William Byrd I, were close to Sir William's private circle, the people were convinced that Berkeley's Indian trading laws were designed to protect the ''monopolies'' of his favorites.

In all the complicated factors involved in Berkeley's reactive attitudes and the people's focusing of their grievances, nothing was as simple as it seemed. Neither Byrd nor Wood was among those who profited directly from the governor's favor.

Abraham Wood, who has been curiously neglected, was America's first outstanding frontiersman in opening up communications with Indians, and his successful trading enterprises seemed always secondary to his interest in Indian relations. Also, unlike the other councilors, he came to Virginia as an indentured servant and belonged among the earliest of America's success stories.

Wood was only ten years old when he arrived in 1620, indentured (apprenticed) in the service of Captain Samuel Mathews, one of the larger planters of the early days. At an unknown age young Wood, as a freedman, moved westward into Henrico County, then the westernmost frontier. There, within the area of present-day Richmond, a precipitous hill had served as the stronghold of the mighty Powhatan, Pocahontas's father, from where the Indians observed all water travel to and from The Falls, which marked the head of tidewater on the James River. At the age of thirty-four Abraham Wood emerged from obscurity as a member of the House of Burgesses from the frontier county of Henrico. Two years later, in 1646, he was placed in command of one of Berkeley's then new frontier forts, at the present site of Petersburg on the Appomattox River.

From here Abraham Wood began his first exploratory journeys of record into the uninhabited stretches of southern Virginia, the territory of the hostile Occaneechis and fierce Tuscaroras. Wood opened trading operations with both nations — trinkets for furs — and established the basis of constantly lengthening trade routes into distant territories. Learning various Indian tongues, Wood negotiated with the chieftains of different tribes as he built the first large-scale Indian trading operation on the continent. By 1675 Wood's assistants had crossed the Great Smokies to the powerful Cherokee nation.

From this contact Wood opened a thousand-mile trail southwest through the Carolinas to the falls of the Savannah River, at the present site of Augusta, Georgia, and around the southern end of the Appalachians to the Cherokee villages. During Wood's rise as the Colony's foremost Indian trader and peacetime negotiator, Berkeley appointed him to the Council and commissioned him one of the three major generals of the combined militia forces in Virginia.

Wood was never active in the exchange of favors among the power group and seemed to be not in sympathy with Berkeley's Indian policies. For a certainty, he did not figure prominently in the governor's counsels during the raids following the summer of 1675 and, if consulted at all, he was not sent to the troubled frontier. Aging and unwell, he remained at his home in the then relatively settled regions of Henrico County, while twenty-three-year-old William Byrd rose as a rival who was destined to develop Indian trade on a far vaster commercial scale than the pioneer.

Possessing in equal parts an outsized acquisitiveness and the ability to expand upon foundations laid by others, Byrd got his start from his uncle's trading post at The Falls and found the pioneered trade routes his road to riches. Although that first William Byrd would exploit the opportunities to power as Wood never had when his turn came to sit with "the men of rank" around the Council table, in 1675 he had not been tapped. But he was socially connected with the governor's coterie by his wife's kinship to Lady Frances Berkeley.

The people might have been wrong in detail about some of their judgments, and there were many shaded areas in the undeclared conflict between the governor and the majority of the colonists, but there was no doubt that Robert Hen's murder on a Sunday morning was the (then unrecognized) "incident" that started the concatenation of incidents bringing the colonists' complaints to a head in the spring of

1676. And as these complaints came into the open, there was no doubt that Governor Berkeley's rigidified attitudes had removed from him the capacity to deal realistically with the conditions which had developed.

Strolling with his lady on his terraced lawns in the lilac dusks, he was too far removed from the temper of the citizens to fear the "multitude agitation" which Lord Digby had warned against. At first, in his scorn of the "base" people, he did not conceive the possibility that a gentleman of his own class would emerge to lead "irregular and tumultuous assemblies of the people." Then, when the people found this leader on the governor's Council, Sir William reacted as if to personal insult. Proscribing the leader as a "rebel," he permitted the passions of his outrage to reduce the whole complicated outbreak to a duel to the death with the presumptuous young Bacon. He seemed totally removed from the reality, with its implications and possible repercussions, of involving the Colony he governed in a vicious civil war, a rebellion of English colonists in the New World, at the very time his sovereign was involved at home in a network of intrigues and shifting alliances in what had become an unremitting struggle between Parliament and King.

The Rebellion of Nathaniel Bacon
the Younger

ON A LANGUID spring afternoon, Nathaniel Bacon was having drinks with three of his new friends on a plantation lawn overlooking the James River. Then twenty-eight, Bacon had come to Virginia only two years before, to settle with his wife on a river plantation acquired for him by his wealthy English family.

Among his companions was Captain Crews, an older man, whose plantation adjoined Bacon's Curles' Neck on the north side of the river. (The river ran there in great loops, or "curls," and Bacon's land fronted on the top, or "neck," of a loop.) Henry Isham, still older, had long been established at Bermuda Hundred, where he was something of the social arbiter on the south side of the river: his daughter Mary was a much courted belle in the scattered plantation "society" of the region. William Byrd, two years younger than Bacon, cultivated large holdings south of the river, from the base of his store at The Falls. He had married Mary Horsmanden, the daughter of a loyalist officer who, after taking sanctuary in Virginia, had returned to England. Mary and William Byrd had a two-year-old son in the bleak house at the trading outpost, where the young mother endured intense loneliness.

Since planters of similar background were few and far between, Bacon — a kinsman of Lord Francis Bacon, a Cambridge graduate, a veteran of the grand tour, and the forty-ninth member of his family to prepare for law at Gray's Inn — had been quickly taken as an intimate into the small group of river planters, and his wife particularly was welcomed by Mary Byrd.

Bacon himself, restless and mercurial, was not cast from the same mold as the men of prudence who had built their own estates. His life before he came to Virginia had followed an irregular course of wasteful self-indulgence. In his Cambridge days, he had been withdrawn from college for a spell because of some youthful extravagance. Elizabeth Bacon's father, Sir Edward Duke, had so bitterly opposed her marriage that he disinherited her. After her brother and Bacon's father settled a comfortable annuity on the young couple, Bacon's extravagances and harebrained attempts to recoup entangled him in such difficulties that his father sent him "to the Colonies." Actually, Bacon could be seen as an early, and high-class, "remittance man" — paid to stay away from home.

In Virginia his money, his background and the established position of his cousin, Councilor Nathaniel Bacon the Senior, opened the way for him at the top. Through a friend and fellow councilor of the older Bacon, Thomas Ballard, Bacon was able to buy at the low cost of £500 a working plantation, fully stocked and equipped, at a coveted spot on the James River. Immediately discontented with his unearned privilege in Virginia, Bacon, with his new friend William Byrd, petitioned Governor Berkeley to form a partnership — amounting virtually to a monopoly — in the Indian trade. Sir William, after negotiating for a while, declined. Perhaps holding some resentment of the governor, and restless in his life of ease, Nathaniel Bacon made friends with highly placed malcontents in the Colony — as well as with his neighboring planters.

He was a slender man of "middling size," darkly handsome, with a suggestion of tempestuousness about him which some acquaintances found disturbing. Men had spoken of his "pestilential talk," referring to his nonconformist opinions and dramatic violence of expression. These irregularities had not been taken seriously by the worldly Berkeley, who showed preferment for his fellow aristocrat from home by appointing him to the King's Council at the first vacancy.

On that spring afternoon, when he and his friends were "making the sadness of the times their discourse," Nathaniel Bacon was agitated over the recent murder of his overseer at a detached plantation less than twenty miles from his house. (The detached plantation, Bacon's Quarter, was in what is now the downtown section of Richmond: into recent times a small creek there was called Bacon's Quarter Branch.) While the planters were discussing the Indian outrages, they espied on the south side of the river a loosely organized force of armed settlers.

Except for wealthy planters, the several hundred armed men looked like a cross section of freeholders from tidewater to the farthest fringes of the frontier. In the mellow sunlight, Bacon and his friends could see the leather jerkins — like long vests, made of hides — of the frontier people, and the tidewater planters' new-style cloth coats falling to the knees, open to reveal waistcoats almost as long, with buttons that caught the light. Many of the men wore leather belts as bandoliers, running diagonally across their chests from the left shoulder. All were armed. Most of them carried a carbine or a flintlock musket called a fusil (from which came England's "fusileer" guards). Here and there fat-barreled pistols were stuck through belts and the sun flashed on the swords of a few militia officers below the rank of lieutenant colonel.

Some of the uprooted frontier settlers, who had been living off the land for weeks, carried packs of provisions collected along the march, and a few had packhorses with sacks draped across their withers. There were more volunteers than militia, and regulation order of march was barely suggested, but the weather-stained men with their familiar weapons somehow looked more like a military force than a crowd. An observer called them "soldiers."

2

Nathaniel Bacon and his planter friends knew this force of men was not an authorized assembly. In the adjoining county of Charles City, Colonel Edward Hill of Shirley plantation had given no order to call out the militia. Charles City was the earliest settled region upriver from Jamestown, where Shirley and Berkeley Hundred plantations were planted before 1620, and yet it was there that the unauthorized drums had rolled in the spontaneous call that rumbled all the way to the frontier border near the Potomac, where Robert Hen had been murdered the year before.

Bacon and his friends also could see that the leaderless force was in no sense composed of a "rabble." Respectable small landholders of the tidewater country had abandoned their profitless toil to join the

tawny-colored men who could no longer work in their clearings surrounded by woods out of which Indian raiding parties might emerge
at any minute. Omitting the small segment of drifters and casuals at
the bottom of the colonial community, and at the other extreme such
families as those of young Bacon and his neighborhood friends, the
"soldiers" could be regarded as representative of the average settler
among Virginia's approximately forty thousand inhabitants.

At that period, only about two thousand Negroes had been imported as slaves bought outright, and the labor system depended upon
the continual stream of white indentures. Six thousand indentures
were then working out their "time," and a large proportion of freeholders planting their own farms on a small or moderate-size scale had
earned the proud estate of "landowner" by serving an established
planter for five years.

In working out their "time" of service, the young Englishmen
who came to the Colony were typical of the age of the apprentice,
when an individual did not expect society to provide him with an
education and opportunities for his start in life. The young man on
his own committed himself to a period of work without pay in which
he would equip himself with a craft or a trade. Captain John Smith
had, in the first years at Jamestown, stressed this point for the new
country: "No man is entitled to a place in America; he must make his
own." The average male indentured servant was, in effect, an apprentice tobacco-planter. After he had learned to equip himself for this life
during five years of working as an indenture, on becoming a freedman
he was provided with essentials for setting himself up.

Artisans and "white-collar" workers, clerks and tutors, who were
beyond apprenticeship, exchanged five years of their services for passage to the Colony and keep while becoming adjusted to the new
land.

Female indentures, not technically apprentices, also exchanged
their services for opportunities in the New World — mostly opportunities to marry. The women worked as "dairy maids" and "lady's
maids" and in general housework. The daughters of yeomen and
artisans did not by custom work in the fields, and in any case, much of
the work in the tobacco fields would have been too hard. When a man
wanted to marry an indentured servant, he bought the master's
"interest" — the price varied with her length of service. In all cases,
marriage was with the woman's consent, and laws and the customs of
the country protected female indentures against misuse. Judging from
the numbers of family units among the humbler settlers, the majority

of female indentures probably married before completing their service.

There was nothing demeaning in this system of contract, and an elaborate code of law protected indentures from overwork, abuse, inadequate diet, poor quarters and clothing, and the like. While some masters could be harsh (as could some employers in England), harshness did not generally characterize the treatment of indentures; some planters indentured younger kinsmen.

The indentures' backgrounds in England have been approximated by a variety of estimates made from incomplete figures, largely from the western part of Bristol and from London. The approximations have been largely substantiated by the recorded careers of those who survived in the Colony. A loose composite of all estimates indicated that as many as eighty percent of the indentures came from the English yeomanry or from the lower class of landless agricultural workers, and that skilled workers — artisans and tradesmen — came from the towns and cities. The larger portion of this eighty percent had been associated with farming, and of those more than half came from landowning yeoman families. Since the average age of indentures ran from eighteen to twenty-four, presumably most of those from yeoman families were younger members who themselves possessed no land in their own right.

Of all who came as indentures, no more than fifteen percent appear to have been unskilled, nonagricultural laborers. Little more than one percent came from the gentry — mostly as tutors or clerks or indentures to kinsmen. Before 1676 England had tried dumping criminals into Virginia during only one period, but the percentage of criminals was infinitesimal among survivors in the Colony.

Estimates of the proportion of the surviving colonists who originally came as indentures were even more approximate. Some calculations estimated that indentures made up as much as seventy-five percent of all those *who came to Virginia*. The same calculations estimated that barely thirty-five percent of the freeholders had come to the Colony as indentures. These apparently contradictory proportions — where three-fourths of all emigrants came as indentures, but former indentures constituted no more than one-third of the landholders — were partly accounted for by the appalling mortality rate among new settlers. Estimates of casualties ran as high as one hundred thousand in the first thirty years, and one estimate — probably high — indicated that five of every six adventurers perished in those first thirty years of the Colony. The heavy death rate came mostly in the "acclimating" period of transition from England: the quick changes in temperature, the semitropical sun of the tobacco fields and the malarial swamps. Indians, too, took an unestimated toll, very heavy in the 1622 and 1644 massacres, which were designed to exterminate the white colony.

Not all indentures who did not become freeholders were mortalities. Some ran away to other colonies before completing their services (in the early days, to Spanish-claimed land south of Virginia) and many on becoming freedmen worked for landholders in various capacities. The majority of the indentures who went on to work their own land blended into the sturdy, self-reliant yeomanry that developed in Virginia — the small-scale freeholders who in 1676 formed the bulk of the Colony's population.

The settlers loosely defined as yeomanry were not conscious of forming a class as the yeoman class was designated in England, but as individuals they existed within the hierarchy of social distinctions brought from England. No one protested when, in 1673, a tailor was fined for racing his mare for a wager of two thousand pounds of tobacco, on the ground that according to English law horse racing was "a sport for gentlemen alone."

While the term "gentleman" was open to the same loose definitions as in England, all understood that anyone who worked for his living with his hands was excluded. In fact, in Virginia as in England, outside the learned professions, almost any gainful employment for which wages were received seemed antithetical to the status of gentleman. When an artisan became an entrepreneur, who directed others, his status could change. The landowner's status appeared to change according to the growth of his prominence in the country. While the average yeoman was not privileged to write "Gent." after his name any more than in England, many would rise to this distinction and be addressed as "Mr."

To some, as to some in England, it was very important to achieve the status of "gentleman." To the majority it was sufficient to achieve, as a tax-paying landowner, the dignified status of "freeholder." To agricultural workers from England, whether of landless families or of families whose land was too limited to be parceled out to them, the ownership of land was a proud state. It gave freedmen a feeling of self-sufficiency and promoted an as yet unarticulated sense of the dignity of individual rights. To the artisans, such as the presumptuous tailor, landowning improved their position in the social hierarchy, as well as opening the way to a financial condition impossible to obtain by wages. Since there were no large cities in Virginia, the land meant more even than in England. For the Colony *was* land, and the general population was characterized by the freeholder — small, large, or middle-sized.

Among freeholders social mobility was more dramatic than in the England the settlers had left. Rises were swifter and higher. Freeholding families who were so little known in 1676 as to be almost unmentioned in recordings of the times, were to emerge into positions to produce three leaders of the Virginia Dynasty — Jefferson, Madison, and Monroe — who would govern the American republic in its formative years.

Andrew Munro (Monroe) was a Scotsman believed, without absolute proof, to have been the Major Munro who was captured while fighting as a loyalist with Charles I and banished to Virginia. For a certainty, he was settled in Virginia in 1650 and his son William, a ten-year-old during the gathering of the armed settlers in 1676, was to be the great-grandfather of the President.

James Maddison (Madison) came to Virginia in 1653 as a ship's carpenter and took patent on six hundred acres in Gloucester County. A minor-scale Richard Lee I, he built small sloops to handle trade in tobacco and grain, brought in several indentured servants, and had acquired eleven hundred additional acres by 1664.

Thomas Jefferson's ancestor was not placed for a certainty in Virginia until 1679, though this first Thomas probably was in Henrico County during the 1676 uprising. In 1679 the first Thomas Jefferson was known to be farming in the area of the James River south of The Falls, where the land had been patented early and grants were harder to come by than on the expanding frontier. He was a totally obscure freeholder and has been placed only by a claim made against his small holding by William Byrd I.

The effect of the fluidity among freeholders was that the men in their spontaneous gathering did not feel themselves to be citizens of an unprivileged class. Feeling discriminated against as English citizens, they defied the authorities only to the extent of looking after the safety of their families.

In taking their defense into their own hands, by carrying the fighting to the Indians, their defiant assembly began as no more of a rebellion than similar protest uprisings that had occurred in England. The year Jamestown was founded, English workers called "levelers" and "diggers" rioted in three counties against high prices imposed at a time of poor harvests, and a few years before that there had been anti-enclosure riots. Around 1630 more violence broke out, and it was reported that the high sheriff of Gloucestershire was "soon and easily repulsed by . . . base and disorderly people." Then, shortly before the civil wars, rioters against enclosure erupted in twelve counties, forest riots broke out in five counties, and roving bands committed public mayhem on the highways and in the towns.

In Virginia it was later, after the fighting started, that the original gathering was joined by runaway indentures, runaway Negro slaves, and "uncouth persons" of unknown occupation, freedmen but not landholders, who came in for pillage. Also, as in any civil conflict, the actual fighting brought out in some of the men their underlying hatred of all wealthy estate-owners. To select a leader, however, the gathering of armed settlers journeyed to the neighborhood of an aristocratic young planter who had never worked a day in his life.

It was not established that the leaderless "soldiers" came to the James River tidewater region of big plantations directly seeking Nathaniel Bacon as their leader. But it was believed that Bacon had been suggested to the men by his neighbor, Captain James Crews. Among the gentlemen of estate who sympathized with the frontier colonists in their purpose to drive the Indians away from the neighborhood of their settlements, Captain Crews was to go all the way as one of Bacon's lieutenants. Then, the armed settlers who halted across the river from Curles' Neck showed no surprise when they were approached by Councilor Bacon. Unless they had been prepared, the men would have had no reason to expect support — let alone leadership — from an English-born councilor whom they would normally regard as one of Berkeley's hated coterie.

3

When Bacon and his friends saw the armed gathering, events began to move with a speed and directness at which no recording witness expressed any surprise. Immediately Captain Crews suggested to Bacon that they take some rum across the river to the "soldiers." Whether or not Isham and Byrd were aware of Captain Crews's presumed recommendation of Bacon, they both supported his suggestion. The four planters walked down to the river to be rowed across, with Bacon apparently unaware that he had been mentioned for leadership. Yet, when his party climbed up the south bank, he showed no surprise when the gathering acclaimed him with belling, echoing yells.

"A Bacon!" they began to chant. "A Bacon!"

It was significant that the men did not say "Nathaniel Bacon," nor "Bacon." "A Bacon" meant a member of the family in the governor's clique, a leader established in *the social hierarchy* associated with political authority. "A Bacon" meant that the people were not choosing a leader from among themselves but one identified with authority in the traditional order.

Along with Crews's probable recommendation of Nathaniel Bacon, some of the more substantial colonists from the tidewater could have known that the young councilor had been unguarded in his assertions against authority on the Indian issue. On hearing of Berkeley's refusal to commission officers to lead an expedition, he was reported to have said: "If the redskins meddle with me, damn my blood but I'll harry them, commission or no commission." After Bacon's typically intemperate words, his overseer was killed. This background was the only explanation for the men's expectation that a councilor would lead an illegally mustered militia, whose force was swelled by what the government would regard as a "tumultuous assembly." It does not sufficiently explain why Bacon, standing slim and elegant in the midst of the work-hardened strangers with guns in their hands, immediately agreed to lead them.

His wife said he was motivated solely by a desire to help the colonists, who were helpless against Berkeley's refusal to change his policy. Elizabeth Bacon wrote her sister in England: "I pray God keep the worst enemy I have from ever being in such a sad condition as I have seen . . . The troublesome Indians have killed one of our overseers at an outward plantation . . . If you had been here, it would have grieved your heart to hear the pitiful complaints of the people — the Indians killing the people daily and the Governor not taking any notice for to hinder them, but to let them daily do all the mischief they can. . . . The poor people come to your brother to desire him to help them against the Indians, and he being so much concerned for the loss of the overseer and for the loss of so many poor men and women and children's lives every day, he was willing to do them all the good he could. . . ."

This wifely view attributed to Bacon a humanitarianism which he had never previously displayed in a life of undirected extravagance. It was possible that gently born Elizabeth Bacon, adjusting to life in the strange, raw land, knew nothing of the influence exerted on her husband by three gentlemen who were very articulate in their anti-Berkeley sentiments. No one knew the extent of their influence on Bacon; but his resentment at Berkeley's refusing him a partnership in a trading monopoly certainly made him receptive to their arguments against the governor's rule, and all three of them were immediately chosen by Bacon as his subleaders. In fact, Berkeley regarded the most sinuous-minded, "the thoughtful Mr. Lawrence," as the plotting brains behind all of Bacon's actions.

With the knowns and the "probables" in Bacon's life before he was acclaimed "leader," and with the erratic, turbulent arc of his revolutionary career, Bacon's actions were far less explainable than Berkeley's. His motivations, like his goals, would never become clear. Unstable and chronically unsatisfied though he was, his acceptance of leadership seemed much more than an impulse. Judged by his reactions alone, Bacon became the people's leader as if he had prepared himself for the role — as if his earlier directionless life had led him to it. It was as if he had waited all his days for that hour, in the lazily bright afternoon, and when it came he was never the same again.

There in the open countryside, where the shallow waves lapped against the river bank, Bacon began by denouncing the old governor as "negligent and wicked, treacherous and incapable." Casting himself as the people's protagonist against the symbol of arrogant, greedy privilege, he promised his enrapt listeners that beyond removing the Indian menace he would redress their many wrongs. The passionate voice showed at once Bacon's gift for arousing men, in loyalty to him and to violent action, and perhaps he had never before experienced the heady sensation of leadership — of throwing a spell over men whose eyes grew hot at his words.

Before the sun went down, the purposeless wastrel had become transformed into "Bacon the Rebel." He ordered the men to take an oath of loyalty to him, and they signed their names in a circle so that the ringleaders could never be known. With this act, Bacon began to rival Berkeley (the former avocational playwright) in making America's first revolution a highly theatrical melodrama. But the struggle that grew around the mortal duel between the two transplanted Englishmen was none the less bloody for being theatrical.

4

At the very beginning, before it became evident that Bacon was not merely leading an unauthorized force against the Indians, William Byrd and other merchant-planters gave their friend at least moral support. These substantial planters revealed their sympathy for what they at first supposed was a movement to bring safety to the border families. When Bacon went on to challenge the governor's authority, Byrd and others withdrew their support. Bacon's followers never placed these early sympathizers among the enemies of the people.

At the same time, the three anti-Berkeleyites came into the open and contributed to an unknown degree toward expanding the unauthorized Indian expedition into a full-scale rebellion. Of these three, one was a man of learning and one was a man of violence.

The learned man was Richard Lawrence, an Oxford graduate and one of the strangest inhabitants of Jamestown. Besides the State House, the red-brick church, the public warehouse, and the storehouse for the mounted guns on the wharf, only a couple of dozen buildings lined Jamestown's two parallel streets, the first of which faced the river. As most of these buildings were occupied by merchants or tavern-keepers (who charged exorbitant prices when the General Assembly was in session), the few permanent homeowners had no more privacy than dwellers in a village. Thus, the mysterious Mr. Lawrence was generally known as the first miscegenist on record: he sought, it was told, "the dark embraces of a blackamoore, his slave . . . as though beauty consisted altogether in antipathy of complexions." Only rumors explained his appearance in Jamestown where, with no need to work, he passed his time in philosophical discourse on the evils of Berkeley's clique.

The man of violence, Giles Bland, was described as "a man of good parts, of courage and resolution," and also as "a man of strong parts, but of great passions, hearty and imperious beyond bearing." Giles Bland was the son of a London merchant in international trade. His uncles had operated in Spain before coming to Charles City County, where in 1654 one of them, Theodorick Bland, established large holdings which encompassed the plantations of Westover and Berkeley Hundred. An educated gentleman of personal presence, Theodorick Bland quickly rose to a position among Berkeley's influential friends and was appointed to the Council. He died in 1671, leaving a widow with three young children. John Bland, Giles's father, held a stake in his brother's Charles City property, and Giles Bland had come to Virginia to settle his father's interests in the estate.

John Bland was sufficiently well established among the London directors of colonial affairs to get his son appointed to the lucrative post of collector of customs, and young Giles was received, with Nathaniel Bacon, into the small group of tidewater elite. In trying to straighten out his father's interests, he ran into conflict with his uncle's widow and entered litigation over the property against her and her children. His aunt-in-law found a champion in her late husband's friend, Secretary Thomas Ludwell, the governor's cousin. Thomas Ludwell and his younger brother Philip were contumacious and arrogant men, with reputations for vituperative powers. In a night meeting with Giles Bland in Thomas Ludwell's Jamestown house, when both "were heated with too much wine and brandy," the secretary indulged his penchant for invective with personal insults to his guest.

No local bumpkin standing in awe of the governor's crony, young Bland, a man "of great passions," cursed Ludwell and challenged him to a duel. Gloves were exchanged and the two Englishmen agreed to meet in the field the next morning. In the daylight, discretion prevailed over Ludwell's truculence and he failed to appear. Bland, who had not gone to bed, in his rage nailed the secretary's glove to the State House door, accompanied by insulting words for the public to see.

Berkeley and his friends rallied around their own. The Council fined Bland the large sum of £500 and Sir William removed him from the office of collector of customs. Bland turned against the governor's cabal in reaction to this "unexampled severity" to — as his mother wrote in a petition to the King — "a stranger, and friendless." Young Bland, whose father had by then died, was not friendless in the high places of the English government. He wrote letters, which reached the King, of "the very distracted posture" of things in Virginia, which he doubted could be settled through "the authority and power lodged in the aged governor . . . without the gracious assistance of His Majesty and his Councils. . . ."

Bland stressed the burden of taxes which bore as heavily on the poorest as on the richest, and suggested, among other remedies for the grievances of the people, an enlargement of their liberty, "in declaring that all such that are born there shall be free borne subjects of England to all intents and purposes."

(Ninety years later Richard Bland, the son of one of the young cousins Giles Bland sought to evict, would write the first clear-headed declaration of the colonies' position on government of their internal affairs.)

The third intriguer was William Drummond. Like Lawrence, he seemed to oppose Berkeley's clique largely on principle, although his approach was less philosophical than that of his Jamestown neighbor. Drummond was a Scotsman who himself had been a colonial governor, of Albemarle in North Carolina, and with his wife and four children kept one of the finest houses in the capital. Not as impetuous as his two friends, Drummond committed himself by degrees. When he felt there was no turning back, ex-Governor Drummond said, almost resignedly, "In over shoes, in over boots."

Captain James Crews, also a family man, became a subleader and stayed to the bitter end. These four men, with high-minded Captain Thomas Hansford, formed the nucleus of leadership around Nathaniel Bacon. Whatever part these most-trusted subordinates had played in bringing Bacon to leadership, once he rode at the head of a body of armed men, the revolution became all his. With all the cloudiness of his motivations, Bacon, finding himself as a swayer of crowd passions, became America's first demagogue.

Nathaniel Bacon was the first leader to use the words "the people" in the later meaning. It was because of his impassioned exhortations on the liberties of the individual — anticipating Patrick Henry and Thomas Jefferson by a century — that he was sometimes called the precursor of the American Revolution. Although the impression he made on Virginia was deep and lasting, and the Colony was never the same again, it seems doubtful that this impulsive young gentleman was guided by the principles of government which later came into being. To the end there remained the unanswered questions: to what extent were the seeds of full-scale rebellion planted in Bacon on the day he accepted the leadership, and to what extent was he carried along by the momentum of violence, improvising as he went?

The seeds were probably planted in his unconscious at the beginning and came to the surface as he was carried along, improvising, with never a clearly defined goal.

5

Given the assumption that young Bacon did not take command with the conscious purpose of fomenting rebellion, the incidents that carried him along were initiated by Berkeley. When the governor discovered that the settlers were determined to defend themselves against the Indians without his authority, and that they had a member of the Council to lead them, Berkeley forgot all considerations except imposing his authority on "the wild beast multitude" and its renegade leader.

First he simply ordered Bacon to disband the gathering. Then he proclaimed Bacon a "rebel." Next he did a foolish thing: he sent three hundred mounted loyalists galloping westward toward The Falls to disperse the "rebels" and capture Bacon.

While Bacon and some of his subordinates usually rode, and occasionally small companies of militia "cavalry" were gathered (mostly for display), Berkeley's followers were the first mounted force employed in Virginia. The sight of the governor's spurred gentlemen on their way to ride men down awakened memories of the bitter distinctions the settlers had left behind in England. To even the second- and third-generation colonists, who knew only Virginia's uncharted lands, the men on horseback recalled tales told of the cruel inequities in the mother country and of the overbearing superiority of titled landlords. Without striking a blow, Bacon suddenly became a people's hero in the early settled county of Henrico — across which the governor's horsemen rode — and adjoining New Kent. From those older regions, sympathy for the new leader, specifically against the governor, began to spread throughout the Colony.

Unaware of the mounted force sent against him, Bacon missed a clash of arms by having started his men southward into the forests before the riders reached the hill overlooking The Falls. While these resplendent horsemen, as they rode back to Jamestown, were arousing the country to Bacon's support, he appeared at that stage to be concentrating only on the settlers' purpose of finding and dispersing the Susquehannocks.

That fierce tribe, after melting into the wilderness late the previous summer, had shifted southward in their raiding along the outskirts from the Potomac to the unsettled, densely brushed low country south of the James River. The only approaches for pursuit were the narrow trails cut by the trading caravans of Abraham Wood. (Major General Wood had avoided taking sides by pleading "infirmities" which confined him to his house. For this, Berkeley reduced the old pioneer's rank to Colonel.) Bacon had in his party several woodsmen familiar with the trails, and they led the strung-out march.

It was early May, before the warm days turned hot, and flecks of dogwood petals showed through the rank vines draping the trees and the tangled underbrush. No one could see fifty yards in front of him. The only breaks in the obscuring woods were marshy-banked streams and spreading swamps. The men began to feel the strain of the march as one monotonous day followed the next, but they knew they were on the track of the Susquehannocks. Some of the woodsmen spoke Indian dialects, and through them Bacon learned from tributary tribes they passed that the Susquehannocks were moving ahead of them.

Then, as the lengthening line of marchers — with stragglers miles in the rear — neared the Roanoke River, at the North Carolina border, an Indian messenger came to the head of the column. He told Bacon, through the woodsmen interpreters, that tributary tribes had been forced to join the Susquehannocks in raids on plantations, and that now these unwilling marauders were ready to turn on the Susquehannocks when Bacon attacked. The Susquehannocks had halted to make a stand on an island in the Roanoke River, where they had built one of their ingenious forts.

Bacon, hurrying on, found when he reached the river that only seventy of his followers were at hand. Provisions had run low as the march grew longer, and the rest of the force had fallen out along the way. While Bacon paused to survey the situation, he observed a nearby village of the Occaneechis. It was built across the traders' trail that led southwest to Cherokee country, and from this strategic position the Occaneechis had long exacted tribute from trading parties as the price of peace. These Indians, Bacon learned, were no happier with the Susquehannocks as neighbors than the northern Doegs had been. Though the Occaneechis themselves were not entirely trustworthy, Bacon entered into a temporary alliance with them. He was also able to open negotiations with those Indians on the island who had been forced to accompany the Susquehannocks.

The fight with the Indians became actually two battles, and only the second battle was involved in the controversy that followed. In the first, the Susquehannocks of fearsome repute were overcome so quickly that the attack on them was almost anticlimactic. They had not been warned by their Indian brethren of Bacon's approach, and apparently trusting in their reputation to awe the Occaneechis, the warriors were lounging about totally unprepared when the white men and the other Indians fell upon them. None escaped. Those not killed in the first onslaught were captured and, to the revulsion of Bacon's men, slowly tortured to death.

The second fight, the real battle, broke out between Bacon's men and their former Indian allies. After the Susquehannocks had been killed, the Mannakins, who presumably had been held captive, drifted in with the Occaneechis; and the actions of this combined force made Bacon's small band suspicious.

In the later controversy, Bacon's supporters claimed that the Indians posted guards over their provisions and the spoils from the Susquehannocks, began to man their own forts, and took a threatening attitude toward Bacon's surviving men, who were then practically without food. Berkeleyites, writing without firsthand information, claimed that Bacon forced the fight on the peaceful Occaneechis. There was probably truth in both claims. The Occaneechis were known to supply weapons — extracted from traders — to raiding parties, and in his insecure position, with his men threatened by starvation, Bacon might well have decided to finish off the tribe he suspected of treachery.

The fierce fight there in the woods by the river lasted into a second day before the Indians gave up, after their chief, Rossechy, fell dead. The surviving warriors put the women and children into canoes. The small party that escaped down the river would never again be enough to maintain their fort on the traders' highway. The Susquehannocks in southern Virginia were finished. And tributary tribes, from which warriors had not always been "forced" to join raiding parties, could be expected to be quiet for a while in the James River country and on the south side of the river.

With the provisions, spoils and captive Indians, Bacon's attenuated fighters started back for The Falls. As of that phase, the settlers with Bacon had accomplished their purpose: safety had been brought at least temporarily to one region in Virginia.

6

The accomplishments of Bacon's force meant nothing to the affronted old governor, who was doubtless egged on by My Lady Frances. He announced the removal of Bacon from the Council, proclaimed "the divers rude, dissolute and tumultuous" persons who had followed Bacon to be rebels, and gathered a force of loyalists at The Falls to pounce on Bacon's worn-out band when the men returned.

Before Bacon reached the James River, Berkeley's advisers in Jamestown urged him to return to the capital for the more immediately important matter of convening the new General Assembly. On his way along the serpentine river road, the governor turned off briefly at Curles' Neck plantation. There he gave himself the satisfaction of telling Elizabeth Bacon to her face that he intended hanging her husband as soon as they caught him.

It had seemed a shrewd move for Berkeley to call the first new election of the House of Burgesses in fourteen years, while Bacon was away in May. The once-adroit executive calculated that the sop of a new election would divert the people from their grievances and isolate Bacon. In this move, Sir William revealed his loss of contact with the

Virginians. He had seriously underestimated the strength of the people's protest. Henrico County elected Bacon, the deposed councilor, along with Captain Crews, as their representatives in the House.

Bacon set off for Jamestown in a sloop with forty of his men as a bodyguard. But he had underestimated the force of the old autocrat's determination to bring him to heel. A large vessel armed with heavy guns ran down the sloop and a naval captain captured the thinned-out and weather-stained Bacon.

The young rebel was in a subdued state when he was brought into the governor's presence in the State House. Berkeley lifted his arms above his head and said in a sonorous voice, "Now I behold the greatest rebel that ever was in Virginia."

Bacon, standing silent with head bowed, gave the former dramatist no help in building a scene. After a baffled moment, Berkeley made one of the few decisions that reflected his previous astuteness. He paroled Bacon on his own honor and turned him over to the advice of his cousin, Councilor Nathaniel Bacon the Senior. This prudent gentleman of the Establishment, shocked at his young cousin's reckless behavior, sincerely urged him to seek pardon and be restored to his rightful position. With unknown motives — perhaps no more than making the best of a bad situation — Bacon agreed.

The next day gave Berkeley the opportunity to milk a scene for all it was worth. The Council chamber was on the ground floor of the State House, and at one end the bewigged governor sat with the councilors on a raised platform behind a railing. A sober-faced young Bacon knelt on one knee at the railing and read his prepared confession. Then Berkeley intoned three times, "God forgive you, I forgive you." With the act over, Berkeley restored Bacon to his seat on the Council and nothing more was said about rebels.

The governor, however, was not finished with crushing the "multitude's" assertion of rights against the King's deputy. Having eliminated Bacon from the House of Burgesses by reinstating him in the Council, he set about to reduce the new burgesses to the position of puppets, in which he had kept the elected members of the General Assembly almost since the Restoration. His ultimate plans for Bacon were not known, but Bacon feared — with whatever justification — that he was to be re-arrested. And he had learned, for a certainty, that Berkeley had no intention of giving him a commission or legalizing further expeditions against the Indians. At this stage of affairs, in June, his legalized leadership still seemed to be Bacon's only concern — except for his personal safety.

On a warm moonless night, Bacon slipped through the shadows of the town to the mainland, mounted a horse, and rode hard through the darkness to Curles' Neck. Word went out across the countryside and followers began to gather. Bacon told them they were not to be allowed to carry their fight to the Indians in other regions. At that point men arrived at Bacon's plantation with news of Berkeley's latest acts. Not only was the existing force not to be legalized for further operations, but Berkeley proposed raising what amounted to a standing army to replace his worthless forts. The burgesses were said to be shocked at the proposal that heavier taxes, to finance this army, be added to the colonists' burdens.

When it became known that Berkeley was set on handling the Indian menace any way except the way the people wanted, new recruits came on foot, on horse and by boat to join Bacon's veterans. In the excitement of this second gathering, more openly defiant of the governor's authority than the first force, Bacon took the turn to revolution. He marched his "hearts of gold," as he called the men, on to Jamestown.

Berkeley was nothing of a coward. Rushing out a call for a quick rendezvous of loyalists at Jamestown, he tried personally to place the capital in a position of defense. Jamestown's fort faced the river, to guard against England's international enemies, and the governor ordered four guns from the fort to be placed at the narrow isthmus connecting Jamestown with the mainland. With only thirty soldiers on hand, he put them to building a palisade across the isthmus.

The soldiers labored alone, as the loyalists showed no speed in marching to a fight with Bacon's toughened Indian-fighters. When the frightened cry arose that Bacon was only ten miles away, Berkeley saw that his few unsupported soldiers had no stomach for a collision. Denied a fight, the old beau still was not to be denied his moment. Retiring into the Council chamber in the State House, he waited the arrival of Bacon's "tumultuous" horde.

It was early afternoon of a bland day in late June when Bacon marched at the head of the hundreds of armed men on to the green parkway between the State House and the steep banks to the river. Hurrying off detachments to occupy the fort and the ferry, he formed his fusileers in double lines facing the State House. Except for the shouts of officers and the rattle of accouterments, the men were quiet. Bacon dispatched a message telling the governor to send out some of the councilors.

When two of them appeared in the doorway, Bacon announced

that he had come for a commission. As the councilors made no reply, Bacon went on to say that the Assembly could not vote for higher taxes to support a standing army. At that Sir William rushed out onto the little porch in the center of the State House.

Gesticulating wildly, he tried to take the scene away from Bacon. Berkeley pulled back his coat to reveal the ruffled linen of his white shirt, and cried, ''Here, shoot me. 'Fore God, a fair mark — shoot!''

Bacon was not to be outplayed. He flung up his arm and shouted that they had not come to shoot anybody but to get a commission to fight the Indians. Bacon has been described by Thomas Mathew, the Northern Neck merchant-planter whose overseer had found the dying Robert Hen. Then among the frightened burgesses, Mathew felt some sympathy for Bacon and was on principle opposed to the governor. But he recounted that the young leader struck ''outrageous postures . . . strutting between his two files of men with his left arm akimbo, flinging his right arm every way . . . often tossing his hand from his sword to his hat.''

At this impasse between the antagonists, Bacon's fusileers spontaneously decided the issue. The burgesses were peering anxiously out of the windows on the second floor, and suddenly the fusileers raised their guns toward the windows. The metallic click of the cocked fusils rattled down the lines as the tough-bitten men shouted, ''We shall have it'' — the commission.

The terrified burgesses shouted back assurances that the commission would be granted. Actually only the governor had the authority to issue a commission. However, the councilors, feeling the futility of their privilege before the explosive armed mob, joined the burgesses in urging the adamant old man to sign a commission. Making no effort to hide his loathing of this coercion, Sir William at last signed a commission for Bacon on June 24. Everyone in Jamestown breathed a sigh of relief.

Bacon remained in command of the capital while the House of Burgesses, protected against Berkeley's intervention, hurried through a succession of laws aimed at destroying the governor's system of privileges tightly held by a few. Though this session is usually called ''Bacon's Assembly,'' in point of fact the people's leader showed little interest and took little part in the laws passed by the ''Assembly,'' temporarily free of Berkeley's yoke.

The fundamental purpose of the new laws was to break the control imposed upon the general population by a central group at Jamestown, and to insure the participation of all freedmen in the operation of affairs at the county level. This was the genesis of the colonists' gradually growing demand for control of their internal affairs.

One of the new basic laws removed the restrictions on the voting franchise which permitted only landowners — or "housekeepers" (operators of a rented farm on which they lived) — to vote, and made eligible all adult white male freedmen. Another basic change involved a legal custom foreign to modern practices. As the Church of England was the church of the State, the parish vestries formed integral parts of the political structure. Except for the quarter sessions of court, a church provided the only center for gatherings in the large, mostly uninhabited area covered by a parish, and the vestries were charged with maintaining the usually isolated building; obtaining ministers from England (a difficult task: it was very hard to get good men) and making assessments for their salaries; providing for the poor, and various other matters, including negotiations with the government. Naturally the educated and wealthier parishioners were placed on the vestries.

The people's complaint arose against the practice of influential families in establishing themselves permanently on the vestries. Since these self-perpetuating members of the vestries were allied with the ruling clique in Jamestown, a parish's affairs were in effect controlled from a central authority, contrary to the operation of the established order in England. The new law ended the self-perpetuation of boards of vestry and opened the vestry membership to election every three years by all the parishioners. This law reflected the Assembly's general underlying intention of bringing the control of parish, and county, affairs to the citizens of the neighborhood.

Several laws were directed specifically at the councilors. The number of appointive (salaried) offices that could be held was limited. Councilors were denied the right to sit with county justices of the peace, and — perhaps the most galling grievance — the councilors' exemption from taxation was removed. Other similar measures revealed the design of the people's representatives to curtail the power and privilege of those hated embodiments of special interests. One law, which (had it been retroactive) would have included Bacon himself, required a minimum of three years' residence in the Colony before an individual could be appointed to any post or the Council.

Later, all the laws passed that June were revoked. But the people's representatives *had* voiced their protests in the forum, and under the specific details of the protests lay an unarticulated concept, an undefined principle of government. The people were not to forget that the protest had been voiced, and the principle was to endure, assuming definition and gathering force.

The passage of the laws, while Bacon's men were in command of the capital, was the high point of Bacon's Rebellion in its significance. From then on, the meaning of the people's protest was overshadowed by the violence and hatred that swept the Colony when the spontaneous movement of that spring degenerated into civil war between Bacon and Berkeley.

7

Late in June word came to Bacon in Jamestown that eight fresh murders had been committed by Indians only forty miles away, though well north of the James River country he had cleared. Using the commission he had exacted from Berkeley, Nathaniel Bacon left the capital to recruit for a full-scale expedition. Bacon himself, with his most persuasive lieutenants, rode across counties on recruiting trips in the sultry July weather.

As the numbers swelled, this new force — unlike the volunteer gathering of May — was prepared carefully with some semblance of military organization. Groups were formed in companies, men who owned horses or had impressed horses were formed into cavalry troops, and supplies — some of which were also impressed — were gathered at strategic points. By the end of July Bacon commanded a formidable force of some thirteen hundred men.

Just as he was ready to mount his decisive campaign against the Indians, Bacon learned that Berkeley was out trying to raise troops again to march against the "rebel." At this stage Berkeley's last responsible acts as governor were behind him. He was obsessed by hatred of the *idea* of the people's assertiveness as represented by Bacon and his followers; the Indian atrocities and the demonstrated sentiment of the people in the House of Burgesses all became meaningless to him. Repudiating the commission given Bacon and again proclaiming him a "rebel," Berkeley apparently believed, despite all contrary evidence, he could raise a force of loyalists willing and capable of taking on what by then amounted to Bacon's army.

When Bacon learned that the governor was trying to rally a force, he turned his troops eastward, toward Jamestown. Very few loyalists came to Berkeley's support. From Middle Plantation (later Williamsburg), the fuming governor could only retire before Bacon's advance. He crossed the York River into Gloucester County, and there suffered a terrible humiliation. While appealing for recruits, he was interrupted by cries of ''Bacon! Bacon!'' It was said that the flushed-faced old man ''fainted away on horseback in the field.''

Sir William probably realized that Bacon would make *him* a prisoner if they met again. Bacon's plan seemed to be to capture and hold the governor, while he wrote the King of the state of affairs. There was nothing for Berkeley to do except abandon his post. Gloucester County faced Chesapeake Bay, and the governor took ship for the Eastern Shore, two counties extending southward from Maryland and divided from the Virginia mainland by the bay. There the people had not suffered from the Indians and, if they were no longer enthusiastic about the governor, they had no stake in the rebellion. They gave sanctuary to Berkeley and his party.

Bacon, seeing that he must control the waters, immediately captured several ships. He impressed their crews and fitted heavy guns on the decks. Giles Bland and Captain William Carver, a seaman, were placed in command of this ''fleet'' which patrolled the bay, isolated the governor, and guarded all approaches to the inland rivers. With his rear protected, Bacon finally turned to the Indian campaign.

This time the enemy was the Pamunkey tribe, long a tributary of the English. From their partisan viewpoints, the Berkeleyites claimed that the Pamunkeys were allies and friends who would not conceivably harm a white person, while the Baconians claimed that the Pamunkeys had given help to the Susquehannocks and the stray bands in the recent atrocities. It was true that the Pamunkey territory opened on Gloucester County, where the latest ravages had just been committed. In that slaughter, the eight victims had been captured and roasted alive, while being subjected to unspeakable tortures.

It was also true that earlier, when Berkeley had brought in the queen of the Pamunkeys for a conference on the subject of the Pamunkey warriors' helping the whites against the hostiles, the impassive old woman — wearing a deerskin ''mantle'' and a crown of black and white strips of wampum — had seemed huffy rather than friendly. As with all the contradictions, there was probably truth on both sides. The Pamunkeys were officially friendly as a tribe, but undoubtedly some of their warriors had gone along with the hostilities. They were certainly aware that the Gloucester marauders had issued from their territory.

Some time before Bacon started out, the Pamunkeys abandoned their villages on the north side of the Pamunkey River and fled across the Mattaponi to hole up in the dismal stretches of the Dragon Swamp.

In the pursuit, the march in the hot weather through the matted brush and then into the tangled bogs of the swamp bore very hard on the men with Bacon, and on him personally. When the reduced force finally found and pounced upon the Pamunkeys, the fight was not very glorious. The Indians seemed more frightened than warlike, and the rout became a chase rather than a battle. Barely 150 men still followed Bacon when he returned once again to Henrico County.

There he received bad news. Berkeley by trickery had captured Giles Bland and Captain Carver with their commandeered ships, and had returned to Jamestown with heavy guns and reportedly 1,000 men.

In gathering his force, the embittered Berkeley had gone all the way toward civil war. He promised recruits rewards from the estates of the rebels along with exemption from taxes for twenty-one years, and granted freedom to any men who were under indenture to any of Bacon's followers. Until this point, the rebels — though using force of arms to gain Bacon's commission — had fought no one except Indians. But now Nathaniel Bacon, appealing to his "hearts of gold," took the final step toward battle with the forces of the Crown's representative.

In a maneuver he believed necessary because of the smallness of his force, the young gentleman brought an opprobrium on his reputation that his defenders could never explain away. He sent off bands to bring in the wives of some of the councilors — including his cousin's wife, also named Elizabeth Bacon, and Anna Ballard, the wife of the man who had befriended him in the sale of a working plantation. Conspicuous in their white aprons, these ladies were forced to walk back and forth upon an earthen barricade while Bacon's men — safe from the fire of Berkeley's heavy guns — built a strong breastwork across the isthmus and brought up guns of their own.

The next day Berkeley's great force was sent in an attack on Bacon's works. At one volley from the seasoned Indian-fighters, Sir William's recruits showed they had no heart in fighting for him. They fled. Once more the governor and his loyal cabal sailed for the Eastern Shore, and once more Bacon's men occupied the capital. There, with most of the available heavy guns on ships commanded by Berkeley, Bacon did not know what to do. For want of any plan, the men set fire to every house in Jamestown, including the State House and the church. With the flames reflecting on the tidal river in the background, the rebels filed off the island.

Three miles away, on September 20, Bacon quartered himself at Berkeley's Green Spring mansion. The storehouses were soon emptied of grain, the cattle slaughtered, and men made merry in the great rooms where Lady Frances had entertained the colonial nobility. That was near the end for Bacon. He had not recovered from the Indian campaigns and the five months of unbroken strain, and he was not a well man.

Then a force from northern Virginia was reported on its way against him, commanded by Giles Brent. Brent was half-Indian, the son of a member of a prominent Maryland Roman Catholic family and an empress of the Piscataways. His purpose seemed vague. Bacon posted a detachment among the charred ruins of Jamestown, left another at Green Spring, and marched to the York River. There he crossed into Gloucester County. Brent's force disintegrated at the approach of Bacon's men, but their brief and ignominious part in the rebellion exerted another strain on Bacon's depleted system.

After all, the slender young man had come to Virginia from the very unstrenuous life of an English dandy and he had competed on equal terms with farmers and frontiersmen, who fell out in droves. Nothing was known of the illness that overcame him in his exhausted state on the Gloucester side of the York River. The only certainty was that he died on October 26. The legends have it that his body was placed in a weighted coffin and sunk in the York River.

. In little more than six months Bacon's career in rebellion was completed, and any purpose for his rebel force was buried with him. Whatever ambitions may have flickered through his mind, beneath the gaudy phrases that served him as a leader in action, Bacon left no plans with his subordinates. After his first unauthorized expedition against the Susquehannocks in southern Virginia, he had largely reacted to Berkeley and a sequence of interactions had been set in motion between the two protagonists. When Bacon was no more, his five chief lieutenants shifted to defensive guerrilla action against the vengeance of a governor who then seemed scarcely rational.

Death sentences were given most casually in Berkeley's day, and in England spectators would gather to view the barbarous methods by which men were executed in public. According to these prevailing standards, there was nothing inhumane about Berkeley's rage to kill those who had presumed to challenge the royal governor's authority. But only total loss of self-control could have permitted a Crown's representative of Berkeley's caliber to indulge this rage with an irresponsibility that reduced the Colony to an arena for his personal vengeance.

Above all things, the destitute colonists needed an end to purpose-

less internecine warfare and a healing of the divisions already revealed. It would not have taken long to restore peace by granting a
general amnesty, as Charles II had done, even though Charles's
pardons had included men indirectly involved in the murder of his
father, a king. But in the aftermath of Bacon's rebellion Sir William
Berkeley, who had begun his colonial career as a conciliator, deepened
and made lasting the divisions. The result was that the repercussions
of the aftermath gave momentum to the individual assertiveness
which had got his back up in the beginning, back when the issue was
largely restricted to Indians.

8

Bacon's force split into five bands and took up positions at strategic points between the York and the James. None of the leaders
showed any capacity for combat leadership. Their only purpose was to
keep out of Berkeley's clutches, and their attention was directed
mostly to victualing the men. It was when the bands gathered provisions that the aura of idealism began to fade from the rebels' activities.

Even in Bacon's day the rebels had grown a little heavy-handed
in impressing food supplies. When November brought chilling nights
and days of lancing winds, the fields had all been harvested, stock was
sheltered in barns, and most of the colonists had put by the hoards of
cornmeal and bacon they hoped would last through the winter. At the
same time the big planters had packed their storehouses with provisions for their private communities — families, indentured workers,
slaves — and for the hospitality they extended to travelers in a land
where inns were few and poor. The rebel bands started provisioning
from the fat plantations, and impressment quickly gave way to
plunder.

Until then, the men who followed Bacon had shown far less
hatred of the wealthy than ''the mean and base multitudes'' who had
rioted in England. During Bacon's leadership only one of the governor's clique, the sourly righteous Richard Lee II, had been molested.
Bacon had taken Councilor Lee a prisoner, probably with the idea of
using him as a hostage. After Bacon's death, while the austere,
scholarly young Lee was kept away from his books, his storehouses
were ransacked, his animals driven off, and his estate plundered.

Now, when the plundering phase began at Richard Lee's, the
bands made for the plantations of other councilors and highly placed

persons. Among the grandees whose homes and outbuildings were looted were Colonel Philip Ludwell and Colonel Daniel Parke, then absent in England; Colonel Nicholas Spencer, one of the "younger sons" of the legends (his son inherited the family estate in England); Colonel Thomas Ballard, one of the staunchest Berkeleyites, and Colonel Edward Hill, of Shirley plantation, one of the haughtiest; high-living Councilor Ralph Wormeley, and inoffensive Councilor William Cole. Sir Henry Chicheley, a deputy governor of the best intentions toward everyone, was imprisoned, and Bacon's older cousin, Councilor Nathaniel Bacon the Senior, was treated very harshly. His rambling house and outbuildings were occupied and stripped.

When the plundering became general, the bands began to descend on any well-stocked plantation, regardless of the owner's status or affiliations. The men grew callous, slaughtering the animals of families by no means wealthy and taking valuables as well as food. They showed a curious desire to steal linen. This must have seemed a symbol of luxury, as tablecloths and napkins would scarcely have been appropriate for meals served on "the boards" — the planks laid across wooden horses set up temporarily in the one main room of a settler's cabin.

More than twenty families well removed from the ruling clique listed losses, and uncounted more did not officially list theirs. Among those outside Berkeley's cabal who put in the loudest claim was Colonel John Washington. A leader in the first fight against the Susquehannocks and a member of the House of Burgesses, he lived far from Jamestown, in Westmoreland County, in the Northern Neck. But as the prudent, acquisitive Colonel Washington was regarded as wealthy, his house and outbuildings were occupied and looted.

These depredations spread as winter set in, chiefly because the leaders were afraid to give up. Desertions drained the separated bands and the only large force was being hacked at by Berkeley's one able commander, Robert Beverley. Beverley was a successful middle-aged lawyer who had acquired a fine estate, and he was attached to Berkeley's order — and to Berkeley personally — rather than sharing in the interlocking financial interests of the large-scale merchant-planters. He was a man strongly moved by partisanship (his Virginia career was to take an amazing turn) and went at any action, military or political, with an uncompromising fearlessness.

Beverley's assignment was to lead water-borne loyalist forces from the Eastern Shore and swoop down on small rebel detachments.

His particular victims belonged to the force commanded by Bacon's successor, Joseph Ingram. Ingram was an Englishman about whom little was known except that he was new in the Colony. His headquarters were at West Point, where the York divided into the Mattaponi and the Pamunkey, and from there he foolishly continued to dispatch detachments from the main force for Beverley to gobble up.

In January the rebellion was obviously falling apart, when naval Captain Thomas Grantham arrived on a warship, in advance of one thousand regular British troops. Although Berkeley was anxious to end the rebellion before the troops arrived to restore order in *his* colony, his blinding hatred would not permit him to negotiate with the rebels. Captain Grantham approached Ingram directly. He promised personal safety to the inept rebel and pointed out that the only alternative to surrender was to shiver and starve while waiting to be run down by British regulars.

When Ingram came in, the other rebel leaders denounced him as a traitor, but their own bands were disintegrating around them. The problem for Richard Lawrence and William Drummond, the original Jamestown conspirators, was that personal safety would not be offered them. Since they could not surrender and neither had shown capacity for commanding men, they combined their bands with that of one Thomas Whaley. Described as "an ignorant, stout fellow," and probably either a former indenture or a seaman who had jumped ship, Whaley had appeared during the course of the rebellion and showed some resourcefulness as a group leader.

The combined force numbered about three hundred men and boys, "besides Concubines and Whores." This motley collection, taking the last of the captured stores, retired westward into New Kent County along the swampy edges of the Pamunkey. The leaders apparently cherished some wan hope of gathering fresh recruits and making it to the frontier. By then the settlers were weary of insurrection, and Whaley's band began to melt away. Seeing the end at hand, Whaley himself and Richard Lawrence slipped away into the gray brush of the swamp. Nothing more was ever heard of the sinuous-minded "Mr. Lawrence."

His friend William Drummond did not fare so well. The former colonial governor was captured, hiding in the swamp, and hustled straight into the presence of Sir William, then staying at the recovered home of Nathaniel Bacon the Senior. Berkeley greeted the prisoner with a line that became historic. Bowing mockingly, he said, "Mr. Drummond, you are very welcome. I am more glad to see you than any man in Virginia. Mr. Drummond, you shall be hanged in half an hour.''

The Scotsman replied steadily, ''What Your Honor pleases.''

After a night in irons on a ship, during which time a ring was torn from his finger and his clothes off his back, Drummond was given a brief ''trial'' and hanged. His wife and children were forced to flee for their lives, and Berkeley confiscated their property.

Elizabeth Bacon's property was also confiscated, to await the King's wishes, and Berkeley began to make persecutory confiscations of the property of men associated with the rebellion.

After the execution of Drummond, Sir William went on a hanging spree. Among others went the men of substance who had been Bacon's earliest supporters — Captain James Crews, Thomas Hansford, and the tumultuous Giles Bland. Along with the hangings and confiscations and clapping of men in jail, Berkeley took a Caligula-like delight in holding threats over the heads of people who could in any way be identified with Bacon. Some of these, afraid to return to their homes, hid out in the forests.

In his compulsion to restore his self-esteem by this assertion of authority, Berkeley perfected the role of the classic villain. With the Colony in the palm of his hand, Sir William had recovered his aplomb when three commissioners from the King arrived at Jamestown in January, 1677.

During the summer's upheavals, Berkeley had written Charles II that he was too old and infirm to continue at his post — confirming Giles Bland's report — and the commissioners had come with directions from the King. Colonel Herbert Jeffreys commanded the British regulars who accompanied the commission, Sir John Berry was in command of the ships, and the third commissioner, Colonel Francis Moryson, was a Virginian who had been representing the Colony's interests in London. As Jamestown was then being rebuilt from the ashes left by Bacon, the commissioners remained aboard ship and requested Berkeley to meet them there.

On board the *Bristol*, Colonel Jeffreys handed Berkeley instructions from the King and the Lords of Trade. He was to return to England to give an account of the insurrection, and he was to publish a royal proclamation granting pardon to all the rebels except Nathaniel Bacon. Colonel Jeffreys was to assume acting control of the Colony. Berkeley, totally in command of himself, treated the commissioners with an airiness which the dramatist in him liked to affect. Refusing to relinquish his authority until he was ready, he used a clause of

Governor Sir William Berkeley (Courtesy of the Virginia State Library)

"conveniency" in the King's letter to postpone leaving Virginia until
he had finished his hangings. He also declared he would not publish
the King's proclamation without including a paper of his own, listing
the men who would not be pardoned.

The commissioners gravely warned him that he was flouting the
King's authority. Berkeley would not listen. He was driven down the
familiar road to Green Spring, to which he and Lady Frances had just
returned, and where dozens of workmen were repairing the damages
left by the rebels' occupancy. By February 20, the work at Green
Spring had progressed sufficiently for Berkeley to convene the General
Assembly at his home.

9

This was a totally different House of Burgesses from the "Bacon's Assembly" of the year before. Its members either were cowed by
Berkeley or owed to the Berkeley cabal their posts of profit (often
invitations to corruption) at the county and parish levels. The session
was devoted to nullifying most of the legislation passed by the so-
called "Bacon's Assembly," especially acts such as the one requiring
rotation in the sheriff's office. With their authority assured among
county officials, Berkeley's clique defied the commissioners and, under
the Green Spring domination, the House of Burgesses opposed the
commissioners in their attempts to execute the King's instructions.

Charles II, faced with his political power problems at home, was
anxious to end the turmoil in the Colony and to remove the causes of
discontent which, he believed, had led to the civil war. But, in examining the sources of discontent, the King used selective perceptual views
to see only those sources which were compatible with his own attitudes. Giles Bland, in his lists of grievances, had mentioned that the
average run of colonists complained about the costs of the General
Assembly — in tobacco handed over for the burgesses' per diem allow-
ances — and that the inequity of the poll tax was bitterly resented.
There were individual settlers who would have preferred having no
representative government at all, to having to support a government
with tobacco they had slaved to prepare for market. Charles II seized
upon the people's discontent with the General Assembly, and the taxes
consequent to its maintenance, as the causes of the rebellion and the
continuing divisiveness in the Colony.

Working on this faulty premise, and only after a bitter struggle,
Colonel Jeffreys and his fellow commissioners could accomplish no

more than a reduction of the per diem allowance to burgesses. Their
futile efforts to abolish the poll tax, in favor of another form of taxation, stirred up resistance to the Crown's interference with internal
taxation. While Charles II might have regarded this resistance as a
baleful effect of representative government — and members of the
General Assembly spoke of the rights of representative government —
the Berkeley-dominated House of Burgesses was "representative" of
the people in little more than name. What that General Assembly was
resisting was *anybody's* interference with the Green Spring control of
taxes and county politics, for which "internal affairs" was a euphemism.

In following the King's instructions to inquire into the "grievances," the commissioners studied the long lists of complaints sent to
them from the various counties. Going beyond, or unrelated to, the
costs of the burgesses and the inequity of the poll tax, many of these
complaints were concerned with corruption among county officials. It
was claimed that Berkeleyite henchmen gave meaningless accounts of
the collections which went to fatten their own pockets. Although some
of the submitted grievances struck at the powers controlling the government rather than at the House of Burgesses as an institution, the
commissioners were under the King's instructions to clip the wings of
the General Assembly.

Also, investigation of the grievances submitted by the counties
was hampered by the absolute power of the Berkeleyites' rule. Many
of the lists of grievances were sent in anonymously, by individuals or
groups fearful of reprisals. Then, when members of Berkeley's clique,
such as Colonel Edward Hill, were specified in the county grievances,
they had the support of Berkeley's government in turning the charges
against the signers of the complaints.

Nor could the commissioners make any progress toward healing
the wounds of civil war. Colonel Philip Ludwell, of "rash and fiery
temper," sat on many of the courts which tried Bacon's supporters,
and he was as vindictive as the governor himself. In fact, some believed that he and Robert Beverley had advised the old man on the
courses which led to the bitterness that grew as the rebellion progressed. The commissioners, watching helplessly as the hangings, im-
prisonments and confiscations deepened the divisiveness, made one
humanistic appeal on personal grounds. When Robert Jones, an honored veteran of Charles I's army in the English civil wars, was sen-
tenced to be hanged, they beseeched Lady Frances to intercede with
her husband. Lady Frances showed herself to be as arrogant as the old

courtier. She wrote to the commissioners that rather than intercede she would wear the canvas clothes "the rebels said they would make me glad of."

The soft-cheeked mistress of Green Spring felt sufficiently secure to treat the commissioners to a turn of her malicious humor. In late winter the three commissioners made another of their futile visits to the governor at his home. On leaving, they walked from the raised ground where the house spread down to the driveway. There they found a dreary-looking conveyance waiting to return them to town: it was the hangman's coach, ordered by My Lady Frances. Spurning the ride, the men glanced back at the house before starting their walk, and saw her gaily smiling face at a window.

When spring came with its sudden burst of green, Sir William Berkeley, holding over the colonists the threat of his return, boarded a ship at the wharf he was never to see again. He was ill when he arrived in London and sent a message to his monarch, asking for an audience in which to explain himself. Before the King acknowledged the message, the old man died, on July 13, 1677 — a little more than two years after the obscure freedman Robert Hen was killed. Charles II spoke the cruel epitaph by which Governor Berkeley was remembered: "That old fool has hanged more men in that naked land than I did for the murder of my father."

When the news of Berkeley's death reached Virginia in the fall and Colonel Jeffreys became lieutenant governor, he was at last able to halt the reign of terror. The rebel leaders having been hanged, all the men who had surrendered themselves were permitted to return to their homes. Somewhere along the way, Robert Jones won a reprieve, and the King pardoned him. Eighty Negro slaves, who had been induced to run off, were rounded up and returned to their owners. The King restored the confiscated property of the widow Drummond and her children, and the widow Bacon and her daughter. Elizabeth Bacon, stranded in the frontier country, solved her plight by marrying a Virginia planter. (The daughter, Mary, was returned to England, where she grew up and married Hugh Chamberlain, physician to Queen Anne.)

But the October session of the House of Burgesses, still dominated by Berkeley loyalists, continued under the thumb of the late governor's cohorts on the King's Council. Led by Philip Ludwell and Thomas Ballard, with support from Robert Beverley in the key position of clerk of the House of Burgesses, the councilors were determined to retain the power and the privileges they had enjoyed during

Berkeley's day, and treated Governor Jeffreys as if he were some transient interloper. With the excuse of making up for losses suffered during the rebellion, "the Green Spring faction" (as it came to be called) dragged into the courts anybody who could be associated with Bacon, and imposed fines or confiscated property. Finally Jeffreys ordered Philip Ludwell to stop his seizures of rebel property.

Outraged at this imposition of authority, Ludwell publicly referred to Governor Jeffreys as "a pitiful little fellow with a periwig," who "was perjured" and "was a worse rebel than Bacon, for he broke the laws of the country which Bacon never did." Jeffreys took this slanderous charge to the Lords of Trade, and this body ordered Ludwell's removal from the Council. This show of strength by Jeffreys only hardened the Green Spring faction — rallied around My Lady Frances — in their opposition to the King's representative as a threat to their control of the Colony. In this power fight, My Lady Frances and Berkeley's political heirs made forthright and final their separation from the welfare of the people in Virginia.

10

While the government was kept unsettled by the struggle, in which Jeffreys made no significant inroads into the Berkeleyites' control, the majority of the colonists returned to looking after their dislocated personal affairs. For many of them times were harder than in the spring, when they had left their holdings to drive off the Indians.

There were no restorations made to the more substantial of Bacon's followers who had already paid heavy fines and suffered confiscations of property. Nothing could be restored to those small one-man plantations which had been neglected for a year. Hogs and chickens had run off, weeds grew in the cornfields, and no tobacco was planted. When crops were put in again, higher taxes would be diverted to reparations for those big planters who filed claims for the losses in property to the rebels.

The "old rebels" muttered among themselves, but nothing could be done while the My Lady Frances–Philip Ludwell bloc represented the only political unity in the Colony. Under the surface, however, scars remained unhealed. And there were memories that went unspoken. Vague stirrings were aroused by the distant crackle of a musket, by the rolling thunder of horses in the night, by a shadowed movement when the evening mists rose before sundown. In these stirrings men and women remembered laws that had been passed when a people's army commanded the capital: though revoked, the laws were forever recorded.

It was not only the people in whom the memories were aroused — the people in the meaning of nine-tenths of the freedmen, a cross section of whom had followed Bacon. Significantly, the younger generation of merchant-planters, then reaching toward power, also remembered. For finally the significance of the rebellion, and the long aftermath, was to be in its future effect on the ambitious men who were rising into positions of prominence during the Green Spring–Jeffreys battle. These newcomers represented the generation that would shape the society then struggling to emerge out of the thousands of isolated clearings in the wilderness.

Old Berkeley himself, with his ego involved in crushing the threat to his version of absolute rule, had never seemed aware that he was trying to stifle the evolution of indigenous forms and attitudes. Nor was there any awareness shown among his successors in the Green Spring faction, greedy frontier despots inflated and made ruthless by their feudalistic privileges. Philip Ludwell was labeled ''an inconsiderable fellow'' by Commissioner Moryson, who also called Beverley a ''pirate'' for his confiscations of rebel property. Although Moryson may have been getting in some insults on behalf of the abused commissioners, even Ludwell's older brother Thomas, then near the end of his road, said he was ''ashamed and amazed'' at Philip's ''madness.'' Their heads turned by power, these transplanted Englishmen (and My Lady Frances, their imperious symbol), appeared to be as oblivious as Berkeley had been to the implications in the colonists' desperately driven assertiveness.

But even though the colonists then seemed subdued, the implications of the rebellion were not lost on the new men rising into political influence. Mostly merchant-planters who had not been partisans during the rebellion, these new figures adapted themselves to the actual frontier conditions — which included recognition of the settlers' justifiable grievances against a government that had failed to promote the welfare of the majority of the inhabitants. Emerging out of the aftermath of rebellion, this new generation would begin the drift to a native governing class that was to be, of all things, responsibly indigenous to its time and place.

The Old Order Passes

WHEN THE YEARS of stress and change began after Berkeley's death, Robert Carter — who would be called "King" — was a fifteen-year-old orphan at school in England. He spent six years with the family of "Mister Baily" (or Bailey) in London, and letters of his later life make it certain that this period of his education came in his teens. According to his father's will, he was being "well educated . . . in his minority . . . for the use of his estate."

John Carter, one of the successful emigrants who had experienced the value of education in the Colony, stressed the importance of a grounding in the classics. He placed equal stress on guidance in deportment, conduct and the development of a character fitted for responsibility. For beyond intellectual development, education was designed to produce the "whole man" (according to the ideal of the day) capable of assuming the obligations, for himself and his society, inherent in the status of "Christian gentleman" — with equal emphasis on the two words.

Education was particularly important for Robert as a younger son, in the very practical meaning of that term: following the English laws of primogeniture, the home plantation and the bulk of the estate went to the firstborn son, John Carter II. John Carter the emigrant had been one of the largest landholders of his day (larger than the first Richard Lee), but of his eighteen thousand acres of choice land extending inland from the river port on the Rappahannock, only one thousand upcountry acres on Corotoman Creek went to Robert. Along with the house and outbuildings at the Corotoman homeplace, Robert's older brother John inherited the animals and equipment, the use of indentures with time to serve on their contracts, and slaves owned outright.

Although African Negroes had first been sold as slaves in Virginia by a Dutch trader as early as 1619, in the following thirty years few planters had bought the black men and none used them as a labor force on a large scale. When tobacco fell to one penny a pound during the 1660's, the more substantial and commercially aggressive merchant-planters began building larger labor forces of slaves as they turned to volume production to make profits at the low prices. John Carter I was among the few who mingled slaves and indentures in some quantity (although at that stage the numbers were small in comparison to the slave labor forces that would come later). One Negro family had been with John Carter long enough for him to grant them freedom in his will.

Robert Carter would also get one-third of the personal estate, valued at £2,200. In England, this estate would have been representative of a moderately well-to-do country family of the minor gentry, or of a moderately successful London merchant. It would have been a pittance in the scale of the great landholding families in the nobility and in the larger gentry. In Virginia it was wealth when John Carter died in 1669. More of the assets were in tangible property than in cash, and most of this property was in the Corotoman house where Robert grew up under the guardianship of his much older brother.

In the elder Carter's generation it had not yet become the fashion to concentrate on silver as symbols of status among the elite. Along with nine silver spoons, two porringers and a large saltcellar, he listed only two pieces by their value: tankards, valued at £13 — the equivalent of one slave and one indenture. The first John Carter had been plentifully supplied with the serviceable pewter, listing 110 pounds of the best, 60 pounds of the "middle sort," and 55 pounds broken. His furnishings showed an absence of the display which Robert grew up to abhor. The fully furnished rooms were stocked with imported pieces, most of fine quality — such as fifteen of the fashionable "turkey-work chairs,'' twenty-one old leather chairs, six Spanish tables, two chests of drawers and ten cushions. He had an unusually large amount of linen. In addition to sheets and curtains, there were tablecloths and napkins which showed that his family dined in high style for their times.

There was an unsolved mystery about the initial V embroidered on some of the linen. None of John Carter's wives had a name beginning with V. As with all the emigrants who came to Virginia with education and means, there were areas in his life — especially before his arrival in the Colony — about which nothing definite was known. Since no facts were available for the time and circumstances of John Carter's landing in Virginia, the legends turned him out in the trappings of a loyalist refugee. One obscure factual item makes it certain that the first John Carter could not be included in the ''cavalier'' convention. A patent for thirteen hundred acres was taken out in Jamestown by John Carter in 1642, before the civil wars produced the ''cavaliers.''

John Carter did not occupy this land in the Northern Neck, embracing the maritime site of Corotoman, until the 1650's, and did not for certain appear again in the records until 1649. Then he entered the House of Burgesses as a representative of Nansemond County, near Norfolk, on the south side of the James River where it enters Chesapeake Bay.

Everything in his life before that was involved with speculation. All the knowns suggested that the emigrant derived from a Carter family well established in the records, but John Carter's precise connection with this family was among the probables. In the shire of Hertford, north of London, the armigerous Carter family owned an unpretentious manor house, Garston, with small landholdings, from 1534 until the place was sold in 1666. Starting early in the seventeenth century, members of this family began to establish themselves as vintners in London, and at least one branch was substantially established: three sons were at Cambridge at the same time and an older son practiced law at the Middle Temple.

Evidence pointed to a relationship between this branch of the family and that of a John Carter, of Christchurch Parish, London, who was also a vintner. Since the records of this John Carter's family were lost in the destruction of the Christchurch records covering the period during which his children were born, the probability — based upon the other Carter family records available — was that John

Carter the emigrant was the third son of John Carter the wine merchant, and a cousin of the successfully established branch of the family.

Assuming that the emigrant was connected with the family of London vintners, his career in Virginia would indicate that he, like Richard Lee I, came first as a trader representing his family, and as a speculator in land. While no record showed any landholdings or planting operations in the Norfolk area, he was sufficiently established in the community, by means and education, to represent his neighbors in the House of Burgesses. Also, when he acquired the thirteen hundred acres at the Corotoman site in 1642, Lancaster County had only that year been opened to settlement by an act of the General Assembly. As the hostile Rappahannocks then made such an isolated spot dangerous, John Carter would have purchased the land only for future speculation. It was an ideal site for a center of commerce, village or city, and he could have selected those precise acres only by making a personal survey by a water journey.

Chesapeake Bay covers about eighty miles of shoreline from the Potomac to the James, at Norfolk, and the inland terrain along the tidal rivers forms a maritime world of this whole "Bay" or "Tidewater" section. About ten miles inland from the great bay, where the Rappahannock was two miles wide, Corotoman was on a point of land on the river between Corotoman Creek and Carter's Creek. The so-called Corotoman "Creek" was itself two miles wide and the angle at which it flowed into the Rappahannock gave Carter a broad stretch of tidal water across the front of his site. Carter's Creek, on the east side, was about three quarters of a mile wide where it flowed past Corotoman into the Rappahannock, and deep enough for oceangoing ships. From this narrow point of land — no more than a few hundred yards on the river front — Carter's holdings gradually widened inland along the east bank of Corotoman Creek.

About eight years after John Carter staked a claim on this magnificent river harbor, Lancaster County had become sparsely settled, and Carter was among the very first (with Richard Lee and Thomas Stegg) to recognize the possibilities in private centers of commerce: the plantation shipping centers. Sometime after 1650 he established his family at Corotoman and built a house on the point of the land, from where he could gaze down the river to the hazy blue opening into the bay.

Up until this stage, some speculation still followed his misty early career in Virginia. From the time that John Carter first represented

Lancaster County in the 1654 session of the House of Burgesses, his career became literally "an open book": it was all revealed in the records.

Between the 1649 and 1654 sessions of the General Assembly, he had permanently established himself as a tobacco planter, listing twelve "tithables." A tithable tax was levied on all free men over sixteen, on all male white imported servants of any age, and on male and female imported Negroes over sixteen. (Later, Negroes born in servitude in the Colony were taxed as slaves.) By the approximately known size of Carter's family in 1654, nine or ten of the tithables would have been workers, either indentured or Negro slaves, or both. Later he imported eighty indentures in one lot, acquiring headrights to four thousand acres.

Along with establishing himself as a shipping-planter and land-acquirer, John Carter I, moving from a settled county in which he had been a person of some position, began to rise as the leader in the new county. The first official recognition of his position came in 1653, when he was appointed major of the county militia and served on the bench as a justice of the peace — an important position in the hierarchy of the Colony's government. One year later, he was appointed "commander-in-chief" to lead a combined force from three Northern Neck counties in an expedition against the Rappahannocks. Two years after that, in 1656, he was appointed chief justice of the county and colonel of the militia — immediately signing himself "Colonel Carter," in ascending to the Colony's equivalent of the peerage.

In practical recognition, he was awarded a contract to construct the courthouse and jail in 1654, and later he contracted to construct Christ Church for the parish. As John Carter, along with his oldest son, naturally served on the board of vestry (that interlocking unit in the framework of government), his place as the county's preeminent citizen was indicated in the vestry book: the names of John Carter I and John Carter II appeared above that of the minister.

When Berkeley had returned with Charles II's restoration in 1660, John Carter I became one of his closest advisers on the Council during the period when the governor was appealing to the King on behalf of the colonials. Among the councilors who sought remedies for the poverty brought by a glut in the tobacco market in 1663, Carter served with Richard Lee I on a commission to cooperate on measures with the governor of Maryland. With other councilors he signed the governor's petitition for protection against attacks on Virginia ships by Dutch men-of-war. In 1667, four Dutch men-of-war and two fire-ships invaded the James River and, after burning a forty-six-gun guard ship and five merchantmen, carried off thirteen vessels as prizes. Although Stuartist Carter did not see this attack (as the people did) as evidence of the Crown's neglect of responsibility to the governed, in his own interests he kept a look-out perch to watch for Dutch or pirate ships entering the Rappahannock from Chesapeake Bay.

He did take a stand against the King when he signed Berkeley's protest against the grants of land Charles II gave in the Northern Neck, encompassing Carter's own property. This petition achieved no more with the indifferent King than any others, but Councilor Carter in his private interests did absolutely nothing to make it possible for the beneficiaries of Charles's largess to claim their grants.

During the years of his rise and power at Corotoman, John Carter's personal life was made turbulent by deaths and remarriages. When he built his house about one hundred yards back from the riverfront, his family consisted of his wife, formerly Jane Glyn, his sons John II and George, and his daughter Elizabeth. His wife soon died, and he married a widow, Eleanor Brocas, from Lancastershire, England. She did not live long and died without having borne any children. Then he married Ann Carter, the daughter of Cleave (Cleve) Carter, thought to be an English cousin of her husband. She also died soon, leaving no children. Then came the wife who produced Robert: Sarah Ludlow was her name, and all known about her was that she was the daughter of Mr. Gabriel Ludlow: the "Mr." was carved on her tomb, and that designation was not used loosely. She was also the mother of Robert's sister Sarah. This fourth wife lasted a little longer than her immediate predecessors. She died in early 1668, when Robert was five.

Late in the year 1668 Colonel Carter took his fifth wife, Elizabeth Shirley (?), a widow from Gloucester County. This last, late venture — for he was near his own end then — seemed to be his first sour marriage. He died June 10, 1669, leaving his new wife about eight months pregnant. Carter's will showed what he thought of the mother of his unborn child and of his progeny by her.

She was to have £500 (which was part of the marriage contract), a Negro boy, "her" necklace of diamond and pearls and "her own books," and share with Carter's sons John and Robert in the residual personal estate. To these bequests he pointedly added two books from the library (which otherwise went to John and Robert): Byfield's treatise *The Whole Duty of Man* and *David's Tears,* an "appropriate legacy for a mourning widow."

Assuming that her child would be a boy, "whose name is intended Charles," and never referring to this future Carter except as "her son," he provided for this heir as meagerly as decency would permit. His executors were to allow the widow £12 a year for his education and "[my] son John is to allow my wife's son necessary clothes." Such was his indifference to the estate of a boy who would bear his own name that he provided for the contingency of the widow putting "her son out [to] apprentice."

By contrast, he wrote in the will, "my son Robert, in his minority, is to be well educated for the use of his estate . . ." and specified that a man servant be "bought for him . . . not only to teach him his books . . . in Latin and English, and to write, but to preserve him from harm and from doing evil."

The widow's child was a boy whom she dutifully named Charles, after which he disappeared from the records. He was presumably alive at twenty-one, for John Carter II made provision for him in his will — one-third of the personal estate — though nothing indicated that he claimed his share. Judging by all the later accounts of and from Corotoman, this posthumous son of John Carter I simply vanished. When the Widow Carter and "her son" left the house, where she had lived so briefly as a wife, was also unknown.

Whenever they did depart, of all the children and women of John Carter's families, whose voices had rung through the rooms of the house between the waters, only John and Robert were left. Robert's sister Sarah and half-brother George had died before their father; his half-sister Elizabeth had married and moved to distant parts. His father was buried under the chancel of the incompleted Christ Church, near his four wives and two children.

Losing his mother and father within a little more than a year of one another, after having lost his companions at the lonely river site, Robert Carter as a boy in his brother's home had to develop early a self-sufficiency. By the time he was in school in London, he showed a self-disciplined purpose to take advantage of the educational opportunities to fit himself for a life with bleak prospects of an estate.

Many sons of wealthy colonials formed expensive habits in London, cultivated tastes for urban pleasures and showed a reluctance to return to the isolated plantations in a frontier community. Robert Carter, perhaps because of his lack of certainties, never seemed to want to be anything except — as he later described himself — "a Virginia planter." This second-generation Virginian totally identified with the place of his birth, "the country," as they called it, and he treated his years of study in London only as a preparation for his return as a responsible helper to his brother at Corotoman.

2

While Robert Carter was in London applying himself to his studies, his guardian-brother was almost equally remote from the post-rebellion agitations in which the Green Spring clique sought to maintain control of Virginia. John Carter II, a misty figure, was among the few second-generation sons of successful merchant-planters who showed no political ambitions. At the local level, he conscientiously assumed the responsibilities of his position in county affairs. He served on the vestry and completed the building of Christ Church, served as lieutenant colonel of the militia and during the rebellion — uninvolved with either Bacon's forces or the governor's — had acted as co-commander of six hundred men stationed in defense against Northern Neck Indians who might have taken advantage of the white man's internecine war. In 1680 he went to Jamestown to take his seat in the House of Burgesses in the rebuilt State House.

His career in the Burgesses was unexplainably brief. Just before Christmas of 1682 he asked to be excused from attending a session, and the following April wrote a deposition stating that Colonel Carter could not come to Jamestown ''by reason of a great deluxion of humors that hath falled upon several parts of him . . . grievous pains and a looseness which hath so weakened him that he is not capable of riding, nor indeed can hardly walk. . . .'' With this, John Carter II disappeared from public life.

It would seem likely that he was a low-keyed man who had no stomach for the political strife and shifting alliances that came to Jamestown in the aftermath of the rebellion. Nor did he have any of his father's commercial aggressiveness or the outsize acquisitiveness that characterized his contemporaries and would form a dominant strain in his younger brother. He ran the Corotoman operations with thorough competence, taking care to protect Robert's holdings, and increased his personal estate (beyond house, land, and slaves) in round figures from £700 to £1,000 while paying for Robert's six years in London and presumably — at least for some period — the £12 a year allotted for the education of his stepmother's son.

He increased the library inherited from his father, showing a strong bent toward religious subjects. When his father's copy of Lewis Bayly's popular *Practice of Piety* went to Robert, John immediately purchased another for himself. This attention to religious matters among literate planters did not necessarily indicate godliness. The authoritarianism of "popery" had not long been thrown off, the impact of disputatious Puritanism was recent, and the new openings for individual evaluations made theology (with theological philosophy) a popular study of the times. The Carters read even the Puritans, probably to find reasons to buttress their faith as Anglicans. However, as John's father and younger brother, whom John influenced, were devout communicants of Christ Church, John appears to have been genuinely of a religious turn of mind.

In his secluded days of managing the planting and shipping on his maritime site, John Carter II did keep abreast of the developments in volume production of tobacco, and increased his labor force of slaves to 106 — a large holding in the seventeenth century. Slaves began to replace indentures as field workers at Corotoman, and Englishmen were brought in more as skilled artisans, tutors and clerks.

While John Carter kept up with the trend toward volume production, contemporaries of his were expanding their planting-trading operations on an entirely new scale and bringing wider diversification to their commercial enterprises. The rise of these new fortune-builders increased the numbers of successful merchant-planters and began to spread individual wealth beyond the small group of Berkeley's surviving clique. These newly rich colonials entered the government without the narrow self-interest of the Green Spring caste. In acknowledging a responsibility for the well-being of the Colony, they were without conscious intent drifting toward the formation of a *class* — in distinction from the caste system inherited by My Lady Frances.

The men prominent in this new generation did not oppose My Lady Frances's continuation of the Green Spring faction. They were simply more flexible and, not directly influenced by the attitudes that had characterized Berkeley's "court," more integrated into the broader life of the Colony. During their upward thrusts, these younger men had held only modest government posts. Themselves caught in the squeeze of low prices and high tariffs, they had hustled like any frontiersmen — though on immeasurably vaster scales.

When William Byrd I, the operator of a successful store, was unable to find customers for one lot of imported goods, he wrote to his London agent: "The country is much overstocked with trading goods." Himself hurt by policies that deprived the colonists of purchasing power, the merchant-planter had the strongest reason to concern himself with the well-being of his neighbors. It was not that

Byrd's generation was fundamentally different in aims from the friends of the late governor so much as that they were more enlightened about the practical terms of the freeholders' lives.

All very prudent entrepreneurs, these newcomers to influence went along with the changes — barely perceptible from year to year — that came with the maneuvers of the Green Spring faction to maintain its political hold under different royal governors.

My Lady Frances's coterie shifted from bitter opposition to Colonel Jeffreys to a cozy alliance with his successor, Lord Culpeper. This was a natural alliance, since Governor Culpeper was a cousin of the mistress of Green Spring, the former Frances Culpeper. But in this change of fronts, the Old Guard suffered some cracks in its solidarity. Prominent persons shifted sides as the Berkeleyites lost their absolute control of the House of Burgesses and as the freeholders' representatives — now including new men of substance — sought to regain the power they had wielded in their brief hour of command.

The people's representatives, leaderless and without clearly defined objectives, asserted themselves mostly by resisting the authority of the governors. On the surface, their resistance could have appeared to be no more than blind stubbornness. Combined with the confusing split among wealthy Virginians and the shifting political alliances — which may have kept John Carter, along with other substantial planters, out of Jamestown — this defiant assertiveness tended to obscure the drift toward a responsible indigenous government.

But the rising powers in the new generation did not need to have any particular astuteness to recognize that the inchoate movement reflected a fundamental change in the Colony since the days when the generation of those first fortune-founding emigrants — John Carter I, Richard Lee I and Byrd's uncle, Thomas Stegg — had produced only a few colonists qualified to run the government, and when the people at large had accepted, with complaints but without effective protests, the rule imposed by My Lady Frances's late husband.

3

My Lady Frances, ensconced in the expanded brick mansion she had inherited, surrounded by its fertile fields and blossoming orchards, was no different from the other women in Virginia when it came to living alone. Three years after her husband died, she married his cousin, Councilor Philip Ludwell. At forty, six years younger than Lady Frances, Ludwell was a recent widower with an eight-year-old son and a younger daughter, and for the second time since he had come to Virginia (twenty years before) he became a lady's third husband. With his marriage to his cousin's widow, Ludwell moved into the Green Spring manor house, the estate of which in time passed to his son, Philip Ludwell II.

My Lady Frances had no children by any of her husbands (at least, none who lived beyond infancy). Records were scant in the days when many women were worn out by childbearing, and by attendant disorders beyond the medical knowledge available in the Colony. "Surgeons," sometimes graduate barbers, were few. While advanced individuals had practiced and experimented with medicine since the earliest Jamestown days, among planter families it was usual for the plantation master to rely on medical books in acting as physician for his own private community. When the planter himself fell ill, he had to serve as his own doctor, with the result that widows were always available for widowers. In the quick remarriages that characterized the life of the Colony, both men and women usually acted with clear-sighted practicality in joining their own estates to those of similar scale. Though sometimes the heart ran away with the head, this was never a weakness among those families which established dynasties.

Before My Lady Frances took Ludwell for her third husband, he and his older brother Thomas, along with Thomas Ballard, Colonel Edward Hill, Robert Beverley (Berkeley's harshly effective leader against the rebels), and other Green Spring stalwarts, formed the hard core of the Old Guard clutching the control of the Colony. Richard Lee II, restocking his estate, seems not to have been active in the post-Berkeley cabal, though they could count on him to support the established order.

Before their position was assured by the arrival of the new royal governor, My Lady Frances and her friends had to wait three years until Lord Culpeper could bring himself to leave London. During this interim the acting governors gave them no serious opposition. Colonel Herbert Jeffreys, who fell ill during the damp heat of the long summers, never gained any effective support against the Green Spring faction, and died in 1678.

His successor as acting governor, Sir Henry Chicheley, was a genuine "cavalier" of the legend. This genial ex-soldier had come to Virginia as a Royalist fugitive in 1649, married a well-endowed widow and became the stepfather of Councilor Ralph Wormeley II. Chicheley was conscientiously concerned about healing the scars left by Berkeley's vengefulness, and sent to the King the continuing petitions of widows for compensations from Berkeley's confiscations. However, growing ill with age and restrained by personal friendships with members of the cabal, Sir Henry Chicheley did nothing that actually curtailed their power.

The sun shone brightly on the Green Spring private paradise when My Lady Frances and Philip Ludwell were wed in the spring of 1680, just when Charles II finally forced Lord Culpeper to tear himself away from his mistress long enough to make a personal tour of his dominion.

Thomas, the second Lord Culpeper, arrived at the high shores of the little river port of Jamestown in May, "after a most tedious passage of eleven weeks and two days, full of death [and] scurvy." From the island his party was driven across the creek to the mainland and along three miles of the only straight road in the Colony, to Green Spring. Culpeper rode between woods blooming in slumbrous, shadowed green, laced with wildflowers and the delicate white sprays of dogwood, and then into the yellow sunlight in the clearing, where terraced lawns of new grass led to the manor house.

He was welcomed by his cousin who, at forty-six, was one year his senior. Either for rent or as a favor, My Lady Frances had arranged for the new governor to make Green Spring his temporary home. After His Lordship was comfortably settled, she was going to London on a honeymoon trip with her new husband. Nothing in his luxurious quarters, the handsome estate or the country around him aroused any response in Culpeper — at least none that he recorded. In a letter to his sister, his only comment was on his cousin. "My Lady B . . . thinks no more of our world."

Culpeper, himself thinking very much of the charms of London, made no bones about the one purpose that had brought him to Virginia — to raise money to support his rightful enjoyment of lascivious and elegant idleness. Culpeper was not only of a class which regarded the world as existing for its pleasure, but through his father he had just claims on Charles II. His father was among those who had lost "all" in serving the Stuart kings, all three of them.

The Culpeper family had long belonged to the larger gentry, producing knights and baronets, professional soldiers, and graduates of Winchester and Oxford and Cambridge, with many attending the Inns where law was formally learned in London. Prominent in county affairs, the various branches of the family had also produced their share of rogues: one was beheaded after becoming the lover of his cousin, Catherine Howard, when she was Henry VIII's queen; a pair of them abducted two co-heiresses whom they married by force in order to share their fortunes. Until Thomas, the second Lord Culpeper, the line was not so raffish.

Culpeper's father, a literate, able and energetic man of ambition with deep loyalties, brought his line of country gentlemen into national prominence. Knighted by James I at the age of twenty-one, under Charles I he eventually became Master of the Rolls. He fought with Rupert's cavalry during the civil wars and in 1644 was raised to the peerage by Charles I. As the first Lord Culpeper, he was in the group which escorted the Prince of Wales (Charles II) to safety out of England, shared the exile, and returned in triumph with Charles to London in 1660. Restored to the office of Master of the Rolls, but having lost his personal estate, he was promised £12,000 by the new King. When the first Lord Culpeper died soon after that, he listed £12,000 as an asset in his will.

The second Lord Culpeper had joined his father in exile when he was sixteen and, though brave enough and smart enough, had followed neither the soldierly nor the scholarly pursuits of earlier Culpepers. Marrying a Dutch lady at the age of twenty-four, he lived until he was twenty-five waiting for the Restoration to return him to lordly privilege. When his father died without estate of any consequence, Charles II — in lieu of paying the £12,000 — gave the young Culpeper the sinecure of captain, then governor, of the Isle of Wight. There the inhabitants complained of the indiscreet manner in which he flaunted a mistress, and in 1671 Charles placed him on the Council for Foreign Plantations. It was in this association with the colonies that the libidinous lord began to see Virginia as the source that could provide an equivalent of the £12,000 he felt was owed him for his father's services.

The first Lord Culpeper had been one of the seven favorites (including My Lady Frances's father) to whom Charles II had, during his exile, granted the domain between the Rappahannock and Potomac rivers, the Northern Neck. When the favorites had started to claim their grants after Charles's restoration, they or their heirs discovered that the Carters and the Lees, among other big planters, had no intention of acknowledging claims to empires they themselves had carved out of the wilderness. In 1672 Charles II further complicated the problems by grandly making other grants that gave away more than half the Colony. When the beneficiaries or heirs of the King's largess began to lose hope of realizing any cash on their grants, Culpeper began acquiring titles to their land grants. Maneuvering for the ap-

pointment of governor at the same time, Culpeper showed the only
single-minded purpose of his life in the stubbornness, along with the
surprising shrewdness, with which he set out to milk the Colony for
his personal benefit.

While Charles had shown egregious ingratitude to the Virginians,
he evidently felt some obligation to Lord Culpeper about the £12,000
he never paid. When he rewarded Culpeper with the governorship of
Virginia, the no-longer-young lord was nearing complete ownership of
the grants in the Northern Neck — called the "Proprietary" — and
another grant, loosely called the "Arlington property." The Arlington grant never figured significantly in the development of the Colony,
but the Proprietary's millions of acres of virgin land, drained by two
tidal rivers, were to exert a most profound effect on the character of
Virginia — and on the career of young Robert Carter.

4

As it turned out for the Green Spring faction, My Lady Frances's cousin was the worst thing that could have happened. Having
come to exploit Virginia, with little interest in the colonists, the
devious nobleman aroused a resistance more subtle than Bacon's Rebellion.

This resistance was not to an individual or his clique, as to
Berkeley's cabal, nor over any one issue, as the Indians. Where
Berkeley, who had himself seemed one of them, became a personal
villain, Culpeper personified an idea — the attitude of Stuart kings
toward colonists. The resistance, undefined and generalized, grew with
an insidious persistence.

Nicholas Spencer, who succeeded Thomas Ludwell as the Colony's
secretary, epitomized the attitude in two statements in letters to
London after Culpeper came to Virginia. "It is plain that Bacon's
Rebellion left an itching behind it," he wrote. Then: "From my observation of the Assemblys since Bacon's Rebellion, their endeavors
have been to lessen the prerogatives" of the Crown.

The efforts of the House of Burgesses were mostly expressed in a
resentment of that attitude of the Crown which eschewed moral obligation to maintain its subjects, while encroaching upon the management of their neighborhood affairs. It was a resentment that reflected
the colonists' growing demand for a reciprocity of rights and obligations within the natural order. The men and women who risked their
lives in creating a new country refused to accept "colonial" as im-

plying subordinate status in citizenship. Their pride as Englishmen had come to encompass a different kind of pride in being citizens of a dominion which they personally were creating.

The pride of the people's representatives was defensive when Culpeper came in 1680, for it was only the year before that elections had been honestly conducted, and the Burgesses could be said to be "representative" for the first time since the rebellion. In any event, the transient governor was not sufficiently involved in the Colony to examine the attitudes of his inferiors. Nothing could have concerned him less than the shifting of political balances, even where the shifts caused a split in the old alliances right in his cousin's circle. Robert Beverley, who had been Berkeley's most ruthlessly effective soldier, went over to "the people."

Among the mixed motivations in all the shifting of alliances, only historical sentiment could attribute to Beverley some awakening to the people's welfare. Robert Beverley had come to Virginia as a lawyer in his mid-twenties in 1663. He possessed the education and background, along with a vigorous and convivial nature, to win the friendship of Berkeley. He was given the important post of clerk of the House of Burgesses, along with a well-paying district in the surveyor general's office and a collector's job in the auditor general's office. Combining these posts with his practice as an attorney, he earned the considerable sum of £425 a year. He acquired holdings in three counties, though he seemed not to have planted on an extensive scale or to have made any considerable use of slaves. He was primarily a professional man who could not be classified as one of the merchant-planter entrepreneurs.

As a close friend of Berkeley's, Beverley had opposed Jeffreys when he first came to Jamestown as one of the King's commissioners, and had become his active enemy when Jeffreys became governor. In an involved clash between Jeffreys and the House of Burgesses, Beverley, as clerk, had refused to deliver records when ordered. As the House of Burgesses had then been subservient to the Green Spring faction, of which Beverley was a stalwart, his identification with the House of Burgesses was an act directed entirely against Jeffreys.

After Jeffrey's death, with unaccountable motivations Beverley continued his identification with the House of Burgesses. By the time Culpeper arrived, he seemed to have become an obstructionist with the habit of opposing royal prerogatives.

His Lordship, doubtless with the intent of pacifying his cousin's incomprehensible friend, showed Beverley, his contemporary, nothing except friendliness. Culpeper could make himself very charming. His florid face was well modeled, with smooth planes and a relaxed expression as of one ready to smile, and his eyes were bright and worldly. His charms were wasted on the self-appointed protector of the customs of the House of Burgesses. Beverley's characteristically vehement actions led him by degrees from guarding the customs of the Burgesses to supporting the broader interests of the population represented in the House.

When Lord Culpeper settled with a few courtiers at Green Spring, the House of Burgesses had been strengthened by newly rising figures of wealth and influence, such as Benjamin Harrison, William Randolph and William Fitzhugh, and it was at this period that John Carter II represented his county in the House. While the appointive King's Council as a unit continued to lord it over the House of Burgesses, the representative body contained some individual members as rich and as strongly connected as the councilors. With these merchant-planters scattered among the freeholders in the Burgesses, a bridge crossed the gap that had existed between the people's powerless representatives and the Council in Berkeley's day.

Though councilors could exert influence by their control of appointments of county officers (many a voluble county representative was quieted by a deal made in a Jamestown tavern), as a body the post-Berkeley Burgesses united against any encroachments made by Berkeley's successor upon their areas of local government and showed the effect of "Bacon's Assembly" in standing up for their fundamental power of legislating taxation.

Concurrently, the very numbers of the families of substance (though still a minute section of the whole population) developed outside of Jamestown, and away from the Culpeper–Green Spring alliance, a communality of interests that transcended the divisions of the two bodies of the government. In the loneliness of even the largest clearings in the riverside forests, the families found their only social life in visiting with distant neighbors of similar station. The men, who could take cross-country rides or make rough trips by boat, went more frequently to talk about planting and the times over a toddy with a planter-friend of their own background. Through this natural gravitation, the new generation began its undirected coalescence into the contours of a class.

Since the social eminence of the newly wealthy was recognized in their communities of loosely scattered holdings, their political leadership more nearly reproduced the familiar order of England than did the superimposed order which My Lady Frances's privileged circle

Lord Culpeper (Courtesy of the Virginia State Library)

tried to continue. In the structure of authority in their time, political authority was inherently associated with the social hierarchy, and the new community leaders, in contrast to the separateness of the Green Spring cabal, were like the country "squires" back home. They did what My Lady Frances's coterie — attached to Governor Culpeper — never thought of doing: *they made themselves acceptable to their fellow colonists.*

The rising leaders may have done this with a mixture of mostly practical motives. But while My Lady Frances's friends tried to go on as if nothing had happened and Culpeper appeared oblivious to what was happening, the leaders rising in the communities made an identification with the whole colony of Virginia that would not have been possible for the caste gravitating around either Berkeley's or Culpeper's Green Spring "court." Through their base in the "country" rather than around Culpeper, with his "easy" smile for inferiors, the new generation of leaders developed an understanding of the implications of power.

Essentially it was this grasp of the implications of power that, separating them from My Lady Frances's Old Guard, made the new community leaders acceptable to their neighbors. With all the attention the rising merchant-planters gave to their personal acquisitions and to looking after their own kind, they would never have been accepted as a ruling order unless the families coalescing into the emerging class demonstrated a responsibility to Virginia not shown at Green Spring in the years immediately before the rebellion or during Culpeper's occupancy.

The rise of these new men, in government and in the commercial diversification of the biggest, was the course Robert Carter observed when he returned to Corotoman from London. Growing into manhood during Culpeper's self-interested administration, he refrained from entering politics beyond the county level while his brother John was head of the family. He was, however, a most observant student of government affairs. Branching off from the classical studies of his London years, he applied himself to reading law books, books on the theories of government and histories of the English government — all useful background for his entrance into colonial politics.

When he worked at Corotoman under the control of his conservative brother, he was also aware of the nature and scale of the operations of the second-generation merchant-planters. At this stage young Carter did nothing with his own thousand acres of upriver holding. He directed his attention to the wharf where Carter's Creek served as a harbor at its entrance into the Rappahannock. This became the center of operations he would develop in another dimension from even the largest-scaled enterprises of his brother's contemporaries. Learning by doing, Robert Carter was the only planter with a library who did not buy at least one of the books, written for the country gentleman, on "how to do" in agriculture. The younger brother had total confidence in his own capacity for mastering detail, combined with the boldest imagination and seemingly illimitable resources of disciplined energy.

It was as if, during the shifting of balances in Culpeper's regime, Robert Carter was given the time and opportunity in his own formative years for preparing himself to exploit across all fronts the changes his brother's contemporaries were bringing in planting-commercial enterprises and in political responsibility — in total, responsible leadership.

5

During the six-year span of Culpeper's administration, His Lordship spent only two brief periods in Virginia. He never traveled about the country and never even glimpsed the land of the Proprietary, his reason for seeking the governorship. In his first stay, of only four months, Culpeper completed his acquisition of the Northern Neck domain, embracing the Carters' Corotoman. He had title to six-sevenths of the property and would eventually come into the remaining one-seventh, held by a cousin who acted as his agent.

On this visit, Culpeper made himself personally affable to the members of the Colony's government and showed a willingness to go along with the House of Burgesses when there was no conflict of interests. The last repercussions from the rebellion had not then quieted — appeals for pardons and reparations were still to be considered — and the conciliatory attitude shown by the new governor was an expression of Charles II's intention to end the divisiveness and unrest left by the rebellion. The conflicts that did arise were caused by Culpeper's instructions, mostly over sources of revenue.

Culpeper acted, as had Jeffreys, under instructions based upon the King's distorted conviction that the General Assembly was the root of discontent. Charles's concern over the "discontent" was entirely practical: contented colonists, undiverted by strife, produced more revenue for the Crown. Culpeper was supposed to ease the tax burden on the small freeholders for those expenses incidental to frequent sessions of the House of Burgesses. Although Charles II did not attack the representative government on principle, of course any weakening of the legislative body would not have been disagreeable to him. Primarily, however, elimination of the poll tax that went for the Burgesses' meetings was aimed at reducing the expenses of the Virginia government, toward the end — as were the body of Culpeper's instructions — of getting more tobacco shipped as a source of revenue for the Crown.

In executing his minute and continuous instructions, Culpeper did not bear down as hard on the merchant-planters as the King desired. The governor was overruled by the Committee of Trade and Plantations when he let pass a proviso in a bill which exempted planters from a duty of two shillings per hogshead on tobacco shipped in Virginia-owned vessels. Taking a partnership in ships was one of the devices by which the big planters sought to defray expenses in their endless plannings to make profits through volume production and diversity.

As part of the King's schemes to increase revenues, Culpeper was ordered to pass laws providing for the building of port cities. Going beyond the general instructions that had been given to Berkeley, Charles II had Culpeper order each of the twenty counties of the Colony to build a town with a warehouse on navigable water. Planters were ordered to ship only from specified points, and ships would collect cargoes only from these points. Had these orders been supported by any practical action from the Crown, the creation of small shipping centers — as bases for manufacturing — could have brought considerable long-range benefits to Virginia. But having dismissed Berkeley's earlier petition, the King merely showed his determination to get revenues from urban taxation without planning, effort or expense.

Under existing conditions, to haul their tobacco to distant and inconvenient locations, as specified, would simply work another hardship on the planters, both small and large. In a tacit, gentlemanly rebellion, all planters simply ignored the new laws. Ships' captains, complaining that no shippers showed up at the designated points, of necessity sailed on to the familiar private wharves.

It was in this kind of detail that Culpeper, on his first visit, chiefly executed the Stuart policies. In his absorption in the Proprietary, however, he demonstrated such superficial interest in the Colony's economic plight that the Council was aroused to protest. After Culpeper sailed for England in September, 1680, the Council wrote the Committee for Trade and Plantations: "Their [the planters'] trade in a more declining condition than ever been known by the low value or rather no value of their only commodity, tobacco . . . and the indigency of the inhabitants, so that if some means be not timely taken to raise their now totally sunk commodity, the inhabitants will be in a most deplorable condition and the peace and quiet of the Government will be hazarded.''

With Culpeper back in his London haunts, and the Council's petition ignored, groups of mostly smaller planters began resolving on measures of their own. It was here that Robert Beverley — in a hatred of governors other than Berkeley — seemed to extend his identification with the House of Burgesses to include the people presumably represented there. Beverley encouraged the freeholders to sign petitions for convening the House of Burgesses, with the purpose of passing laws for cutting back tobacco planting.

The House met while sick, old Sir Henry Chicheley was again acting governor during Culpeper's absence. No group of planters could establish a line of general agreement either in the full sessions in the State House or in small gatherings in the taverns. When the Burgesses failed to offer any relief by law, small mobs gathered in Gloucester and New Kent counties. In May, 1682, bands of knife-wielding men began cutting tobacco plants in the fields. The militia was called out. At the approach of the organized armed forces, the tobacco cutters scattered after only several hundred crops had been laid waste. But this little flare-up, coming so soon after Bacon's Rebellion, caused the British authorities to denounce Chicheley for calling the assembly at Beverley's instigation, and Culpeper was ordered back to Virginia.

At this turmoil, some of the Green Spring councilors began fearing Beverley's popularity with the people and turned on their old friend. He was arrested. Although Beverley was then too worn to be another Bacon, the people were so strongly behind him that twice he was able to ''escape.'' He was released on his bond of £2,000, very high, with no charges having been placed against him. Beverley was only suspected of having incited the plant-cutting, which was certainly in his nature. But all that existed as evidence were loose words he had spoken in drink. Even Culpeper said that he could ''find no evidence against him except general sauciness.''

With the country in this unsettled temper, Culpeper returned in the bleakness of December, 1682. This time, bringing along a cargo and some indentures in order to make a profit on his journey, Governor Culpeper evinced none of his earlier surface affability. He was angry in his frustration over the Proprietary.

Having, for all practical purposes, gained control of the land grants, he found it next to impossible to collect quitrents from the Northern Neck planters, such as John Carter and the Lees, who refused to recognize his claims. The tangle of quitrents, fallen long in arrears, was a complication which threatened to deprive him of any profit for all his scheming. Also, the unsettled legal conditions created by the Proprietary's claim to the land discouraged settlers from patenting in the Northern Neck. As his agreeableness to the House of Burgesses had gained him nothing, Culpeper indulged his native feelings by treating that body of colonials with contempt.

First he doubled his own salary to £2,000, gave himself other emoluments, and then, after harshly altering the bill passed in the House, adjourned the Burgesses. In this visit Culpeper revealed his self-interest so baldly that in 1683 even Charles II felt forced to recall him. When Lord Culpeper was removed from office that August, Charles, as a final gesture to his own conscience, allotted him a cash pension for the Arlington grant in Virginia, and this controversial property reverted to the Crown.

The Proprietary was left suspended, and Culpeper was never to gain a profit after twenty years of conniving.

6

Lord Howard of Effingham, Culpeper's successor, was almost a cutout of the high-living peer of late seventeenth-century England. He was a dark man of flaccid features, with an expression of haughty fatuity. He came of one of those families of the nobility who had fallen upon the need of cash to support their style of living, and Charles II looked after Lord Howard by foisting him off on Virginia. By his own self-indulgences and by his personal zeal in executing Charles II's policies, this product of the Stuart court inadvertently gave impetus to the emergence of a native ruling class.

Like Culpeper, Effingham came with instructions designed to relieve the average freeholder specifically of the costs of frequent Assemblies, and in general of those county and parish levies for which Charles II, through Culpeper, had ordered "a particular full and perfect account" from church wardens and justices of the peace. But Effingham came when the House of Burgesses, several years free of the Berkeleyites' yoke, was forming the habit of resistance to the imposition of any authority which tampered with their institutions and customs. And the overbearing Effingham, who would have been at home in any despotic government, was scarcely the type to win the cooperation of frontier settlers in an assertive mood. Regarding any form of popular representation with aversion, he seemed to feel contempt for the mostly unpretentious colonists who composed the House of Burgesses and, in dealing with these inferiors, he had no scruples about using deceit when threats and browbeating failed.

Effingham's troubles with "the meaner sort" had no effect on his personal life during his exile in the Colony. Approximating the pleasures of London as best he could with those councilors who shared his taste for high living, he ate and drank with a favored few and played cards all night. His particular intimate was Ralph Wormeley II, who installed His Lordship in one of the smaller houses at Rosegill.

Councilor Wormeley, who was thirty-three when Effingham became his guest, probably came closest of any Virginian of his generation to capturing the Renaissance ideal of "gentleman" as defined in Castiglione's *Courtier* and Henry Peacham's *Complete Gentleman* — both books in his library. A happy hedonist, Wormeley served ably on the Council, ranking high in influence, and was extremely enterprising in operating his 5,000-acre plantation on the south bank of the Rappahannock. This he had inherited, along with four indentures, thirteen Negroes, cattle, sheep, and twenty-four horses branded with his stepfather Sir Henry Chicheley's coat of arms.

Wormeley's slaves were trained to weave linen and wool, turn out leather in a tanyard and run a flour mill. Wormeley seemed not to have engaged in trading operations to any extent — certainly not like the planters newly rising to wealth — though he doubtless shipped from his own wharf on the south bank of the Rappahannock. His concentration was on home manufacturing from products grown along with tobacco. A French Huguenot refugee who visited Rosegill while Effingham was staying there, said, "When I reached his place, I thought I was entering a rather large village."

The manor house at Rosegill was, except for Green Spring, one of the very few plantation houses of the day built with some grandeur. Immediately inside, a gallery ran the width of the house, with stairs at each end leading to three bedrooms above. Downstairs there was a large reception room which served for parties, an intimate room and a dining room. All service units, such as the kitchen and laundry, were in outside buildings.

Since Wormeley's father's day, "feasting and carousing" were continual at Rosegill. While Effingham was there, at least one titled visitor from England came, perhaps a friend Wormeley had made when he was a student at Oriel College, Oxford. Having inherited about twenty pieces of silver service (a large collection for his father's

Lord Howard of Effingham (Courtesy of the Virginia State Library)

day in Virginia), Wormeley entertained with a style and taste rare in the Colony in the 1680's.

In conforming to the ideal of the *Complete Gentleman*, Wormeley had a library of nearly four hundred books, probably the largest of his generation. In spreading his interests laterally, Wormeley was not the classicist that Richard Lee was and never became regarded as an erudite man. He was typical of the gentry of his time in Virginia and England in reading widely on religious subjects, particularly those relating to the Church of England: he kept abreast of the writings of the outstanding Anglican churchmen and, of course, ordered fresh copies of the *Book of Common Prayer*. In secular subjects his tastes ran to history and travel, and instead of Lee's scholarly books on logic and philosophy, he read modern plays — Beaumont and Fletcher, James Shirley, William Cartwright and such. Though Wormeley was lightly stocked on law books in comparison to the law library young Robert Carter was building, he had the newly published *English Horseman* and, unlike the austere Lee, a book on wine making and one on beer brewing.

As a matter of fact, Wormeley, with his addiction to showiness, spread himself so thin that the time would come when Robert, the young brother of his friend John Carter, would have to help straighten out an entangled Wormeley estate. But in his days of glory, the native-born "complete gentleman" made an ideal host for Lord Howard of Effingham. When other councilors joined them for a night of high-stake gambling, it would seem unlikely that the problems and policies of the Virginia colony figured largely in their conversations over the heavy wine Wormeley imported from Portugal.

The members of the House of Burgesses saw none of this light side of His Lordship. In all truth, from the new governor's first encounter with the General Assembly, the Burgesses had showed an obstructive attitude to Effingham's proposals on the touchy subject of meetings of the Assembly. Under the existing laws, a General Assembly had to be called for every passing emergency and for any legislation concerning taxes. Several counties had earlier petitioned for a change which would permit — as Berkeley and his Council had been permitted immediately after the Restoration — the governor and the Council to levy taxes for an emergency. Charles II approved of this and Effingham, following instructions, submitted the proposal for a five-year period to the first Assembly he met in the new State House in Jamestown, in the spring of 1684. His Lordship assured the gathering that the King desired only "your ease and benefit."

After a quarter of a century of struggling against low tobacco prices under Charles II's Navigation Acts, the freeholders not unnaturally received the assurances of the King's regard for their "ease" with some skepticism. Secretary Spencer believed their distrust was exploited by such troublemakers for the King as Robert Beverley, who aroused fears that the Assembly's rights were in danger. Whoever instigated the response to Effingham's proposal, the Burgesses' somewhat irrelevant answer was a memorial protesting the Crown's infringements on the rights of the General Assembly. From this unhappy start, the meetings between the governor and the Burgesses degenerated into quarrelsome scenes.

The Burgesses stood firm on their determination not to yield on any point that even appeared as if it might diminish the power of their weapon to legislate taxation. Where they could perceive no threat, the Burgesses finally agreed to a duty on spirits imported into Virginia from other than English ports. This was designed to lower poll taxes, by applying indirect taxes for the maintenance of Virginia's government, and over a period of years the revenue from the direct poll tax was gradually decreased. But despite complaints of fraud and corruption in the administration of county levies in some localities, the Burgesses steadfastly rejected any measure which threatened the independent powers of the counties and parishes to levy taxes — any measure that threatened local autonomy.

Confronted by this (to him) mulish opposition, Effingham became very dictatorial in his dealings with and manner to the Burgesses. He dictated the laws he expected the House of Burgesses to pass, denounced the members when they refused to follow his orders, and declared "void" the laws he disapproved of. Where he could impose his will upon them, Effingham removed from the House of Burgesses their rights to elect their own clerk, to receive judicial appeal, and to control revenues, and levied an assortment of fees over their angry protests. Effingham was following instructions based on Charles II's mistaken belief in the need to limit the General Assembly's power, but the measures taken by the governor, as well as his authoritarian behavior, could not fail to give the impression that he was using every device available to him to subvert representative government without abolishing its forms. When the resistance to him had hardened to the point where every session meant a bitter conflict, Effingham claimed that the Burgesses "rudely and boldly disputed the King's authority."

When the governor made this accusation in 1686, Charles II was no more. He had been succeeded the year before by his foolish brother

James II. Too dull to bother with Charles's type of schemings to retain the power of the Crown, James asserted himself as a divine-right monarch exercising a one-man rule such as England had not seen since before Henry VIII. Applying this absolutism to Virginia, while knowing little of the actual conditions, James ordered the "rude" General Assembly to be dissolved, and settled upon Robert Beverley as a scapegoat. Beverley, having survived persecutions that had dogged him until 1684, was then back at his post as clerk of the House of Burgesses and was still continuing to encourage the people's representatives to manage their own internal affairs. James ordered Beverley to be removed once again, and this time finally, from his post. A year later the prematurely aged lawyer died.

Beverley's death led to another break in the political solidarity of the Green Spring faction. Philip Ludwell, then deputy surveyor of customs, gave Beverley's son his father's old position as surveyor (collector) — "the best in the country," according to Secretary Nicholas Spencer. For befriending Beverley's son, Ludwell was removed from the Council by Effingham. When Ludwell had been removed earlier by Jeffreys (and restored to his seat by Culpeper), he represented only the Berkeleyite Council in its fight for its own privileges. But such was the generalized resentment of Effingham that Ludwell was elected as his county's representative in the House of Burgesses. My Lady Frances watched the power grow diffused as her husband was caught up in the changes that dissolved old alliances and formed regroupings.

The basic change underlying all the shiftings was one of those nameless "forces," not personalized by any hero or articulated by any philosophical observer. It had to do with money — the means of getting it in relation to the standards of living of the colonists.

By 1682 British merchants had begun to unload on world markets the tobacco accumulated in their warehouses. This brought an increase of buyers for Virginia tobacco, without bringing a rise in the price. The expanding market, at the same prices, gave big merchant-planters the opportunity to make fortunes by enlarging volume productions, and accelerated the drift toward replacing transient white indentures as field workers with Negro slaves.

At that stage the purchase price of a slave to be owned outright was only about three times the cost of five years of an indenture's work, and the Africans were better adapted than the average English emigrant to the hard labor in damp fields under a broiling sun. While it was not until after one decade of Charles II's ruinous policies that the number of slaves had increased to 2,000, during Effingham's term (1683–1690) the number was multiplying, and by the end of the century it reached 6,000.

The real significance of this increase in slaves in the Colony was less in the growth of large labor forces used by a few rich colonials than in the spread of the use of slaves by planters of modest operations. These tobacco growers cut themselves loose from the ways of the average freeholders and turned to slave labor in adopting on various scales the big producers' methods of acquiring and cultivating expanding landholdings with a permanent labor force. This change in method began a division among the freeholders — dividing the yeomen, who did their own work, from the planters, who did no physical work themselves. Bringing changes in concepts and standards and, most of all, in attitudes, this broad spread of slave labor was the genesis of the "planter class."

Technically, every tobacco grower was a "planter": in Virginia usage, "planter" became distinguished from "farmer" generally through association with slave-operated plantations. During Effingham's day the line of demarcation between the small planter and the yeoman was very blurred (and never sharply defined). The "planter" working 200 acres with a couple of Negro slaves would be in all practical ways closer to the yeoman family working their 200 acres with healthy sons than to the merchant-planter working fifty slaves on 10,000 acres and shipping from his own wharf. But there were less than twenty of the large-scale merchant-planters who held more than 5,000 acres, and nine-tenths of all landholdings were less than 1,000 acres. What the spread of slave labor created was a gradation from the biggest planters to the smallest, in which new planters tended to identify themselves with the masters of the great plantations. The big planters were the models who, showing the way to make profits by volume production, established the customs and the values, the styles and the tastes, and, most of all, the attitudes. For attitudes distinguished the "planter," in its local meaning, as much as the use of slaves.

The class grew, from its beginnings in the late years of the Stuart regime, into an approximation of the English country gentry. By the nature of the frontier, the colonial class was more diffused, less clearly defined, than its English model. Not all tobacco growers who worked with slaves aspired to the planter class, in the sense of gentry, and no statistics could compute the proportion of tobacco growers working with a few slaves who remained plain farm people. But in the changes when Effingham was governor, the emerging planter class *as Virginia gentry* was composed of tobacco growers who worked with slaves.

The newly forming class was also more in ferment than its English model. As families rose out of the yeomanry with aspirations to the gentry, other families rose within the gentry by an increase of estate, more pretentious standards of living, advantageous marriages into other families on the way up and, by attaching themselves to the men of immense influence, positions in the county governments. And always, where substance was accompanied by at least some education, the personal force and ambition of the heads of well-connected families continually brought new men into positions in the ruling group.

The lines of demarcation also grew fuzzy near the top, between affluent, educated planter families and the forming native aristocracy in the classic meaning of those who ruled as a qualified minority. With the continual recruitment (as in England) of new families into this colonial aristocracy, the blurred line of demarcation did not exist as a definition of any permanent stratification. In the continual flux in the almost totally rural population, families seemed to find their own levels from day to day, and men and women had no difficulty in recognizing others of their own "degree."

Unlike anything before Bacon's Rebellion, unlike anything familiar to rigidly set English-born imports such as My Lady Frances and Lord Howard, this germinal planter class gave an ever broadening base to the emerging Virginia ruling class, which — not detached from the Colony like the Green Spring "court" — became the apex of a pyramid growing out of the life of the Colony.

When a tobacco grower rose, by using slave labor, out of the general run of freeholders, who were still dominated by the yeomanry, the elements seemed to be the same as in any earlier economy: ambitious inclinations supported by enterprise, careful management of money and time, and the absence of bad luck. The primary requisite for beginning the shift to slave labor was a small sum of accumulated cash. While an indenture could be brought in for the £5 of his passage (and the majority of freeholders could not save up even this), a slave at that period cost from £12 to £18. From that line of demarcation on, it was a case of the more one had, the more one could get. For a planter with as many as three slaves, it was easier to squeeze out enough profit by volume production to buy three more slaves than it was for one man, doing his own planting, to save enough to buy the first slave.

Excluding the shiftless and the inefficients simply not equipped for the life, as in any society in any time, a variety of individual reasons explained why the majority of freeholders did not make the shift over to volume tobacco growing based on slave labor. Some were not good planners, some were poor bargainers, and others — who might work their fingers to the bone — were improvident with time. It was no great chore to make hard cider and peach brandy from easily picked fruits, and the fifty-acre farmer could enjoy a night of hard drinking with companions as heartily as Ralph Wormeley with the governor. The difference was that the next morning the yeoman had to pick up the hoe himself. Then, ill health was financially ruinous.

Probably the largest proportion was composed of those who simply desired modestly and asked no more than self-sufficiency on their own land. Those families had realized the dream that beckoned them, or their parents, to the New World. Hard times might come and food be scarce, but their snug houses were truly their castles and they walked, as did noblemen, on their own property. Having wrought such heroic changes in their own destinies, these men and women were not concerned that others did better or aware that the upward thrust of some of their neighbors was beginning a Virginia version of the English class structure.

The majority of the population, these families continued as a strong strain of self-reliant, self-respecting people, of personal dignity and a gentle courtesy, in the Virginia communities. Though their political influence would wane in time, as the planter class grew in numbers and in the self-consciousness of making up a gentry, during Effingham's day the non-slave-owning freeholders formed a solid segment of those gradations which doomed the outwardly imposed order represented by Lord Howard and the declining Green Spring circle.

7

While there were no heroes in the nameless "forces" that caused a subsurface shifting in the balances of political weight, there were prototypal entrepreneurs who exploited the hard times by combining volume planting with large-scale trading operations. William Byrd, William Fitzhugh, and William Randolph had all been newly arrived unknowns in the Colony when Sir William and My Lady Frances flourished in the regal days of the Green Spring "court." Too young to be caught up in the old order, each brought the same combinations adapted to the conditions of the post-rebellion changes that

John Carter I and Richard Lee I had brought to the more primal conditions of their smaller Virginia.

All three were younger than the first empire-founders had been when they arrived, about 1670, in the first full flush of young manhood. Byrd was eighteen, Fitzhugh and Randolph around twenty or twenty-one. Though not native-born Virginians, because of their connections with established families and their political and social intimacy with men and women who had grown up in the Colony, the three emigrants were usually associated with the second generation of plantation families.

None of these three fortune-builders ever seemed "young." All appeared mature men of large affairs when they were first noticed in their mid-twenties. Obsessed with personal advancement *through* wealth, as millionaires of later American generations were obsessed with amassment of money, they worked themselves into premature old age. Fitzhugh felt old at thirty-five and died at fifty. Byrd lived one year longer, and Randolph lasted until he was sixty-one — outlived twenty-four years by the wife who bore him nine children.

Nothing was known of the beginnings of the three emigrants, or of their arrival in the strange land and the start of their new lives, except that they all came to work hard for success in the New World. Byrd started at his uncle's trading post and landholdings at The Falls in the James River, but nothing was known of the circumstances that brought him or of what determined his career on his uncle's death. Records placed Randolph and Fitzhugh in the Colony at certain dates, with probable English backgrounds, though nothing detailed their ways of gaining the footholds from which they rose to appear among the families of prominence.

One certainty was that none of them passed through the yeomanry stage. Byrd started with the estate left by his highly placed uncle, and Randolph came with family connections which he built upon. William Fitzhugh, alone of the three, began without the initial advantage of local connections. He quickly made his own. The phrase "his eye on the main chance" could have been invented for this businessman as planter, the one who most clearly outlined the course that would later typify the rise to riches in America.

8

Of all the dynasty-founders of the second generation, William Fitzhugh showed most obviously a sense of insecurity derived from the effects of dislocations in early life. He came of an armigerous family of maltsters in Bedford, where they had been locally prominent for two centuries: Fitzhughs had served as mayors since 1487. William's father, not following the family trade, was a woolen draper who married the daughter of a Bedfordshire rector. When William was only six, his father ran into financial trouble and died seven years later, leaving his widow and children in hard case. What William, the youngest child, did between the ages of thirteen and twenty-two was a particularly puzzling mystery. When his appearance in Virginia became recorded, Fitzhugh was sufficiently grounded in law to be practicing as a lawyer, sufficiently schooled to write the letters of an educated man, and sufficiently assured to be at ease with gentlemen of substance.

His looks were not prepossessing. His irregularly arranged features were dominated by a sharp nose, and between a rounded point of chin and black eyes of metallic brightness his mouth was incongruously full. Though his face in repose gave little hint of his driving force, probably Fitzhugh's vitality was reflected in his expression when he became animated. He was a man of good temper, adroit in personal relationships, and had no trouble in winning the friendship of important personages.

Fitzhugh's upward rise began with a curious marriage which, without contrary evidence, seemed to be of the coldest pragmatism. Fitzhugh was first placed definitely in Virginia in 1673, though it has usually been presumed that he arrived around 1670. Almost certainly he had been settled for a while before he appeared in the 1673 court records as receiving the power of attorney for Mrs. Rose Gerard. This twice-widowed lady had an eleven-year-old daughter, Sarah Tucker, whom Fitzhugh married when he was twenty-three.

According to family tradition, the child bride was sent to school in England for two years before the marriage was consummated. Long before she returned, Fitzhugh received Sarah's share of her dead father's estate, which included a Negro couple, a bay gelding, six ewes and a ram, hogs, and the household furniture, utensils and dishes to set up a house. Later, five thousand pounds of tobacco came to the couple, and very probably some land. Given this head start over the average freeholder — who began the struggle with fifty wilderness acres, a parcel of clothes, a gun and a few tools — Fitzhugh eventually expanded his holdings to fifty thousand acres.

His home plantation was in sparsely settled Stafford County — where Robert Hen had been killed — the westernmost settled area bordering on the Northern Neck. As soon as Fitzhugh was settled, he

*William Fitzhugh. From a portrait copied by John Hesselius
in 1751, owned by Mrs. Robert H. Stevenson, Boston, Massachusetts
(Courtesy of Mrs. Robert H. Stevenson)*

established an intimacy with his neighbor Nicholas Spencer, then very influential and soon to be secretary of the Colony. It has been assumed that Spencer, also from Bedfordshire (his son inherited the Spencer family's estate at Cople), had known Fitzhugh's family in England. Through Spencer he became friendly with other established planters in the western region on the edge of the Northern Neck, such as the burgess Thomas Mathew, who recorded Bacon's Rebellion. Possibly also through Spencer, he became engaged as Robert Beverley's lawyer. Doubtless self-taught in law, Fitzhugh did not do too well for Beverley, but acting as attorney for the people's hero brought him into general prominence in the Colony. Even before that, when only twenty-six years old, he had been sent to Jamestown as Stafford County's representative in the House of Burgesses.

In Jamestown, while he took a strong position for the rights of freeborn English citizens established at a distance from the home country, Fitzhugh ingratiated himself first with Culpeper and then with Effingham. Fitzhugh's property lay within the controversial Proprietary, and as Effingham was trying to help Culpeper collect the long-overdue quitrents from the recalcitrant settlers, Fitzhugh's purpose was evidently to obtain an appointment as agent for the Proprietors.

Before this plum fell to him, Fitzhugh seemed to turn cash from his law practice into the purchase of land and slaves: he was one of the early users of slave labor on a large scale for that period. When he died, he owned about fifty, who he said were good breeders. He was extremely efficient in the employment of slave labor. Using tobacco as a money crop, Fitzhugh raised cattle, corn and wheat (operating his own gristmill) on a scale to produce sufficient surplus, after feeding his own community, to conduct an "inland trade." Trading foodstuffs to small planters for their tobacco, Fitzhugh, with his backwoods plantation, soon became a one-man commercial enterprise.

He frequently acted for London merchants trading in Virginia, and brought bold ideas to his shipping activities. He proposed to load at his own wharf cargoes of from 200 to 250 hogsheads of tobacco, which he would collect from neighbors and sell at the going rate of ten shillings per hundred pounds. This plan would save the English ships the time and expense of sending sloops up the tributary rivers to collect small lots. Evidently it was too simple for the London agents, who probably suspected that Fitzhugh would pay a little less for the tobacco he contracted for.

In Fitzhugh's scheme, he would have squeezed out his own profit

with an actual saving to the London merchants and at no loss to the
small planter. For while Fitzhugh would have paid slightly less for the
tobacco than the London agents did, the small planters would not have
shipping charges deducted by Fitzhugh. Nor would they suffer the
long wait, sometimes two years, between the actual shipping of tobacco
and the accounting which advised them of the amount of their credit
with the London agents.

Shipping represented a continual and deadly game between English merchants and tobacco growers, and — as the evolved custom
eliminated the merchant class as such in Virginia — only the big merchant-planters were qualified to hold their own. Ships came in the fall
to load tobacco, and space was always scarce for two reasons: the
merchants were careful not to bring back light cargoes, and the
planters tended to give low figures in the estimates they mailed in the
spring, for fear of driving down prices. The ships tarried until spring
to recross the Atlantic, beginning there the planters' period of waiting. It was in sparing the small planter this period of uncertainty that
Fitzhugh and the big shipping-planters — for the least idealistic motives — did a real service to the yeomen tobacco growers.

The merchant-planters who operated stores — as the Carters,
Byrd and the Harrisons — also, and quite incidentally, performed a
similar service by providing immediately needed goods for farmers'
families against the future sale of their tobacco. If Fitzhugh operated
such a store, it was not important in his calculations. He concentrated
on his "inland trade" for tobacco, estimating that he handled stock
nearly as high as sixty thousand pounds. Roughly the equivalent of
£300 in cash, this was about forty times as much as the yeoman would
gross by doing his own work. With nearly two-thirds of the yeoman's
gross sale deducted by the expenses of marketing, his net cash income
was a pittance which he could not use for expansion. Fitzhugh's more
than £100 net — since volume would reduce his marketing costs —
enabled him continually to grow bigger.

In developing his inland trade with farmers, Fitzhugh gave more
attention to planting than did some of the other merchant-planters.
But it was Fitzhugh's intentness on providing his own sufficiency of
food that indicated his vestigial fear of want resulting from earlier
insecurities. He was proud of stocking "all sorts of goods" sufficient
for the needs of his family and slaves for two or three years, and his
home plantation of one thousand acres was a completely self-sustaining unit.

Around his house were scattered such dependencies as four cellars, a barn, stable, dairy, henhouse and dovecote, and within view cattle and sheep grazed, and horses and mares. In addition, he mentioned "stocks of cattle and hogs at each [slave] quarter," and pointed out that the distant quarters were "well furnished, with all necessary houses ["necessaries" were privies], ground and fencing. . . ."

His attention to fences, enclosing sections of the home plantation, also reflected his need for a sense of security. A locust fence "as durable as most brick walls," he wrote, enclosed an orchard of twenty-five hundred apple trees, and a stout locust fence enclosed a garden and house yard.

As a forerunner of the later-day type of millionaire, Fitzhugh wrote that he felt at times that the final gratification eluded him. An indefatigable correspondent, Fitzhugh was more self-revealing in letters than his contemporaries. Occasionally sorry for himself in "my declining age" (thirty-five) and suffering pangs of loneliness for England, where his mother still lived, he wrote: "Society that is good and ingenious is very scarce, and seldom to be come at except in books."

Judging from the books he ordered, in addition to books on law (such standards as Coke's *Reports* and *Institutes*), his tastes ran to scientific study and history, with sprinklings of Virgil, Horace, Tacitus and Juvenal: he preferred translations, though he could read the Latin. His store of religious books was comparatively small and commonplace. His wife chose those for herself in her "relinquishment of dower," and along with the Bible and the *Book of Common Prayer*, listed only five religious books. These included the two staples in every literate Anglican household, *The Practice of Piety* and *The Whole Duty of Man*.

Despite the company of books, Fitzhugh wrote that what bore "the greatest weight" upon him was "the want of spiritual help and comfort." This would seem to indicate an absence of emotional rewards and companionship from his family. He never referred to his wife in his personal letters; every reference to his home was in terms of "I." In his most intimate letters to kinspeople in England, he only referred to his five sons when discussing the problem of education for the oldest two. They both studied with a nearby French tutor, and the second oldest was sent to school in England. Even his concern over their schooling reflected his own ambition: "Good education of children is almost impossible [here], and better never to be born than to be ill bred."

Fitzhugh completed the pattern of the later type of millionaire by acquiring the tangible symbols of wealth. By Effingham's term as governor, Fitzhugh's house had been expanded to thirteen rooms, nine of which were, he wrote, "plentifully furnished with all things necessary and convenient," but "four of the best [were] hung" — with tapestries and leather hangings. Curtains and valances draped the windows, which had diamond-shaped panes shipped from England, and framed portraits decorated the walls. Turkish carpets covered the floors, brass and iron andirons glistened in the wide fireplaces, and the matched furniture was the best that could be imported from England. Until his death Fitzhugh steadily increased his acquisitions in silver, the standard symbol among the new rich.

He wrote that with his building finished and his "plantations well settled and largely stocked with slaves . . . I esteem it as well politic as reputable to furnish my self with an handsome cupboard of plate which gives myself the present use and credit, is a sure end at a dead lift without much loss, or is a certain portion for a child after my decease."

At the period when less than seventy families in Virginia used, or owned, silver, Fitzhugh displayed fifteen plates, two dozen spoons, nearly a dozen basins, large candlesticks and "lesser candlesticks" and "the smallest candlesticks," snuffers, large porringers and "second best" porringers, "the great silver tumbler" and smaller tumblers, tankards, a chocolate pot, bread plates, a salver, casters, a snuff dish, an extinguisher, and a number of unspecified dishes. All were engraved with the family coat of arms, although he and his brother could not agree on what the coat of arms was.

Fitzhugh liked to think that circumstance forced him to his materialistic ends. "Our estates here depend upon contingencies, and to prepare against that causes me to exceed my inclinations in worldly affairs." Yet, when important visitors came, Fitzhugh outdid his contemporaries in the lavishness of his hospitality. When the Frenchman who had visited Ralph Wormeley arrived with a party of twenty, Fitzhugh put them all up (two to a bed), served good wines and all kinds of beverages, and brought in three violinists, a jester, an acrobat and a tight-rope dancer. They "caroused" until after noon of the next day. Lending them his boat to cross the river, the host sent servants with a silver punchbowl of wine to the party at the shore.

Fitzhugh appeared to derive little pleasure from the "carousing" part of the entertainment he provided. In a letter to a London friend he wrote that he could not join in toasts to his health as often as did their mutual friends in Virginia, who "now exceed me more at this sort of exercise . . . neither my brain nor my constitution will admit me to go too far in these bacchanalian exercises.'' On hearing that his brother was drinking heavily, he wrote that his brother could not long continue in good health ''if he drinks so hard.'' Extending hospitality gave Fitzhugh the opportunity to display the symbols of his hard-won status: on a later visit from Governor Effingham he brought out his newest shipment of silver to show his guest.

With all his striving, Fitzhugh's early death deprived him of the most significant rewards of his struggle — the marriages of his children. The grandchildren of the financially ruined Bedford woolen draper united with families then among the most prominent in Virginia: William Fitzhugh, Jr., of Eagle's Nest (as the home plantation came to be called) married Ann Lee, daughter of the scholarly Royalist, Richard Lee II.

9

It was William Randolph, however, whose children's marriages intertwined the descendants of this emigrant with so many families who had or would gain position, that he and his wife Mary have been called ''the Adam and Eve of Virginia.'' To take only those most generally known to history, their descendants included Thomas Jefferson, John Marshall, John Randolph of Roanoke, and R. E. Lee.

Like Fitzhugh's, William Randolph's family were armigerous gentry who had fallen upon hard times. In the fashionable explanations for the low financial estate of emigrants, Randolph family tradition attributed their plight to losses they had suffered as loyalists during the civil wars. Actually, the first Randolph in Virginia was William's uncle Henry, a merchant who came to the Colony at about the age of twenty in 1635, before the civil wars could have affected either his family or himself.

That this first Randolph was educated was indicated by his appointment as clerk of Henrico County soon after his arrival, and in 1659 he became a clerk of the General Assembly. He was a friend of William Byrd's uncle, the councilor Thomas Stegg, Jr., witnessing Stegg's will. Without acquiring the large estate and power of Byrd's uncle, Henry Randolph was well established in Jamestown and among the planter families on the south side of the James. It was probable that William Randolph, like William Byrd, was encouraged to come to the Colony by his uncle. Randolph's father died in Dublin in 1671 (his mother having died two years earlier), and young Randolph came to Virginia either shortly before or shortly after his father's death.

As with Fitzhugh and the other successful emigrants, nothing is known of when and where William Randolph left the ship after his three months' voyage, or of how or where he first lived. Also like Fitzhugh, Randolph suddenly appeared in the records in 1673: on the death of his uncle, he was appointed to succeed him as a clerk of the General Assembly. Then twenty-three, Randolph also began to study law on his own. While he did not practice law as early as Fitzhugh or as widely, and never seemed very learned in the law, his legal self-training helped advance his career. (When at forty-four he was appointed attorney general, Randolph compensated for his lack of background by a conscientious application of intelligence with a knowledgeable interest in the Colony, to do his job extremely well.)

A year after his appointment as clerk at the capital, Randolph imported twelve indentures to the Colony, the headrights to whom gave him a property of 500-odd acres on Swift Creek, well inland from the James River. An oral tradition was that William Randolph, coming to Virginia with a broadax on his shoulder, earned the money for the passage of twelve persons by building barns. Evidence indicated that he did work at building whatever came to hand, though he was never identified as a "carpenter." The probability was that, coming to Virginia without cash, he was physically strong and willing to use his strength as well as his brains for a quick advance into the colonial society for which his background fitted him. By 1676 William Randolph had built a house and stocked it with furniture and goods. He was a neutral during the rebellion, but the quality of his establishment attracted bands of Bacon's men, who made impressments beyond the necessities for victualing themselves. Randolph reported detailed losses in sheets, tablecloths and similar imported material.

Judging from his stock of linens, Randolph was then planning for his marriage to Mary Isham. This charming young lady, known to play a musical instrument called a "cittern," was the much sought-after daughter of Henry Isham, the community social leader and a friend of the late Captain James Crews and Nathaniel Bacon. Randolph, who evidently had a personable presence, became first a friend of Mary Isham's father. The young gentleman emigrant chatted with the older planter as they smoked pipes together, lighting the tobacco with a coal lifted from a brazier and held with silver tongs. Wholly acceptable to her father, Randolph won the prize belle of the sparsely settled neighborhood, and they were married in 1680.

As with William Byrd, Randolph's marriage gave him important social connections; as with William Fitzhugh, Randolph's marriage brought property. He and his wife received the bulk of Henry Isham's estate a few years after their marriage. Before 1680 he sold his Swift Creek plantation and bought land on what was to become the fashionable north side of the James River. At first Randolph was able to get only 150 riverside acres at Turkey Island, later the name of his establishment. He expanded this into 1,000 acres, half of which he bought from the heirs of Captain James Crews. On this he built an unpretentious one-and-a-half-story house, with gabled roof and enormous outside chimneys. In addition to his home plantation, Randolph acquired about 10,000 acres. Only half the size of Byrd's and one-fifth of Fitzhugh's landholdings, it was in another bracket entirely from the average good-sized holding.

A planter with diversity of agricultural operations, who augmented his income by a law practice and government posts, Randolph was representative of the new powers primarily because of his genealogical contributions. Where it was the practice for the offspring of his contemporaries to marry into other dynasty-founding families, William and Mary Randolph surpassed them all in the number of descendants who through marriage crisscrossed the lines of the families emerging into wealth and position. Eight Randolph children produced thirty-seven grandchildren, and from them the spread of the Randolph strain became geometric.

One son, Richard, married into what was beyond all question the oldest family in Virginia: Jane Bolling, the great-granddaughter of Pocahontas, was directly descended from Powhatan, the great chief when the first settlers arrived at Jamestown. Richard acquired Curles' Neck, the former holding of Nathaniel Bacon.

Two of the sons married Beverley sisters, granddaughters of Robert Beverley; and one of those sons, Sir John Randolph, was among the very few colonials knighted by the King of England. Two grandsons married granddaughters of Benjamin Harrison III, who joined the north-side movement with the acquisition of the Berkeley Hundred property formerly owned by the Blands. A daughter married Richard Bland, whose family had relinquished Berkeley after the litigation caused by Bacon's lieutenant Giles Bland. It was the Bland line of William Randolph's descendants that married into the Lee family.

It was also in the Bland line that intermarrying most noticeably involved cross-marriages with other Randolphs. When Frances Bland married John Randolph of Curles' Neck, her father-in-law was her first cousin and her husband's mother-in-law was his aunt. When their children also married cousins, to judge from the eighteenth-century scandal at Bizarre and the neurotic malformations of John Randolph of Roanoke, inbreeding had reached a point of diminishing returns.

(There were also widening branches from the descendants of Uncle Henry Randolph, though apparently most Randolphs prefer descent from William and Mary — even when Uncle Henry was manifestly the progenitor.)

Good fortune had to be an element in William and Mary Randolph's being blessed with a brood of healthy children who used advantageously the fruits of the founder's ambition, hard work, and resourceful acquisitiveness. There was also another intangible element. When the Randolph children followed the natural practice of marrying into families of similar background in the small society, some combination of genes and home conditioning gave the young Randolphs a particular prudence in selecting their mates. When they married into other established families, they picked the winners in those families. Even when two granddaughters strayed outside the confines of the emerging class of planter–political powers to marry relatively unknown young men, they produced John Marshall and Thomas Jefferson — destined to be the greatest political figures of them all. There was also an indefinable genetic element that made the immediate descendants of William and Mary Randolph good breeders. At basis, as in all the unpredictable factors of frontier life, they had to have luck.

William Randolph's luck began in his proximity to the Isham family. After he won Mary Isham against scattered competition, the rest was unflagging attention to business and the astuteness and personality to make the most of social and political connections.

10

Of the three young emigrants, William Byrd was the only one who could have enjoyed a life of ease with little effort. He was the only one whose family had suffered no financial reverses, nor had he been thrown on his own with the insecurity experienced by the others. His father earned a modest income as a goldsmith, the London family was intact, and Byrd remained on intimate terms with them: he was deeply moved when, in his thirties, he visited his brothers and sisters in London. There was nothing in Byrd's background to account for his outsize acquisitiveness, already fully flowered when he began with the best position of any emigrant among the fortune-builders.

The first of Byrd's line in Virginia was his maternal grandfather,

Thomas Stegg, Sr., who sailed a trading ship back and forth between England and the James River as early as 1637. More frequently in those days than later, a ship's captain was also owner or part owner of the vessel and its cargo, which he took up the rivers to trade at the private landings. Getting to know the people, who welcomed him as an emissary from home, Stegg developed a position as an influential agent. In time, he acquired land on the James River, where he set up one of the stores, and was appointed to the Council. As he continued his Atlantic crossings, his son came over to look after his Virginia affairs. After his father's death, Thomas Stegg, Jr., shifted the store to the south side of the river at The Falls, shifted from shipping to the Indian trade, and succeeded to the Council. Having no children of his own, Stegg brought over his sister's eighteen-year-old son, William Byrd, and shortly after Byrd's arrival, his uncle died.

At that time it never seemed to attract attention when a young Londoner made an immediate adaptation to the wilderness. Byrd's uncle had built his isolated house of stone as protection against Indians, and there were still no large clearings to the west of the Stegg land when Byrd took up his lonely residence in 1670. Wolves howled at night and deadly water moccasins slithered through the underbrush. In the semitropical summers the rank green brush enclosed him, and in the damp winters his only vista was the naked woods where animals prowled. His companions were mostly the rough, wild illiterates who drove his trading caravans along the five hundred miles of trail to the Cherokees. Bands of drivers led as many as one hundred horses loaded with cloth and kettles, muskets, powder and shot, trinkets, and the inevitable beads, to be traded for deerskins. Tinkling bells attached to the bridles announced the peaceableness of the caravans. Though drivers were sometimes killed, it was always easy to find landless freedmen who, having no hand for farming, took to the backwoods life with all its hazards.

When young Byrd sought relaxation, he journeyed to the plantations of his uncle's friends, families of established position. Among them he met Warham Horsmanden, the grandson of a baronet and a Royalist army officer who had abandoned Cromwell's Puritan England and remained in Virginia until the mid-1670's. Byrd married his daughter Mary. The significance of "cavalier" connections was in their effect on the Byrds' children. When Horsmanden returned to England, his son — Byrd's brother-in-law — graduated from Magdalene College, Oxford, and became an Anglican rector. When the Byrd children went to England for their education, they came under the influence of persons of quality in their uncle, grandfather and cousins.

Of more immediate consequence, Warham Horsmanden was also a cousin of My Lady Frances, and Byrd's marriage brought him into the good graces of the mistress of Green Spring. In 1680, when Lord Culpeper came, Byrd ascended to the Council and from this vantage point he won the consequential and well-paying post of colony auditor and receiver general. From his initial advantages Byrd became the most successful of the three emigrants. The prototype of the merchant-planter as financier, he operated from the base of his plantation as an international trader.

He showed none of Fitzhugh's insecurity or, during the first twenty years of his successful acquisitiveness, any desire to acquire the tangible symbols of wealth. There is no record of his having provided impressive entertainment, although he practiced the customary hospitality which visitors noted in all planter families in a land with few public places. After he became auditor general, Byrd rented a "chamber" (apartment) in Jamestown, which he stocked with claret — evidently to be served to fellow politicians.

William Byrd I made few more references to his family than did Fitzhugh, except on one occasion: when his five-year-old daughter sailed for school in England, he showed his concern by constantly writing to ask assurances of her safe arrival. Both the daughters and one son were sent at early ages to England, since the gently bred Mrs. Mary Byrd preferred to suffer the loneliness of the isolated outpost rather than expose her children to the rude conditions of frontier life.

For the girls, education seemed of secondary importance. The problems concerning them arose over proper quarters for young ladies in London being fitted for the world of fashion. Ursula, whose safety had caused Byrd's anxiety, returned to the Colony at an early age. She married the second Robert Beverley, but died shortly after giving birth to a son, just before her seventeenth birthday. Susan married an Englishman, John Brayne, and evidently never returned to Virginia.

The son, born in 1674 and sent to England at the age of seven, came more under the direction of the practical father. As a proper background for a young "gentleman" destined for the great mercantile world, William Byrd II was first sent to a highly regarded school where he received a fine classical education: he read Greek, Latin, and Hebrew for pleasure the rest of his life. Then, when he was sixteen, his father started his commercial training by sending him to Holland to learn Dutch business methods. Though it is nowhere specifically stated, it seems possible that the elder Byrd hoped his son would represent the business in international trade, as the Lees and the Corbins, among others, had family representatives in London.

When the younger Byrd expressed a dislike for Holland, his father placed him in the offices of his London agents, Perry and Lane, the most powerful mercantile house then trading with Virginia. But the second William Byrd had no liking for trade, then or later. In his formative years in England, hobnobbing with the educated young gentlemen he met through his well-connected Horsmanden kinspeople, he had developed a taste for a dilettante's life in London. Determined that his son be useful, in something of a compromise William Byrd I had him entered at eighteen in the Middle Temple to prepare for law. Byrd's heir, however, even after he was licensed to practice law, showed his preference for remaining a colonial expatriate in London.

Whatever the unreflective older man thought about this turn of events, Byrd was all business, and nothing distracted him from his complicated operations. The center of his affairs was the store. From this trading post Byrd's system ran something like this: with the tobacco from his plantation, sometimes shipped in vessels of which he was part owner, he bought ''trucks'' (as he called it) for the Indian trade; trading these trinkets and goods for skins, he sold the skins for merchandise which included everything from wearing apparel bought in London to rum bought in Barbados and Negroes bought from ships' captains. Sometimes he underwrote a ship's whole cargo. He traded the goods to the small planters for their tobacco — though occasionally he sold Negroes for cash — and the circular operation grew more profitable with each complete turn.

All of the operations had to be conducted in the uncertainties caused by the long delays in communication with England. As enormous as was Byrd's account, he once asked for facts from his agent, with whom he was on excellent terms. ''Not knowing how my account stands, I dare not send for goods, though my wants are very great and pressing.'' Very few men would have the heart or the head, or the cold nerve, to keep that many balls in the air day after day, month after month, with unceasing attention to details from which the eye could never glance away for fear of everything collapsing in total ruin.

The store could be run by a single young indenture. When one boy was working out his time, Byrd wrote his agent for a replacement, ''trusty and capable of business,'' who would be ''put to no hard work.'' The store gave Byrd constant trouble with the sharp merchants of England. He continually wrote his London agent about prices, whose rise and fall he followed like a stockbroker. He also wrote continually (and apparently to little avail) about the customers' complaints about the quality of the goods. "His duffields" (duffel was a coarse woolen cloth much in demand among the yeomanry) were never satisfactory; usually the material was "too light" when the customers wanted dark blue. Stockings, hats, thread were equally unsatisfactory, and "nails the worst ever saw." When he ordered hats for himself for special occasions, he fumed: "The French hats I sent for extraordinary for myself were worse than those I had from others [agents] for the store."

Yet, these were small worries compared to the risks he assumed in handling other planters' tobacco. Once he contracted for it, the risk of delivering the tobacco in London was his, as was the risk of getting safely to Virginia the goods he ordered against the tobacco. The only anxiety he revealed in his many letters to his agents was over the whereabouts of ships of which — or of whose cargoes — he was part owner.

With the scope and complexity of his operations, Byrd gave the same attention to a fraction of a penny as to pounds in three figures and, with twenty thousand acres, he would maneuver to gain a tiny profit from the smallest parcel of land. After Byrd became a councilor, he adopted his fellows' practice of patenting virgin land which, in evasion of the law, he neither settled nor paid quitrents upon. To evade the escheat laws governing patented land which remained unsettled or on which quitrents were not paid, one of Byrd's friends would repatent the escheated land and then reassign it to the original patentee. It happened that the first Thomas Jefferson in Virginia settled a homestead on 167 acres which, originally patented by Byrd, had reverted to the Crown in escheat. He was a "squatter" on public land. Before the lonely settler knew what was happening, a friend of Byrd's repatented the land in the escheator's office and assigned it to him, and the great merchant-planter forced Jefferson to pay him for the property.

Byrd never waxed philosophical, as did Fitzhugh, about the "contingencies" of planting and trading. He absorbed the inevitable losses and endured the bad times without complaint. One batch of Africans brought smallpox with them, which spread among his people. Fifteen slaves and his small daughter caught it, and three slaves died of it. Such a calamity would have wiped out a small planter, many of whom did lose the few slaves who represented their life savings.

In 1684, though he enjoyed "a good season" in tobacco, the small planters brought less to him for shipping: "I never knew so little made in these parts in my life." The following year the James River flooded, rising twenty feet, and carried away Byrd's fences and tobacco plants, and poured into his house. He wrote that the flood "did me and my neighbors much damage," without repining at all.

It was probably after this river flood of 1685 that he built his second house on the north side of the James. Sometime after his marriage in 1673, he had moved from his uncle's old stone house on the south side of the river, though retaining land on both sides. His second home — to which in the new style he gave a name, Belvedere — was built back from the river on the crest of a bluff which is now in the city of Richmond. Instead of buying tapestries and silver to give elegance to his new house, Byrd wrote the most detailed specifications for pieces of iron machinery he wanted for a sawmill he planned to install.

Like most of the big planters, he wanted books on practical subjects: these men all showed the greatest (and frequently justified) confidence in their ability to educate themselves for all manner of undertakings. Byrd's special interest during Effingham's administration was in ore. With this practical turn of mind, he showed not the slightest interest in people, not even when he wrote warm letters to his family. The only human behavior that he recorded as disturbing him was when the widow of a cousin of his in Virginia married a man he did not know. For months Byrd invariably referred to him as "a Stranger."

This reaction indicated the close-knit quality of the planter community, however widely separated their homes. Byrd would go by boat ten miles to Randolph's house, where he occasionally mentioned "drinking toasts" with his friend, and Randolph presumably exchanged the afternoon visits for quiet talks over a toddy. Byrd evidently did not share his friend's interest in horse races, where Randolph (placing no wagers himself) sometimes officiated. Byrd would usually see his other friends, or allies, when the General Assembly met in the Public Times at Jamestown. Isolated on the very edge of the frontier, he was probably not visited as frequently as those who lived near the passageways to and from Jamestown.

William Byrd, however, never mentioned being lonely, even after his affecting trip to his kinspeople in England. Alone of the three young dynasty-founders, and rare in the community, William Byrd was sufficed by the financial manipulations which gratified his acquisitiveness. His growing power seemed always a means to greater wealth, rather than the other way around.

11

None of the prototypal entrepreneurs revealed any awareness of influencing the drift toward a native ruling class, an aristocracy, arising out of a colonial gentry. Exploiting the crises for profit in efforts to realize the ambitions which had brought them to the New World, they went along with the changes and represented, rather than consciously introduced, the new nature of responsibility in wielding power. The fundamental difference between what they represented and the practices of the dissolving Green Spring faction was in the communication growing between county governments and Jamestown.

In "Bacon's Assembly" the chief objective had been to break the control centralized at Jamestown and to permit all freedmen to participate in the operation of affairs at the county level. Though this ideal was far from being attained under Effingham — and would never be attained in the full meaning of democratic representation — the counties' representatives carried more authority in the General Assembly when the people began to send men of the standing of Fitzhugh and Randolph to the House of Burgesses. The majority of the burgesses were not men of Fitzhugh's and Randolph's position but Effingham managed to unite them all in common purpose.

In his retreat at Ralph Wormeley's Rosegill, the governor and his host had developed a custom of dining at two o'clock in Effingham's quarters, where he served white wine from Spain and claret from Portugal. At the end of the day His Lordship would go to the manor house for supper, where Wormeley added beer and homemade cider to his imported wines, and pleasure-minded friends gathered. When called away from this rural idyll to Public Times at Jamestown, the governor seemed to find some outlet for self-expression in the dictatorial attitudes which hardened the Burgesses' resistance to all he represented, at the time when the freeholders came to look to the House of Burgesses to represent their interests at Jamestown.

When Effingham had first arrived, for a number of reasons the House of Burgesses was not as strong politically as similar bodies in some of the younger colonies. Even before the House of Burgesses was made helpless under Berkeley, it had been overshadowed by the Council and further weakened by the county courts' handling many functions which in other colonies were the responsibilities of legislative bodies. But during Effingham's administration, as control ebbed from the Green Spring faction which had dominated the Council and as powerful merchant-planters increased among the Burgesses, members of the House — actually representing the people — began to reveal the urge to extend its spheres of authority. Effingham kept the Burgesses too much on the defensive for them to make any concerted thrust toward an extension of their powers. But around their core of power — control of the general tax levy — the Burgesses' habit of resistance developed attitudes of another nature entirely from those of their days as puppets under Berkeley and under the Berkeleyites immediately after the rebellion.

There was nothing rebellious in the new spirit, no echo of Bacon. But when a political change came in England, the House of Burgesses was ready to shift suddenly from their defensive resistance to an aggressive move against Effingham.

In England the people had had enough of Stuart divine right for the second time, and this time for good. As reaction against the Cromwellian government had restored Charles II, counterreaction reached a climax under James II, with his personal government and his Catholicism. With some undercover maneuvering (including the disloyalty of Culpeper), James II was deposed, and Parliament established its supremacy when it brought James' Protestant daughter Mary to the throne with her husband, William of Orange.

Himself of Stuart blood (a grandson of Charles I), William III, the actual ruler, had established a reputation in Europe as a defender of the Protestant faith. Ascending the English throne after "the glorious revolution" of 1688, William accepted newly defined powers of Parliament and opened a new era of English constitutional government.

When Virginians learned of the changes in London, they decided that the time was propitious for petitioning the new King for Effingham's removal. Philip Ludwell, whom Effingham had removed from the Council, was selected to take the petition to William III. William handled the petition adroitly. Recognizing that Effingham, a vestige of Stuart attitudes, could serve no useful purpose in the Colony, he recalled His Lordship to London. To save face for a well-connected peer, William permitted Effingham to retain his title and his salary. As deputy governor, to act as de facto governor at Jamestown, he appointed Francis Nicholson, a professional soldier and career colonial administrator.

Nicholson, an honest man and efficient executive, left the ship at

Jamestown in the mellow warmth of June, 1690: only one decade had passed since Lord Culpeper was welcomed by My Lady Frances as the supporter of her Green Spring faction. In the year that Nicholson came, My Lady Frances died, and with her passed the personification of centralized government imposed from the top without the consent of the governed.

Her widower, the contumacious Philip Ludwell, seemed to have spent his capacity for hating after Effingham left Virginia, and a new order began to take shape. As age came on, Ludwell relinquished Green Spring to his now adult son, and left the land of his violence to end his days in England.

With the passing of the attitudes reflected in the Stuart–Green Spring order, in 1690 the patterns were already formed, the framework laid, for the native ruling class — the apex of the pyramid evolving out of an indigenous order — to assume responsible control of the Colony's internal affairs.

Also in 1690 John Carter II died, opening the way for Robert Carter, then twenty-seven, to assume his position among the Colony's leaders. During his long preparation for "the use of his estate," the changes in Virginia prepared an order as favorable for Robert Carter's career as the post-rebellion period had been for Byrd, Randolph and Fitzhugh, and as the earlier period had been for John Carter I.

Chronologically Robert Carter was of a cross-generation. Younger than the men of the second generation — such as Richard Lee II and William Byrd — he was older than their children, the third generation. In 1690, Byrd's son was a sixteen-year-old beginning his unwilling study of Dutch business methods, and Thomas Lee, who would be the most outstanding of Richard Lee's children, had just been born. By this accident in time, Robert Carter began his career in Jamestown during the first year of Nicholson's pivotal regime — just as his father had arrived in Jamestown contemporaneously with Sir William Berkeley, when that governor, then in his prime, had introduced a new order. Robert Carter and the era that led into Virginia's "golden age" began together.

· 5 ·

A "King" Is Born

ROBERT CARTER emerged as the prototype of the eighteenth-century dynast, the fully evolved aristocrat, during Francis Nicholson's two terms as governor (1690–1705). Nicholson's administration was a fulcrum period between the unarticulated gropings toward a colonial order, and the establishment of a solidified, self-aware ruling class. In this transition, the influence of the ruling class on the character of the Colony developed those attitudes of mind and designs of living that brought forth the flowering of an aristocratic order in the "golden age" of the eighteenth century.

Nicholson's era developed the attitudes and the life-styles to the point where the "golden age" appeared in its first budding, tentative and incomplete, in a state of exposure to the elements before the full flowering. Concurrently, Robert Carter advanced from the obscurity of a younger brother into a position among the dominant powers, with his own life on the verge of ultimate fulfillment as *the* dominant figure in the flowering of eighteenth-century Virginia society. In this colonial version of England's order of rule by those "best qualified" for leadership through estate, social position, and political responsibility, the country was run by the men with the biggest stake in it. Robert Carter had the biggest stake of all.

When Corotoman came to him, he was all ready to expand his planting-commercial enterprises along the principles developed by his brothers' contemporaries, then in the fullness of their financial and political power. Doing nothing essentially different from these older men, he conceived in larger dimensions and took up where they stopped. Combining in his own operations all of theirs, he refined each aspect of the vast complex and at the same time made *each* aspect of his whole operation larger than the main operation of his three prototypal predecessors — William Fitzhugh, William Byrd, and William Randolph.

While Fitzhugh was the largest landholder of his generation, with 50,000 acres, Carter's more than 300,000 acres was about four times as much as the other three held together. Where Fitzhugh was pleased when his slaves numbered more than 50, Carter owned upwards of 1,000. While raising more than two thousand cattle, along with sheep and hogs and horses, he operated forty-four tobacco-producing plantations in a dozen counties, and his store made him the biggest importer and exporter in the Colony. Where Byrd's store had been the center of his trading interests, Carter discounted notes like a banking house, invested in mortgages and developed his shipping into an enterprise in itself.

When Robert Carter's contemporaries began to refer to him as "King" — during Nicholson's administration — there was a question as to whether the soubriquet was given in derision or respect, or a mixture of both. But there was no doubt in anybody's mind what "King" meant.

Unlike his immediate forerunners, Carter fitted no part of the model of later-day millionaires. Hating ostentatious display — he regarded Ralph Wormeley's expenditures on frills and vain show with cold disapproval — he had almost a fetish for quality in everything he produced, sold, bought or used; whatever he touched had to be the best. With the scope of his activities as planter and merchant, shipper and financier, he was so intensely proud of the quality of the tobacco he sent to the London market that he would personally inspect a single hogshead if anyone questioned the quality of "Carter tobacco."

He was typical of his time and place in receiving daily affirmation of his ways from his comforting religion. As the Virginia community, embraced in the Church of England, was a structure ordered according to "priority and degree," in which each individual experienced the security of his place in the order of things, this earthly order in turn belonged to the Divine Order of God. Following the admonition "work, for the night is coming" kept Robert Carter in the graces of the God who controlled the universe, and none followed quite so successfully the Biblical advice: "Seest thou a man diligent in his business? He shall stand before kings."

In subscribing wholeheartedly to this Protestant ethic, Robert Carter was annoyed with the rituals of the Anglican Church as with any other kind of fol-de-rol. Wanting only to get to the heart of the matter — "the comfortable words" — he was prominent among the planter-class powers who debased the high church ceremonials and led to the low church practices in Virginia.

Carter's total commitment to work for the success his religion encouraged acted as an integrating center for his personal growth into "the complete man." In his "transcendent security," with none of his psychic energies wasted in self-doubts or inner conflicts, he was able to engage himself fully in multiple facets of life. In the breadth of his interests, his capacity for enjoyment, his love of learning, and the scope of the lives he affected directly and indirectly through personal involvement — along with the sheer size of the domain he acquired and the might of the power he wielded — King Carter was larger as an individual than the older men who were in power when he came to Jamestown.

In living itself he was also a heartier man. He took relish in eating, he was a knowledgeable and regular drinker of wines and brandies and a good companion in the taverns during Public Times, and his house was always open to visitors. He did nothing special for his guests: he provided handsome quarters and a fine table, and talked to them when he was free. He liked particularly to talk at night to ships' captains. He was, of course, absorbed in his endless figurings over pounds and pence, and in assuming personal responsibility in government, he enjoyed the play of power in politics. Along with these activities, he found a constant source of pleasure in reading, and took a participating interest in education, for his children and the Colony.

Most of all, he was deeply occupied by his family: his oldest son became a close friend, as did one of his sons-in-law; he was cruelly hurt by one of his daughters and extremely close to another daughter. Ultimately it was his concern for his children that made King Carter the greatest, the archetype, of the dynastic founders.

Tobacco wore out land in a few years, and volume production by slave labor spread the soil exhaustion widely and rapidly. Where the custom of primogeniture awarded the home plantation to the firstborn son, the leftover parcels of land would not last long for younger sons.

King Carter conceived of founding a dynasty by endowing each son with an extensive plantation of his own; when his daughters married, their families were helped by gifts of cash and slaves.

In England primogeniture was adhered to because it had been found that the perpetuity of a family's position depended upon the concentration of its assets in the home manor, as a dynastic seat, which passed without divisions to the oldest son. Though hard on younger brothers, the practice was justified by achieving its purpose of perpetuity in the family across centuries. Only in Carter's precise time, in his precise place, was his plan feasible. By it he entrenched the wealth and privilege of the generations following him more securely than did any of his contemporaries.

It was highly possible that Robert Carter was impelled to endow all of his children, in a drastic break with primogeniture, because he himself had been a younger son. He was by no means pauperized by his heritage — a backwater holding of one thousand acres, his mother's hoop ring and crystal necklace, one-sixth of his father's books and one-third of his father's personal estate. But it was little to build on for a younger son orphaned at the age of six and dependent upon the goodwill of an adult brother with a family of his own.

The portrait of Robert Carter as a young man revealed anything except a forceful figure who would dominate his time. It showed a soft and malleable-looking face, grave in expression, with a well-formed mouth suggesting sensitivity and dark eyes holding an oblique, questioning glance. The portrait caught him at a stage to capture all the uncertainties of a younger brother.

The years of uncertainties could not have been happy ones. In all his later recollections of his youth, Robert Carter never once referred to the years in the complicated household before he was sent to Mr. Baily's school in London. Nor did he ever make a reference to his father. He seemed to have blotted out childhood from his memory.

His one point of similarity with the second-generation Virginians was that he never seemed young.

2

Robert Carter's older brother had been, in effect, his foster father, and John's two wives were at once Robert's sisters-in-law and his foster mothers. Also in the sprawling brick house at various times were a stepmother, a full sister (who died), a half-sister (who married and moved away, out of his life), two half-brothers (one died and the other vanished), and Robert's young niece Elizabeth — John's daughter by his first wife. The mother of John's first wife was a family friend, and her stepson John Lloyd came to court Elizabeth.

All of these people had an interest in Corotoman, and the one whose presence continued a threat to Robert was the second Mrs. John Carter II. She was the former Elizabeth Travers Chinn, a widow and the daughter of another substantial Lancaster County planter — Colonel Raleigh Travers, a member of the House of Burgesses. By his father's will the land and house of Corotoman would go to any of John's "male issue." Along with growing up in such an unsettled household, with its inherent personality conflicts, Robert Carter lived like a prince with uncertain prospects of succession.

When Robert was twenty-five, he further unsettled the household by bringing to Corotoman his own bride, Judith Armistead, the daughter of a councilor. She gave birth to a son, another John. In beginning a possible "line of succession," Robert's wife became something of a rival mistress of the establishment to the still childless Mrs. John Carter II, between whom and Robert there was no love lost.

The layout of the house would not have offered much privacy. Not one of the designed manor houses, Corotoman grew by additions, and changes were made according to the exigencies of the moment. No part of the original house seems to have been destroyed, but old rooms came to be used for different purposes. As with most of the early Virginia houses, bedchambers were everywhere — downstairs and upstairs and over outbuildings. The chambers over outbuildings were always used for guests; since the time of John Carter I county officials had sometimes gathered at Corotoman. In 1688, the year he married, Robert had become one of the justices who met in the monthly court, and probably continued to invite Lancaster officials to stay.

Then, when John died, the new master of Corotoman wasted no time in getting the entangled domestic arrangements straightened out. Robert Carter's niece, then in her teens, moved out the year after her father died and married her grandmother's stepson John Lloyd. Soon the widow, who received short shrift in John's will and no claims on Corotoman, moved out in a huff.

Mrs. Elizabeth Travers Chinn Carter took Christopher Wormeley as her third husband and, in 1692, had "a complaint exhibited against" her ex-brother-in-law in the General Court. Robert Carter was then a burgess, and the House granted his request to waive the privileges of the House in order to answer her complaint. Shortly thereafter she died, and her husband sued Robert Carter for his late wife's one-third share of John's estate. Neither of them got any satisfaction, and that line passed out of considerations of Corotoman.

Robert's niece Elizabeth died very young in 1693, and he entered a caveat against her husband, John Lloyd, as administrator of her estate. She had received two-thirds of John's personal property. But nothing came of the caveat, and this property, which yielded £40 a year in interest, was the last money to be diverted from Corotoman. The plantation on the point of land became Robert Carter's wholly and completely, including the symbols of the plantation master's status — his brother's sword, periwig and cane.

As if in a symbolic act of coming into his own, Robert Carter stood for the House of Burgesses. When he was elected to represent the county that had grown along with the Carter fortunes, he never seemed to "begin" his career in politics: by his total preparation, he appeared full-blown in the governing bodies, confident in the self-sufficiency developed during his years as younger brother.

3

From his earliest recorded memories Robert Carter had consciously "educated" himself, as his father's will directed, "for the use of his estate," and he was the product of an early formed self-model. As the activities and character formation of Robert Carter's adult life confirmed his remembered impressions of adolescence — and he was the most factual minded of men — there was no possibility that his memories were colored by "the pathos of distance."

Everything in his life bore out his statement that in Mr. Baily's house in London he had formed a lasting estimation of the value of a classical education: "On the wisdom of the ancients was to be found a way of life suitable for young Virginians to imitate." The goals and youthful values that had guided him were consistently revealed in the later letters to and about his sons, his grandson, and the Wormeley boys whose estate he helped administer after their father's death. To his grandson, he summarized his own credo: "You are now growing toward manhood. It is not fine clothes nor a gay outsight, but learning and knowledge and virtue and wisdom that makes a man valuable."

Contrasting his sons' luxurious habits in London with his own, he wrote: "I lived with old Mr. Baily for six years [and] I never stood my brother in £30 in any one year of the time." Constantly he contrasted his own serious-minded and single-minded purpose in his youth with the attitude of those who played at being princelings instead of fitting themselves to run the plantations back home.

About the Wormeley boys he wrote: "Too much finery, and too

much pocket money, raises in young folks such opinions of their estates that they hardly know how to take up when they become their own masters. . . . From my own observations when I was in England, those boys that wore the finest clothes and had the most money in their pockets . . . went away with the least learning in their heads.'' To Francis Lee, the Virginia agent in London, he wrote of the Wormeley boys' desire to extend their stay: ''. . . to keep them too long in England will give them a disrelish of their [occupations here] all their lives after . . . make the drudgery of Virginia a trade too mean for their thoughts, and the remembrance [of the pleasures] they have left behind them lie too [near] ever after. This is what I have always observed of those who have been kept in England until their manhood. When you send them [home], let them be equipped suitable to their circumstances, not too gaudy or rich, yet genteel.''

He always retained a strong feeling about young men fitting themselves both for the responsibilities of their stations and for a fruitful life *according to their stations*. In his detestation of ''finery'' he revealed a lifelong aversion to sons taking the big estates for granted and growing into manhood with a sense of irresponsible privilege. As he wrote about the Wormeleys, ''to be somewhat acquainted with plantation affairs before they come to be men might be of extraordinary use to them.''

Unlike the British landed estates, where income flowed in from tenants' rents, no commercial plantation could be self-sustaining. His long years as a younger son may have contributed to Robert Carter's freedom from any illusion about the nature of the application required to stay on top in the mercilessly competitive system based upon low and fluctuating tobacco prices. But always, included with the requirements necessary for maintaining the estate, there was the emphasis on personal responsibility to make of the self a whole man — of learning, wisdom and virtue.

In his commitment, education transcended its value in self-advancement. While all the newly wealthy plantation families were aware of the advantages of education in colonial society — though few devoted Carter's thought and consistent efforts to the full education of their children — beyond that Robert Carter esteemed learning for its own sake. In another of the innumerable letters about his sons' education, he referred to their English schoolteacher, Mr. Solomon Low.

''I could wish Mr. Low had kept in the old understanding of Lillie's Grammar and of the old school books that we and our forefathers learned. There is one book which did me the most service of any that I was acquainted with, to wit — the *Jannua Linguarum Trilingus,* in Latin, English and Greek written by John Comenius. . . . It is so much in my esteem that I would desire you to give positive direction to Mr. Low that my son, Landon, be made a perfect master of this book in all three languages. . . . If they [boys] do not meet with a thorough improvement in their learning, such as will stick by them and be useful to them in their riper years, all our cost is thrown away, and the greatest part of their work is to do after they have left school. It is not by reading a few scraps of the poets and the classics that makes boys understand the scope and designs of the authors.''

His concern about education, never restricted to his own children, extended to a concern over educational opportunities for the coming generation in Virginia. In a letter to Francis Lee, he wrote of the ''country, which to my sorrow I will complain to you, having drawn my first breath here, does at this time labor under a very thick cloud of ignorance. Pray God send the next generation [that] it may flourish under a set of better polished patriots.''

When his own brief formal education was completed, Robert Carter had access to his brother's library, composed of their father's books and John's continuing additions. Along with the large proportion of religious books — which included theology, dialectics, Anglican church history and guides to individual conduct — John had owned the standards of colonial planters' libraries of his day.

There were informative books on farming, such as Gervase Markham's *Way to Get Wealth.* This had nothing to do with making money. It was a useful compendium of practical directions covering all aspects of running a plantation : growing crops and raising animals, planting orchards and gardens, preserving and brewing, and practicing ''physic'' and surgery. John's particular interest in medicine was reflected in eleven costly medical books. There were also books specifically on training horses and studies in soil fertilization, both to increase fertility and to restore exhausted lands.

As a militia colonel, he had two books on military discipline and tactics. He had dictionaries of Greek and English, French and English, Spanish and English, and two of the best English dictionaries of his times — Thomas Blount's *Glossographia* and Edward Phillips' *New World of English Words.* He had translations of the *Iliad,* Virgil's *Works,* Ovid's *Historical Epistles* and Plutarch. His collection included little history and few romances, as John's reading com-

forts had derived mostly from spiritual books. There was one volume
found in every educated planter's house: King James I's *Basilikon
Dorn*, a guide for the education of a gentleman.

Undoubtedly Robert began to buy books in building up his own
library before his brother's death. Not only were his tastes different
from John's — he liked to read Greek, Roman and especially English
history — but his brother's books reflected no interest in theories of
government or in law. Robert built one of the best law libraries in the
Colony and, judging from his quickness to lock horns over legal
matters with his sister-in-law, her husband and his niece's husband, he
had been reading in the law for some years before he was twenty-
seven. As a justice sitting on the monthly courts, he would certainly
have prepared himself.

His law books included treatises on the duties of the justice of the
peace, on wills, on the laws and customs of England, on writs; a
compilation on case law, citing more than twenty thousand cases; Sir
John Fortescue's popular book on the common law; the *Commentaries*
of Edward Plowden, the famous sixteenth-century lawyer who designed the hall of the Middle Temple; and John Perkins' legal treatise
The Practical Booke, which was so highly regarded that it remained in
print for three centuries, from 1530 to 1827. He bought collections of
statutes, of transactions of the Court of Chancery, and an abridgement
of Sir Edward Coke's *Reports*. Books on the law merchant were of
particular interest to Carter in their treatment of international phases
of mercantile law. On a basis of the old standards, he bought new
books as they came out all of his life, including the manuals on special
aspects of law practice and various handbooks on general guidance.

One aspect of his self-education could not have been planned:
having waited until he was twenty-seven to become the head of a
family at Corotoman, the element of time was never a consideration in
his goals. No delays or frustrations ever swerved him from a project
once he committed himself to it, and in the fluidity of his many-
faceted activities, his genius for the "management of effort" made
him a master of time — and timing.

4

In beguiling April weather, the new master of Corotoman and his
horse took the ferry trip across the broad stretch of the Rappahannock
to the flat south shore. By sandy, leaf-layered roads and byways, the
expert horseman rode across country, ferried the York River, put up

with a friend, and splashed across the creek onto the island of Jamestown. He took lodgings in one of the crowded taverns on the broad
street facing the James, where his father had landed in the sparsely
settled colony of fifty years before.

When the embryonic "King" climbed the stairs in the State
House to take his seat in the House of Burgesses, Francis Nicholson
was nearing the end of his first successful year as governor. The first
efficient career administrator to represent the crown, Nicholson had
won the respect and even affection of the Virginians in government. A
friendly bachelor in his mid-thirties, Nicholson rented a house in
Jamestown, where he entertained members of the General Assembly
and sometimes dined a party in one of the expensive taverns.

Nicholson not only showed a genuine interest in the Colony, he
showed an accepting understanding of the new social order in which a
planter class was emerging with the wider spread of families of means.
As a colonial careerist without associations with the post-Berkeley
Stuart era, the new governor would not miss the significance of the
rapidly growing use of slave labor.

In round figures, 1,700 of the 5,000 landowners were working
with slaves, and there were actually more slaves in the Colony than
there were heads of landowning families. England did not make a
systematic census for another hundred years, and only gross estimates
could be made for the total population of Virginia. As 60,000 would be
a composite figure for the decade of the 1690's, in thirty years slaves
had risen from one in twenty of the population to one in ten. When
Nicholson came, there were almost as many planters using slaves as
there had been slaves in the Colony before Bacon's Rebellion.

The trend represented by the spread of slave labor was so clearly
of a permanent nature that it would not have been possible for Nicholson to think in terms of "the people" in Berkeley's meaning of "the
great beast multitude." While the yeoman families outnumbered
those generally of the planter (slave-owning) class, and a rabble
shifted restlessly around the fringes, one-third of the tax-paying
landholders identified themselves with the big planters. Adapting
themselves for acceptance among the gentry, the astutely ambitious
maneuvered to get on a parish vestry and the county court as a justice
of the peace, showed diligence in the militia gatherings to win an
appointment as captain or major, and from there worked for election
to the House of Burgesses.

In the 1691–1692 session of the General Assembly, Nicholson
could have observed the beginning of another trend. The interlocking
family interests between the King's Council and the House of Bur-

gesses, a Virginia version of England's "web of kinship," were producing the nucleus of an oligarchy — a core of power at the top of, though within, the ruling class.

In that session, newcomer Robert Carter was appointed to fifteen committees, including the most powerful Committee of Propositions and Grievances. These appointments, while showing a recognition of his capabilities in taking over the big Corotoman operation, also showed the respect in which his family was held in Jamestown — even though it was nine years since his brother had served in the Burgesses. Men of John Carter's generation in the House when Robert Carter came in were William Randolph and William Fitzhugh.

Robert Carter did not gravitate to these older men. He associated himself with a family bloc which, with him and others, would form the nucleus of the oligarchy. Three members of this family bloc were on the Council: Benjamin Harrison II, who had made an unspectacular rise into substantial wealth on the south side of the James, and his sons-in-law — Philip Ludwell, Jr., the commercially enterprising heir to Green Spring, and James Blair, a new arrival who represented the Bishop of London in Virginia. A fourth member of this family, Benjamin Harrison III, in the House of Burgesses, was married to Elizabeth Burwell, whose father was the half-brother of Philip Ludwell II. The young Harrison was about as close as anyone came to being a friend of Carter's in the meaning of a personal relationship.

Carter in time had scores of intimate acquaintances, whose companionship he enjoyed and who enjoyed his hospitality, and developed close political alliances with the Harrison family bloc, but though his allies and pleasant companions formed the world of his very active social life, he never seemed particularly attached to any individual outside his family.

Of Carter's new associates in Jamestown, except for the older Benjamin Harrison, all were his contemporaries, and with no exceptions all were motivated by a love of power.

There were other interlocking families whose communality of interests with the upper order of the burgeoning planter class made them part of the "web of kinship" then in evidence in Jamestown. Burgess Edmund Jenings, the last English-born gentleman of influence in the Colony's government, was, through marriage into the English-Virginia Corbin family of merchant-planters, brother-in-law of Councilor Richard Lee II. The clerk of the House was Robert Beverley's son Peter: he married the daughter of Sir Edward Peyton, baronet, and his two daughters married sons of William Randolph, who was appointed attorney general during the 1690's. Peter Beverley's brother Robert, Virginia's first native-born historian, married Councilor William Byrd's daughter Ursula, whose passage to England as a child had caused her father to make one of his rare displays of concern.

Among Robert Carter's contemporaries in the House of Burgesses were John Custis and Lawrence Washington. Custis, like Carter, was on his way up from a solid foundation: one of his sons married the daughter of the raffish Daniel Parke and Jane Ludwell. Part of Custis's wealth would go to his grandson's widow, Martha Dandridge Custis, and her second husband, Lawrence Washington's grandson.

Confronted by this type of interchange, Nicholson found it the point of wisdom to adopt an attitude that led to cooperation and conferences between the Council and the House of Burgesses. Though the House of Burgesses remained a secondary branch during that period, the governor's recognition of the General Assembly as essentially a body of respresentative government was a significant change from the rule of the Stuarts' proconsuls.

Where Charles II had delivered his unrealistic orders for the sudden creation of urban centers, in Robert Carter's first session in the House Nicholson offered proposals for building towns and ports, along with suggestions for the encouragement of linen and leather manufacture — then being done on a limited scale in a few of the plantation centers. What most ingratiated the governor to the House, however, was his active support of a college.

The Colony's first college and its first planned city, Henricus, on the south side of the James River, had been destroyed in the great massacre of 1622, and thereafter education had become a private concern. Berkeley had strongly opposed education for the people during his reign, saying, ''I thank God there are no free schools nor printing, and I hope we shall not have these hundred years; for learning has brought disobedience, and heresy, and sects into the world, and printing has divulged them, and their libels against the best government. God keep us from both.''

Since Bacon's day individuals had established an unrecorded number of public schools, open to anyone who could pay a small tuition, and a larger number of private schools for the more privileged. For colleges, all families who could afford it sent their children to England. In Nicholson's support of a plan for a college, through an odd incident he financially contributed to it. The General Assemb'y showed its appreciation of the deputy governor by the unprecedented act of voting him a gift of £300. As the governor was forbidden to accept gifts, Nicholson petitioned the King to be allowed to receive the

£300 on the condition that he contribute half to the new college. The petition was granted.

The planning stages of the new college showed the precise status of Mr. Robert Carter — not yet "Colonel" — at this stage of his political career. In the first plan, which was soon abandoned, Robert Carter was included in a list of persons whom the House considered to be entitled, by virtue of wealth, position and capacities, to serve on a board of trustees. In the final plan for selecting a site and preparing for construction, a different kind of board was to be formed, of four members from the Council, four from the clergy, and nine from the House. To choose the trustees from the House, each member submitted his list of nine. In the final count, not enough members submitted the name of the first-year burgess for Carter to be among the trustees, but he was among those considered.

As his personal contribution to the college fund had been too modest to have influenced his consideration one way or the other, he was regarded as *among* persons of influence at twenty-eight, when he had been liberated from his younger-brother status less than one year and had occupied his seat in the Jamestown State House less than one month.

5

At the end of the 1692 session of the House, Virginia temporarily lost her friendly governor. In London, Effingham finally resigned as official governor, and when the new governor, Sir Edmund Andros, came to Virginia, Deputy Governor Nicholson was sent to another colony. Andros, another professional soldier and career administrator, came to Virginia from the northern colonies. Unlike Nicholson, he was not at all sympathetic to the attitude he encountered in the General Assembly. Not a throwback to the divine rightists, and an able, conscientious administrator, Andros had come up in the Stuart tradition with its autocratic attitude to popular government.

However, though he remained six years, Governor Andros exerted no significant effect on Virginia. In his stiff-necked authoritarianism, he was remembered for foolish things: he imposed newly passed English statutes — which had no application to the colonies — on the body of "customary laws" built up in the Colony, and he derived some weird satisfaction from telling the people that they held no real titles to their land.

Robert Carter did not go to Jamestown for the 1693–1695 session of the House of Burgesses under the new governor. His temporary absence from the House had nothing to do with Andros, with whom Carter was friendly enough on the surface. His absence might have been involved with the operations of the Northern Neck Proprietary, for which a Virginia agent was appointed in 1693.

Systematic action had finally begun on this controversial land grant after the death of Lord Culpeper in 1689. Though Virginia's one-time governor died without ever turning a profit from his twenty years of conniving, the year before Culpeper's death James II had validated his claim to the Northern Neck. In Culpeper's will he left the bulk of his personal estate to two illegitimate daughters and palmed off on his widow and her daughter Catherine the profitless Proprietary. Then Catherine Culpeper married the fifth Lord Fairfax, and things began to stir.

Thirty-three-year-old Fairfax, another peer in need of cash, applied himself to the entangled estate of his wife and mother-in-law, Lady Culpeper, and brought some order to the pursuit of profits from the land grant Charles II had carelessly given nearly half a century before. Fairfax was given more active support by King William than Culpeper had ever received, for the new King had reason to be grateful to both the Culpepers and the Fairfaxes.

Even though James II had validated Culpeper's claim, one of Culpeper's last acts had been to betray the Stuart king and contribute to the ascension of William and Mary. Fairfax himself, as a lieutenant in the 2nd troop of Life Guards, had been second-in-command of the Yorkshire cavalry which secured the north for William and Mary, and had served in the Parliamentary Convention which gave them the Crown. In his gratitude to the Culpeper-Fairfax family, William coldly rejected all the Virginians' petitions to remove the Northern Neck from the claims of the Proprietary, and supported the Proprietor in placing the region of the Carters and the Lees under what amounted to feudalistic control.

It still remained for Fairfax to collect the quitrents from such Northern Neck landowners as Robert Carter. For this he turned to prominent Virginians on the scene, first trying Secretary Nicholas Spencer and then Philip Ludwell without success. With an eye on the agency, William Fitzhugh had been cultivating governors since Culpeper came, and Nicholson, to escape the damp heat of his first summer, had journeyed to Eagle's Nest and Fitzhugh's spectacular hospitality. With his connections, Fitzhugh won the goal of his long-held ambition when, in 1693, Lord Fairfax appointed him and his law partner, George Brent, to act as his agents.

Two years after Fitzhugh's appointment Carter was back in the House of Burgesses, from where he could conduct his personal war against these first vigorous agents of the Proprietary. Significantly, he won the appointment as chairman of the powerful Committee on Propositions and Grievances, which was then investigating the practices of the Fitzhugh-Brent agency. Brent and Fitzhugh had been pushing the claims of the Proprietary, and the aggressiveness of George Brent had aroused a lot of feeling in the Northern Neck planters. Fitzhugh was a man of tact, and not only were the older landowners — like Richard Lee and Secretary Spencer — his intimates, but he preferred to move with the adroitness by which he won and held friends. Brent, inflated by the authority, became highhanded and threatening.

In terms of cost, the landholders would pay no higher quitrents to the Fairfax Proprietary than to the Colony. Their resistance was to acknowledging the dominion of the Proprietary. Brent threatened to double the quitrents and, instead of winning converts, stiffened the planters' resistance. Then, as part of his general policy of asserting the Proprietary's claim to all land fallen into escheat, he rejected Robert Carter's petition for a section of the escheated land in his (Lancaster) county. It was this that set Carter off.

At some stage during the 1690's he developed his own ambitions for the Proprietary agency, but in his violent reaction to Brent's refusal of his claim, Carter seemed enraged only at the effrontery of a colonial lawyer who would deny him land. His first counteraction seemed designed to discredit the agents, Brent and Fitzhugh, in order to maintain the ineffectiveness of the Proprietary's claims.

When he returned to Jamestown in May, 1695, Carter delivered from the floor of the House a free-swinging attack against the "abuses" of the agents' "strange and exorbitant practices." At thirty-two, there was nothing left of the grave and questioning mobility that characterized his early appearance as a younger brother. The cheeks had thickened, transforming the earlier planes into a solidified square, across which cut his firmed mouth, formed in indomitable resolution. The dark eyes, with steady self-assurance replacing the young questioning, held a gaze that looked the world straight in the face. It was the gaze of a man coming at life. In the next few years he would be called "haughty," and though Nicholson would say that after they became enemies, there may have been then a suggestion of imperiousness of will in Carter's unyielding expression.

In his charges against the agents, Carter selected points that had some basis in fact and distorted them, like a criminal lawyer building accusations upon slight evidence. He translated Brent's "threats" against recalcitrant landowners into "demands" for double the quit-rents allowed by the King in the Proprietary charter. He revealed the personal nature of the attack by condemning one practice which he later followed himself.

To discourage speculation in land and encourage the settlement of the Colony, strict laws forbade the holding of land which was not actually "seated" — occupied and cultivated. Carter charged the agents with placing no limitations on lands lapsing into escheat "for want of seating." By the agents' methods, he said, "a man may hold 50,000 or more acres of land by a secure title, and that without as much as actually seating or building upon any part of it." This possi-bility (which Carter himself later exploited) was implicit in the method of establishing the Proprietary's claims to unoccupied land. Though neither agent took extensive advantage of it, for that germ of fact, Fitzhugh and Brent each did take patent on something over five thousand acres, unseated, for themselves.

The force of Robert Carter's exaggerated picture of the ruin being visited upon the Northern Neck swayed the Burgesses, and the House voted to present a protest about the agents to the Crown. But the older Fitzhugh had too many friends among his contemporaries on the Council, including Richard Lee II, who as a Northern Neck land-holder himself resisted the Proprietary's claims. The Council refused to support the protest, and it died as far as action in the General Assembly was concerned.

Carter probably did not expect any more than this. His public charges had accomplished his purpose of maintaining the resistance of the Northern Neck landowners. The agents could get no large land-owners and few small ones to "attorn" — acknowledge the Propri-etary. It was not a profitable enterprise for Fitzhugh and Brent. Both the Proprietor's agents and the adamant Northern Neck landowners needed the support of the Board of Trade in London.

Fitzhugh could gain no influence with the Board of Trade, and Robert Carter had not then been master of Corotoman long enough to win the friendship and support of the powerful London factors. To judge from the working alliance that soon developed between Carter and Micajah Perry, the merchant of vastest influence on colonial affairs, Carter evidently was cultivating London allies in the period of the 1695 clash — as well as political allies in the General Assembly.

The reckless force he had exhibited in taking on the most solidly entrenched men of the generation then in power impressed the Burgesses. When the General Assembly convened the following year, in September, 1696, Robert Carter was chosen speaker of the House. He assumed duties similar to those which had evolved for the presiding officer in the House of Commons as that branch of Parliament grew in strength.

Originally the squires elected to represent the English counties did not speak to or before the House of Lords. The House of Lords in those earlier days gave the burghers a list of questions, usually on the amount of taxes their districts could produce, and the "commoners" retired to arrive at the answers in debate among themselves. Then a chosen lord served as the "speaker" to convey their answers to the superior House. When thirty-three-year-old Robert Carter became the gowned speaker of the Burgesses, he presided over all deliberations, voiced the determinations of the Burgesses, cast the deciding vote in the event of a tie, issued warrants for execution for those orders that required a legal form, and himself communicated the House's resolutions to the Council.

6

The most significant event for Robert Carter, during the two years he served as speaker of the House, was the overthrow of a royal governor by James Blair, of the Harrison family bloc who became Carter's most important political friends. The representative ("commissary") of the Bishop of London to the Church in Virginia was just about the trickiest, most ruthless behind-the-scenes operator to appear in the Colony. In taking on Governor Andros single-handedly, James Blair was also the boldest. He rushed suddenly into a dominant position with a new kind of power exercised in a new and deadly method of opposition to whatever he was against — beginning with Governor Andros.

Robert Carter's contemporary, Blair had been in Virginia only since 1685, when he had come as rector of Varina parish in Henrico County. The son of a Scots clergyman, his Scottish background profoundly affected his destiny and was of considerable consequence to Virginia's. After he received his master's degree from Edinburgh, Blair was ordained by a bishop of the Church of Scotland. Though the ordaining Bishop Wishart had received his consecration from bishops of the Church of England — continuing the Anglican apostolic succession — he had been consecrated specifically to be a bishop of the Church of Scotland. Thus, Blair had never actually been ordained in the Church of England, and this was the happenstance that changed the course of his life.

Probably nothing would have come of this circumstance if Blair, after serving two years as a clergyman in the Edinburgh diocese, had not been "deprived" of his ministry for refusing to take an oath demanded by James. This was in 1681 when the future King James was acting as commissioner for Charles II in Scotland. Out of a job, the twenty-six-year-old Scotsman set out on the beckoning road to London. There, because he was not an ordained priest of the Anglican Church, Blair was forced to take a clerical position in the office of the master of the rolls. This chance became the turning-point in his life.

In the three years he held this position Blair made the friends in high places who were to determine his career and influence the course of Virginia politics. A spare man, with square bony jaws, an inflexible mouth and zealous eyes, humorless Blair did not win people by charm. But he could make himself agreeable by persuasive earnestness, flatter when it served his purpose, and he knew the guiles of insinuating himself into another's graces. What won him the respect and support of highly placed Londoners was the determination and intense application he brought to any purpose. Ambitious and undistracted by frivolities, Blair inspired trust in his sense of responsibility as well as in his obvious abilities. The reward for his diligence was that he came to the attention of the powerful Bishop of London, Henry Compton, whose diocesan authority extended to the colonies.

Blair's dubious Church of England status could be overlooked in the diocese of Virginia, chronically hard put to obtain enough first-class clergy, and Bishop Compton gave him a license to hold a parish in the Colony. At twenty-nine, Blair obtained the comparatively plush Varina parish in Henrico County, then extending to both sides of the James River. Near Nathaniel Bacon's old holdings, the country church was built on the north bank of the James River, and was accessible to communicants coming by water. Less than ten years before Blair came, the forested neighborhood of the church had been along the edge of the Indian-infested frontier, and the unsettled country to the west was still not safe. A man had recently been killed at Byrd's plantation and two of Byrd's people carried off. But what was of consequence to the newly arrived rector was the prominence and wealth in his parish of such families as the Randolphs and the Byrds.

In England, the social prestige of the rector was low in the scale. Often he ranked at the level of an upper house-servant and ate his meals in the servants' hall. In Virginia the rectors were more respected, partly because they were among the few educated men,

James Blair. From a portrait owned by the College of William and Mary
(Colonial Williamsburg photograph)

though their positions were by no means exalted. They were at the will of the powerful vestries, and the less affluent parishes showed no conscience about paying inadequate salaries and providing poor quarters, or none — forcing the clergyman from England to find lodgings in the scattered community. In the richer parishes, the rector had to contend with the sometimes overbearing men of new position who made themselves heard in the vestries.

Blair, with his flinty kind of strength, began with an advantage in the rich Varina parish. Since his important vestrymen subscribed to the Protestant ethic which glorified success in business, the young veteran of London politics knew how to handle himself and, by ability and ingratiation, became accepted as one of them. Soon he became a visitor to the home of Councilor Benjamin Harrison II, and such was the scarcity of eligible gentlemen to marry the daughters of the rising merchant-planters that — two years after leaving a clerical job in London — Blair won the hand of Sarah Harrison.

In terms of personal happiness, Blair's elevation into the ruling class came at some cost. At the wedding, the eccentric Miss Harrison showed a highly assertive spirit by disrupting the ceremony with a refusal to agree to the "obey." Every time the bewildered minister, Mr. Stith, repeated the question, Sarah Harrison firmly repeated her answer, "No obey." Finally the ceremony was completed with her impromptu proviso, and in the marriage Mrs. Blair made good her declaration of independence. Domestic bliss was not to be included in the clergyman's amazing career.

For this price, his entrance into one of the politically powerful families completed James Blair's fitness for the assignment to which everything before seemed to lead with a curious inevitability. As Virginia remained in an informal missionary status within the diocese of London, and no bishop was to be provided, the Bishop of London appointed Blair to represent him in Virginia as commissary, generally in charge of the Church and its clergy in the Colony. At that time no man in the Colony was equally at home with persons of consequence in Jamestown and in London, as Blair was. In addition, through his partly frontier parish, he was familiar with the problems of the Church in Virginia at all levels.

Blair's appointment had been brought by Nicholson, when he first came in the spring of 1690, and an immediate friendship developed between these contemporaries. They worked together on the founding of the college, of which Blair was to become the first president, and Blair was appointed to the Council. Blair himself went to England to complete the details for the charter of a college that was to include a grammar school and an Indian school. While in London the busy cleric, winning the Queen's support in a personal audience, also got a gift from Sir Christopher Wren of a set of plans for the main building of the college. On Blair's return he found that his friend Nicholson had been replaced by Andros.

Two such men as Andros and Blair were not designed by nature to get along together. Blair was as dictatorial in his way as the governor was in his, and they were bound to fall out over something. The issue of conflict arose over the clergy. None would deny Blair his honest zeal for remedying the abuses in, and to, the Virginia clergy, and for improving conditions for the individual rectors. It meant nothing to him that Andros, representing the Church of England in his capacity as royal governor, occupied an incomparably stronger position than he did in the Church as well as in government. Nor did he hesitate to make his fight over a dubious principle — although, as a zealot, he may not have recognized the unsoundness of his principle. He made his fight with tactics, taking advantage of the autocratic Andros's mistakes.

By the King's orders the grants for the building of the college and its operations were to come out of the revenues from quitrents and taxes. At the same time Queen Mary, under Blair's spell, had also directed the general fund from quitrents — something under £1,000 a year — to be used to increase the clergy's salaries. As clergy's salaries were paid by parishioners, this would have established the unsound practice of using government funds for churches.

Not attacking the principle, Andros, supported by the Council, protested on the practical grounds that after the grants to the college were paid, the general fund was needed to pay government salaries and expenses. King William compromised by withholding the execution of the Queen's directive for three years: in that period the Virginia government would try to maintain itself without drawing on the general fund, and if successful, then the revenues from quitrents would be applied to the clergy's salaries.

According to Blair, Andros ordered payments out of this fund for expenses never before charged against it. He was not politic in his accusations. In front of some of the prudent gentlemen in the Council, he recklessly accused the governor of diverting the use of the fund in order to avoid following the King's orders. His violent show of temper was so unseemly to the councilors that they went along with Andros in suspending Blair.

At this turn in 1695, Blair, in the Colony only ten years, forced a test of power between himself, the mere commissary of the Bishop of London, and the career administrator who represented the Church of England. Through the influence of his London friends, Blair was restored to the Council by order of the King. From there he kept the government stirred up by continual attacks on Andros, especially blaming him for the poor condition of the Virginia clergy, and the governor again removed him from the Council. By then the controversy had begun to disturb authorities in London, and at a most propitious time for Blair's cause.

All during the 1680's Bishop Compton had presented the Lords of Trade with petitions about the abuses suffered by the church in Virginia and accused the governors of laxness. In 1695 the Lords of Trade was reorganized as the Board of Trade, a more effective commission. At one of its first meetings, in 1696, the new Board heard the petitions of two London merchants, charging that Virginia planters on the Council could not be compelled by law to pay their just debts. The Board of Trade called in Edward Chilton, a Virginia lawyer then in London, and he testified that the councilors were, indeed, exempt from legal action. This started the members of the new board on a close examination of conditions in Virginia, though on a broad scope in which the councilors' practices were incidental. With Bishop Compton's complaints about the Colony's governors on record, the Board of Trade took a hard look at Andros.

In this atmosphere James Blair arrived in London in the summer of 1697. Leaving his Virginia post ostensibly on church business, he had come to carry his case against Andros to the top. Such was his persuasiveness that he engaged first the interest and then the support of John Locke, the philosopher then famous for his *Essay Concerning Human Understanding* and — of more significance to Blair — *Two Treatises on Government*. In the book on the theory of government, Locke had written pointedly to King William on the sovereignty of the people: "our great restorer . . . to make good his title in the consent of the people."

As Locke wanted to put his theories into practice, and since the colonies offered a useful place to experiment, he took very seriously his advisory position as commissioner on the new Board of Trade. Then sixty-four and suffering from bronchitis in cold weather, the eminent philosopher stayed in London only during the summer and early fall. Blair's visit coincided with Locke's stay in rooms at Mr. Panley's house in Little Lincoln's Inn Fields. For most of a week Locke questioned Blair. Blair gave articulate, well-organized answers, supplying specific details to support his theories on the flaws in Virginia's government and economy. Most of these, in Blair's view, led back to Governor Andros.

From these sessions, Locke wrote a paper on Virginia and, to verify Blair's statements and get other viewpoints, sent a list of queries to the Board of Trade. Made into an official paper, these queries were submitted to Henry Hartwell, another London lawyer with offices in Virginia, whom Locke regarded as a "discreet person." Then Edward Chilton was called to appear before the Board, and both he and Hartwell confirmed the impressions Locke had gotten from Blair. From this material, based on Blair's representations, Locke developed a thirty-nine-page brief for reform in Virginia: *Some of the Chief Grievances of the Present Constitution of Virginia, With an Essay Towards the Remedies Thereof.* ("Constitution," having no reference to a written document, meant loosely the conditions of the society and its government.)

Locke's recommendations for reform deeply influenced the government in Virginia, beginning with and related to Robert Carter's rise, and continuing after his time. When Blair, Chilton and Hartwell were asked by the Board of Trade to write a précis on conditions in Virginia, the clergyman and two lawyers, themselves under Locke's influence, wrote *The Present State of Virginia.* This short book established itself as a permanent standard in the literature on Virginia at the end of the seventeenth century.

All the reports pointed to a need to reduce the area of responsibility of the royal governor and to curtail the privileges of the Council. On the first point, the Board of Trade made known its disfavor for Andros. The curtailment of the Council's privileges, stressed in Locke's suggested reforms, was deferred for later action in the Colony, and the immediate issue came down to the fact that Virginia was not big enough to accommodate both Andros and the commissary.

Andros's defense was undertaken by William Byrd II, two years after his admission to the bar. Shortly after young Byrd had completed his studies at the Middle Temple, his father had brought him back to Virginia and, through the elder Byrd's considerable influence, his dandified son was elected to the House of Burgesses for the 1696 session.

By the time William Byrd II came home, his father had moved from the outpost at The Falls, where Mary Byrd had endured such bleak loneliness. Closer to Jamestown in the more settled region of the plantations lining the north bank of the James, his Westover adjoined

Berkeley Hundred, newly acquired by Carter's friend Benjamin
Harrison III. For the frame house he built there Byrd ordered a
dozen of the best Russian-leather chairs and three tables, and instructed his agent to buy from Rotterdam "handsome and neat"
bedsteads, curtains, looking glasses and such, "but cheap." The
younger Byrd, then twenty-two and seeing the Colony for the first
time since he was seven, found nothing in the new house or in his
colonial contemporaries in the Burgesses to compensate for the London he loved.

During his years at the Middle Temple he had won the friendship
of several distinguished gentlemen of parts, scholars and literary men
of social position, and had also formed an abiding addiction to
pleasures of the flesh, cheaply bought in London. In his family's new
home on the broad tidal river, while he showed no inclination for
commerce or planting, young Byrd did display his smoothly developed
talents for cultivated urban society. He was learned and witty, he had
style and presence, and in his own right was an embryonic man of
letters. His return to London at the time of Blair's campaign was
probably involved with the Blair-Andros feud.

William Byrd I, comfortably established in power in the existing
order of the older generation, was among Andros's supporters as specifically against Blair. Perceiving his son's gifts for the great world,
and recognizing the intelligence behind the legal training, evidently
the elder Byrd allowed the younger to return to London with a mission. Whatever the arrangement between father and son, the second
William Byrd's defense of Andros was more of an attack on Blair.

Both the Byrds underrated the steely commissary. In December,
1697, the Archbishop of Canterbury and Bishop Compton held an open
meeting, where Blair made a strong presentation of his case. Between
the influential ecclesiastics and Locke's influence on the Board of
Trade, the Scots clergyman, unordained in the Church of England,
was able to force the recall of Andros, a royal governor appointed by
the Crown.

Nor was that the end of Blair's show of strength. In response to
an appeal from former Deputy Governor Nicholson, Blair — with the
Bishop of London — gained Locke's support for the appointment of
Nicholson as full governor. When the appointment went through, in
May of the following year, 1698, James Blair returned to Virginia
with the awesome reputation of king-maker.

Acutely aware of the power he then wielded, Blair seemed unaware of the implications of all of Locke's suggested remedies for

Virginia and her government. He wanted his own way in controlling the clergy and the new College of William and Mary, and he expected no opposition when his friend Nicholson returned. But the unhappily married commissary — whose wife took to drink — apparently was burdened with inner hostilities which he had to vent on authorities.

In Virginia, James Blair could be seen as representing the fundamental changes in the twenty years since young Bacon had used force to defy a royal governor. In his test of strength, Blair used political maneuvering with unrelenting purpose and a most unchristianlike guile, with which he encountered in London a newly favorable interest in the conditions in Virginia. This lesson was not lost on the Colony, particularly not on Robert Carter.

In Blair's next feud, Carter worked with him in the formidable alliance which — as the older group began to die off — stood ready to establish an oligarchy in the new generation of the ruling class.

The Reality of Power

IN 1699 ROBERT CARTER lost his wife, Judith, her death continuing the melancholy roll call that had marked life at Corotoman through all his memories. She left him with four children: John, Elizabeth, Judith and Anne. John was then his favorite child, though he deeply loved his three daughters, and their relationship (despite a break with Elizabeth late in life) was close as long as he lived. John was trained from the beginning to assist in the management of the growing empire, with its seat at the eight thousand acres of the home plantation fronting on the point of land.

If Ralph Wormeley's enterprises had made Rosegill appear like a village to a visiting Frenchman, Corotoman would have appeared like a shipping-manufacturing town. Along the riverfront of Carter's Creek, near its entrance into the Rappahannock, skilled indentures and freedmen worked in a boat-building yard. Three sloops, three flatboats, a pinnace, a yawl and a canoe were built there as an inland fleet. Back of the wharves were buildings housing warehouses, the store, a spinning house where indentured weavers worked, and an office where indentured clerks copied correspondence and kept records of what each field produced, what products sold for, purchases made, and the details of shipping and the warehouses. Teams of oxen pulling tobacco hogsheads plodded past the buildings to the boat landing. Carter had abandoned horses for the heavy hauling because of "the sad spectacle of sore-backed horses and poor jades," and searched to find experts to break in the oxen.

Scattered inland were separate groups of workers — wheelwrights and carpenters and joiners, millers at the gristmills, sweating indentures firing forges and bricklayers working at kilns. It was a running chore for Carter to get these skilled artisans, either as indentures or freedmen for wages, and another chore to keep most of them (especially bricklayers) conscientiously at their tasks. Farther inland, field hands raised hogs, slaughtered cattle and made tallow, hayed fields and pitched the hay into barns to carry the animals through the winter. Stretching on inland were the fields of wheat, most of which was sold, and fields of corn, the bread staple for the community. On and on spread the fields of tobacco, dotted with tobacco sheds and flanked by the rows of quarters. Field slaves worked in groups of fifteen or twenty under a Negro "captain" (foreman). One overseer at the home plantation was responsible for the work of the field hands.

Each of Carter's forty-odd smaller plantations also had its own overseer responsible for grading the tobacco and packing it into hogsheads for market. He was also responsible for the cattle, hogs and corn with which each separate unit was supplied for subsistence. These outlying plantations were formed into groups, with a head overseer in full charge of each group.

Carter had the usual trouble with keeping good overseers, although these men as a lot were not the coarsened casuals from the white communities that appeared on absentee plantations of a later day. The head overseer of a group had to be, in Carter's scheme, a highly qualified and responsible agricultural executive, who drew the highest wages in the Colony. In addition to his quarters, Carter paid him £35 a year. By contrast, for "a barber surgeon, a young fellow just out of his time [indenture], that can bleed and shave and dress sores; a sober towardly young fellow [who] will be very useful in my family . . . I can't give him more than £8 or £10 a year."

At the home plantation John, like his father and his father's brother before, learned by doing. Beyond this practical experience, formal education for ten-year-old John and his younger sisters was provided by indentured tutors. Robert Carter gave his personal attention to imparting a love of learning in the children. When Judith was an adult she was praised for her well-informed mind, her love of books

and her encouragement of mental inquisitiveness in young people. All
four of the children grew up to become intelligent parents, producing
children who assumed responsible positions in the community of
Virginia.

While manifestly a good father, Robert Carter would be forced to
be frequently absent from home beginning in 1699. That was the year
of ascension for his fortunes: Francis Nicholson was then back in
Virginia as full governor, resuming his warm relations with Commissary James Blair in a period of good feeling in the government.

The year before, Robert Carter had not been reelected speaker of
the House of Burgesses in the short fall session of the General Assembly, but had lost out to Captain William Randolph, of the older
generation. In October of that year, 1698, the rebuilt State House at
Jamestown caught fire and burned to the ground. The next session of
the General Assembly, convening on April 27, 1699, met first in a
private home in Jamestown and then in the main hall of the nearly
completed Wren Building of the new College of William and Mary. In
that session, Carter fought hard for reelection as speaker of the
House. It was a tough campaign, and a tie had to be broken before he
was restored to his position. But from that victory, everything followed.

Within one month, he was appointed to the newly created post of
treasurer. This post came about through the decision to move the
capital from Jamestown to Middle Plantation, where William and
Mary College was located. Midway between the James and the York
rivers, at a narrow waist of the Peninsula, Middle Plantation was a
former stockaded settlement which had sprawled into a village. In
addition to the new college building and the handsome small brick
church of Bruton Parish, it consisted of an ordinary, a smith's shop,
two mills, a few stores and the grammar school. The idea of moving
the capital there was presented to the General Assembly by several
students of the college, one of whom summarized the advantages with
reasons that were profoundly to affect the education of the new aristocracy for rule in government.

''Another great benefit to the students at this place, would be the
conveniency of good company and conversation: For in such a retired
corner of the world, far from business, and action, if we make
scholars, they are in danger of proving mere scholars, which make a
very ridiculous figure: made up of pedantry, disputaciousness, posi-
tiveness, and a great many other ill qualities which render them not so
fit for action and conversation; except the muses naturally shame-

faced and bashful learn to put on a decent confidence by seeing and conversing among men and being acquainted with action and business.''

For a largely elective body of representative government, the General Assembly voted with remarkable dispatch to build a new capital city. Two hundred and eighty-three acres were set aside as the ground on which a city would be laid out according to a design. The college building faced to the east, overlooking a horsepath along which were strung the few scattered buildings of the town. In building a new capital in a careful design, four of these buildings were to be dismantled in order that a wide street might run in a straight line for nearly a mile. At the eastern end of this street, to be called Duke of Gloucester Street, the new capitol building would be erected, to face the college at the western end of the street. Side streets were laid out with equal care (one was to be named for Governor Nicholson), with provisions controlling the placement of houses on half-acre lots.

Jamestown as a city was not abandoned. Shipping continued at its two landings, worship continued at the church and the dwellings remained occupied. Gradually its inhabitants died off or moved away, and the streets became those of a ghost town. During the building of Williamsburg, however, the only physical change was the gaping foundation where the old State House had stood.

Robert Carter's new post grew out of the plans for building an imposing new capitol. After having appointed directors for the settlement and encouragement of the new ''city,'' and having formed committees to contract for and supervise the capitol building, the House of Burgesses passed acts to tax indentures and slaves imported into the Colony, and liquor, to finance the building of the capitol. As a treasurer to handle personally all the money collected, and give bond for £5,000 sterling (a lot of cash in Virginia then), the House of Burgesses appointed their speaker. Robert Carter's new official position — which he assumed May 19 — was unique in that the treasurer was equally responsible to the House, the King's Council and Governor Nicholson. He had also to consider, unofficially, the building committees and the city's directors, which included the familiar faces of Benjamin Harrison, Philip Ludwell, and Edmund Jenings.

Little more than two weeks after he became treasurer, Robert Carter ascended into the Colony peerage when Nicholson appointed him, on June 3, colonel and commander in chief of the militia in his county and adjoining Northumberland County. Within a few months after becoming ''Colonel'' Carter, he was appointed by the governor

(October 24) to succeed Ralph Wormeley as naval officer and receiver of the Virginia duties in Rappahannock River. This lucrative post was no sinecure, and Carter assumed its duties while serving on the county court as a justice, on the vestry of Christ Church, in the House of Burgesses as speaker, establishing procedures of operations in the treasurer's office — and supervising the infinite details in his shipping-planting-trading complex.

That epochal year 1699 in Robert Carter's career was to be crowned by the Colony's highest honor: on December 26, Governor Nicholson received, in response to his recommendation, a letter from the King "commissioning Robert Carter and John Custis, Esquires, to be sworn members of His Majesty's Honorable Council of State of this Colony and Dominion of Virginia." Robert Carter was appointed to the Council on June 5, 1700, but, for unexplained reasons, did not come to Jamestown until July 10. Then he went with a prepared statement to the members of the Council who were assembled. The Council would consist of twelve when Carter and Custis were sworn in, though rarely were all members present.

Thirty-seven years old then, standing at the middle height and beginning to thicken, Robert Carter gave an impression of stockiness with his widening waistcoat reaching just above the puff at the knee of his knee breeches and the skirts of his open coat flaring out at the tops of his stockings. Above the lace collar at his throat, the broadening of his face, with the resolution in his well-formed mouth and the surveillant brown eyes, gave altogether an impact of solidity to his presence. He wore a diamond ring, carried a gold watch valued at £30 in the low pocket of his waistcoat, and in the large, low-hung coat pocket he carried a silver comb for his wig, a snuffbox and a handkerchief. His brief address to the councilors went beyond the customarily modest disclaimers: he presented real reservations about accepting a place on the Council.

"I cannot but with all thankfulness humbly acknowledge to your Excellency and this honorable Council the great sense that I have of his Majesty's high and royal favor conferred on me in appointing me one of the members of his honorable Council of State of this his Majesty's Colony and Dominion of Virginia and must not forget my gratitude to your Excellency for the character you have given of me to his most sacred Majesty which I conceive has been the instrumental cause of this conferred honor, an honor which (I confess) the best of men have been ambitious of.

"And tho' none perhaps can be more desirous and ambitious to serve his Majesty than my own self must beg leave in all humility to lay before your Excellency and this honorable Council these following reasons in my excuse and submit the same to your consideration:

"1st — The distance of my habitation is so great and so far remote that the same may occasionally be some impediment in the prosecution of my duty in so high and honorable a place.

"2ndly — My personal disabilities and infirmities with which I am too well acquainted renders me an unfit object of so high a favor.

"3rdly — And which is of greatest weight, as I have had the honor several times heretofore to be a member of the House of Burgesses in this His Majesty's Colony, in which place have always made it my care to discharge my duty with all faithfulness to God, my Sovereigns and my Country, so particularly at this time I am not only a member of that house but have also the honor (though too much above my demerits) to be Speaker and how I can dispense with my duty in that station and the obligation of that oath I already lie under, that remaining still a whole body without dissolution, I must leave your Excellency to judge."

It was true enough that, like many of his contemporaries, he experienced debilitating attacks of various illnesses, and the journey to Jamestown (or to Williamsburg) was hard and time-consuming. While he liked water travel on the rivers, Carter preferred not to travel by boat from Corotoman to Jamestown. Going by way of the choppy open waters of the bay — in that period menaced by pirates — and the long pull up the James, evidently took too much of his time. He continued his cross-country rides and, as there were no public places along his way, he put up with the friend nearest to where darkness caught him. Since he liked to ride, Carter was probably bothered less by the physical exertion and inconvenience than by the time away from any profitable or personally rewarding activity. The trip must have become a bore to him.

These were not hazards to loom forbiddingly when weighed against the appointment that he could only regard as the first pinnacle in his political career. The illustrious and influential position — he was *officially* one of the twelve rulers of the Colony — offered opportunities for his total advancement in all areas that were well-nigh limitless. He evidently presented his reservations to avoid appearing eager to the older members entrenched in power, even though his relations were friendly with most and he was an intimate of Ralph Wormeley, the ranking councilor. Wormeley's second wife was the sister of Carter's recently dead wife ("Sister Wormeley," as Carter referred to her).

Colonel William Byrd I, the auditor and receiver general, was next in rank. Richard Lee II had been second until 1699 when, pleading ill health, he had resigned, actually making the opening for Robert Carter. Edmund Jenings, connected to Lee by their marriages to the Corbin sisters, had earlier ascended to the Council from the House, where he had been acquainted with Robert Carter.

After recording his reservations, Robert Carter joined his contemporaries and political friends, James Blair and Philip Ludwell, Jr., on the august body. With the elder Benjamin Harrison (whose son was then attorney general), they formed the nucleus of a new inner group ready to supersede the older. Ralph Wormeley died the next year and William Byrd I in 1704, but the new power bloc was not to wait for the death of the elder Byrd to take over.

2

With Robert Carter's political career established, his initiative combined with circumstance to win him the big prize for his financial expansion — the Proprietary's agency. This was the key that opened the door to his landholding empire.

In 1699 the contumacious George Brent had died, leaving William Fitzhugh as sole Proprietary agent. Fitzhugh's association with his friend Richard Lee had become closer through the marriage of William Fitzhugh II to Lee's daughter Ann, and the next year Lee broke the back of the Northern Neck resistance to acknowledging the Proprietary. Lee made a private legal arrangement ("composition") with Lord Fairfax, in which he recognized the claim of the Proprietary.

Second to none in eminence among Northern Neck landowners, Richard Lee II was so Old Guard that for a time he had relinquished his Council seat in refusal to recognize William and Mary as the rightful rulers, after James II had been forced to abdicate. When this embodiment of the status quo abandoned the position the Northern Neck landowners had held for half a century, his attornment caused a general movement throughout the region to acknowledge the Culpeper-Fairfax feudalistic claim.

Lord Fairfax had never intended to assert de facto ownership of the occupied Proprietary land; in practice acknowledgement of the Proprietary merely meant paying quitrents to Fairfax instead of the Colony. Where escheated land reverted to the Proprietary instead of to the Colony's escheator, this concerned only politically connected land accumulators who would miss the parceling out of escheated land among friends in office. The troublesome area was in the patenting of the unoccupied lands.

Because of the long uncertainties over the Proprietary, settlement was lagging in the fertile Northern Neck. A settler taking up new land there could not buy it outright. Grants to new lands in the Proprietary were made in fee, usually paid in tobacco, and were subject to a composition and the agreed payment of "rents." Beneath all the Proprietary's legal provisos, a patentee did in effect own the land he patented, and rents paid to the Proprietary's agents amounted to no more than quitrents paid to the Colony.

The whole object for Lord Fairfax, and his agent on the scene, was to get the — then larger than two million acres — tract occupied by settlers whose rents would bring in cash to His Lordship — and incidentally to the agent representing him. When Lee's private composition with Fairfax led the landowners then in the Northern Neck to attorn, it was the agent's job to encourage other settlers to see that the landowning situation was resolved and to take up land within the Proprietary.

Before William Fitzhugh could benefit appreciably from his friend's act, he died, in 1701. When Lord Fairfax sought to replace him, he asked the advice of Micajah Perry, then the most powerful agent in London for the Virginia trade.

Perry and Lane had been active in the Virginia trade since the early 1670's, and Micajah Perry was the dominant figure of the firm in dealing with Virginia merchant-planters. Perry's services were these: first, to sell the planters' tobacco to the highest European market; then to purchase all goods required by the planter, either personal or for his store; continually to act as a post-office exchange, as a banker, and as an employment agent — sending indentures and craftsmen. In addition, he performed an indefinable assortment of favors for the planters' children in England: he changed the elder Byrd's daughters from a school to the home of his brother-in-law, and personally entertained and accommodated Robert Beverley's three sons during a stay in London — for which he charged Beverley's estate £40.

Perry charged for all of his services, and for all favors that cost him a penny in pocket. At the same time, along with his extremely profitable business he performed many favors on which no price could be put. One of these was to use his influence on behalf of his clients when he provided the Board of Trade with information on the colonies. A very specific favor to a favorite client was Perry's recommendation of Robert Carter to Lord Fairfax.

The new master of Corotoman operated in every way to please the great London agent. He sent a volume of business, in both tobacco for market and purchases for Virginia; he was specific in his correspondence and meticulous in his accounts, always keeping his balance ahead — a sure way to the heart of any London agent. He did not ask for favors. Carter never gave all his business to Perry, never placed all his eggs in one basket, and the older man probably respected the Virginian for his independent shopping around. With thirty years' experience of trading in the Colony, Micajah Perry would readily have recognized Carter as the rising star. Then, a personal accord developed between them out of their mutuality of respect. Following Perry's recommendation of his younger friend for the Proprietary agency, they worked together like allies.

When Robert Carter's careers in politics and finance were established, it was significant that his first allies — the London merchant and the Church's representative — were not selected from among the locally established. There was never any working alliance, or personal cordiality, between Carter and Richard Lee II (sixteen years older), whom the younger man was challenging for the position of ranking citizen of the Northern Neck. It was through his cultivated connection with Perry that Carter reaped the fruits of Lee's act of opening the Proprietary during the agency of his in-law, William Fitzhugh.

Robert Carter never made a reference to his own damning attack on the Proprietary system when he signed the contract to act as Lord Fairfax's agent in the spring of 1702. With his usual business methods, Carter converted one of the buildings at Corotoman into a land office for the Northern Neck Proprietary, installed clerks, appointed subagents to move about the countryside and engaged men with some training in surveying. When an application for a new patent was entered in Carter's land office, the tract would be surveyed at the patentee's expense.

The fee paid for the composition was 13s. 4d. per one hundred acres, which was higher than the price to patent land outside the Proprietary. However, all the good land in Tidewater was then taken up, and it would usually have come to more than 13s. 4d. to acquire Tidewater land by purchase from a landowner. The land west of the fall line (head of tidewater) on the great rivers was still sparsely settled, particularly in the northern areas between the Rappahannock and the Potomac, where the danger from Indians had not entirely ceased. The Proprietary fee, if not paid in tobacco at six shillings per hundred pounds, could be paid in pounds sterling — of which not many were around — or in the relatively commonplace Spanish pieces of eight, valued at five shillings per piece.

Handling the tobacco paid to the Proprietary, also acceptable for quitrents, or the cash, Carter took a commission in addition to a salary. The exact amounts of these arrangements he never recorded. During the first period — ten years — of his agency, he recorded earning more than £500 for one year, and for two other years wrote that he had not earned "more than £300."

It would be impossible to reach a modern equivalent of that figure. Any cash estimate would mean little because of the absence of comparative monetary standards in the Colony. With no industry, banking, urban real estate, transportation and communication, or the like to deal in large sums, and with the mercantile interests of planters not involving considerable cash sums, the *money* Carter cleared at the agency — over and beyond the *wealth* accumulated in his other operations — represented a kind of income uncommon in Virginia on that scale.

Broad comparisons could be made with money (as cash) earned in England in the late seventeenth century. The highest average annual earning was £400 by 2,000 "eminent merchants and traders by sea." Eight thousand "lesser merchants" averaged £198, and 10,000 "persons in law," £154. Five thousand "persons in greater offices and places" averaged an annual income of £240. In this general income bracket, 12,000 of the landowning gentry — whose incomes derived from tenant-farmers and renters and employed agricultural workers — averaged an annual earning of £280. Three thousand "esquires" (locally prominent gentlemen, or squires) averaged £450. Only 1,560 heads of families, all in the landowning gentry — except 26 "spiritual lords" (as bishops) — averaged more than £450 a year. Of these 1,560 landowning gentry, 160 "temporal lords" had an income of more than £1,000 annually, and the wealth of some of these was immense.

In the averages, the income of an "eminent merchant" such as Micajah Perry would be much higher than the mean figure. This would apply to some extent in all listings, although the range would not be very broad at the lower levels of earnings, such as the £72 averaged by 2,000 "eminent clergy," the £80 averaged by naval officers and £60 by military officers. Many positions outside these listed categories, such as colonial administrator, paid £1,000 and more a year. Carter's annual earnings of approximately £400 from the Proprietary was only a cash addition to the wealth he was accumulating at Corotoman.

It was noticeable that the additional income from the agency did not seem to elate the broadly based operator. But then, he never seemed elated about any one thing. Each pound pouring in might mean no more than one sip of wine to a heavy, chronic drinker. Yet, each "sip" had its welcome part in the glow from the volume, as Carter turned his attention, very discreetly at first, to the patenting of Proprietary land for himself and his children.

He stated very plainly that this acquisition of land would provide the separate estates for the nonprimogenitary dynasty he was to found. At the same time, he was also impelled to acquire as an end in itself. Acquisition was an appetite which did not exclude other appetites; he savored his glasses of wine with and after meals as thoroughly as did hedonistic Ralph Wormeley, and he was known to stay with drinking parties when they got rolling. He went from one appetite to another, allowing none to take over. While there was no doubt that the dominating lust was for wealth in all its forms, it never possessed him: he controlled and manipulated it as the center of a broad pattern of gratifications.

Coming into the period when he would be called "King," Robert Carter really was outsized in the scope of what he could accomplish *and* enjoy in one day, and in his growth as a person, as an accumulator and as a political power. Day after day, he grew totally and steadily and — as it seemed to his contemporaries — inexorably.

3

From the 1699 spring session of the General Assembly, when Governor Nicholson showed his favor of Robert Carter, until the spring of 1702, when the land office for the Northern Neck Proprietary agency was opened at Corotoman, Francis Nicholson on the whole enjoyed the harmony with the General Assembly that had characterized his earlier term of office. Yet, somehow things were not the same. He had wanted to come back and was happy to be back (he wrote John Locke an effusive letter of gratitude for his part in securing the appointment). But he had changed some, Virginia had changed some, and he carried new instructions which presented a conflict between his duty and his sympathetic understanding of the "constitutional" problems unique to the Virginia colony.

Nicholson's own personal change, revealed by a new violence of temper and unpredictable irascibility, was regarded as no more than the eccentricity of a man getting along in years. (He was forty-four in a society where geriatric factors often appeared early.) There were also excuses for him. He was cramped in temporary quarters in the college building, and life in a village being transformed into a city was not as convenient or pleasant as in the other days in Jamestown, on the broad street facing the river. Then, most members of the General Assembly were inclined to shrug off his uncertain temper — even the occasional rages in which he lost control of himself completely — because of their earlier regard for him and his friendly attitude to the House of Burgesses.

The governor was obviously suffering from some personality disorder of which his outbursts were only symptoms. Another symptom was a "mad passion" he conceived for sixteen-year-old Lucy Burwell, the lovely and sought-after daughter of a family prominent in the plantation society. It was not merely the hopeless and fevered love of an older man for a young girl, but in pursuing Lucy Burwell ("pursuing" quite literally) Nicholson's behavior grew irrational.

With his own changes, he observed without pleasure the hardening of the character that was making Virginia different from the other colonies. He wrote to London of the self-awareness of these colonials as Virginians and complained that they "begin to have an aversion to others, calling them strangers." He wrote that there no longer was any "encouragement for men of good parts to come" to Virginia, as all the best land was taken up, and "if there be any widows or maids of any fortune, the natives for the best part get them. . . ." (This last observation might have been a little personal with the governor, since his chosen maid of fortune selected a native for herself.)

Nicholson reproached the Virginians for their self-centered interests and indifference to England's struggle for power against her European enemies — among whom both France and Spain occupied large territories on the same continent with Virginia. When the French were established in Canada, claiming the lands drained by the Mississippi, in 1696 Louis XIV had issued an edict ordering colonists to take wives and settle families. Nicholson was farsighted in recognizing that the French claims to the Mississippi threatened to restrict the English colonies to regions east of the Alleghenies. He recommended trade as a countermeasure and formed a trading concern. This won no subscribers, and when he tried to interest London merchants, the Board of Trade wrote him that the "business of Virginians is to plant tobacco."

With this attitude in those charged with colonial affairs, Virginians did not feel any more self-centered than the other colonies in looking after their own interests. In the twenty-eight years under Charles II and James II, the colonists had been forced to adopt the principle that if they did not look after themselves, nobody else would. Nicholson was encountering the assertive self-awareness of people who *were* looking after themselves according to their own pragmatic adaptations.

Along with the hardening of the Virginia character, there was also a hardening of the mould of the ruling group — and this was the point of conflict with Nicholson's instructions. The suggested reforms of John Locke (which Blair passed over lightly) concerned the power concentrated among the councilors. Special attention had been given to the councilors' channeling of wealth, which supported their power, by apportioning lucrative posts to themselves and their friends. When Nicholson returned, Auditor and Receiver General William Byrd had for his James River collectors William Randolph and Colonel Edward Hill of Shirley and, for the Potomac, Richard Lee II and Lee's brother-in-law Edmund Jenings.

Nicholson realized it was one thing for the Board of Trade, without firsthand knowledge of the Colony, to make recommendations suggested by a philosopher of government, and something else for him to impose legislation on a working system which had evolved out of the conditions of the country — including adaptations to the Stuart rule. If a small group was growing richer through offices apportioned by the councilors, Nicholson knew that for the most part the officeholders were the best-qualified men. He liked and respected these men, and found none of them acting in narrow self-interest. After all, since wealth was England's weapon in the struggle for position among world powers, its citizens' individual goals were personal wealth, and these Virginians — as Berkeley had written home forty years before — were performing a very real service for the nation in following the national goals in a colonial expansion.

Then, practically, as the small group was only a part of a growing class, it would be difficult to isolate and regulate influence among the entanglements of the "web of kinship." Where the plantations were the centers of commerce, the plantation *families* became the units of power, like corporations. Alliances of interests between these families, as well as intermarriages, produced what amounted to interlocking directorates in control. They might fight among themselves, engage in bitter rivalries, but the older men then in positions of power had risen during the years of growing resistance to assertions of Royal preroga- tives in Virginia, and all the councilors had before them — as Nichol- son had before him — the example of what had happened to Andros as the representative of a weakened Crown.

It was clear to Nicholson that the harmony of his administration would come to a quick end if he antagonized the councilors. Any legislation he might impose over their opposition would bring unpre- dictable consequences to the present peace in the Colony and its stable course of development. For as the councilors had come to represent a ruling class, similar to the peerage in England, the economy and the government of the Colony became inextricably involved with the operations of the whole planter class. In settling for harmony, Francis Nicholson was the first governor to base his actions on considerations of the nature of the Colony, with its laws of custom and its customs as strong as law.

Still, the governor had to do something about his instructions. One of his instructions concerned a practice which he sincerely be- lieved constituted an abuse: this was the holding for future use, or speculation, of large tracts of idle land. Since measures to break up these large unsettled holdings were not aimed specifically at the coun- cilors, no serious objection was made to his order that patents be voided on landholdings on which quitrents had not been paid for seven years. When he demanded the names of all holders of more than twenty thousand acres, and ordered that no surveys for more than one hundred acres could be made without his permission, this came closer home to some of the councilors, including Robert Carter. As these laws would not be effective in the Proprietary, they did not restrict Car- ter's acquisitions in the Northern Neck after he became agent in 1702. But the idea did not sit well with him, nor with some others.

Then there was another measure which went against the grain with Robert Carter and other large-scale planters, even though the acreage involved did not constitute a large part of their land opera- tions. Nicholson abolished the system of granting fifty-acre headrights on imported indentures and slaves. This measure, cutting down on the incidental land accumulations of planters investing extensively in slaves, was primarily aimed at closing the market on headrights. This small though very active enterprise was engaged in mostly by ships' captains, slave traders and the dwindling number of dealers in indentures. Working with nonplanting land speculators — Nicholson's main target in this measure — the traders managed sometimes to sell a single headright as many as three times, bringing a fifty-acre grant with each sale.

In his total land policy, Nicholson's chief purpose was to open land for purchase so as to encourage settlements in the vast silences of the forests. The big merchant-planters who held these idle tracts contended that they did not handicap individuals who wanted land to work, since there were not enough settlers to pay quitrents on the thousands and thousands of acres of primeval forests. While this argument was beside the point of Nicholson's policy, it held its own logic, and, except for closing the headrights market, Nicholson moved with moderation in executing his larger policies.

It was in the small details, particularly in dealing with the Council, where Nicholson was undiplomatic. In following his instructions to curtail the councilors' power, Nicholson, with his inner disturbances, began to act without following the procedures customary in working with the Council. Most of his actions, like making appointments at county level, might have seemed unimportant to the Colony's operations, but they were vital to the power structure being solidified by the group of Robert Carter and his allies. Also, the dignity of these councilors was affronted by what they considered the governor's "arbitrary" behavior, which tended to reduce the Council to a subordinate body. Basically, the instructions which Nicholson executed clumsily and the attitude of the new bloc in the Council represented conflicting philosophies of government. At the point of conflict, no one articulated these philosophies: the growing clashes came between personalities whose purposes reflected the philosophies.

The effect of these differences, each small in itself, was cumulative, and in the early years after his return Nicholson aroused no consolidated opposition. Before the bloc of Carter, Blair, Ludwell, and the elder Harrison united against him in 1702, opposition to him was scattered and was caused more by his torrential outbursts than by his policies. He enjoyed the continuing friendly support of the House of Burgesses and the lasting gratitude of the bay country inhabitants for his hero's role against pirates in the spring of 1700.

4

Ships bound to and from Virginia had been attacked by pirates since 1621, when the Turks started the raids, but it was not until the

1680's that pirates began to make inland excursions to plunder and terrorize plantation families. Unknown numbers of pirate ships made a haven of the shadowed inlets and small islands in the area of Chesapeake Bay, where the crews provisioned their vessels at leisure. In 1682 a pirate ship had landed at the mouth of the York River and its crew sacked two plantation homes, taking silver plate and cash as well as victuals. Until then, the colonists had traded with the pirates, but in 1684 a proclamation prohibited "the King's subjects from trading, harboring or corresponding with the pirates."

In the year following the proclamation, pirates robbed householders in the Isle of Wight County, on the south shore of the James River, and later in 1685 Governor Howard executed the chiefs of "some pilfering pirates [that] have done damage to the inhabitants." Evidently, considerably more unreported plundering was done, for in 1688 a small ship was captured in the James River, containing four pirates with their cash booty, on their way to "retire" in the Colony.

They were three white men and a Negro, Peter Cleiss, the servant of the captain of the pirates, Edward Davis. The retirement sum of the three white pirates amounted to wealth: 1,900 Spanish pieces of eight worth a total of £475, plus three bags of uncounted cash. In addition, they had more than four hundred pounds of assorted silver plate (exceeding even William Fitzhugh's collection), along with cloth, linen, lace, ribbons, and four pairs of silk stockings.

Their interminable trial took a strange turn. Cleiss talked freely of many pirate exploits in faraway places during his nine years with Davis, and soon he was listed by Captain Davis as "a Negro since dead." After he died — he was probably murdered as an informer — the three white pirates changed their pleas of innocence and petitioned for inclusion in the King's proclamation which offered pardon to pirates who surrendered and gave security for their future good behavior. The Virginia General Court claimed they had not surrendered and only petitioned after they were captured. The well-connected pirates engaged the services of Micajah Perry to represent their case to the Lords of Trade, and in 1690, during Nicholson's first term, they were shipped at their own expense to England for trial.

As the trial dragged on, several of their accusers died, and though Davis revealed familiarity with Virginia, proof was lacking for any specific robbery in Virginia which would not come under the legal definition of "piracy" on the seas. In 1691 the Lords of Trade freed the "great villains" (as Governor Howard had called them), who immediately began to petition for the restitution of their retirement fund. William III ordered their property returned, with the proviso that £300 be subtracted, to be applied to the building of William and Mary College. A story goes that James Blair promised to use his influence to get their property restored if they donated a sum to the new college. In any event, "Davis, Delawafer and Hinson" were listed as contributing £300 to William and Mary College.

That famous trial was Nicholson's first actual experience with pirates in Virginia. Before he came for his first term, an order had been issued for outbound vessels to wait for a convoy ship, unless they were sailing with a sizable fleet. As soon as he arrived for his second term, in 1699, British warships began cruising off the coast under orders to be alert for pirate ships, "more especially to look after Kidd the pirate." Kidd was rumored to be off the Eastern Shore.

In July an unidentified pirate ship captured two vessels in Lynnhaven Bay, and in October Colonel John Custis reported that pirates had landed on Smith's Island and were slaughtering his cattle. Then in April, 1700, a French pirate ship, *La Paix,* opened operations on a scale to defy the whole Colony and the English warships. *La Paix* seized nine trading vessels in a period of ten days.

Ex-soldier Nicholson went into action himself. Writing England that "we are in a state of war with the pirates," he sailed down the James and boarded the English warship *Shoreham.* With the governor on board, the *Shoreham* cruised between the capes — where Chesapeake Bay entered the Atlantic — until *La Paix* was discovered, late in April. The pirate ship was lying at anchor close to the shore of Lynnhaven Bay when sighted at first light.

Captain William Passenger ordered a broadside fired and demanded the ship's surrender. *La Paix* answered by hoisting sail, running up a blood-red pennant and returning the fire. The ships maneuvered and fired at one another until two o'clock in the afternoon. The pirate ship was no match for the man-of-war. Most of her masts and rigging were shattered, several guns had ceased firing and the hull was almost smashed. At two o'clock the pirates struck their colors. By then the ships were so close to the shore that hundreds of people had gathered near the water.

After both ships had ceased to fire, several men leaped from the deck of *La Paix* and swam to the *Shoreham.* Hauled aboard, the frightened men told Nicholson that they represented a number of English prisoners on *La Paix.* They said that the pirates were arranging thirty barrels of powder to blow up the ship, having agreed to die together rather than to have their ship boarded. Governor Nicholson personally wrote a dispatch assuring the pirates that quarter would be granted and the men placed under His Majesty's mercy if they would surrender as prisoners of war. Accepting his assurances, about one hundred pirates came ashore, bringing twenty-five wounded and leaving twenty-five dead on the ship.

The joy of battle had returned to Nicholson during the engagement and, storming about under Captain Passenger's sour gaze, he was not at all reticent in pushing himself into the center of attention. It was indeed a big adventure for him, the first governor in the Colony's history to take personal action against pirates, and it had big consequences.

Captain Guitter and his crew were sent in manacles to England for trial. Three captured pirates who had not surrendered were tried in a quickly called court of admiralty, found guilty and publicly hanged in chains. Following Nicholson's actions, large-scale pirate operations abruptly ceased off the Virginia coast. Minor raids occurred from time to time, beef cattle were slaughtered and goods stolen, but the families in the bay area no longer lived under the threat of what amounted to small invasions.

It is very possible that Governor Nicholson was partly impelled toward his heroics by his desire to impress young Lucy Burwell, for at the time when the pirate menace became big news Nicholson was in the throes of his middle-life passion.

5

Sixteen years old in 1699, when the forty-four-year-old governor first fell under her spell, Lucy Burwell was one of the beauties of her day, of charming presence and social assurance. Lucy's family on both sides had been established among the influential planters since the early days of Berkeley's administration. Her mother had been a niece and legatee of Nathaniel Bacon, the Senior, and her father, Councilor Lewis Burwell II, was the half-brother of Philip Ludwell II. After Burwell's father had died, his widowed mother married Philip Ludwell, before his marriage to My Lady Frances. In fact, the Burwell network of family alliances was about as dangerous an enemy as could be made in the Colony.

Lucy Burwell's sister Elizabeth was married to Robert Carter's friend Benjamin Harrison III. As the daughter-in-law of Councilor Harrison, Elizabeth was, through the close relationships of kinships by marriage in Virginia, the equivalent of a sister to her husband's brothers-in-law, Councilor Philip Ludwell, also by blood her uncle, and Councilor James Blair. Through the same close relationship of kinship by marriage, young Lucy herself (Ludwell's niece), as sister of the elder Harrison's daughter-in-law, would be regarded as a member of the Harrison-Ludwell-Blair family. Lucy's brother Nathaniel would in the not distant future marry a daughter of Robert Carter; later the son of Elizabeth Burwell and Benjamin Harrison III would marry another of the "King's" daughters.

When the governor started calling on Lucy at Fairfield plantation, in Gloucester County, Major Burwell had recently built a new and impressive house there. With its massive walls, it was more like a small English manor house than any other home of that period in Virginia. Fairfield was famous for elegant parties, but Nicholson had eyes only for the young lady whom he addressed as "my saint," "my dove," and to whom he poured out his turbulent heart in verse.

By all accounts, Lucy conducted herself with remarkable composure during the five years of the obsessed bachelor's siege. She seems not to have discouraged him with any finality until she fell in love with Edmund Berkeley, a gentleman nearer her own age.

Edmund Berkeley and former Governor Sir William Berkeley came from separate lines that had branched off from the Berkeley Castle family, for whom the 1619 colony at Berkeley Hundred had been named. Berkeley plantation, with busy wharves on its three miles of James River frontage, was then the homeseat of Benjamin Harrison III, brother-in-law of Edmund Berkeley's fiancée. With Berkeley plantation between Colonel Hill's Shirley and Auditor General Byrd's Westover, and not far from William Randolph's Turkey Island, these home plantations were the future manorial seats that formed the grandees' row of James River mansions. Edmund Berkeley belonged in this society. Not among the very rich, he was among the very proud, with the education (he owned one of the Colony's finer libraries) and strong-willed ability to support his ambition to advance politically to the top, where he would participate with these grandees in government. He was in all ways a suitable match for Lucy Burwell.

Governor Nicholson refused to see it that way. When he learned that his "most angel" had committed herself to another, the governor first wrote her truly piteous letters. When these appeals availed nothing, he revealed the depths of his disturbance by attacking the motives of Edmund Berkeley, and carried his case to her father.

March 14th 1700/1
About 6 o'clock in the morning

Major Burwell
    Sir

 I desired my very good friend Coll: Ludwell to speak with you concerning the most important affair of my whole Life, being for aught I yet see, twill despatch me into another world, or make the small remainder of my life most unfortunate and uncomfortable in this: unless you, Sir, be pleased to give me leave to make my addresses to yor Daughter, Madam Lucy who by her beauty, many extraordinary vertues and rare accomplishments &c hath charmed me to a degree beyond expression &c.

 The person who pretends to her I am sure cannot really be in love with her any otherwise than for his own Interest. . . . If you and Madam Lucy are resolved upon my ruin I pray God forgive you; but for his sake, Dear S^r, be pleased to have a good Settlement made for her wch to hear of, will be a great satisfaction, to . . .

Yo^r most affectionate, tho at
present most melancholy, friend
[Not signed]

 Major Burwell wrote him that he was sorry for the Governor's "extasy of trouble" but could not help him. Nicholson replied that "nothing keeps me from sinking under the great weight of my misfortune, but that thing is not yet fully done." Since Lucy was not yet married to Edmund Berkeley, he still hoped to obtain "the fair and virtuous lady's consent. . . ."

 Then Nicholson complained of Major Burwell's behavior, and in early January, 1702, Lucy's father wrote him a strongly forthright answer: "And as to inviting you to my house on purpose to affront you, I cannot conceive what reason you have to think so, for I am satisfied my behaviour showed no such thing, but since my civil intentions are so misconstrued, I hope I shall be excused for the future (if I endeavor) not to affront your Excellency in that manner any more. I hope this answer will be sufficient for what past and for the future. . . ."

 On receipt of this the possessed man wrote quite wildly to Lucy:

Madam Lucy

   Vertuous Soul

   God Almighty bless keep protect direct & guide you in all y^r ways intentions designes and undertakings whatsoever & make you one of the happiest & fortunatest women in all respects, and after you have lived as long as you please here, may you be conducted by y^r Sister Angels to those eternal mansions of bliss & glory. And if it please God that I should be so happy & fortunate as to be any ways the least instrumental in y^r attaining those things, it would be most acceptable to me in this world. . . .

By then Lucy was preparing to go ahead with her wedding to Berkeley, and when Nicholson learned the dread event was to take place, he was beside himself. He threatened to kill the bridegroom, the minister who performed the ceremony and the justice of the peace who issued the license. In the derangement of jealousy, the governor frightened a young minister into fleeing from Virginia.

Nicholson was lurking on his horse outside the Burwell plantation when he encountered the Reverend Mr. Stephen Fouace, leaving after paying an afternoon visit to the family. Nicholson rode up to him and, with no other greeting, bellowed that he was not to speak to the young lady in the Burwell house. The startled minister protested that he would not have the "foolish presumption" to speak or act in any way that would occasion the governor's jealousy. To this Nicholson roared at him: "You are an impudent rogue, a villain, a rascal. You are insolent and proud now but I'll humble you and bring down your haughtiness. When you came hither, you had more rags than bags."

When Fouace remained silent with fear, Nicholson suddenly jerked the minister's hat from his head and denounced him for riding covered in his presence. The more he raged and the more Fouace cowered, the more Nicholson lost control. Finally he spun his horse as if to ride down his imaginary rival. At this the parson broke his horse into a gallop and rode out of Nicholson's sight.

The last seen of Fouace was when he boarded an outward-bound ship, riding off the landing at Jamestown. He hid in the hold of the ship until his parish and Virginia were far behind him.

During these didoes, poor Nicholson had one more grand moment in the public view. News reached the Colony that King William had died on March 19, 1702. Since Queen Mary had died before, her sister Anne, a devout member of the Anglican Church, was hurriedly crowned before her brother James (''The Old Pretender'') had a chance to bring his Roman Catholicism to the throne. For a memorial service to the King and proclamation to Queen Anne, the governor planned an elaborate ceremonial to be staged in the new capital on a Thursday late in May.

Three grandstands were built in front of the college, tents were erected and armed militia turned out with mounted troops and two batteries of artillery. The college building at that time had balconies across the front. On these and on the ground musicians took their places in three tiers — buglers from warships on the top, oboe players on the middle, and violinists on the bottom. During the morning, while the grandstands filled up, the musicians on the three tiers played, sometimes separately and sometimes together, always mournfully. By noon, when about two thousand colonists from all parts of tidewater had gathered, Nicholson appeared at the head of a procession.

The stocky governor, impressive in mourning clothes, rode a white horse draped in black. The English flags, woven with gold, were covered with crape, with their carriers dressed in mourning. The secretary was given the honor of announcing the death of the King. Then the riflemen, with reversed arms, escorted members of the clergy to one of the tents, where Commissary Blair delivered a funeral oration.

During Blair's oration, the governor slipped away for a change of costume. When Blair finished, the riflemen returned to their previous places, the musicians began to play lively tunes, and Nicholson reappeared — this time turned out in a dazzling blue uniform covered with braid.

The secretary read a proclamation stating that the second daughter of King James II was now Queen Anne, and hats were waved as the crowd three times shouted hurrah. Then the militiamen fired their rifles in crackling volleys and the cannons blasted three salutes. With the acrid smoke still hanging in the spring air, the crowd dispersed in gay spirits to points where Governor Nicholson had stationed attendants to serve rum and brandy with sugar.

During the warm afternoon everybody was served food provided by the governor, and while toasts became louder, rifles intermittently volleyed and the cannons roared again. As far as his romance was concerned, the show was all in vain for Francis Nicholson; Lucy was not among the revelers. This may have been just as well, for the celebration ended in a miserable anticlimax.

The governor had planned an elaborate fireworks display for the climax of the day, when darkness fell. One of the masters of ceremony had officiously claimed that he was an expert on fireworks. The self-appointed expert somehow managed to set a fire which, instead of starting a succession of crackles, caused all the fireworks to explode at once in a frightening blaze. Rockets shot off in all directions, sizzling over the suddenly scattered crowd and hissing to the ground near individuals fleeing into the night. When the sudden blaze had burned down and the last rocket fizzled out, only a pungent-smelling smoke was left of Nicholson's elaborately planned display.

The anticlimactic ending of the governor's celebration could have served as a symbol for the end of his one-sided love affair. Nicholson's behavior, following the announcement of her wedding, drove Lucy to break off acquaintanceship with him : she was no longer "at home" to the governor. The possessed man, unable to accept the reality that his own conduct had estranged Lucy, could attribute her refusal to receive him only to a motive to harm him. He wrote a melancholy memorandum about "Madam Lucy," in which he referred to himself in the third person as "His Excellency."

"His Excellency was once in hopes that though she would not admit him as a lover, yet she would be an honest virtuous friend : but it seems she declines them both alike, and so he must look upon her as an enemy, and such a one as designs not only his ruin in this world but the next. . . ."

Apparently a little uneasy about his behavior, Nicholson confessed "himself very much given to passion," but it never "made him do an unjust thing not becoming a gentleman, which he thinks he might justly challenge before ever he saw Virginia. . . ."

This was all rather sad, even though he was totally deluded about himself, since his weird behavior was used against him when his harmonious relationship with the Council also came to an end amid bitterness on all sides. In fact, Nicholson's behavior over Lucy Burwell led to the break with the Council coming when and as it did.

Stephen Fouace, the clergyman whom he had frightened into flight, was literate and respected, a trustee of William and Mary College, and his friends included James Blair. Nicholson's encounter with Fouace became, in the quickly spreading gossip, blown up into a physical attack upon a minister of the Church. Unfortunately for Nicholson, nothing in his overall conduct tended to discredit the distorted version. Major Burwell's personal anger was shared by the elder Benjamin Harrison, and this brought to a head the grievances of the Harrison-Ludwell-Blair family bloc in the Council — and of their ally, Robert Carter.

When this group came into the open against the governor, they would write in a petition that his behavior "is more likely down right madness than anger of passion." Whether or not this extravagant charge showed a flash of insight into Nicholson's condition, the enemy councilors seemed not to have associated the torments of unrequited love with his outbreaks of hostility towards innocent parties. At some minor encounter with a student in the hall of the college, Nicholson shouted a torrent of curses and horrendous invectives that aroused everyone in the building. Commissary Blair, professors and trustees (including councilors), appeared to consider this unprovoked rage as another instance of a governor who could not govern himself.

Whether the love frustrations caused his furies to possess him, or whether both were manifestations of some deep disorder, ultimately it was his personality that brought on the break with the new power bloc, as this group bid for supreme control of the colonial government.

6

Commissary Blair now became the vehement leader in the move to depose another governor. Though a variety of causes led Blair to turn against his former friend, the genesis of their clash lay in the personality exacerbations that arose from the frustrated lover and the miserable husband sharing the same building.

Nicholson gradually took more space in the college's Wren Building for offices for his staff, and Blair, as the president of William and Mary, began to regard each encroachment as an affront. Had the governor acted with his earlier amiability, probably Blair's resentments would have rankled less. But along with Nicholson's irritability and rages — which were growing harder to bear for everyone in frequent association with him — he had become dictatorial in his personal dealings. In his frustration at trying to become Lucy's lord and master, he took to domineering everyone who crossed him.

Blair characteristically charged the man who riled him with improper consideration for the clergy. Along with the personality conflict, Blair recognized only one right way — his — and Blair's desired organization of the Church in Virginia was, in fact, not entirely realistic. The Church of England organization, which he wished to follow, could not be applied to the conditions where dwellings were scattered over large areas and where the centers were private plantations rather than the crossroads where churches were built.

When Blair had been struggling to depose Governor Andros in 1697, he presented a realistically negative report of the conditions in the Church in Virginia. With only twenty-two permanently established clergy for the fifty parishes, some parishes were physically too large for one church and others were numerically too small to provide adequately for a minister. Among these small parishes either one minister served several parishes or some parishes had no minister at all. Few of the parishes provided comfortable houses on the "glebes" supposedly established for the minister, and most of the clergymen from England were forced to makeshift expedients as "boarders." As bad as the living conditions was the lack of tenure, caused by the tight control held by the vestries. All of that was true enough, along with low salaries in most parishes.

When the then friendly Nicholson returned in 1699, Blair introduced a proposal for changes. Many of his points were sound, and his definition of the requirements for a minister's glebe house held a special historical value: it gave one of the clearest surviving descriptions of the standards of living for the modestly placed families that were above the yeomanry but not high on the ladder that led to the great merchant-planters.

The glebe house, Blair's proposal specified, should be frame, with cellar and garret, and the main story would consist of two rooms with a minimum pitch of ten feet, and a large closet. The inside walls would be plastered, the windows "glass" with casements, and there would be brick chimneys and a shingled roof. The kitchen would be outside with other outbuildings. Four or five slaves with an overseer would be supplied. Since the Negroes were not specified by age or sex, or listed as field hands, presumably they would work the vegetable garden, orchard and cornfields, attend to the seven or eight milk cows that went with the glebe, and perform sundry outside and domestic chores. (A planter with four or five slaves and an overseer would, obviously, work most of them in the tobacco fields.)

There was no record as to how many glebe houses for ministers were built according to Blair's specifications, but there was no appreciable increase in salaries for the clergy and their insecure tenure remained subject to the will of the vestries. The weakness of Blair's general proposal came from his continued disregard of the actual conditions, and his differences with Nicholson came from Blair's identification of himself with the Supreme Representative of the Church. As commissary, Blair lacked real authority and was supposed to work with the governor in strengthening the organization of the clergy in Virginia. But anything involving his power became very personal with

Blair, and he brought to bear the influences of his political connections to support his official position in the Church.

For Nicholson's part, actually he had always given careful consideration to the clergy. He had left a fine impression with the clergy of the other colonies he had governed, and the Virginia clergy supported him against Blair. There was, however, his "attack" on Fouace, which Blair used as an "example" of Nicholson's disrespect when the commissary made the clergy one of the issues in his second campaign to unseat a royal governor.

On the Council, Blair had only four totally committed supporters: his brother-in-law Philip Ludwell, his father-in-law Benjamin Harrison, his ally Robert Carter, and John Lightfoot. Nicholson charged that Lightfoot had been recommended for the Council by the Carter-Blair faction only because he would do their bidding. Later Matthew Page came in as the sixth member, making it impossible for the Council ever to gain a majority against them.

Why Robert Carter joined the governor's enemies, and became himself the most bitterly forceful antagonist in the group, was never explained by any of those involved. Unlike the two original antagonists with their tormented emotional lives, Robert Carter had in early 1702 married a seventeen-year-old widow, Betty Landon Willis, with whom he was — and would remain — gratifyingly happy.

Born in Herefordshire, England, Betty Landon had come as a child with her parents to tidewater Virginia, in Middlesex County, across the widening Rappahannock from Corotoman and near the bay. In this settled section of fine estates, Thomas Landon, Esq., established his family among the colonial gentry. Betty married a Mr. Richard Willis, who soon died, leaving her an estate valued at about £1,000 after his debts were paid, and a fine assortment of wines that went into the wine cellars at Corotoman. Betty, within a year of Willis's death, brought her goodness of heart to the thirty-nine-year-old master of Corotoman and his four children. Carter wrote of her: "in every relation wherein she stood, whether considered as a Christian, a wife, a mother . . . or a friend, her conduct was equalled by few, excelled by none."

With his personal life complete, Robert Carter most likely reflected the attitudes then dominant in England's ruling class. When fragile and sickly Queen Anne showed no strength in governing, diminishing further the power of the Crown, Carter could see in action the truth of the axiom "France is ruled by kings, Spain by priests and England by gentlemen." In his participation in forming the controlling bloc within what had become Virginia's governing class, Carter was experiencing the authority traditionally exercised by the English models, precisely at the period when those models were supreme in the government of England.

Always of his time and place, Carter, as the fully evolved native-born aristocrat, had a far stronger feeling than had the preceding generations for the dignity of Virginians in the scheme of the British Empire. He also had a stronger feeling of the importance of his position in the whole English scheme. As his sense of power within Virginia's enhanced status came simultaneously with the diminished might of the Crown, Carter viewed Nicholson only as an individual in an official capacity, stripped of any "awe" as representing Her Majesty. In this attitude, Carter reflected the difference of the Colony's native evolved authority from the transplanted English: he found personally unacceptable the harsh-tempered arbitrariness of the English career administrator in *his* country. His dignity as a councilor was violated by the executive's behavior.

Carter may or may not have been motivated, in his repudiation of the governor, by his alliance with the Harrison family bloc. But once he declared himself, his antagonism seemed personal and was irreconcilable. There was nothing of mere defiance of, or resistance to, the governor. He forthrightly opposed Nicholson and set the authority of his bloc within the Council against that of the royal governor. When the controversy broke into the open, it was observed that King Carter (as he was then called) addressed the governor as an equal. While he followed the forms of respectful address due the office, his arguments were made without equivocation, in hard, personal directness.

Simultaneously the governor was arousing opposition in the formerly friendly House of Burgesses by using the same arbitrariness with them. He had been an efficient administrator, changing the King's revenue from a deficit of £4,600 to a surplus of £1,000, at the same time lightening the tax burden. In 1701 his blundering personal tactics undid his good works. When it became obvious that war with Louis XIV was inevitable (the War of the Spanish Succession), Nicholson was instructed to raise £900 and a military force to be sent to aid the defense of New York. Instead of proposing this to the House, he high-handedly demanded that the Virginians cough up the money and send their militia to a distant colony. The balky Burgesses responded by preparing a protest to be delivered to the King.

At that time William Byrd II was still in London, acting as an "agent" to represent the Council. This appointment had been obtained for him in 1698, probably by his father, and his occasional appearances before the Board of Trade had justified his otherwise idle existence among the literati and fleshpots of London. When the Council approved the Burgesses' petition of protest, the younger Byrd was given the duty of presenting it in 1702 to the new sovereign, Queen Anne. The Queen refused him an audience. Byrd then took the petition to the Privy Council, which forwarded it to the Board of Trade. The Board denied the protest and reinstructed Nicholson to enforce the ruling.

The House, without entering a formal refusal, simply took no action to raise the funds for New York or to send off troops. The Burgesses could get away with this defiance through procrastination because the governor had no support from the Council. Beyond the Carter-Harrison bloc, Nicholson had clumsily touched a nerve of the elder Byrd by striking at his purse. The governor had showed his disapproval of the younger Byrd's acting as "agent" in London by refusing to allow the government to pay him, and the expenses had to come out of Councilor Byrd's pocket. When William Byrd II went about London making protests over Nicholson's discouragement of the colonists' growing cotton and flax for clothes at home — though Nicholson's instructions had originated with London merchants — the governor took up the personal vendetta in Virginia. He tried to make two separate offices of Byrd's lucrative post of auditor and receiver general of revenues.

Councilor Byrd was then one of the few survivors of the prudent elder generation, and with him stirred up against Nicholson, by the spring of 1703, the six councilors of the Carter-Blair bloc felt sure enough of themselves to make the move to depose the governor. On May 20, 1703, they drew up a bill of complaints to be sent directly to the Queen (with no "agents" involved), requesting Nicholson's removal.

The long petition listed dozens of charges, many wholly unjust and some showing Carter's technique of exaggerating and distorting an element of truth. Although the petition was designed to demonstrate Nicholson's unfitness to serve as governor, the document (running to nine printed pages) essentially revealed the signers' affronted dignity at being subjected to treatment unbefitting their status as a governing body of English-Virginia gentlemen. The forming native oligarchy, composed of six councilors, had come a long way since the unorganized colonists selected Nathaniel Bacon, a high-born English remittance man, to represent such fundamental grievances as starvation and vulnerability to Indian ravages.

Only those six signed the petition to the Queen. Edmund Jenings, who then demonstrated his detachment from partisan alignments, disassociated himself from it altogether. He wrote Nicholson a personal letter assuring the governor of his support against the bloc.

The petition accused Nicholson of being "so abusive in his words and actions as not only to treat our best gentlemen with the scurrilous names of dogs, rogues, villains, dastards, cheats and cowards, and our best women with the names of whores, bitches, jades, etc., but . . . in a most public, insolent and tyrannical manner. . . . His haughty, furious and insolent behavior to the best gentlemen in the country is more likely down right madness than anger of passion.

"His ordinary housekeeping is most scandalously penurious, not any suiting the dignity of Her Majesty's Governor, having but one dish of meat at his table, though at public times, when he has any flattering address to procure or any other design in hand, he prepares such feasts as he thinks may best contribute to the carrying on of his sinister purposes." This referred, among lesser occasions, to the vain celebration at the death of William III and ascension of Queen Anne.

Nicholson was accused of making "her Majesty's name cheap and contemptible by using it to every frivolous, unnecessary or arbitrary command." If he wanted to speak with a man, if he wanted a horse or a boat with hands, the message was brought with the words "His Excellency commands you in the Queen's name to come to him instantly."

The petition listed numerous cases of his allocation of authority on minor matters, "to engross all power into his own hands and to render the Council [an] insignificant cypher, which is a great alteration of government . . . very dangerous and unsafe to Her Majesty's service."

Here the petition went on to justified complaints against Nicholson's practice of acting on his own without going through the customary consultations with the Council. The petitioners stressed his nomination of justices and sheriffs without following the custom of seeking the Council's "consent and advice." Since there he struck at the base of the political structure of the ruling class, it looked as though Nicholson's own disturbances caused him to follow general instructions in obliviousness to the political realities.

As with his crowding Blair in their shared quarters, many of his blundering measures could have been softened in their effect with a little of his former tact. But resentments were fanned by "his usual high, haughty, passionate and abusive way of browbeating, discouraging and threatening all that speak anything contrary to his opinion."

Along with showing resentment of Nicholson's manners in his undiplomatic practices, the petition mentioned two specific protests in which Robert Carter's hand was seen as representing the great land-owners. "Rules of limitation in taking up land have been prescribed to surveyors, against both Law and Custom, and without any advice in Council. Surveyors of lands have been directed, limited and totally restrained in the execution of their offices, against Law and without any advice in Council, to the great prejudice of Her Majesty's subjects." Though these specific measures were relatively mild implementations of Nicholson's general instructions to curtail private empires — and, except for Robert Carter, few of Her Majesty's subjects were prejudiced by the measures — again the governor used bad tactics in taking this action independently of the Council.

Despite the wording of the bill of complaints, it was clear that Nicholson's independent actions had been maladroit rather than "sinister" in design. However, his actions did reflect his personality disturbances. By 1703 he had reduced his relations with the Council largely to a personal level, and developed resentments of his own at the presumptuousness of the newly sprung colonial aristocrats. When, instead of curbing their wealth and power according to his instructions, he found himself on defense against their removal proceedings, Nicholson began to attack the characters of his antagonists, especially Robert Carter.

Nicholson's first complaints were directed at Carter's absence from Council meetings. This was petty, as Carter's attendance record was at least average and his reasons for missing meetings were always legitimate. "I was setting out for the last Council meeting on Monday, but some goods just then coming to my landing stopped me until pretty late next day." No merchant-planter could know when a ship was going to arrive. Then, "I can not possibly be at the next, having appointed some [ships'] masters to be at my house to give me bills of lading for some tobacco I have on board." He could not keep the shippers' vessels idly waiting at his landing while he absented himself for days.

Soon Nicholson went on to accuse Colonel Carter of bad character. In 1704 he wrote that among Carter's traits "are his extraordinary pride and ambition, using several people haughtily, sometimes making the Justices of the Peace of the County wait two or three hours before they can speak to him, etc. He is likewise famed for his covetousness and cowardice; to people that will flatter, cajole and as it were adore him, he is familiar enough, but others he uses with all the

haughtiness and insolence possible; in contempt of him he is sometimes called King Carter and other times Robin Carter, even to his
face.''

This character sketch has been used out of its context — the
intemperate words of a man of habitually violent speech fighting to
hold his position. No other contemporary mentioned Colonel Carter
being called ''King'' to his face. ''Robin,'' a family diminutive, might
have been used by intimates, though not in a derogatory sense. In the
other traits, Carter doubtless did appear haughty and insolent to a
governor possessed of a late-life compulsion to domineer those around
him. But the ''cowardice'' charge — as a part of their personal inter-
changes — actually revealed more about Nicholson than about Carter.
For it was Carter who stood up to the governor face to face in the
Council room when the conflict came into the open.

Blair, the former friend who had been the first to turn against the
governor, had written a separate petition of his own, in which he made
the wildest charges and found evil ''designs'' in manifestly innocent
actions of Nicholson. Where Blair had earlier condemned Governor
Andros for neglect of the militia, he accused Nicholson of foul purpose
in calling out the militia too much. Evidently recognizing the lack of
substance in most of his attacks, Blair went to London and collected a
number of affidavits from individuals who could cite instances of the
governor's inappropriate behavior. The affidavit of the Reverend
Stephen Fouace was particularly damaging.

After the Queen had referred the petition for Nicholson's removal
to the Board of Trade, the Board and the Queen sent the material
(including the affidavits) to Nicholson with directions for him to
deliver a reply to the councilors' charges. Nicholson called in the
signers of the petition and demanded that Carter, Ludwell and Lightfoot swear oaths to each of their allegations (Blair was away in
London).

They told him coldly that, as their case was pending before the
Queen, they did not feel required to answer him in the Council. Governor Berkeley would have hanged a councilor who gave him such an
answer: Nicholson went into one of his rages and shouted at them that
he thanked God the case *was* pending before the Queen. Carter, in
coldly assured self-control, replied by requesting that it be entered in
the journal of that Council meeting that he, Ludwell and Lightfoot
''likewise thank God that it was so.''

After this head-on confrontation in 1704, when his violence broke
against the Council bloc, Nicholson lost all poise and began to hurt his

own cause. He tried to round up affidavits contradicting those made against him and, in Williamsburg, he acted at a low personal level, sometimes with almost childish spitefulness. Then he sent to London countercharges crammed with intemperate broadsides as insubstantial as Blair's. Throughout the accusations he made to the Board of Trade ran a thread of veiled threats against the signers. By other sources the Board of Trade was also informed of open threats he was making in Virginia.

In mid-August, 1704, the Board wrote Nicholson of receiving information of the "great heats expressed by his Excellency against private person or persons," and advised him, for the good of the Queen's service and the peace of the Colony, to forbear personal resentment, prosecution or molestation while the complaints against him were under the Queen's consideration. This was the handwriting on the wall. It meant that the Board was not going to support its own expressed policy of diminishing the power of the councilors. Nicholson's personality derangements might have been largely responsible for solidifying the bloc against the implications of his instructions, but the Board (perhaps with advice from Micajah Perry) realistically accepted the solidarity of the new power group and all it represented.

While poor Nicholson was concentrating his animadversions on "King" Carter, Ludwell and Lightfoot "the tool," in London James Blair was doing some private politicking with Bishop Compton and other dignitaries of the Church. By 1705 Blair was able to inform Carter that the end seemed near for the governor. When Blair was returning on a man-of-war, the rest of the bloc called a meeting at Ludwell's home, ironically Green Spring. At the last minute, "pressing" matters — apparently the arrival of a ship at Corotoman — prevented Carter from attending the meeting, and he wrote Ludwell a note to affirm his position.

Saying that Blair had done his work so well that he was sure Nicholson would be recalled, Carter warned that they must be prepared for Nicholson's last acts. "I remember out of the Apocalypse we are told that Beezlebub near the end of his reign will arm himself with double furies for the destruction of his enemies, and just such I take the violence of our devils to be." However, "I think all concerned have reason to bear their present sufferings with patience, seeing they are like to be but for a moment." Let the "fiends grate their teeth if they will," as the violence would be "but like a dog on a chain. . . ." After this philosophizing, the "King" ended his note by saying that, nonetheless, "I am desirous of a meeting to give the finishing stroke."

The ugly episode came to an end on August 15, 1705. Nicholson called a meeting of the Council, held — sadly for him — in the newly finished Capitol whose building he had done so much to make possible. In the shadowed summer coolness of the high-vaulted room, Governor Nicholson was shorn of all his histrionics. Without words, he passed a letter he had received from Queen Anne to the councilors seated at an enormous table covered with green cloth. They silently read that he was to be relieved of his duties as governor with the arrival of his successor, Edward Nott.

Nicholson was not relieved, Queen Anne wrote, either because of the information against him or because of Her Majesty's displeasure. His removal was for the good of the Queen's service. This was completely true. The Board of Trade never condemned Francis Nicholson for his failures in executing his instructions. The Board withdrew from its own policy, with all the implications of recognizing the authority of the Carter-Harrison group as leaders of a new ruling class.

This could have happened only in the changed conditions since the departure of James II. Not only was Parliament asserting its post-Stuart powers, but the successful European land war — which broke the power of Louis XIV — established the influence of the monied interests in government. The new Board of Trade, uninterested in extending royal prerogatives to the governor representing the Crown, regarded Nicholson as an executive in a profit-making concern. As such he was jettisoned. Along with him went the policy which, deriving from Locke's principles of government, had been applied hastily, without the details of a program evolved in advance, and dependent upon the extemporizing of an erratic individual.

When Nicholson sailed from Jamestown, to the last he breathed threats against those who had unseated him. He never seemed quite sure of what had happened. As in his romance with Lucy Burwell, the deposed governor never took into account the effects of his own conduct. Nevertheless, it was a pathetic departure for an honest man who had, by mechanisms then undiagnosed, grown unbalanced in interpersonal behavior.

If Robert Carter and the other councilors who had caused his removal showed any triumph, or any compassion for the man, there was no record of either. Robert Carter acted as if the deposal of a royal governor by a few councilors — inconceivable in his youth — was a matter of course. Five days after the order of Nicholson's withdrawal was read in Council, he wrote a London merchant: "Thank God the divisions have grown less and less every day by the mild and

prudent, and will be quite at an end in a little time if Coll. N——n not
be allowed to perplex things at home [England].''

7

The impersonal casualness with which Carter regarded the accomplished end, dismissing a two years' struggle as all in a day's
work, revealed the completeness of his identification with a governing
class that had been established in the Magna Carta signed by King
John five hundred years before. It had taken just about one century in
Virginia for a ruling class, as established in 1705 by King Carter and
his allies, to become a branch of the historic stream flowing from
Runnymede.

The Carter group entered the tradition at a time when the governing class of England was undergoing profound change. With the
Crown weakened, the old ''cavalier'' party of landowners, emerging
as the Tories, had to fight for and share power with the progressive
Whigs. In the mélange of factions forming the Whig party, the new
monied interests (not primarily associated with land) were allied with
the surviving yeomanry in the eastern, southeastern and southwestern
shires, with the Protestant Dissenters of all types (who had secured
toleration during the War of the Spanish Succession) and the ''free-
thinkers,'' including the intellectuals of the day. As in all political
alliances, an amalgam of considerations formed strange partnerships,
and shifts were constant within and between the parties. Essentially
the status quo Tory landowners (and the dependents on whom they
could impose their political will) represented the old — though the
''old'' contained many strong personalities who were new to the
peerage.

Robert Carter personified the reflections of the English changes
in Virginia both as landowner — representing a landowning class,
however new — and as merchant — representing the monied interests.
As these separate elements in England formed the governing power in
Parliament, in Robert Carter they were combined in his own person
and personal power in the government controlling Virginia's internal
affairs. He was both traditional and progressively new as the archetype of the colonial ''aristocrats'' who had succeeded the second
generation in power. Most of all, he was less local, less parochial, in his
outlook than the generation that passed out of power with the deaths
of Ralph Wormeley, William Fitzhugh and William Byrd I, the last to
die, in 1704. (Richard Lee II remained in retirement until his death
in 1715.)

Although this older generation had been responsible to their offices, were (as Nicholson said) usually the best qualified for the appointments, and were mostly honest within the broad interpretations of the practices of their time, they had been largely preoccupied with building their fortunes and establishing their personal positions, and had directed much of their power toward developing an exchange of favors on a local scale. Without any pronounced sense of partaking of the functions of the English governing class, they had limited the exercise of their power to Jamestown. Fundamentally, they were transplanted Englishmen making a go of it in the colonies.

Robert Carter, with his native-born identification with Virginia and the class of Virginians in power, looked outward from his secure base to a mercantile world in which his private domain was an established unit and his public sphere of influence was recognized. When he and five other councilors took their petition for the removal of a royal governor directly to the Queen, they had received no support from the rest of the Council or the House of Burgesses, and the clergy had come out in support of Nicholson. When the Queen, the Privy Council and the Board of Trade removed the royal governor because of the displeasure of those six councilors, Robert Carter was confirmed in his sense of the relative importance of Virginia's fully evolved aristocracy in the scheme of England as an empire.

He never used the word "aristocrat," and probably never thought of it. In common with his contemporaries, Carter was interested only in the reality of power, and he was never known to object to being called "King."

The Oligarchy Takes Root

THE CHANCE OF accidents gave King Carter and his political friends the opportunity of five years in which to entrench their party as the core of an oligarchy that would control Virginia's government throughout the rest of the life of the Colony, into the Revolution. Major Edward Nott, the governor who followed Nicholson, lived only one year after coming to Virginia, and a successor did not arrive in Williamsburg until four years after Nott's death. During this hiatus, when Virginia had in effect no royal governor, the position of dominance that the oligarchy had won in overthrowing Nicholson became fixed in custom. Rule in Virginia became a habit to Robert Carter and his allies on the Council.

It was a responsible rule, growing as it did from the broadening base of politically influential families in control at county levels, and supported as it was by the expanding planter class. As the men at the top grew secure in their power, some of them — not Robert Carter — developed an arrogance about their personal prerogatives, as if sanctified by long tradition. Any familiar ways in the Colony became quickly established as "what hath been the ancient custom."

Major Nott had no effect on the councilors of the new power bloc, except possibly to confirm their sense of security in position. The new governor arrived in Williamsburg in the breathless heat of mid-August, 1705, when the colonial capital seemed like a partly deserted town. With the General Assembly not in session, the councilors and burgesses were all away on their plantations, large and small, and there was little movement around the taverns and inns and shops that had sprung up along the broad, shaded Duke of Gloucester Street. The frame houses, where lodgers were put up during Public Times, were shuttered against the sun. Major Nott took quarters in one of these houses and established himself in offices in the Wren Building of William and Mary College.

He was an agreeable gentleman and showed from the beginning that he had no intention of interfering with things as they existed. When Williamsburg stirred out of its summer lethargy with the fall session of the General Assembly, the new governor did not change from his quiet unobtrusiveness. He was tactful in meetings with the councilors in the high-ceilinged room on the second floor of the new Capitol, and his attitude to the House of Burgesses was as friendly as Nicholson's had been in the early days of his administration.

There were no items of importance with which he had to involve himself. The chronic discussions about establishing port towns came up, and Governor Nott had instructions on this point. As the English manufacturers feared that the growth of towns might turn the colonials from tobacco growing to manufacturing, the governor gave no support to this tired measure, and passed on the Board of Trade's disapproval of planting cotton and flax. None of this concerned anybody very much, and the only ripple of conflict came at the local level, in debates that arose during conferences between the Council and the Burgesses.

The point at issue was the self-perpetuating vestries, which maintained in the parishes the influence of the same, relatively few families. The non-slave-holding planters who numerically still dominated the House of Burgesses, and regarded themselves as representing all freeholders, could perceive the drift of power spreading from the oligarchy on the Council toward a controlling majority of the whole General Assembly.

As the slave-owning freeholders of the planter class identified themselves with the most influential of the big merchant-planters, the political aspirants among them already were extending the control of the oligarchy into every courthouse and parish vestry — with the same men serving on both. In the joint conferences with the Council, some of the burgesses seized upon the self-perpetuating vestries as one means of breaking the interlocking control of the prosperous families who were coalescing into a class which would dominate Virginia's whole government. In a reprise of "Bacon's Assembly," the Burgesses argued for vestry elections every six years.

The reply of the councilors bluntly expressed their honest belief that the general run of uneducated people were not qualified for responsibilities involving decisions which affected others. They made the "aristocratic assumption" that they knew better than the majority what was good for the whole, and they made no bones about voicing the opinion that their inferiors were unfit to serve on the vestries. They denied the proposed elections on the grounds that the elections would be "made by all the freeholders and housekeepers promiscuously, the greater part of which are mean people, and not always the most considerate, they will be like enough [by numbers] to carry the election in favor such as themselves."

That settled the vestry issue and, along with it, the attempt to halt the drift toward control of the Colony's government by a ruling class. In the generation of Robert Carter's children, the ruling class would spread to incorporate the dominating majority of the House of Burgesses.

With this local matter disposed of, the councilors and richer burgesses met in the Capitol yard to talk about the dangers from French privateers, from a fresh eruption of pirates, and about the effects of the bad tobacco market in London. Slaves were coming into the Colony at the rate of nearly seven hundred a year (by 1710 they would come in at the rate of about nine hundred a year), and the men talked of overextended planters running into debt to Micajah Perry.

Robert Carter was not affected by the fluctuations that kept the smaller planters insecure, but — as his father had — he kept lookouts with spyglasses watching the Rappahannock to the east where the broadening river entered the blue mists of the Bay. Carter was also kept informed about ocean and Chesapeake Bay traffic by the large number of ships' captains with whom he did business and whom he entertained in the evenings. For them and similar visitors, he kept in his cellars huge quantities of ale that he imported from Dorchester, sometimes ordering as much as four hogsheads of bottled ale — two thousand bottles — at a time.

His own tastes ran to wine, usually red, as white wine did not keep well. He wrote: "It turns brown and loses the briskness of its taste." He loved brandy but even through the best agents he sometimes received inferior shipments. "Stark naught," he wrote of one shipment. "Such I never met with that bare the name of French brandy."

Some of the ships' captains traded in slaves, bringing cargoes to his wharves on Carter's Creek. He would stride down to the wharf and personally inspect the black people. For his own plantations, he thought "Gambers slaves" were the best. He acted as agent for neighboring planters, mostly small, who were starting in volume production with from one to four slaves, working fields that averaged (in his county) 165 acres. Since many of these small planters had no ready cash, Carter assumed responsibility for all payments, for which he charged a ten percent commission.

The master of Corotoman was held in considerable esteem by the ships' captains, and not only because of his riches. He had a straightforward way of doing business, which they liked, and the man whom Governor Nicholson had found "haughty" was friendly with the rough, shrewd seamen. In 1704, when twenty men slaves staged a revolt on a ship, one young Negro defended the captain and had his arm severely injured. By the time the ship reached Corotoman, the surgeon had healed the young man's wound, and the captain, setting him free, turned him over to Carter. The captain wrote: "A very worthy gentleman, Colonel Carter, took him into his service, till he became well enough acquainted in the country to provide for himself." Carter saw personally to preparing the young freedman for his new life in the Colony.

Whether from humanity or cold practicality, or a combination of both, Carter was always careful about looking after the physical well-being of all his slaves. With his "people" numbering in the hundreds, scattered on separate plantations, he gave attention to the proper clothing for each Negro. He charged the overseers on the separate plantations with the responsibility of obtaining at Corotoman the clothes for each slave, by name, and distributing them. He wrote angrily about an "arrant cheat" who sent him shoes of a smaller size than the size marked on the outside, and he was continually concerned about getting shoes to fit his "large people."

According to the customs of the time, when criminals were branded and publicly pilloried, runaways and recalcitrant slaves were whipped and branded. As the T branded on a white criminal was to warn all that he was a thief, the R on a runaway was to proclaim him as private property. Having the power of life and death over the Negroes, Carter meted out such pragmatic punishments — "to fit the crime'' — as impersonally as when he served on the General Court dealing with white malefactors. In one hard case, whom neither whippings nor brandings kept from running away, Carter obtained a court order for a doctor to cut off his toes.

The punishments of runaways were the only means he, and all planters, knew to protect their investment in slaves. Carter was buying and using slaves on a larger scale than anyone in the Colony. Working with his inspired gift of organization, in which all the separate plantations were coordinated into a single operation under his all-seeing supervision, he brought in labor forces as he bought up new tracts of the choice land he was continually acquiring in Tidewater. Many of these holdings were evidently bought from small-scale planters who had run into debt trying to imitate the Carters of the Colony. With the unstable tobacco market in Major Nott's year, Carter's immense — and immensely complicated — enterprises kept expanding as his party's political power was entrenched under a governor who discreetly left the big merchant-planters alone.

2

The greatest event in Major Nott's one-year administration occurred during October, when his first General Assembly was still in session. During Public Times, all sorts of people crowded into the town, now in the awkward process of growing into a small city. Tradesmen brought in their wares, performers came to do their acts in the Public Square, thieves and prostitutes and vagrants drifted in with the crowds that came to see the sights. The councilors and burgesses slept anywhere they could find accommodations. As the Capitol had been completed only the year before, various government offices and chambers remained in the college. These also were used as temporary lodgings, and Colonel Edward Hill was sleeping in the speaker's chambers at the south end of the main building.

This Colonel Hill, the son of the haughty councilor of Berkeley's cabal, was the owner of Shirley plantation, and he had provided himself handsomely with necessities and comforts for his stay in Williamsburg. One October night, between eleven and midnight, Colonel Hill was awakened in his ground-floor chambers. Pulling on breeches over his nightshirt, he ran out on the piazza and into the yard. Several men were gathered near the smokehouse and, following their gaze, he saw the glare of fire in the hall in the center of the building. The lurid light from the flames was already halfway to the roof. Out on Duke of

Gloucester Street hastily dressed members of the General Assembly stood watching the fire. Nobody was doing anything.

Colonel Hill ran back into the chambers where smoke was then drifting. The blaze had not begun to approach the south end of the building, and he took a quick look around, ''considering what was most valuable to save.'' His eyes settled on the large chest which held most of his clothes. Ordinarily two servants were required to move it, but the James River plantation master dragged the heavy bulk out on the piazza and then to the ground. Gasping for breath, he puffed back into the chambers. He threw his saddle over one shoulder, grabbed up his sword from the window ledge, a silver tankard, and several odd objects. With his arms clutching the trophies, he reached down one free hand for his portmanteau, containing toilet articles and papers, and staggered out.

By the time he returned to his chest in the yard, the flames had reached the roof and the cupola was blazing above and lighting the whole east front of the building. Several men were running past the college gates, most of them ''in pretty good apparel,'' and all with hats. A mounted planter, who had earlier given the alarm, rode past. Beyond the college gates, a small crowd gathered in Duke of Gloucester Street. A few of these approached at a discreet distance, but nobody did anything. Colonel Hill saw Councilor Henry Lightfoot wandering around, and got him to help pull the chest away from the building.

After a century in Virginia, the colonists still stood helplessly before a big fire. Colonel Hill's inspired energy in personal salvage was the only useful act during the long burning of the interior of the building and of the piazzas where Nicholson had had the musicians play during the ceremonies for Queen Anne. With little more than the shell left of the gracefully designed building, William and Mary College — one of the reasons for placing the capital at Williamsburg — had to be rebuilt. For fire prevention, the rules against lighting candles or smoking were strictly enforced in the new Capitol at the other end of the street, and though the building grew terribly damp during the winter, chimneys remained forbidden.

Since the governor's temporary offices were destroyed with the Wren Building, the fire — along with his unregal lodgings in a frame house — probably prompted Major Nott to propose the building of a substantial brick dwelling to serve as a permanent residence for royal governors. When the project was undertaken, work progressed slowly on the new house, and Governor Nott was unremembered in association with what became ''the Palace.'' The mild gentleman, who died in August of the year after he came (1706), was scarcely remembered for anything. Yet he was historically significant — as a later governor would recognize — for his inadvertent contribution to the habit of power developed in Robert Carter and his allies in the oligarchy.

After Nott's death, a weird accident left Virginia for four years without any governor at all. Colonel Robert Hunter, on his way to Williamsburg, was captured at sea by a French ship and when finally released, went to govern the New York colony.

Colonel Edmund Jenings, then president of the Council by seniority, became acting governor. Only four years older than Robert Carter, he had won the respect of the older generation as an English gentleman of "quality," the son of a member of Parliament, and he had come to the Colony when Richard Lee II, his brother-in-law, was a power on the Council. He had been awarded the prestigious post of secretary by the generation that had passed from the scene by 1706 and, as Council president and acting governor, he was officially the most important political figure in Virginia. Yet, by continuing his personal policy of remaining unattached from any political groupings or partisan maneuvers (he had disassociated himself from the petition that removed Nicholson), in effect he abdicated the power of his office to the oligarchy.

Jenings had built an estate, Ripon Hall, after the fashion of the modest English manors, and his land produced some of the best tobacco in Virginia. Not as efficient in management as the big merchant-planters on the Council, he was among those tobacco growers who were getting in financially over their heads. He needed the revenue from his post as secretary and, in his congenital neutrality, he made the miscalculation of looking to London instead of to the Colony's de facto powers for the security of tenure. By this practical disassociation from the oligarchy — with whose individual members he was friendly enough on the surface — Colonel Jenings settled for the honor of being titular governor while Robert Carter's party grew habituated to running Virginia.

3

During the 1705–1710 hiatus, in the changes on the Council caused by death, Robert Carter found a new drinking companion in William Byrd II. The elegant expatriate, eleven years younger than Carter, had been forced by his father's death to return to Virginia. As the elder Byrd's wealth was entirely in the business he had operated, his son would have to take up the management of the plantation and trading post. Although a dilettante with a pronounced distaste for business, Byrd could bring to a going concern a trained intelligence, good health and a sanguine disposition.

Making the best of his exile from London's beguiling streets, at the age of thirty-one — having spent only one year in Virginia since the age of seven — he "succeeded" to his father's honors and emoluments, and moved immediately into the social world which included King Carter and the oligarchs. He had to wait until 1709 for his appointment to the Council, as two natives had precedence in filling vacancies, but the younger Byrd from the first associated with the councilors as though one of them.

Because of his and his father's feud with Nicholson, Byrd would receive only half the revenues his father had enjoyed as auditor and receiver general. In one of his last acts, Nicholson had divided this post into two offices, and William Byrd II succeeded only to the post of receiver general. Such was Byrd's self-assurance, however, that in 1709 he tried to buy the office of deputy governor of the Colony, attempting in one step to supersede the power bloc built by Robert Carter and his allies.

Before this vain maneuver, in 1706 Byrd married Lucy Parke, one of the daughters of Daniel Parke, a rakish gentleman who cut a gaudy swath in Virginia before he left the Colony. His father, the first Daniel Parke, had been a councilor during Berkeley's reign, and died in 1679, when Daniel Parke, Jr., was ten years old. As the only male heir to his father's estate and position, the young Parke had matured early and arrogantly. At about the age of seventeen he married Jane Ludwell, when she was living at Green Spring with her father and his third wife, My Lady Frances. Soon after two daughters had been born to this union, twenty-one-year-old Parke went to England for a couple of years, and returned with a mistress, a married woman, whom he referred to as "Cousin Brown."

Colonel Parke was a handsome man of overbearing self-assurance, violent and tumultuous, and for the next five years he flaunted his disdain of his fellow colonials while the powers, out of class loyalty, conferred on him the posts of collector and escheator, sent him to the Burgesses, and had him appointed to the Council. He had a particular hatred of Governor Nicholson and of James Blair, his brother-in-law's brother-in-law, and went so far as to pull Mrs. Blair bodily from her pew in Bruton Parish Church. In 1697, when Blair was working to supplant Governor Andros with Nicholson, Parke more or less abandoned his wife and two daughters, and left for England with his mistress.

In England the swashbuckling colonial won important friends, including the Duke of Marlborough, who appointed him aide-de-camp and gave him the assignment of carrying the news of Blenheim to Queen Anne. Parke was rewarded with the governorship of the Leeward Islands. There he had a spectacular amorous career and acquired a new mistress, by whom he had illegitimate daughters. Making no effort to support his family, who were living at Green Spring with his wife's brother, Philip Ludwell II, he wrote his daughters advice on the proper behavior of young ladies and gave them notions of exalted position. In 1705, the year before Byrd married the younger daughter, Lucy, Parke's abandoned wife wrote a piteous letter of appeal for help in maintaining the then young women in the style their absent father thought fit for them.

Ill and worn out with life, she wrote: "As your daughters are grown women, and we live in the notion of your wife and daughters, it is expected we should live equal with the best in the country," but it was impossible to keep "any sort of kindly acquaintance with gentility." It "makes me many times wonder how you think we live, especially you that have lived so like a man of quality all your life, and know so well how a gentlewoman should live. . . . As you know, I have never had anything to be called a living from your hand, but what I have shifted and charged and toiled for here, which I was so unable to do in my sickness that had it not been for the assistance of my friends and relations [I] might then have suffered the greatest want imaginable." For herself she only desired "to be happily released from all worldly care, quietly to sit down with as small a competence as you please, I having done all the service I can for you and your children, who, I thank God, are better able to keep themselves than I can them or myself. And being so tired from a sickly life, the least thing in the world is become burdensome to me, which makes me the more earnest to quit it all on any terms whatsoever."

Mrs. Parke lived for three years to see her daughters well married: Frances, the older, to John Custis IV, and Lucy to William Byrd II. While their mother had none of the Ludwell contumaciousness, her daughters seemed to inherit their father's tumultuousness of character. John Custis came to boast of the hell in which he lived with his wife; and although Byrd enjoyed many rapturous moments with Lucy, he clashed with her tempers and her willfulness, and life with the fiery young woman was not bland.

However, Byrd's marriage placed him in the center of the power
bloc then in control of Virginia. Byrd had little personally in common
with his wife's uncle, Philip Ludwell II, who was a grasping man with
a provincial's assertive jealousy about his privileges and was not
among those planters distinguished by a love of learning. But they
were natural allies through a mutuality of class interests: Ludwell
entertained heartily at Green Spring, and the adaptive Byrd got along
well with his strongly placed in-law. Byrd established a more personal
intimacy with Ludwell's brother-in-law, Benjamin Harrison III, a
friendly neighbor at adjoining Berkeley plantation. Between the
friendly alliance and personal friendship with these two brothers-in-
law of James Blair, Byrd, at least on the surface, buried his former
hostility toward the commissary. Completing the Harrison-Blair-Lud-
well family group was the commissary's brother Dr. Archibald Blair,
established in partnership with Philip Ludwell in a successful store.

While at ease with these colonial squires, Byrd became friendly
with Robert Carter through more natural affinities. Carter did not
establish a deeper intimacy with Byrd than he did with any other
man, but they enjoyed each other's company. When Byrd first returned, he and Carter seemed not to visit each other's homes, and they
were thrown together mostly during Public Times in Williamsburg.

Before Byrd was on the Council, he frequently went (as he said)
"to pay my court" to President Jenings, and he would be in Jenings'
lodgings, or in the secretary's office just inside the entrance to the
Capitol, when Robert Carter and other councilors dropped in on their
way to a meeting in the Council room. When Council meetings adjourned, and Jenings stayed behind, Byrd was around to join Robert
Carter for dinner in one of the taverns. Sometimes other councilors
joined them, and they drifted from dinner into serious drinking.

Unlike Carter, Byrd was not a daily drinker at meals. As a social
drinker he was often present when a few rounds led to a big party,
and he privately recorded some gruesome hangovers. One bright
Saturday in April, 1709, Byrd left Williamsburg with Colonel Carter
and Philip Ludwell for a break in the business of government at
nearby Green Spring. That night, in the manor house built by Sir
William Berkeley, they "danced and were very merry."

The next morning the gathering rode in carriages the three miles
to the Jamestown church, where Commissary Blair preached. Despite
his new amity with Blair, Byrd could not keep from falling asleep
during the sermon. Back to Green Spring they rode for a midday
dinner, the party growing in size all the while. After eating, the men

(as was customary) took a walk. Then young John Custis (Byrd's brother-in-law) entered two horse races, during which Robert Carter and the other councilors forgot for a while their august estate. It could be observed, however, that when the rest of the party prepared to go back into the mansion for supper, Robert Carter and Benjamin Harrison rode back to Williamsburg to be ready for the business of the day on Monday morning.

4

From his early forties to late forties, during the 1705–1710 period, King Carter was adjusting to changes in his growing family. A better sire than his brother had been or even his father with five wives, by 1710 Robert Carter had had three more boys by his second wife, and the end was not in sight. These new sons — Robert, the oldest, Charles, the most colorless, and Landon, the most brilliant — were all being prepared to be sent to England for their education. As the fresh batch of children's voices rang through the rooms and across the grounds, Carter's first son, John, went off to Trinity College, Cambridge, and his oldest daughter, Elizabeth, left Corotoman as the bride of Nathaniel Burwell. Carter's first of many sons-in-law was a brother of the famous Lucy Burwell Berkeley and of Elizabeth Burwell Harrison, the wife of Benjamin Harrison III.

In 1710, Carter lost his friend Harrison, who died when only thirty-seven. He left a young son, Benjamin Harrison IV, a childhood friend of Anne Carter, the last child born of Robert Carter's first wife Judith. When they grew up, these children of the friends married, although young Harrison had to ask the help of his neighbor Byrd in approaching his future father-in-law.

Benjamin Harrison III died two years before his father, the old councilor and family-fortune founder. Born in 1645, Benjamin Harrison II had started with a legacy of a furnished plain house, five hundred acres, and an entrée into the county's political organization. From him there passed to his sons and grandsons, and to the grandson of Benjamin Harrison III, a gift for practical politics and a love of political maneuver that no family in the Colony surpassed.

When the two Harrisons died within two years of each other, and Benjamin Harrison IV was still a youth, Carter experienced his first losses in the group of allies with which as a young burgess he had identified his political future. By then King Carter was himself becoming one of the senior leaders in Virginia's government and in plantation society. As such, he took on personal responsibilities that extended to the families of the merchant-planter community. Nothing revealed more about Robert Carter as a man than his handling of the unrewarding chores that came to him as joint guardian of Ralph Wormeley's sons, whose widowed mother, ''Sister'' Wormeley, was the sister of Carter's first wife.

Wormeley's resplendent style of living, which Carter had regarded as vain show, had left an entangled estate for his widow and children. After the debts were settled, the broadly based operations at Rosegill plantation, with the considerable tangible property at the handsomely equipped homeplace, would still be wealth in the Colony, but the Wormeley estate would no longer be among the very rich trading plantations, as it had been when the second Ralph Wormeley came into it during Berkeley's rule. As with Byrd's estate, without active and skillful management the property would not support the young Wormeleys in the manner to which they were habituated and which they wished to continue in London.

Carter wrote to Francis Lee, the Virginia agent in London: ''Ralph in prospect will have a fine estate, John a valuable one; yet it will hardly be compatible in either of them to follow their father's steps in all things. . . . If you can retrench their expenses what reasonable you can, twill be a kindness to the boys. . . . No doubt the continuance of careful education will render them accomplished men qualified to preserve the character of their father, and fit for the service of their country. . . .''

In July, 1705, he wrote Thomas Corbin, the other joint guardian, saying that Francis Lee had intimated that the boys wanted to come home and their mother was anxious for them ''to come in'' (return to Virginia). ''Considering that Ralph grows to manhood apace, and seeing his fortune promises none other than a Virginia life, too long a taste with your town may do him harm, and to be somewhat acquainted with plantations affairs before they come to be men might be of extraordinary use to them.''

The boys put off returning and the following year, in August, Carter wrote Corbin: ''I am sorry master Ralph is angry with us; if it be for ordering him keeping within suitable limits, we must take no notice of it: he will in time see his own folly.''

That year, 1706, Carter began to get more trouble than he relished from the guardianship. Sister Wormeley had married again, in 1703, and her husband, Colonel William Churchill, Gent., seemed to be at the root of the difficulties. Although Carter and others had forced Churchill to sign a marriage agreement stating that he could not be willed any part of the estate due the widow's children, Churchill had fixed himself (Carter wrote Corbin) "absolutely in the government of the estate," and trying to manage for Sister Wormeley had become a confusion "for all concerned."

When the boys planned to come home that year, Carter wrote with growing irritation: "It's high time they were here to look after their own affairs." They could get an accounting themselves from Colonel Churchill. Revealing the state of affairs at the Churchill-Wormeley ménage, he wrote: "I have done the best service I could at the distance I live [downriver on the other side of the wide Rappahannock], but am of late very much a stranger in their affairs, as so I believe is everybody else concerned."

The two young men finally arrived in December of the next year, 1707, and Carter found their equipment "a great deal too extravagant." There was evidently little cordiality between the guardian and the young gentlemen, and Carter had too many affairs of his own to intrude where he was not useful. He expressed his disapproval to Francis Lee in a short, choppy note dictated, apparently, in an irritated hurry to wash his hands of the whole thing: "If others are pleased, I have little to say; only wish their incomes may keep their goings out, else will prove imprudent prodigality at the end."

King Carter had given his time and energy for six years on the behalf of his friends' children. Yet, with no reflections on human ingratitude or the waste of his efforts, nine months after the Wormeley boys were home, he wrote off the whole business like a bad debt. In September, 1708, in a business letter to Corbin, he included his last words on the subject of his troublesome and largely fruitless involvement: "I have done concerning myself with young Wormeleys' affairs; their estate is entirely under their own government and indeed tis time they addict themselves to business. So I take leave of it from any further writings on their account."

When an episode was complete for Carter — whether deposing a royal governor or withdrawing from six years' involvement with the finances of a fellow councilor's family — it immediately belonged in the forgotten past. Ralph Wormeley III lived only five years after coming into the Rosegill estate. His brother John married and had a daughter, Elizabeth, who would in Carter's lifetime marry his son Landon.

Such conflicts between members of the ruling class, almost always involving money, property and administering estates, seldom affected

the relationships permanently : they were like quarrels between individuals in a large family. Carter's comments on closing episodes of
this kind were included in the commercial letters he dictated to one of
the clerks in the office at Corotoman. When he wanted to make a more
personal comment, he wrote in a diary. Even in the diary, the personal
items mostly concerned some aspect of business. There were accounts
of his visitors (when they came and went), but his guests, like ships'
captains, were usually associated with business. When his children
grew older, married, and moved to their own homes, his accounts of
their visits often referred to some personal details, and these references noted in greatest brevity any conflicts that had occurred or were
occurring. Though his deep, continuing involvement in the welfare of
his children could not have left him unaffected by differences, the
references were as emotionlessly factual as his dismissal of his involvement with the Wormeleys' affairs.

The one subject he wrote on fully was his experiences with illness.
Especially when he suffered from the gout among other afflictions as
he grew older, Carter recounted at the greatest length and in the most
minute detail every stage of his feelings, every symptom, the quantity
and nature of his bowel movements, his precise place in the house
during all the hours of the attacks, and described every mouthful of
liquid or food that he touched.

This too might be regarded as business, since all his wealth and
power resided in him as an individual, all deriving and flowing from
his own person. Not calling in doctors, or visitors or help of any kind,
he concentrated his attention upon the physical entity which was the
source of empire, and studied himself with the same meticulous attention he brought to the details of his business affairs.

While he charted the progress of his illnesses in the emotionless
tones of commercial correspondence, he did specify the intensity and
duration of his pains and intestinal disturbances. He suffered stoically, without lamentations, but when prolonged, the suffering en-
gulfed him.

Beyond chronicling the minutiae of his days with illness, Carter
evidently recorded items of a personal nature in a second diary. This
he referred to only as "the other book." Unlike those writers of secret
diaries who subconsciously intended their words to be posthumously
deciphered for an oblique sort of immortality, Carter manifestly
intended to keep his private reflections forever secret. No human eye
save his own ever saw "the other book."

Carter never revealed an introspective turn of mind, nor indicated any hint of a bad conscience. He was called some hard names for the gains he made out of operating the Proprietary's agency, but all of his correspondence relating to the Proprietary suggested that he was acting within the commercial conscience of his day. This conscience held a morality, within the Protestant ethic, which did not necessarily include fairness in interpreting to his advantage the letter of a contract or of the law.

In his first period as agent, which encompassed the 1705–1710 interlude, Carter patented land for his family on the modest scale of fifteen thousand acres — considerably less than the tidewater land he was acquiring by purchase. On the Proprietary land he patented, the Fairfaxes in England would receive quitrents minus Carter's commissions, the same as if other settlers occupied the land, and through the steady increase of patents which Carter issued to new settlers, the Proprietors received far more revenue than ever before.

With from £300 to £500 cash coming in yearly from the agency above all his other profits, sometime during the 1705–1710 period Robert Carter began to build a new house on the point of land. This house, begun at an unknown date, would be the mansion that has usually been associated with Corotoman as a plantation homeplace.

As with most of the rich merchant-planters of the early eighteenth century — like the elder William Byrd at Westover and Benjamin Harrison III at Berkeley Hundred — Carter did not attempt to build a baronial dynastic seat like the larger gentry in England. He built solidly, using brick made on his own plantation, a rambling two-story house about eighty-five feet across and twenty-five feet deep, with a stone-paved cellar five feet below ground. Not intended as an English basement, it contained enormous wine cellars, with passages guarded by locked iron-grill doors. The thick-walled house was massively comfortable rather than ostentatious, though of course everything in it was of "the very best." The six-inch H hinges on the inside doors and the seventeen-inch H L hinges on the doors to the outside were finely wrought and made to last.

With kitchen, laundry and all service units in separate buildings outside the house, the use of the rooms was not strictly defined, except for the dining room and Carter's own bedchamber on the first floor. Other bedchambers were scattered all over the Corotoman center unit — in the new "mansion," the "old house," over the office and over the brick store, even over porches. It was like a small hotel, where transients were continually coming and going, staying from overnight to several weeks, and with permanent guests who themselves were frequently absent. Books were everywhere, with no room designated as a "library." The largest collection was in the closet of the "lower chamber," presumably the master bedroom. Books were kept in the closets of other chambers, in the chamber over the brick store and in a large black walnut case in the office of the store. Many of the chambers had closets, as did the dining room, a feature which curiously was not included in the dynastic mansions built a few years later.

Highly skilled craftsmen had not then achieved individual reputations in Virginia as master builders, except Henry Cary in Williamsburg, and no single architect was known to have been responsible for the building of Corotoman. Master masons, master carpenters, and joiners worked probably under the supervision of one or more master builders, and the supervising builders themselves may have changed during the slow building of the mansion. Nothing of record indicated that Robert Carter and his contemporaries planned their own houses in detail. However, each of the houses reflected the personality of the owner and — with a few exceptions — the prevailing architectural fashions, or practices, of the day in Virginia. The massive solidity of Corotoman perfectly reflected its owner.

While the manor house was being completed, the interlude between English governors came to an end in the summer of 1710.

5

Before the "golden age" came into full flowering under the oligarchy, Robert Carter and his allies were forced into a struggle over who was to rule Virginia's internal affairs along with the strongest, most resourceful governor yet to appear in the Colony. Colonel Alexander Spotswood, a professional soldier turned professional administrator, came in like a new executive concerned with making a success of a corporation in his own way.

As a tactful, mannerly new executive, he came in quietly. When Robert Carter met the newly arrived governor on a rainy June day at Green Spring, where Ludwell was putting up His Excellency, Colonel Spotswood was courteous and friendly. None of Carter's friends felt any premonition that they were to be confronted with the ultimate threat to their positions. For not only their power in running the Colony according to their lights was at stake, but their whole patterns of life as plantation masters were by then inextricably interwoven with their political rule.

On the day Robert Carter and his fellow councilors met the new governor, the total pattern of the Colony's day-to-day life reflected them and they reflected it. There was no way to change their positions of authority in government without changing the whole structure that had been a century in evolving. It never occurred to the councilors gathered at Green Spring that anyone would try.

The Struggle to Final Decision

THIRTY-FOUR-YEAR-OLD Alexander Spotswood had something significant in common with the councilors he met, though no one quite saw it
that way: he was commited to winning fortune and influence in the
New World by his own abilities and efforts. This similarity of motivation was obscured by the surface difference between colonials and an
English governor.

Colonel Spotswood was a personal case of the mobility in the
English gentry. His family having fallen from higher estate, his
purpose was to regain position on his own.

The Spotswoods were Scottish Anglicans whose history had been
associated with the Reformed Church of England since the break with
Rome. One of Spotswood's ancestors had been admitted to orders by
Thomas Cranmer, the Archbishop of Canterbury and the principal
authority for the *Book of Common Prayer*, and his great-grandfather,
a historian of Scotland, had been the Archbishop of St. Andrews. His
grandfather, Sir Robert Spotswood, was secretary of Scotland during
the rise of the Covenanters who, in opposition to the Church of England, supported the anti-Royalists eventually led by Cromwell. Because of Sir Robert Spotswood's loyalties to the Anglican Church, he

was put to death in 1646. The decline of the family fortunes followed.

Spotswood's father, a physician, was a quarrelsome man who settled for the modest post of doctor to the garrison at Tangier. England maintained this outpost on the African side of the Straits of Gibraltar before the Rock of Gibraltar came into English possession. Alexander Spotswood, born in Tangier the year of Bacon's Rebellion (1676), lived there only the first seven years of his life. Just before the outpost at Tangier was abandoned, he was taken by his mother to England, in 1683.

He presumably went to school in England, as he was an educated man habituated to the society of cultivated people. He first appeared in the records at the age of seventeen, when he was appointed ensign in the Earl of Bath's infantry regiment, then stationed in Flanders. During the War of the Spanish Succession, Spotswood advanced to the rank of lieutenant colonel, serving under Lord Cadogan as lieutenant quartermaster general. When he was captured at Oudenarde, Marlborough personally negotiated for his exchange. He was wounded in the great victory at Blenheim, and with the critical phase of the war over, in 1710 he turned to England's relatively new career field of professional colonial administration.

His friends tried to dissuade him from taking the post in Virginia, on half the pay he drew in the army, but Spotswood, like the forebears of the Virginia oligarchy, saw the New World as the land of opportunity. He made this explicit in a letter he wrote later to Nathaniel Harrison: "Every man that is endowed with a common share of thought and understanding to forecase his worldly affairs (and I presume none that know me will exclude me from that number) certainly forms to himself some apparent comforts, when he unconstrainedly embarks in an undertaking that must quite change the scene of his life."

He was to be deputy governor, the de facto viceroy in Virginia, while the sinecure of titular governor went to the Earl of Orkney, who would divide the salary with Spotswood. Orkney had been influential in the Act of Union which joined England and Scotland in 1707 in the kingdom of Great Britain, and the English government still used the colonies for rewards to the politically deserving. Orkney, however, was not uninterested in the Colony, and he was Spotswood's official superior in more than a titular sense. Yet, though Spotswood observed all the amenities in exchanges with Orkney, his actual superior was the Board of Trade.

During the war the English government had paid little attention to the colonies, and colonial interests — the maintenance of a balance of trade for the benefit of Great Britain — had been left to the mercantile class which dominated the Board of Trade. While the welfare of England (especially its merchants and manufacturers) was the Board's primary consideration, its members were far removed from the shortsighted policies of milking the colonists that had prevailed under Charles II. As practical men of business, they recognized the importance of maintaining Virginia as a prosperous source. With the war causing financial tightening in the Colony as well as in England, the Board's concern about Virginia was essentially pragmatic : its operations should work profitably. In Alexander Spotswood, the Board had the ultimate pragmatist.

Striving to advance his own career, Spotswood committed himself to operating a successful colony like any executive committing himself to the efficiency and prosperity of the firm. With seventeen years in the army, Spotswood was accustomed to working through the channels of authority in a complicated organization. At the same time, independent-minded and shrewd, he could act flexibly in his own sphere, had no fear about assuming the responsibility for making decisions, and was so bold in taking the initiative that he pushed his instructions to the border line of discretion. He behaved with a forthrightness in manner and action which obscured a capacity for using in civil administration a military commander's method of plotting a campaign : he would make a reconnaissance of the enemy, coldly evaluate his own forces, and then devise a cause-and-effect strategy for achieving his objective with the most careful attention to tactics. To gain ends in which he believed, the Scotsman could be devious and unexpectedly expedient.

Spotswood's capacity for maneuvering was not suggested in his bluntly featured, soldierly appearance. His face, a thick-cheeked oblong, with a straight mouth of resolution and a straightforward gaze in his eyes, gave a false impression of stolidity. It also gave a very true impression of self-assured solidarity, which was not unlike that of Robert Carter. In fact, though they never became really intimates, there were many points of similarity between these two titans who were somewhat unwillingly to lock horns in the decisive struggle over the rule of Virginia.

2

There was no shadow of a conflict when Colonel Spotswood arrived in the James River on Her Majesty's ship *Deptford*. The man-of-war had come to convoy a homeward-bound tobacco fleet, protecting the merchant vessels from the enemy's privateers, and Spotswood spent the night of June 20 on board. The next morning he landed in the old capital of Jamestown with a pretty kinswoman, Mrs. Russell, who was to act as hostess of the bachelor governor's home. They were driven along the three miles of road built by Sir William Berkeley more than sixty years before, to the grassy terraces rising to the brick mansion of Green Spring.

In the great room where My Lady Frances had held her private court not too long before, British army Colonel Spotswood and his niece were received by colonial militia Colonel Ludwell and his lady. Nothing of a courtier, Ludwell (himself admitting his inadequacies for "polite conversation") soon braced the new governor on the subject of his replacing Edmund Jenings as secretary of the Colony. Though later Spotswood complained of Ludwell's crudeness as a person, on their first meeting the governor evidently found the master of Green Spring agreeable enough. Without committing himself, Spotswood privately favored Ludwell for the secretary's post.

During that day and the next, members of the Council and other persons of consequence arrived to pay their respects to Colonel Spotswood and Mrs. Russell. The governor was noticed for his fine military bearing and his courtesy. William Byrd, whose formal appointment to the Council coincided with Spotswood's arrival, formed the impression that he "seemed to be a very good man." That evening when Ludwell brought in musicians and the party danced a minuet, the governor showed himself to be a gallant with the ladies. The windows were open to let in the summer night air, and the governor and his niece showed social fortitude in appearing to ignore the Tidewater mosquitoes, of whose bites even the natives complained.

The next morning, June 23, Robert Carter and the other councilors escorted the governor to Williamsburg. Council President Jenings, who had not joined the party at Green Spring, formally met Colonel Spotswood outside of town, and the cavalcade passed a crowd of people gathered to see the new governor. Without bands, the dignitaries moved past the college building, now in the process of being rebuilt, and turned into the broad Duke of Gloucester Street.

In the mile between the college and the facing Capitol, and along the two parallel side streets, new houses gave the pleasing impression of a prosperous rural center. The homes, set back from the street in gardens then in full flower, were mostly frame, one-story and dormer in lines of simple grace. Scattered among them, with no divisions between business and residential, were several one-story ordinaries,

The College of William and Mary (Courtesy of the Virginia State Library)

*Bruton Parish Church
(Courtesy of the Virginia
State Library)*

The Capitol, Williamsburg (Colonial Williamsburg photograph)

The General Court Chamber, the Capitol, Williamsburg
(Photographed by Stephen M. Toth, Colonial Williamsburg)

The Council Chamber (above) *and*
the Meeting Hall of the House of Burgesses (below),
the Capitol, Williamsburg (*Colonial Williamsburg photographs*)

the coffeehouse where councilors met when government business was over, and larger taverns and inns which, like rooming houses or small residential hotels, provided lodgings for members of the General Assembly during Public Times. Various artisans, such as bootmakers and wigmakers and armorers, hung out pictured signs from the doorways of their shops. The small brick church of Bruton Parish faced a green which jutted off from Duke of Gloucester Street and led to the beginnings of construction on a new house for the governor. Ahead of the party, fine crested carriages, drawn by two or four or even six horses, pitched and rolled on the sandy street beside produce-laden wagons, and among them rode horsemen, keeping their mounts' unshod hooves out of the ruts.

At the end of the street, the governor's party turned into the courtyard of the new two-story red-brick Capitol, imposing by local standards. The H-shaped building in modified Renaissance style (without colonnades or an elaborate facade) was rounded in the front of the two wings, with arched windows, and above the connecting center rose a cupola, with the town's clock that struck the hours. No one could guess what the new arrival had expected in a colony, or his reactions to what he saw.

Inside, they mounted the stairs above the General Court to the handsomely paneled Council room. There Spotswood made a brief "courteous speech," saying mostly that he had come to do the Queen and country service, and hoped the councilors would all concur with him in that "good design." Then President Jenings treated them all to dinner at a public place, and from there they went to Jenings's house to drink French wine to the Queen's health. During this informal and friendly induction, it can be assumed that Alexander Spotswood made the same appraisal of the men with whom he was to govern as he had of Ludwell.

Shortly after he was settled, the governor received a surprising visit from Edmund Jenings. It would appear that the Council president, in his disassociation from King Carter's group, was trying to establish a quick alliance with the royal governor. He privately offered his services to Spotswood and presumed to advise him on methods of handling the Council.

Already knowing that Ludwell was after Jenings's post of secretary, Spotswood needed no great astuteness to recognize that the Council president was maneuvering in his own interests outside the oligarchy. Spotswood wrote of Jenings's "advice" to Nathaniel Blakiston, the Virginia agent in London and a friend of Ludwell. Blakiston immediately wrote Philip Ludwell that Jenings had advanced to Spotswood "some schemes of politics how he was to manage the Council, but they were so preposterous that Col. S. must have held him in much contempt for his wild notions."

Jenings's maladroit maneuvering did sour Spotswood on him as secretary. The new governor had a fetish about efficiency and he placed no confidence in the president for the important post which carried with it an office on the ground floor of the Capitol. Jenings justified Spotswood's judgment when the following year he took leave to look after private affairs in England. As he prepared to sail, Spotswood urged him to appoint Philip Ludwell as deputy secretary during his absence. Jenings refused.

At this point in his life, not quite fifty, Colonel Jenings began to reveal that his growing debts were impairing his judgment. It turned out that among his "private affairs" in England was the obtainment of the agency for the Northern Neck Proprietary, then held by Robert Carter. The fifth Lord Fairfax had died in 1710, leaving a sixteen-year-old son. Fairfax's widow, the daughter of Lord Culpeper, felt that her son was too young to be able to get more revenues out of the Proprietary and, in chronic hard straits, turned for advice to R. Clayton. Wanting to justify himself by action, Clayton wrote Lady Fairfax that she was not well served by Micajah Perry, "a sharp man," and "his friend" Robert Carter. Actually, at that period Carter was turning over to the Proprietors £684 a year.

When Lady Fairfax directed Clayton to change agents, he went to Thomas Corbin, who suggested his brother-in-law Edmund Jenings and his nephew, young Thomas Lee. It was not established that Jenings went to England with the specific purpose of obtaining the Proprietary agency, but the changes being made by Lady Fairfax were certainly known to him when he sailed. Jenings agreed to pay the Proprietors a set annual fee of £425, and as this was £159 less than Carter paid in commissions, presumably Jenings agreed to pay some percentage in addition.

It was a foolish move by Jenings, whose freedom from "entangling alliances" had apparently given him the delusion that he was also free of the reach of the men in the alliances. Already deeply in debt to Micajah Perry, he stayed in London to straighten out his finances and tried to supervise the Proprietary from there. To Thomas Lee, twenty-one the year he received Jenings's power of attorney (1711), went the job of removing the books and records from Carter's offices at Corotoman.

Young Lee was a throwback to his grandfather, Richard Lee I, and similar to middle-aged Robert Carter in his ambitious concepts of personal empire. The transfer of the Proprietary papers from Corotoman was the first of many exchanges, unmarked by warmth, between him and King Carter. Carter and his clerks evidently did not put themselves out to help Lee sort and cart the papers away, for although Carter relinquished the agency in 1712, the new agents did not issue their first patent until September, 1713.

Robert Carter expressed no displeasure at losing the cash income and land acquisition from the Proprietary agency. But Colonel Edmund Jenings had grown very confused indeed if he thought, as he apparently did, that the "King" accepted his removal from the agency in kindly spirit. Jenings so lost touch with the realities that he later turned to Carter to borrow money on mortgages against his property, and signed the papers for his own ruin.

More immediately Spotswood, supported by Blakiston, recommended to the Board of Trade that Jenings be removed as secretary on the grounds of his absence, and be replaced by Dr. William Cocke. Since Dr. Cocke had the advantage of permanent residence in Williamsburg, the Board gave him Jenings's job in 1712. Before that, in order to advance Ludwell, Spotswood and Blakiston had supported him for the post of auditor, the other half of the job formerly held by William Byrd I. Ludwell was appointed in 1711.

In this first move, Spotswood acted without regard to the oligarchy members on the Council or to the powerfully connected families in the ruling class. Dr. Cocke was no more a part of any combine than Jenings and became a warmly personal supporter of the governor. In his commitment to building an efficient operation, Spotswood removed Gawin Corbin, of the Lee-Corbin merchant family, from his post as naval officer (collector) of the Rappahannock. He charged Corbin with forging a date on a royal license to permit the *Robinson,* of which he was part owner, to sail without a protective convoy. Corbin went to England in an effort to clear himself of the charge, but he was not restored. Later Spotswood removed the collector of the Lower James for "incompetence."

When Robert Carter and his friends showed no resentment at these isolated measures, Spotswood began his administration by underestimating the unified strength that could be mustered by what he came to call "the party." It happened that the oligarchy felt no direct threat from Spotswood's early moves. Gawin Corbin, with all his powerful connections, was not allied with any of the families in the network spreading from the bloc in the Council. Nor, in this period of amity, did the new governor show any more disposition to challenge the oligarchy's control than had Major Nott. He was still feeling his way with the colonial government while concentrating his attention on problems which he regarded as consequential to the well-being of Virginia, and indirectly to the interests of the whole colonial system.

3

In his first meeting with the House of Burgesses in October, 1710, Alexander Spotswood showed outwardly a friendly attitude, which did not fully reflect his feelings about these outspoken representatives of colonial government. In no way reverting to royal prerogative, the European simply judged the colonial Burgesses to be, as a body, unqualified to exercise the responsibility he knew they insisted upon. By the standards of Spotswood's cosmopolitan view, many of these weather-beaten Virginia freeholders were not qualified to execute the broad continental policies Spotswood had in mind. Nor would their attitudes, expressed in a system evolved from local custom, qualify the Burgesses as a body to function efficiently in the organization he demanded.

Spotswood recognized that the Burgesses felt the same sense of self-sufficiency shown by the Council and indeed came close to regarding the General Assembly as the equivalent of Parliament in managing their internal affairs. Though no member made such a direct claim, the Burgesses — as Spotswood later accused them — acted as if they arrogated to themselves the rights of the House of Commons.

In the proper system of organization, as Spotswood conceived it, the provincial body was subordinate to and not collateral with Parliament.

Also, Marlborough's ex-deputy quartermaster general very definitely regarded the burgesses as individually inferior to English M.P.'s. While the House of Commons drew its members from an established gentry, many deriving from younger branches of the peerage, the burgesses would come largely under the English classifications "Freeholders of the Larger Sort" and "Freeholders of the Lesser Sort" (yeomen) — and colonials at that.

In that 1710 meeting on the ground floor of the Capitol, there were a number of colonial gentlemen of substance and education, belonging to or allied with the most powerful families in the oligarchy. William Randolph II would later become a councilor, as would Henry

Harrison and Peter Beverley, whom Spotswood liked. Henry Fitz-hugh's brother would rise to the Council, and Nathaniel Burwell's father, Major Lewis Burwell, was a councilor when he died that year. The local prominence of individuals, however, did not influence Spotswood's opinion of the shortsighted provincialism of the Colony's representative body. And their capacity for assertiveness was evident in the self-reliance in their tawny faces, the straight-on gazes in their resolute eyes, the confident movements of their lithe, toughened bodies — developed not in grouse shooting or cross-country canters, but in tobacco planting in all weather, in Indian fighting, even in four-day rides on horseback to Williamsburg.

They were a breed who were beginning to refer to men like Spotswood as "Englishmen" and no longer spoke of England as "back home." They were Virginians, whose parents and kinspeople had begun to emerge as a separate people during Bacon's Rebellion. With their interests and allegiances following their identification with the local, they were products of a New World who looked without deference at a "gentleman" of an Old World culture.

Yet Spotswood wanted to work with them. He wanted them to go along with his system of organization for his large-scale plans for building a successful colony. He gave only one warning. They passed laws vainly, he said, "if they square not either with the prerogatives of the Crown or with the interests of the country which protects us." For the rest, he talked of simple matters: he recommended improving the militia, strengthening defenses against England's enemies, and speeding the work on building the house for the governor.

Shortly before Spotswood had come, a Negro and an Indian had been convicted of plotting an insurrection on Easter and had been executed. Their severed heads had been "set up" for public display, the Indian's in Williamsburg. Referring to this event, Spotswood advocated laws to prohibit slaves from meeting in large gatherings.

Then, coming closer to the Virginians' deepest interests, he explained that the recent drop in tobacco prices was caused by "the unhappy state of Europe," a concatenation of factors resulting from the long war. England's war with Louis XIV (which would not end until 1713) curtailed the tobacco market with France at the same time that the support of armies demanded more government revenue. The war between Charles XII and Peter the Great had hurt the Baltic market, while Holland was beginning to grow tobacco in some volume for the European market. When Virginia shipments to England increased, the London merchants had been caught in a squeeze.

The merchants were required to post a bond for duties to be paid within eighteen months on the tobacco they handled. In those eighteen months, a merchant had to pay the costs of unlading and relading tobacco, port and warehouse charges, and similar costs. When the tobacco was sold, the merchant was reimbursed for these charges, and he paid the duties which cancelled his bond. However, if the tobacco remained unsold in England more than the eighteen months, the merchant was required to pay interest on the amount of the bond covering the duties. To stay within the eighteen months, the merchants got rid of the tobacco as quickly as possible. When they had to accept less for the tobacco in order to make a quick sale, the planters got less for their crops — since every expense was paid before the tobacco grower got his share.

The Virginians contended that the high government revenues — 6½ pence per pound of tobacco — were responsible for the low take left over for the tobacco growers. This was true enough, but as Spotswood and the home government saw it, sacrifices were necessary to maintain England in her international struggle, the outcome of which would affect the colonies.

The colonials were hardest to reach on the subject of the effect on themselves of England's European involvement. Spotswood tried to bring it home by pointing to the French on the same continent. While Holland had long since withdrawn from New York and Spain was not aggressive, France was established in Canada and the Mississippi Valley and was determined to build a North American empire. England's naval superiority was the guarantee of the colonies' protection. Though this left to the colonists the burden of defense against all manner of land attacks, the English men-of-war were a symbol of England's protection.

In talking of this background, the main impression Spotswood gave to the General Assembly was of his genuine interest in Virginia's welfare. There was nothing political in his approach: he was speaking with complete sincerity. William Byrd recorded that the speech was delivered "with the best grace I ever saw anybody speak in my life."

During the following period, while the General Assembly remained in session, the new governor continued to strengthen the favorable personal impression he had already made on the councilors. Kindly in all his dealings, the "polite scholar," as an admirer called him, entertained at his house in a manner not seen for years and — as he proudly pointed out — at his own expense. The governor occasionally had Robert Carter in for dinner and served French wine and claret to the connoisseur. Other councilors were also well dined by the governor, and Byrd — who was experimenting with a diet of a one-dish meal — noted that ''we had eight dishes besides the desert.''

Spotswood had become friendly with Byrd before the General Assembly convened, visiting him at Westover on the occasion of presenting the new councilor to the county militia as their colonel and commander in chief. A few days after the governor's opening address, Spotswood and Byrd served as godfathers and Mrs. Ludwell as god-mother at the christening of Daniel Parke Custis, son of John Custis and Byrd's sister-in-law, Frances Parke Custis.

The governor was frequently present at impromptu social gather-ings of the other councilors in Williamsburg. He seldom joined them at the coffeehouse where Robert Carter and William Byrd usually ate their supper together, often with one or more of their fellow counci-lors. Sometimes they played cards, and though the stakes were not high, an evening's casual losses would have equaled the year's earn-ings of a hard-pressed yeoman.

During the winter Spotswood gave a great ball on the occasion of the Queen's birthday. In a heavy rain, the ladies and gentlemen began to arrive in their coaches at his house during the day. Colonel and Mrs. Carter brought one of their daughters with them. Mrs. Byrd was still smoldering from having been overruled in her desire to pluck her eyebrows, and her husband was sniffling with a cold. After the party had supper at seven o'clock, they all drove in their coaches through the rain the short distance to the unheated Capitol. The musicians were ready, and the governor opened the ball by dancing a French dance with Mrs. Byrd. Byrd then danced with Mrs. Russell, the gov-ernor's pretty niece. After a time, they warmed up with country dances and, as always, Colonel Spotswood ''was very gallant to the ladies and very courteous to the gentlemen.'' The party did not break up until two o'clock.

Robert Carter and his wife and daughter took Commissary Blair in their carriage, as Mrs. Blair's addiction to the bottle had kept her away from the affair. The wind in the rain frightened the Carters' carriage horses and they became too unruly to drive. One of the gen-tlemen present volunteered and led the horses out of the Capitol yard and down the dark street to the Blairs' house. Colonel Carter did not keep a house in Williamsburg. When alone in town at Public Times, he rented a chamber in one of the houses which served as residential taverns; when his family came in the ''chariot'' to a social function, they stayed with friends, as was the general custom.

In the relaxed atmosphere of that first session in Williamsburg, Colonel Carter had nothing more momentous to report than that he had ordered militia to patrol the head of the. Rappahannock, where Indians had been seen. Spotswood wrote to Carter approving of the action and suggested that he send immediate notice if the Indians "should commit any acts of hostility, that further care might be taken for the protection of the inhabitants."

During this stage, Governor Spotswood was being drawn into those intercolonial problems that were to occupy the center of his attention for the next three years of his administration.

4

Adjoining Virginia's illy defined southern border, North Carolina was under a separate administration from South Carolina and in all practical aspects a separate colony under the Proprietors (of Charles II's grant of 1663). While the port city of Charleston, built in 1670, became a trading center for the prosperous plantations in South Carolina's low country (similar to Virginia's Tidewater country), North Carolina did not have a port of its own for oceangoing vessels and thus did not develop a stable plantation society. What little tobacco North Carolina did raise was sold to New England trading vessels plying the sounds between the coast and the Atlantic, and other produce for export went through Norfolk, on the south bank of the James where the Virginia river entered the bay. Under these conditions, North Carolina was weakly administered, its backcountry scarcely at all — and this concerned Virginia.

Because of the loose administration of the backcountry, this area had long been a sanctuary for runaway indentures from Virginia. With easier terms for settling land than in Virginia, the backcountry also attracted those borderline-subsistence families who wanted few or no restrictions; many settled as no more than squatters. Since the border between the colonies was uncertain and disputed, these mostly slovenly, unambitious settlers subsisted in a shadowy world of their own. Spotswood had sent a commission, headed by Philip Ludwell and Nathaniel Harrison, to meet a North Carolina commission over settlement of the border, but nothing came of it.

Then in 1711 an insurrectionist named Thomas Cary tried to overthrow North Carolina's new governor, Edward Hyde, and incited the fierce Tuscaroras along with a number of Negroes, some of whom were fugitive slaves. Spotswood acted promptly. He sent marines to

Pamlico Sound where Thomas Cary had fled. When Cary slipped away and came into Virginia, he was captured and sent to England. By then the Tuscaroras were literally on the warpath. The Indians ravaged North Carolina's western frontier, killing two hundred settlers and making a prisoner of Baron Christoph de Graffenreid, who had established a settlement of Swiss. When famine and pestilence began to spread, the backcountry denizens appealed to Virginia for help.

Finding Virginians unmoved by this appeal, Spotswood determined to help for reasons of "enlightened self-interest." (The Board of Trade commended him for his decision.) Spotswood saw that with North Carolina collapsing, Virginians were not safe from the Indians, and their trade with the Cherokees — a strong factor in the Colony's prosperity — would be threatened. As it was, South Carolina officials were already making trouble for the Virginia traders crossing their western territory.

With no support from the General Assembly, Spotswood ordered out the militia to prevent the tributary Indians from joining the hostiles. Then he managed to separate the peaceful Tuscaroras from those on the warpath. After making a separate treaty with the peaceful Tuscaroras, Spotswood planned to send the militia into North Carolina to help the settlers against the Tuscaroras still ravaging there. At this point Spotswood came up against the shortsighted, self-centered local interest which he found prevalent in all the colonies.

The House of Burgesses, with a tricky maneuver, made it impossible for the governor to get the money for the troops to leave Virginia. When Spotswood appealed to North Carolina, Governor Hyde refused to provide either money or supplies for the Virginia militia (he was probably unable to), and Spotswood was powerless. South Carolina dispatched a force which drove off the Indians, without a decisive defeat, but the next year (1712) her governor took the House of Burgesses' attitude that the North Carolinians deserved any misfortune which befell them. By this time rumors were reaching Williamsburg that the Tuscaroras were to be joined by the Five Nations from New York and that the French were encouraging the Iroquois to rise. It was then that Spotswood, unable to get money to provide for the militia in the field, wrote to London his true opinion of the colonial representative government.

The constitution, he wrote, "allows to every one, though but just out of the condition of a servant, and that can but purchase ½ acre of land, an equal vote with the man of the best estate . . ." with the result that "the mob of the country . . ." usually elected "repre-sentatives of their own class."

Without trying to be tactful, Spotswood made a second appeal for money, only money, to help the neighboring colonists. Though the House of Burgesses grudgingly voted £1,000 for relief of the North Carolina backcountry, Spotswood could do nothing to arouse the General Assembly to "enlightened self-interest." The truth was that since the Colony's exploitation by Charles II the people, as Governor Berkeley had said, regarded any "good" done them by the Crown as done against their will. By Spotswood's day the General Assembly had become thoroughly experienced in thwarting governors' attempts to encroach on their control of the power to disburse revenues.

Spotswood did not look back to the genesis of the representatives' resistance and, besides, all the colonies were local-minded. However, with his international point of view, the governor was very clear-sighted in recognizing the danger that would be presented to the colonial system by the collapse of North Carolina. A physical gap would be opened between Virginia and South Carolina, in which the French could infiltrate from the west, and the coastal region would provide a haven for privateers and pirates. Working independently, Spotswood opened negotiations with South Carolina to initiate joint operations to remove the Indians from North Carolina's western frontier.

After a South Carolina force inflicted a heavy defeat on the hostile Tuscaroras in 1713, when the Indians shifted north to harass the Virginia border, Spotswood was ready with tributary tribes formed under white scouts. The hostile Tuscaroras were divided and tracked down. Having earlier made peace with some of the Tuscaroras, Spotswood made a treaty with the die-hard elements and allotted them a hunting ground.

When the Tuscaroras broke the treaty within a year, the Bur-gesses were willing to vote for an all-out war against them. Spotswood, humanely as well as practically concerned about developing good rela-tions with all Indians, appealed to the Burgesses' interest in trade. He had already discovered a new route to the Cherokee villages which would avoid South Carolina's territory. Since the power of the frag-mented Tuscaroras was declining, Spotswood correctly believed that it would be sufficient to establish a fort facing the Tuscaroras' approach from the south. The Burgesses went along with the building of a fort and a school for Indian children beside a Saponi Indian village on the Meherrin River.

Spotswood had then achieved his purpose of making North Carolina safe. Between South Carolina's fighting the Tuscaroras and Spotswood's success in separating the Indians, many of whom were contained, a larger contribution to the Colony's welfare had been accomplished than Spotswood's contemporaries appreciated. Besides the colonials' typical indifference to their fellows, the governor's operations with the Indians led to his passage of an Indian Act (1713), which antagonized the Burgesses. In time, the Indian Act, which formed a Virginia Indian Company as a controlling agency for trade and relations, would be joined by an act for the control of shipping tobacco, which antagonized just about everybody in the Colony.

While the two Acts were part of Spotswood's policy for Virginia's welfare and progress, the ambitious Scotsman was a man in a hurry, and — with the intercolonial problem behind him — he made the fundamental mistake of moving against the country's unwritten laws of custom.

After his great, and greatly unappreciated, accomplishment outside Virginia, from the day he was free to concentrate his energies on the Colony, all harmony between "the polite scholar" and the General Assembly ceased.

5

Robert Carter and his councilor friends were not directly involved in the governor's clash with the Burgesses over the Tobacco Act. Spotswood claimed that they secretly incited the Burgesses, and there was no question about the general distaste for the Tobacco Act passed in 1713. For one thing, Spotswood's timing was bad.

The war with Louis XIV ended that year, without bringing any relief to the tobacco growers. Shortly after Spotswood had come to Williamsburg, the English government, in its pinch for revenues, had demanded that London merchants pay duties on imported tobacco as soon as the duties fell due. This meant such a big layout of cash before the merchants collected anything on the tobacco that some merchants could not even have the ships unloaded. Micajah Perry informed the Board of Trade that ships with more than six thousand hogsheads on them had lain in the Thames as long as twenty months. When the tobacco was either not sold or sold for little more than the duties and fixed charges, the small planters could establish no credit against which to import needed goods. To keep themselves out of rags, some colonists turned to homespun — which, of course, displeased English manufacturers. After the war ended, the tobacco duties measure was rescinded for the relief of the merchants — who were again allowed eighteen months — but the effect was not yet being felt in Virginia when Spotswood came forward with his revolutionary change for tobacco shipping.

Spotswood's Tobacco Act called for the mandatory use of forty public warehouses, to be built at or near shipping points, where all tobacco was to be brought and examined before being exported or offered for legal tender. Examining agents would give certificates specifying weight and type of tobacco, oronoco or sweet-scented, and they would be empowered to eliminate inferior tobacco. In theory, the plan would serve two basic purposes: as legal tender, the standardized certificates would simplify the payment of quitrents, clergy's salaries, officers' fees and the like; and the elimination of inferior tobacco would decrease the volume of exports and tend to raise prices more quickly. Also, ship-loading from the vicinity of the forty public warehouses would make exporting a more efficient operation and simplify the supervision of the naval collectors. While this whole conception reflected Spotswood's need for system, at the same time he was aware of the people's resistance to anything like a government agency supplanting their accustomed practices.

Before he presented the bill to the General Assembly, he made the first large-scale use of patronage in the first body of popular government in North America: of the forty agents to be appointed to the job, which paid £250 a year, he chose twenty-seven burgesses — a majority in the House. Not knowing of this maneuver, his advisers on the Board of Trade thought his act had no chance of passing. When his measure went through, Spotswood wrote that it was "looked upon to be the most extraordinary one that had ever passed a Virginia Assembly." Not incidentally, Micajah Perry — who had the ear of the Board of Trade — contracted to sell the huge weighing-scales to the newly appointed agents, who had to pay for them out of their own pockets.

The act was approved by the councilors largely because they would not be personally disturbed by it. The big merchant-planters among them would continue to ship from their private wharves, and they grew little or no inferior tobacco. Also, Robert Carter had received favors from Spotswood before his temporary loss of the Proprietary's agency. Spotswood, he wrote, "always favored me . . . in the nomination of our northern sheriff, which is some kindness to me in getting in our quit-rents.'' Anyway, Carter and the other shippers may well have suspected that government red tape would soon bring about the collapse of Spotswood's system designed for efficiency.

Things in Virginia seemed to work best when they evolved of themselves. While nothing had come of any of the Crown's orders to build ports, where good harbors existed towns came into being — as at Norfolk on the south bank of the James, Yorktown on the south bank of the York, and Hobbes' Hole (later Tappahannock) upriver from Corotoman on the south bank of the Rappahannock. Since William Byrd I had died there was public shipping on the north bank of the James at The Falls, an outpost which soon would grow into the city of Richmond.

Spotswood's coup was the costliest victory with which he had ever been associated. Except for the very big planters who shipped from their own wharves, everybody complained about the trouble of rolling tobacco to inconvenient warehouses, the extra charges, and the losses of revenue on the poorer grades of tobacco. What had seemed a fine scheme to boost tobacco prices in the future, by decreasing exports, resulted in a lack of immediate income to the small planters in a year (1714) when the subsistence crop of corn happened to be low all over the Colony. A general resentment over the whole idea quickly spread, and the government's agents were looked upon as objects of personal disfavor. In 1715, when a new election was held for the House of Burgesses, twenty-one of the twenty-five counties demanded a repeal of the Tobacco Act in whole or in part.

Spotswood's reaction revealed a weakness within his system of efficiency: he took it very personally when the people's assertiveness opposed him as the Crown's representative. On the coming meeting of the General Assembly he wrote to Secretary Stanhope in July, 1715: ''I cannot forbear regretting that I must always have to do with the representatives of the vulgar people, and mostly with such people as are of their stamp & understanding. . . . So long as half an acre of land (which is of small value in this country) qualifies a man to be an elector, the meaner sort of people will ever carry the elections, and the humor generally runs to choose such men as are their most familiar companions, who very eagerly seek to be Burgesses merely for the lucre of the salary, and who, for fear of not being chosen again, dare in Assembly do nothing that may be disrelished out of the House by the common people. . . .''

With all his realism and real abilities, and his own personal in- volvement in Virginia — he began privately taking up land on his own in 1714 — Spotswood shared his predecessors' failure to validate the colonial representatives' sense that they should have "rights" different from those he thought they should have. Although Spotswood did not use royal prerogatives so much as a principle, he did rely on the Crown's authority to support him in getting his own way in measures he believed would restore Virginia's prosperity.

He was dealing with people who believed they knew more about their own colony than a "foreigner" did, and to whom "the Crown" was an abstraction. When Queen Anne died in 1713, the Stuart line, with which Virginians had been familiar since the founding of the Colony, came to an end. While George I, the new King, was a great-grandson of James I (a second cousin of Anne), he was a German-speaking Hanoverian who could in no sense be regarded as topmost in the English nobility. The Virginians might give their loyalty to the symbol of what had become the British Empire, but this symbol had nothing to do with the price of tobacco — which was where they lived.

In his denunciation of the Burgesses, Spotswood reflected the personal conditioning in England which had given him an aversion to a representative body answerable to "the mob." Much of what he complained of would have been true of any representative body. But in their generalities, Spotswood's lamentations told more about him than about the House of Burgesses.

There would have been few, if any, burgesses who needed the small per diem allowance for their sessions in Williamsburg, and the richer members of the House definitely did not fear the "disrelish" of "the common people": their county neighbors looked up to them. Actually, in using the generalities characteristic of men in political positions (and in his time men spoke with hyperbole and extravagance), the governor was outraged that the Virginians weighed his acts in the measure of their own experience rather than according to the perceptual views he had acquired in Europe. The gall of it was the colonial bumpkins' belief in the views formed by their own frontier experience, and their refusal to defer to his European enlightenment.

The agent Blakiston, who tried to keep on the good side of everybody, wrote to Philip Ludwell of the Governor: "That gentleman had really capacity and talents to manage in a high sphere but he adheres too much to his own sentiments sometimes and thinks himself ill used if everybody will not think as he does."

The ex-soldier Spotswood showed his rough side to the House of Burgesses in 1715. Once the burgesses got the idea of resistance in their heads, they became obstinate and assertive without much point. Spotswood dropped his courtier's tact. Speaking out of anger, he denounced the House with blunt invective. When they met his anger with stony stares, he dissolved the Assembly and sent the burgesses on their way with his insults ringing in their ears.

After this it was only a matter of time, two years, before the Assembly got his Tobacco Act repealed. It might have happened sooner, except that Micajah Perry did not support the repeal to the Board of Trade until the warehouse agents had paid him for the scales — souvenirs of their brief careers in a government agency. The Virginia Indian Company, formed by Spotswood's Indian Act, also was nullified by the obstructionist Assembly. The company, creating a monopoly, had run counter to the financial interests of too many individuals who were indifferent to the humane aspects of the governor's plan.

Ultimately, however, Spotswood's policy for efficiency was gutted when the governor aroused the opposition of the members of the oligarchy on the Council.

6

Spotswood made few tactical mistakes in his political maneuvers, but he made a major blunder when he took on the power bloc in the Council precisely when he needed the Council's support for his Tobacco and Indian acts.

These faulty tactics, reflecting Spotswood's hurry to introduce his own system, aimed at an objective which revealed his English-conditioned perception of colonials. Viewing Virginia as one detached dependent among other small dependencies in the great growth of the British Empire, he was annoyed at the people's defense of all their inefficient methods and at their laws based on the grounds that such-and-such "hath been the ancient custom." As the so-called King's Council had come to embody all the most virulent attitudes of local autonomy, Spotswood felt compelled to reduce the power of the party in the Colony to subordination to the representative of the King of the whole empire. When Spotswood reached this decision, he unintentionally brought on the deadly struggle over who was to rule Virginia's internal affairs.

Robert Carter's party and the Board of Trade thought that that question had been settled with Governor Nicholson. But Colonel

Spotswood, after three years in Williamsburg, came to believe that the presence of the power bloc on the Council was detrimental to the operation of his system for progress. As he àlways identified his measures with the Crown's prerogatives, he refused to accept the local situation in which Virginia, "the most English of the Colonies," declined to stand in awe of the King's prerogatives.

His specific grievance began when he found the councilors working hand in glove with the burgesses. He claimed that the councilors made a private distinction between their obligations as members of the King's Council and as members of the General Assembly. When assisting the governor on King's business, they acted as Englishmen loyal to the Crown; when operating with the burgesses in the General Assembly, they acted as Virginians with local loyalties. Indeed, he wrote home, when acting as members of the General Assembly, the councilors of the party "lay aside the obligations of those oaths as Councilors which give them title to act there. . . ." They were not willing ". . . to defend all jurisdiction and authorities appertaining to His Majesty." Instead, they agreed with the House of Burgesses in "matters prejudicial to His Majesty's prerogative and interest when these interfere with . . . the liberties which, by a long custom, without any lawful foundation, they have been used to. . . ."

Again and again, Spotswood wrote of his growing resentment at the power of custom. Virginians "look upon all persons not born in the Country as foreigners, and think that no other qualification is necessary for an employment . . . but that of being born in" the Colony. Though the members of the oligarchy took oaths of Supremacy, by "their actions they seem to allow no jurisdiction, civil or ecclesiastical, but what is established by laws of their own making. . . ."

Admitting that only three councilors held remunerative offices — those of secretary, receiver general, and auditor, among whom the secretary was actually an outsider of the governor's own appointment — he claimed that the widely spread connections of the oligarchy used the influence of nonprofit posts, such as militia officers and vestrymen, in opposing external authority. When the death of a councilor left a vacancy in 1714, Spotswood was outraged that the oligarchy's influence with the London merchants weighed more than his with the Board of Trade. He had recommended a man outside "the web of kinship," but the Board appointed Edmund Berkeley (Nicholson's former rival), of the Burwell-Harrison clan. Spotswood wrote the agent Blakiston: "I think it is doing little honor to the Gov't to have its council appointed in the Virginia Coffee House" in London, where merchants have "no other rule to judge of a man's merit than by the number of his tobacco hogsheads. . . ."

7

Spotswood chose for his test of strength the superficially simple issue of the councilors' exclusive right to compose the oyer and terminer courts. Simultaneously, however, he became embroiled in separate controversies with Ludwell and with Byrd, and these private feuds created an atmosphere of strife in which his test case with the party appeared more complicated and involved with personalities than, in actuality, it was.

His conflicts with Ludwell and Byrd began, justifiably enough, over the inefficient administration of their offices, those of receiver general and auditor general. Both men treated these positions as if they were sinecures. Spotswood's efforts to bring order to these important departments led first to personality clashes with the two gentlemen, and then to open enmity. The conflict with Ludwell ran parallel to the test case and was never involved with it. But Byrd sought to embroil the Council in his private feud by making common cause with the showdown over the oyer and terminer courts issue. For a couple of years there, Spotswood seemed to be fighting on all sides at once.

Yet neither Byrd nor Ludwell ever gained the support of the other councilors in their private fights. Robert Carter opposed Spotswood only as a member of the oligarchy and only over the specific issue of the courts. Though Spotswood, like Nicholson, regarded him as "haughty," King Carter never intruded any personality elements into the essentially political test of strength. The courteous Spotswood had not offended his sensibilities, his dignity of position, as had the intemperate Nicholson, and Carter was defending the status quo rather than, as against Nicholson, attacking to change the order.

He seemed to like the governor, and clearly he liked the heavy drinking conviviality of Public Times in Williamsburg as he had enjoyed them during the first years of Spotswood's administration. Before the controversies, Byrd recorded in his diary glimpses of the "King" after the Council meetings were over for the day.

He was happily "almost drunk" in his lodgings one afternoon in a party with Mrs. Churchill, his sister-in-law, Peter Beverley's wife, President Jenings, and John Clayton, a politically connected attorney. Another time his friends were "very merry with Colonel Carter" over a bowl of punch. Then there was the big night after the governor had dropped in on Carter and his friends at the coffeehouse. After the governor left, the councilors went on to Carter's lodgings where he served them a punch of French brandy with oranges. "We talked very lewdly and were almost drunk, and in that condition we went to the coffee house and played at dice and I lost £12. We stayed at the coffee house until almost four in the morning. . . ."

The next day, Byrd reported, "Colonel Carter and several others came to my lodgings to laugh at me for my disorder last night." After an informal session in the governor's house, Carter and his friends put away two bottles of claret each, and the next morning Colonel Carter "was very sick."

There were other days when he was sick without having been very merry. The diet of heavy food and wine was beginning to take its toll as he approached fifty. It was a time also when he was deeply concerned — even agitated — over the education of his older children, while his second wife Betty was giving him a new family of little children.

It was not that any elements in his personal life would have diverted Carter from locking horns with Spotswood, or anybody, if he had been aiming at some objective or had felt threatened. But though strain inevitably developed between the governor and the councilors, Carter's defense of the party's position did not engage him personally at the time when Ludwell and Byrd stirred up personal animosities.

Spotswood's conflict with Ludwell was two-pronged — over the way Ludwell handled his post and over that sensitive subject in Virginia, land. Philip Ludwell II had come into the valuable Green Spring estate through his father's marriage to Berkeley's widow. In Berkeley's time, the government had allotted 3,000 acres for the use of the governor, to which Berkeley had added 2,000 acres as his own property. Philip Ludwell II was as land-hungry as Carter, as the elder Byrd and Fitzhugh had been, and he had never refuted the charge that on importing forty indentures, entitling him to 2,000 acres, he had added a zero to increase the grant to 20,000. Among Ludwell's holdings was property in and around Williamsburg, where he would build a handsome brick house in 1717. This property included fifty acres near the governor's house, then being completed under Spotswood's direction. The trouble started when Spotswood applied to England for permission to exchange the fifty acres adjoining the governor's house for fifty acres in the government's demesne at Green Spring.

Though this was agreeable to all, when the Green Spring property was surveyed the government's 3,000 acres were discovered to have shrunk to 2,400. As the government's demesne was enclosed by natural boundaries on three sides, adjoining Ludwell's private property on the fourth, Spotswood concluded that the land had "eroded" to Ludwell. This was in the fateful year of 1713, when the governor threw down the gauntlet to the party.

At the time when the governor and Ludwell were carrying on their Green Spring dispute, which led to a law suit in 1716, Colonel Spotswood began to demand of Ludwell and Byrd more system in handling their accounts as auditor general and receiver general. These demands were part of his total reforms for increasing revenue, particularly through the proper collection of quitrents. Toward that end, the orderly-minded Spotswood had put through various land acts designed to get vacant areas under cultivation. Spotswood had no objection to large landholding as such: all during his controversies, his own holdings were growing in central Virginia in what was then the western part of the Colony. For reasons of colonial development as well as revenue, he passed laws that required holdings to be actually settled (not given just the token "seating" of a shack and a few hogs running wild), and he felt that the governor should control the right of disposing of escheated land.

In connection with Byrd's and Ludwell's collections of quitrents, Spotswood pointed out the haphazard methods of collecting practiced by sheriffs' deputies, and the leniency of sheriffs toward "concealed lands" (holdings on which no quitrents were paid). Spotswood discovered that county officers were apt to look the other way for the small landholders during hard times, and for the big landholders all the time. Also in hard times the collectors were inclined to accept inferior grades of tobacco from the small freeholders as quitrents.

As the sheriffs' reports were handled in bulk and not broken down by individual taxpayers, so the auditor general and receiver general handled their accounts in bulk, without a breakdown for individual sheriffs' lists. Spotswood ordered the sheriffs to break down their reports, so as to uncover concealed lands and poor-grade tobacco, and ordered Ludwell and Byrd to provide accounts in detail. In demanding that the auditor general and receiver general do actual bookkeeping, Spotswood was asking only that the councilors do the work for which they received the revenue. Byrd protested at the imposition in fairly purple prose, while Ludwell simply ignored the instructions and went on as before.

This was the official situation between Spotswood and Ludwell when the governor's law case against the Green Spring property came to a strange kind of trial in 1716. A jury of freeholders went down to Green Spring to look over the land, to form their opinion of the instructions for the surveyors. Spotswood lost his temper at them as they debated the matter, and denounced them as a "Chickahominy jury"— from the upper waters of this river, where the low-lying ground was swampy and offered refuge to various undesirables of the Colony. Ludwell accused Spotswood of browbeating the jurymen and spoke angrily to the governor in a highly inappropriate manner.

Spotswood wrote the Board of Trade that he was treated "with more rudeness and ill manners than I believe any governor ever was treated," and asked "a suitable reparation for an affront done me in my public capacity, which I should not have acquiesced under had it been offered to me as a private person."

No reparation was made, nor did Ludwell heed his kinsmen's advice to apologize. The Board of Trade let slide the profitless dispute over Green Spring, in which no honor accrued to either man. By then Spotswood and Philip Ludwell had developed a deeply personal antipathy. Spotswood wrote the Board of Trade that the Ludwell family "have never suffered any governor to be at ease after he once began to enquire into their title" to Green Spring, and they had "fomented and carried on . . . all the clamours raised against" former governors.

Then, returning to the auditor-general matter, he sent Ludwell a copy of his instructions, which required that the accounts be kept in separate, orderly books and specify each sum raised and disposed of. Ludwell ignored him. Spotswood asked if he intended to comply. Ludwell evaded by saying that he could not change his methods without instructions from William Blathwayt, the colonial auditor general in London. At this, Spotswood suspended Ludwell (May 24, 1716) and Blathwayt removed him from the office.

Spotswood gained personal satisfaction and efficiency in the auditor general's office, at the cost of increasing his enemies. Ludwell's nephew John Grymes became auditor general and, while scrupulously following instructions, became the governor's bitter opponent in the House of Burgesses. Ludwell was implacable.

8

While Ludwell (whom Spotswood regarded as "uncouth") was a truculent colonial squire accustomed to getting his own way in his

William Byrd II (Courtesy of the Virginia State Library)

own neighborhood, William Byrd was a subtler man of a larger world, whose ambitions were both grander and vaguer.

At a time in Western Europe when men newly ascended into the status of gentleman obscured their origins and invented backgrounds, the second William Byrd developed an "image" which, by writing his own epitaph, he palmed off on posterity.

As Byrd saw himself, among his greatest achievements was his friendship with titled Englishmen of letters. He gave two lines in stone (in his epitaph) to Charles Boyle, the third Earl of Orrery, and no mention of his own father. "This well-bred gentleman," he wrote of himself, was "born to one of the amplest fortunes in this country." That is to say, his father, the son of a London goldsmith, had made a fortune as a frontier trader in anything from slaves to weapons for Indians. "He studied for some time in the Low Countries" was Byrd's euphemism for the year his merchant father forced him to study Dutch business methods. "Thus eminently fitted for the service and ornament of his country, he was made Receiver-General of His Majesty's revenue here." This was Byrd's version of being forced by his father's death to leave London for Virginia, where, after first finagling in vain for the post of governor, he inherited half of the office held by his unmentioned father. He omitted his later sale of this office for £500, which "the splendid economist" — as he called himself — needed for debts.

"To all this were added a great elegance of taste and of life." Though he had copulated with streetwalkers in London parks and could not keep his hands off house-servants, these habits of lust would not conflict with elegance of taste in the bawdy age in which he grew up and ultimately, his "great elegance . . . of life" formed the totally real elements in his self-image.

In his idealized version of himself, Byrd envisioned the complete Renaissance man. But he was not a builder. Actually, he was a custodian of the mercantile-planting estate his father had developed, and his personal diaries contained extremely sparse references to business. When a ship went down off Margate Roads with twenty hogsheads of his tobacco and seven of skins, he wrote: "The Lord giveth and the Lord has taken away." Months went by without another reference to shipping or the plantation.

As a second-generation rich man, Byrd had rare gifts of self-expression, in speaking and in writing, and he had acquired, through his early intimacy with English peers, the tastes usually associated with the "aristocrat" of ancient pedigree. Not a typical product of

Virginia, he was a learned, charming, witty, returned expatriate who happened to inherit powerful home connections: essentially he was, as he saw himself, ''an ornament'' to the Colony.

Those councilors who, like Robert Carter, found him a genial tavern companion and a good man at a party, did not regard him as fundamentally different from themselves. They had all enjoyed the same advantages, including school in England, and had chosen for themselves careers in the Colony's ruling class. Byrd's brother-in-law, Robert Beverley the historian, looked on him, with his English pre-dilections, as an ''arrant social climber.'' Himself a cold man, over-bearing to those considered his inferiors and grasping for fees, Beverley might have resented Byrd's graces. For Byrd was unlike the busily occupied merchant-planters who had solidified the power structure in the oligarchy, in that he used the command of time — which he inherited — to pursue his dilettante inclinations, his cultivation of elegance, and to indulge himself in a love of pleasure.

Regularly reading Greek, Latin, Hebrew and Italian, Byrd liked to play at writing. Not sufficiently secure in his gentleman-scholar's status in the great world to risk publication, he wrote constantly in his diary and experimented with various prose pieces. ''I read,'' he recorded, ''some of my own work to the ladies.''

He also recorded his less savory episodes with the ladies. Once, during a Public Times in Williamsburg, he returned to his lodgings to find his sister-in-law, Frances Custis, and Mrs. Charles Chiswell with his wife. They played at some game which led him to kiss Mrs. Chiswell. ''I kissed her on the bed till she was angry and my wife was also uneasy about it, and cried as soon as the company was gone. I neglected to say my prayers, which I should not have done, because I ought to beg pardon for the lust I had for another man's wife.'' After this obeisance to his conscience, Byrd, sanguine and unintrospective, typically recorded: ''However I had good health, good thoughts, and good humor, thanks be to God Almighty.''

Lucy Byrd was by no means neglected by his lust for others: he faithfully recorded his episodes of making love to his wife at all hours of the day and night, and in any place that happened to be convenient.

In no sense addicted to gambling and never losing heavily (in proportion to his means), Byrd passed considerable time with dice and at card-playing. At home he played piquet, and also liked to play billiards. And he was always ready to turn a casual gathering — as when several visitors appeared near mealtime — into a party that could go on into the next day. He was most intimate with his Harrison neighbors, at adjoining Berkeley Hundred, and across the river at

Brandon, with Richard Bland and William Randolph's family, and with Colonel and Mrs. William Bassett of the Burwell-Harrison clan. Joanna Burwell Bassett was the sister of Mrs. Edmund Berkeley, of the widow of Benjamin Harrison III, and of Nathaniel Burwell, Robert Carter's son-in-law.

The social movement of William and Lucy Byrd at the very center of the oligarchic families could give the impression that Byrd personally was a stronger force than he was in actuality. One of the powers by virtue of his inherited position and wealth, he was prominent among them by virtue of his social presence, and historically he became disproportionately prominent by virtue of posthumously published writings and deciphered diaries. But Byrd was something of a personal adventurer, not motivated by a steadfast sense of obligation to the society. Always there was the element of the dandy, in it for himself. Being clever as well as highly articulate, on the Council he acted as an intelligent collaborator — up to a point. This point was soon reached when he indulged in an indiscreet comment concerning the governor, and was betrayed by his own self-image into the delusion that he was larger than Spotswood.

Since Byrd had tried to get the governorship for himself, from the beginning he had regarded Alexander Spotswood as an equal who had been his successful rival for the same job. In the early days of Spotswood's administration, in 1711 when everything was cozy, Byrd had for self-interested reasons opposed a tax on skins which was intended to provide revenues for the fighting against the Tuscaroras. The following year, when Spotswood aroused the House's opposition by asking for £20,000 for the Indian wars, Byrd indiscreetly remarked to Will Randolph (William Randolph II) that no governor should be trusted with £20,000. Randolph repeated Byrd's words. As in a small society there would always be someone who hoped to advance himself by getting the remark to the governor, soon Byrd heard on all sides that Spotswood was angry with him. After worrying a good deal about how to make amends to the governor, when the General Assembly convened in January, 1712, he decided to brazen it out.

The governor treated Byrd with marked coldness then and later when the councilors attended him at his house. At Spotswood's customary dinners for the councilors and their wives, Mrs. Russell also was chilly towards Byrd. Byrd's sister-in-law, Frances Custis, helped nothing by spreading some gossip about the governor's niece.

It was in this strained atmosphere that Spotswood demanded that

Byrd as receiver general correct the inefficiencies in the collection of quitrents and the sale of tobacco paid in quitrents. Byrd countered with the suggestion that four deputy receivers be appointed who, at an added cost to the Colony, would do the work, while he continued to enjoy the revenues of a sinecure. Spotswood dismissed this proposal and in 1714 offered a new procedure to the Council: first, sheriffs would no longer collect quitrents on the land, but at appointed places; second, sheriffs would settle directly with the receiver general at his office in Williamsburg; third, the collected tobacco would be posted in Williamsburg on a given day and bid upon. With only Byrd and Ludwell voting against the governor's proposal, it was passed in the Council. Going into effect immediately, the scheme brought larger revenues and gave Spotswood one area in which his passion for order had prevailed, at least to his own satisfaction. There were the usual complaints about change, and John Grymes wrote that "this hasty altering the old methods has drawn on a great deal of confusion."

Byrd reacted by taking the position that his integrity had been questioned. Spotswood made it clear that he accused no one of dishonesty. He had ordered a change because Byrd (like Ludwell) headed a poor system which cost the Crown revenue. To the Board of Trade he wrote that he did not think it was His Majesty's intention for a receiver general to be a formal officer whose work was done by others. Byrd, having come into everything without effort on his part, and influenced by his English friends who merely collected rents, felt it inconsistent with his image to do the work.

By 1715, when Byrd would be required either to run his office himself or to resign, he had conceived a deep dislike of the governor at a time when his own affairs had become entangled beyond his capacities to straighten them out. The "splendid economist" had gotten himself in this fix out of pride and vanity over his status as a large landholder.

It had started in December, 1710, when Byrd's father-in-law was murdered in an uprising in Antigua. Daniel Parke's will left, Micajah Perry said, "a stain upon his name forever." His holdings in the Leeward Islands were left to an illegitimate daughter; his holdings in Virginia and Hampshire went to Frances Custis, who was to pay off all her father's debts; and Byrd's wife Lucy was (as Byrd said) "fobbed off" with a cash settlement of £1,000. As Colonel Parke had never paid Lucy's dowry of £1,000, this amount was listed as a debt to be paid off by Frances Custis out of her father's estate. Such short shrift was not at all pleasing to Byrd, who had not needed cash in 1711, and he entered into a complicated deal with his sister-in-law's husband, John Custis.

Early examinations revealed debts of £6,680 against assets of Parke's Hampshire property, valued at £4,000, and the Virginia property, about which he had grandly written Custis's father: "You may easily inform yourself that my daughter, Frances, will be heiress to all the land my father left." Byrd, in his desire for the landed estates in Virginia (some of which included slaves, a few cattle, and horses), did not make a careful investigation of Parke's affairs before arranging with Custis, in effect, to assume the debts in exchange for the Virginia and English properties. After the transaction, more of Parke's debts were uncovered, approaching £10,000 before accumulated interest, much of which was owed to, of all people, Micajah Perry. While the Hampshire properties went for less than the estimated £4,000, other debts kept coming to light as the interest mounted, and in exchange for the vain satisfaction of extending his Virginia holdings, Byrd was burdened with a debt that was to hang over him for years and color all his financial affairs.

(The shrewd Custis did not get off as easily as he had expected. Debts against Parke's Leeward Islands property were revealed, and since Parke's will stipulated that Frances Custis was to pay "all my legal debts and bequests," Parke's distant heirs charged Custis with the obligation. He was saddled with lawsuits for the rest of his life, and his son after him, and then his son's widow, Martha Custis Washington.)

Partly to try to bring some order to his oppressive financial situation and partly to get away from the governor, Byrd asked for a leave of absence in 1715 to go to England. There he sold his office of receiver general for £500 and began working to undermine Spotswood when the governor's test case with the oligarchy reached its climax.

9

Spotswood's choice of ground — the courts of oyer and terminer — for his fight to reduce the oligarchy's power, seemed a very simple showdown for all the antagonism it caused. But the implications of the issue were clearly recognized by Spotswood and the councilors.

It was the custom for the General Courts, on which the councilors sat as judges, to meet in October and April. Early in his administration Spotswood had called for special meetings of the oyer and terminer courts in between, to hasten bringing criminal cases to trial and prevent the long waits of prisoners in the verminous jails. At first he did not exercise the right, contained in his instructions, to appoint special judges. Until 1712 he went along with custom and appointed only councilors. Then, when a man was on trial for his life, the governor threw down the gauntlet and appointed judges other than the councilors.

It was over this, and only over this, that Robert Carter took a strong position opposing the governor. With other councilors, he protested to Spotswood against this violation of the ''ancient custom'' by which men would be tried by ''more inferior judges than their fortune.'' Sure that the law was on his side, the governor remained courteously adamant.

The oligarchy on the Council had then grown to eight, and these councilors wrote a petition presenting their case to the Board of Trade: the substance was that ''it would be hard that men's lives should be tried'' by inferiors. The only councilors who did not sign were Dr. William Cocke, Spotswood's personal appointee as secretary, and President Edmund Jenings. Having cast his lot outside the oligarchy, Jenings became a sycophant of the governor.

The Board ruled (June, 1716) that Spotswood had the right to make his own appointments unless a colonial law existed to the contrary. This aroused Robert Carter and his allies to a defense of their customary rights. At their continued protests, the Board appealed for a ruling from the Attorney General of Great Britain, Sir Edward Northey. In October, 1717, Northey gave his opinion that Spotswood had the law on his side. In transmitting this opinion, the Board advised Spotswood to use discretion. Before Spotswood received the warning, he had appointed an oyer and terminer court on which four outsiders were to sit with five councilors. Except for Edmund Jenings, the appointed councilors refused to sit on the court.

Robert Carter, Ludwell, Blair and the other members of the oligarchy (except Byrd, then in England), wrote their strongest petition to the Board, protesting the governor's action. To support their case they introduced other, more general charges. One such charge, suggested by Ludwell, was that the change of the old methods of collecting quitrents reflected on the Council and its president, Jenings.

This petition was not aimed at removing Spotswood; personally, Robert Carter and other leaders still liked him. They wanted to clarify the situation and promote an understanding with the governor in which, of course, they would retain their privileges according to the ancient custom. Edmund Berkeley, Nathaniel Harrison and William Bassett, then on the Council, all signed this petition with the Carter bloc. Again Jenings and Dr. Cocke abstained.

It was at this stage that Byrd made common cause between his personal feud and the oyer and terminer issue. "I am glad to find the Council is fairly engaged with the Lieutenant Governor," he wrote Ludwell. "They have a good cause and I hope I shall be able to procure justice done them."

Before this Byrd had represented the General Assembly to the Board of Trade on several of Spotswood's measures which both houses opposed — the Tobacco Act and the Indian Act, and a misguided effort of Spotswood's to place revenues from quitrents directly into the Royal Treasury. Since these measures had been nullified, the councilors had confidence in Byrd's presentations of their grievances.

Spotswood, his position made secure by the Board's support and the Attorney General's ruling, countered by moving directly against Byrd. Once before, in 1702–1703, the Board had rebuked the Council for permitting Byrd to act as an irregular agent, and Spotswood complained about "private agents." Nathaniel Blakiston, he pointed out, served officially as the Colony's agent. Ludwell, knowing of Blakiston's friendship with Spotswood, brought all his hostile energies to the oyer and terminer fight and induced the House of Burgesses to appoint Byrd as its official agent. Spotswood vetoed the appointment. The House voted to pay Byrd out of its own funds, and Byrd carried the oligarchy's protest to the Board. "We have nothing to fear if we miscarry," Byrd wrote Ludwell privately, "for he can't be more our adversary than he is already."

When Byrd carried the new protest to the Board, however, he had weakened his own position by earlier writing a defense of Ludwell's auditor generalship and his own receiver generalship. The literary strain in Byrd had taken over, and in the sharp, clear statement he had indulged in those sarcastic turns in which he excelled. As both Byrd and Ludwell were then out of office, that argument was academic, and the Board had dismissed the whole matter. When Byrd came back again, using the Council's official protest as a weapon in his private fight to remove Spotswood, he began to wear out his welcome. By then the law had resolved the matter in Spotswood's favor, and the governor was bringing the conflict under control in Virginia.

Spotswood ended the fight with the ultimate pragmatism. When in early May, 1718, he read the Attorney General's ruling to the members of the oligarchy on the Council, the governor asked them flatly if they agreed that he had the power to appoint judges in the oyer and terminer courts along with councilors or even to the exclusion of councilors. Robert Carter and his friends refused to give a direct answer which would acknowledge Spotswood's authority. They had it entered in the Executive Journals that they acquiesced in the determination of the Board of Trade.

From the councilors' unyielding expressions and cool civility on parting with him, old soldier Spotswood recognized that he had won a fruitless battle in what had become a war, which he was losing. Those seven determined men had won the total support of the House of Burgesses and had mobilized the strength to resist all the governor's legislation that must pass through the General Assembly.

Despite Spotswood's description of the Burgesses as "rabble" owning half an acre of land apiece, the richer members of the growing planter class were multiplying in the House. Daniel McCarthy, the speaker, was a big planter in the Northern Neck and a distant neighbor of Robert Carter; Gawin Corbin, another friend of Robert Carter's, had never forgiven Spotswood for removing him from his post of naval collector, and he was one of the governor's most forceful enemies in the House. With the oligarchy working hand in glove with the Burgesses, Spotswood's most important legislation had already been gutted, and it was clear that his reduction of the eight councilors' power in the oyer and terminer test case came at the cost of his own authority to enact legislation.

The councilors' grimly set opposition extended into the social life on which the governor prided himself. Later in May, 1718, after his confrontation with the councilors over his authority, Spotswood made overtures to the councilors with one of his elaborate parties. For this occasion he used the new governor's incomplete house, which was being built under his supervision at such public expense — "lavishing away the country's money," the Burgesses complained — that people began to refer to it derisively as "the Palace."

In all truth, the building designed by Spotswood was palatial, at least by colonial standards. Spotswood designed with a splendor and elegance befitting the official residence of the royal governor. He provided the architectural vision and superb taste in the directions given Henry Cary, Williamsburg's master builder, and the total structure, in which the main house was the center unit in a formal design of dependencies, emerged on a scale of magnificence never before seen in Virginia. A wide green about one hundred yards long (later called "the Palace Green") led off from Duke of Gloucester Street to the imposing entrance of the buildings that would establish the style for the dynastic seats on Virginia plantations.

Spotswood had achieved a curious blend in his architecture. In basic design the house and its dependencies suggested the English

The Governor's Palace, Williamsburg
(Photographed by Stephen M. Toth, Colonial Williamsburg)

country houses of that day (which came to be called "Georgian"), and at the same time captured so completely the indigenous aspects of Virginia houses as to serve as the ideal for later plantation houses. What most impressed the big plantation owners was the manorial forecourt, where the central house was flanked by two handsome, smaller brick buildings, the guardhouse and the governor's offices. All the service buildings — kitchen, scullery, laundry, smokehouse, salthouse, stables, servants' quarters — were off to the sides and in the back, and were screened by a complex of shrubs and gardens. There were gardens of box, fruit and vines, holly, flowers and vegetables, and "the falling gardens," sloping down to a private canal, which flanked the property from front to back. At the back a huge mound ("mount") rose over the icehouse, which was approached by narrow steps to a space ten feet deep.

The main house presented a square front of two high stories and a third story, with dormer windows, topped by a balustraded roof above which rose a stately cupola. For the night of Spotswood's party, ostensibly in celebration of the King's birthday, the lantern in the cupola was lit, illuminating the imposing facade. Also for this occasion the governor arranged for a play to be acted by a troupe who were the first professional players in the colonies.

William Leviston, a merchant in New Kent County, was more interested in giving dancing lessons around the countryside than in merchandise, and to help him he indentured a couple, Charles and Mary Stagg. Charles Stagg, listed on his indenture papers as a "Dancing Master," evidently had some experience on the English stage, as did his wife. Soon after the Staggs' arrival, in 1716, Leviston obtained permission to use rooms in the College "for teaching the scholars and others to dance until his own dancing school in Williamsburg be finished." When Leviston started to build the house for his school facing the Palace Green, he freed the Staggs from their indenture, built a theatre, and sent to England for actors and musicians. The Leviston-Stagg acting company was ready to give its first performance at the time of Spotswood's party celebrating the birthday of George I.

Spotswood's spectacular party shared the fate of poor Nicholson's celebration, when the explosion of the firecrackers had brought the day to an embarrassing anticlimax. None of the oligarchic councilors showed up at the party. What added insult to the injury was the sound of boisterous gaiety drifting to the stately house from the Capitol. The Burgesses had also picked the King's birthday to give a party of their own and, Spotswood wrote bitterly, "invited all the mobs to a bonfire, where they were plentifully supplied with liquers. . . ."

The governor was deeply outraged by this gesture of disrespect from the oligarchy and wrote an enraged letter to the Board. Then, as the summer passed, the ex-soldier began to face the reality that he was in a war he could not win. Always pragmatic, he suppressed his feelings and started to use his neglected skills.

10

In preparing a new, practical campaign, Spotswood first isolated his personal enemies and put them on the defensive. In Williamsburg he won over Nathaniel Harrison. Succeeding his late father, Benjamin Harrison II, on the Council, Nathaniel Harrison was of great influence as a member of what Spotswood referred to as "the very Family" — Harrison-Ludwell-Burwell-Blair-Carter.

An enterprising merchant-planter at his south-of-the-James plantation, Brandon, thirty-six-year-old Harrison was brought to view Byrd less as a collaborator than as a man looking after his own ambitions. He wrote his kinsman Philip Ludwell: "I consider the consequences if Col. Byrd should ever obtain his end [and] come here Governor and we should be so unfortunate as to differ with him. Now that Col. Byrd will come here in that station I have much reason to think, and therefore we should act so as not to give him any advantage against us by which he might keep us in awe."

Harrison's apprehensions were groundless. At the time when Byrd in London was trying to get support for the governorship, Spotswood was directing the attentions of Lord Orkney and the Board to the agitation of a few individuals. Referring to the oligarchy on the Council, he wrote to the Board: "A Governor cannot contrive a surer way of gaining their disfavor than by strictly pursuing his duty and faithfully discharging his trust. Your Lordships' determination about the disputes of the Courts of Oyer and Terminer remains deeply rooted in their minds, and they have publicly declared at the Council Board that, though they could not help acquiescing therein, they were not convinced of the legality of that decision. Their behavior towards me ever since has been far from owning themselves in the wrong in that controversy. When the minds of some of the Council, heedlessly drawn into that dispute, began to waver on seeing their pretensions condemned, and were thereupon willing to return to a good correspondence with me, Mr. Blair and Mr. Ludwell, the chief engines of faction, found it necessary to keep up their spirits by a new invention. . . .''

If "the party," he wrote, succeeded in removing another governor, the consequences would be grave, since already he considered "the power, interest and reputation of the King's Governor in this dominion to be now reduced to a desperate gasp. . . ." To Lord Orkney also he wrote of his concern for the future government of this province, and listed Ludwell and Blair of the Old Guard, and Byrd and John Smith of the newer councilors, as the "turbulent" who fomented trouble "in the country." Spotswood suggested to Orkney that he act to remove these four troublemakers from the King's Council.

Orkney did propose to the Board the removal of those four from the Council, and Spotswood followed this (September, 1718) by proposing directly to the Board that Byrd be removed on the grounds of his absence. In his letter, he made shrewd use of Byrd's "employment" by the House of Burgesses and, not giving Byrd the title of "Colonel," minimized his position in London by local identification. "Mr. Byrd, one of the Council here, having been gone from hence three years and a half, and seeming, by his letters and the new employment he has got into of being constituted Agent for the House of Burgesses, to incline to a much longer continuance in England, I hope your Lordships will think fit to move his Majesty to appoint another Counsellor in his room, and I humbly recommend to your Lordships for that purpose Mr. Cole Diggs, a Gent. who lives very convenient to the seat of government, of an ample fortune, good parts, and a fair character, and whose father was also of that Board."

This was just the beginning of Spotswood's series of letters to Lord Orkney, the Board, and other authorities. While Byrd as kingmaker failed to gain the influential support that Blair had had in London, Spotswood was in a far stronger position than either Andros or Nicholson had been. He wrote John Cragge, England's newly appointed Secretary of State, of the evils of "the Party" whose agent, "Mr. Byrd," was trying to remove both Spotswood and Orkney.

Spotswood's campaign against Byrd was more skillful than Byrd's against him. By adroitly using against Byrd his own behavior — his absence from the King's Council, his serving as "irregular agent" for the House of Burgesses, his "malice" in seeking to remove both Spotswood and the titular governor — Spotswood managed to spread the impression that Byrd was the chief cause of the insurgence of "a formidable party here, who have long aimed at raising their own power by lessening that of their sovereign. . . ." In suggesting the removal of Ludwell, Blair and John Smith, along with Byrd, he associated Byrd with a chronic governor-deposer in Blair and with an inefficient administrator in Ludwell, who was himself identified as a troublemaker by the Board.

While isolating Byrd, by the end of the year (1718) Spotswood was making peace with the other councilors. He had never included Robert Carter or Nathaniel Harrison among the "fomenters" who should be removed. In referring to Carter's "haughtiness" in his stand for the ancient rights of councilors — the "King" was one of the drafters of the generalized petition — Spotswood did not single him out as a personal enemy. Also, newly on the Council was a new son-in-law of Robert Carter, young Mann Page, who that year had married Carter's literary-minded daughter, Judith. Page was clearly a supporter of Spotswood, and it was evident to Spotswood that Page's father-in-law, along with Nathaniel Harrison, William Bassett, Edmund Berkeley and John Lewis, were holding out only on the oyer and terminer issue.

On this principle Spotswood could not give in. Instead, he found a graceful retreat. He selected a time when he had just won some personal popularity.

"Captain" Robert Teach, the pirate called "Blackbeard," had recently flashed into a gruesome notoriety along the coast of Virginia and North Carolina. Though pirates no longer enjoyed the sanctuaries in Virginia's bays and inlets as they had before Nicholson's victories, there was still a reluctance in some planters to be hard on pirates, and Blackbeard always managed to find a haven. Spotswood, entirely on his own initiative and at his own expense, hired two sloops, manned them with sailors from a British warship, and sent an expedition after Captain Teach among the sounds off North Carolina's coast. The pirates were conquered in a fierce battle in which Blackbeard was killed, and his bloody head swung from the bowsprit of one of the sloops returning to Jamestown. The fifteen captured pirates attracted local attention when they were crowded into the cold jail in November, 1718, and thirteen of them attracted even more when their bodies hung in chains along the road to Queen Anne's port.

A month after this diversion, Spotswood called in the full Council and made his proposal. If the councilors would publicly agree that they owed appointments on the oyer and terminer courts to the governor, and were not chosen by virtue of being councilors, then he would agree to appoint only councilors to the oyer and terminer courts.

The realistic councilors, caring less about the abstract right than the reality, were perfectly willing to allow the governor the dignity of theoretical authority. They readily agreed to the compromise.

However, there was no jubilation on either side at this pragmatic settlement. The conflict had gone on too long, for six years. There was too much strain still in the atmosphere and too much generalized opposition in the Colony — which the councilors themselves had helped promote. Also, Spotswood's personal enemies on the Council were, as he said of Ludwell, "inveterate," and the governor himself was too stubborn to back off from a fight, even when further controversy would be disadvantageous to the position he had established at the truce in the oyer and terminer conflict at the end of 1718. While not growing out of the oyer and terminer test struggle, Spotswood's new encounter with Ludwell, then working in a private alliance with Blair, extended from the same period and kept hostilities alive.

11

Philip Ludwell had lost his ally in London when Spotswood's campaign against Byrd reduced the would-be governor to petitioning the Privy Council for the retention of his position as councilor. The Board of Trade, in denying Byrd's presentation against Spotswood with rebukes for "the extraordinary manner" of the presentation against all royal instructions, recommended to the Privy Council that Byrd be removed from his seat. Byrd shifted quickly from trying to supplant Spotswood to an appeal for permission to stay one more year in England to straighten out his debts. His wife had died in England, in 1716, and he was trying to find an heiress who would marry him.

He wrote to the Board, in March, 1719: "To convince their Lordships that he is sincerely inclined to peace, he promises to employ all the credit he has with the Council to dispose them to a sincere pacification upon the terms of the Lieutenant Governor's own plan. . . ." While this capitulation did not incline him peaceably toward Spotswood, from whom he feared a vengeance, as a political enemy of the governor Byrd had been silenced. The Board wrote Spotswood that he had their complete support.

In Virginia, Ludwell joined another vindictive enemy of the governor, his brother-in-law James Blair, this time in a dispute over the power of vestries. The commissary, in bristly vigilance against any encroachment on the Church in Virginia, took on Spotswood over "benefices" — the right of the governor to place clergymen in parishes and give them tenure.

Considering his troubles with the councilors and the burgesses, Spotswood could not be seen as a skillful campaigner in spreading his fight to the Church vestries. Rather, it appeared that a stubbornness goaded him to display his lack of fear of that bugaboo "custom," and to encounter every aspect of it simultaneously. In this stubbornness, he brought up dry principle to fight a tradition that reflected the very heart of the attitudes by which Virginians lived.

In their opposition to giving clergymen tenure, the vestries practiced self-government in their religion as well as in their internal affairs. In adapting the Church of England to their frontier communities, the people had evolved a religious practice of moderation in all things in which they were comfortable. Without theories or doctrines, the parishioners by habit and custom had made a working reality out of Church and State to fit the conditions of their lives. When Spotswood began to insist upon his power of "collation" (the bestowal of benefices), he was striking at something more than "what hath been the ancient custom." Threatened by his imposition of an English principle on their New World communities, the vestries simply refused to present their ministers to be inducted by the governor.

At this deadlock James Blair made of himself a test case. After a series of skirmishes involving the Jamestown Church, Blair, as rector of Bruton Parish, refused to present himself to the governor for induction. Spotswood, in allowing himself to be drawn into this fight, put his legal authority on the line against the weight of custom. Whatever Blair's personal motives — and he demonstrated a lifelong vindictiveness toward Spotswood — the commissary was, for totally practical reasons, in effect committing all parishes to a stand on self-government for the Church of England in Virginia.

In April, 1719, a few months after the settlement between Spotswood and the councilors, the governor and the commissary clashed in a convention of the Virginia clergy. The majority of the clergy, wanting tenure, naturally supported the governor. In the course of bitter arguments, a demand was made that Blair show proof that he had ever been ordained in the Church of England. Having been ordained in the Church of Scotland before the union of Scotland and England, Blair actually held his ministry at Bruton Parish illegally, since ecclesiastical law required a minister to have been ordained in the Church of England. Blair refused to produce proof (as he had none to produce), and took a defiantly lofty attitude about the question. The convention degenerated into a clamorous spectacle of name-calling, out of which Blair and Spotswood emerged in a stalemate.

The General Assembly agreed to provide funds for an attorney to make a ruling on benefices, and there the matter ended. Blair had the support of the Council and the Burgesses, the vestries and the parishioners, and once again Spotswood had been checked by the immovable object of ''what hath been the ancient custom.''

Robert Carter and the other oligarchic members of the Council, in supporting Blair's position, did not (except for Ludwell) take any active part in the church controversy. As Blair obviously did not have the backing to try to overthrow another governor, he and Ludwell could only continue to simmer on the Council as a minority of men of personal ill will toward Spotswood.

Robert Carter and the others clearly wanted a return to harmony. Edmund Berkeley had died and been replaced by Cole Digges, a councilor of the governor's choice, and the younger oligarchic councilors wanted to get on with the business of running Virginia rather than support fights against an able man whose tests of power had already damaged his enlightened programs of efficiency.

When this stage was reached, Spotswood took the initiative toward promoting a full reconciliation. In late May (1719), when dogwoods were blossoming in Williamsburg gardens, he called the councilors to a formal meeting in the Capitol and addressed them in obvious friendliness. He asked them to agree to submit future differences to the Board of Trade with impartial statements drawn up by both parties; there would be no separate solicitations, such as Byrd's ''agency'' (which Spotswood had devoted considerable time and energy to undermining), and questions of law would be referred to the Board to get the opinion of Crown lawyers. The councilors agreed.

Then Spotswood asked that each write letters to the Board of Trade announcing the reconciliation and negating all former representations of one another. Again the councilors agreed, although more in their official capacities than in personal warmth. However, if cordiality was not restored — not as long as Blair and Ludwell could prevent it — the councilors were sincere in their political reconciliation.

Robert Carter in particular was in a mood for reconciliation, for that summer he suffered the death of his wife Betty. Extending the long roll of funerals at Christ Church, Betty Carter was buried in July at the age of thirty-six. The outwardly contained man wrote a year later, at fifty-seven: ''I remain a mourner to this day, and propose to myself to continue in my single state until the time comes when I must put on immortality.''

Carter also had, along with the other councilors, a less personal reason for ending the controversies. During the period of fruitless political conflict, the tobacco market had been restored and good times were back again. "We don't know how to think of tobacco than eleven pence for our crops," Carter wrote Micajah Perry. Of that, after freight charges and duties, the planter got twopence. Then Carter added a prophetic note: "Am afraid the blessing that attends us in a plentiful year will have the consequences of a decline upon our market which of necessity must make us lower our topsails."

While Spotswood could not truly claim credit for the return of good tobacco prices and easy money, these developments reflecting the end of war in Europe did occur during an administration which he tried — and, in some measures successfully — to make efficient. Carter could not remain antagonistic to a governor under whose administration he was able to sell twenty slaves for between £1,200 and £1,300 — four times the price of the past century.

These high prices endeared Spotswood more to the big merchant-planters like Carter than to the yeomanry, working without slave labor. Declining numerically and in influence, these farmers doing their own work had begun to perceive the threat of slave labor to their own evolved patterns, and considerable discussion was raised in the General Assembly about prohibiting slavery, or at least restricting the importation. The antislavery element succeeded in raising the tariff on slaves to £5 (about the full price of an indenture), and this bill passed over Spotswood's veto. Spotswood was under specific instructions from London to forbid any restrictions on the importation of slaves: huge sums were owed the Royal African Company for slaves bought on credit and the merchants wanted no unsettling of the market.

The planters investing their savings in their first slaves, or in only a few slaves, had no established credit with the large English agents, such as Perry, and sometimes bought from the New England slave traders plying the rivers with their cargoes — slaves, rum and goods. These were small dealers, regarded by the big merchant-planters with the disrespect that the established store would feel for itinerant pedlars. Some of the small planters, however, ventured aboard the New England trading ships and tried bargaining with these "foreigners."

It had been no intention of Spotswood to divide the yeomanry from the planter class but that was the drift of the economy, and in his ambition to build his own fortune, the governor had himself followed the way of the big merchant-planters. At the very time he was fighting them over the technicality of authority, he was acquiring land on a continually increasing scale and was privately trying to develop mines in central Virginia. What was happening, without announcement, was that Spotswood was joining the merchant-planters of the oligarchy.

Spotswood's own course, in fact, invalidated the theories that could be advanced (and they have been) about the democratic implications in the councilors' "resistance" to the authority of a royal governor. Only on the surface could the councilors' apparently solid stand be viewed, retrospectively, as a fight for "liberties" against the encroachments of a representative of the British King. The details of the power fight show clearly that except for the oyer and terminer test case — itself a test of strength only between the executive and the Council — the chief resistance, by Ludwell and Byrd, had nothing to do with liberties.

These two somewhat self-inflated gentlemen became the governor's personal enemies because, in the interest of imposing a system on the gathering and disbursing of the Colony's revenues, he demanded that they do the work for which they drew a commission. When Spotswood isolated Byrd and put him in the defensive position of having to save his Council seat, there was no rallying by the councilors to protect him from the governor's counterattack. Ludwell, more one of them than Byrd, got no support on the Council when Spotswood introduced his new methods for a more efficient handling of quitrent tobacco. In fact, during Ludwell's opposition, Spotswood was amused to see Robert Carter and Ludwell quarrel in front of him. During all the controversies, Edmund Jenings, the Council president, remained, as Byrd wrote, "the devoted creature of the Governor."

Blair's successful battle against the governor's exercising the right of inducting ministers with tenure was a resistance to the State's authority encroaching on the Church's, although Blair's record would scarcely indicate that he was motivated by libertarian principles. Spotswood, on the other hand, was sincerely interested in improving the position of the clergy. One of the most brilliant clergymen, Hugh Jones, an Oxford graduate teaching at William and Mary, who also had the Jamestown Church (probably due to Spotswood's influence), wrote a highly complimentary defense of the governor in which he spoke for the majority of the clergy.

All in all, Spotswood was not reflecting any attitude of the Crown to encroach on colonial "liberties." He invoked the King's name to gain his ends, growing indignant that the Virginians did not stand more in awe of "the Crown," and in his involved struggle with the oligarchy he shrewdly wrote the Board of Trade that his opponents were determined to undermine "His Majesty's authority."

But in England, where the ministers were running the government for an indifferent German who could not speak the nation's language, and where mercantile interests dominated the direction of colonial affairs, the Board of Trade began to feel that Spotswood's controversies might be ending his usefulness. Advising him to move more quietly, to be discreet, Spotswood's superiors showed themselves to be more concerned with the support that Virginia's General Assembly failed to give the governor than with supporting the governor in the face of a generalized opposition. Since Spotswood's days as governor were numbered by the time peace was belatedly made with the councilors, he could not well be seen as representative of the Crown's attitude.

Nor could a governor who joined the councilors in amassing landholdings, and established himself among them as a Virginia planter, be realistically viewed as representing repressive Old World prerogatives. Instead Alexander Spotswood could be seen as a careerist who came to the New World to make his fortune and, after failing to impose methods formed of his European experience, came to view the Colony as did the natives. For the final turn in Spotswood's career vis-à-vis the Council was that, still retaining his "enlightened self-interest," he indulged in all the practices over which he had fought the oligarchy.

12

Colonel Spotswood was far more devious than he appeared. In his manly, straightforward letters to the Board of Trade and Lord Orkney, about "the party" reducing the government's authority "to a Desperate gasp," nothing had indicated his own deepening commitment to the way of life of the big merchant-planters. In this, Spotswood was not the "hypocrite" which he had accused Blair of being. In a case of the right hand's knowing what the left hand was doing, Spotswood managed to combine his vigorous interest in the Colony's progress with the advancement of his own affairs.

More mindful than the colonists of the uncharted country to the west — occupied in the distance by the French — Spotswood continually exerted efforts to encourage expansion beyond the fall line of the big rivers, toward the Blue Ridge Mountains and the great valley, the

Shenandoah, beyond. In the midst of all his controversies in 1716, he conducted a party across the Blue Ridge on an expedition that entered legend as the journey of "the Knights of the Golden Horseshoe."

The image of "knights" and the "golden horseshoe" became one of those frills in the Colony's history which, like the mythical aspects of the "cavaliers," gave little suggestion of the hard core in men like Spotswood and the ruthless competition of the life they mastered. Spotswood's trip combined personal business, a gesture toward westward expansion, and an escape from the damply smothering August heat of Williamsburg.

As he was then battling the councilors, the thirteen companions he selected included none of the titled gentry, the "Colonels." Fourteen gentlemen, including the governor and his friend Robert Beverley II, were accompanied by twelve rangers with a large number of servants, making a party of sixty-three men. Seventy-four horses were taken, most of them laden with luxurious supplies — including all kinds of alcoholic beverages — which Spotswood provided as for an elegant picnic. The expedition headed first for Germanna, a community which represented Spotswood's commercial venture in Virginia.

Spotswood had started in the Germanna enterprise by giving financial and political support to Baron Christoph de Graffenreid for a German colony which would develop mining. Baron de Graffenreid, in association with other promoters, had first settled a Swiss colony in North Carolina, but after his experience with the Tuscaroras had returned to an earlier scheme of mining in central Virginia. Just west of the falls at the head of tidewater on the Rappahannock River, west of the present city of Fredericksburg, the location was in the region later famous as the Wilderness. It was typical of Spotswood that his personal involvement with the German colony coincided with his official interest in developing mining, and he presented de Graffenreid's settlement as a public enterprise.

Keeping his own part secret from the General Assembly, for several years Spotswood corresponded cautiously with the Board of Trade, and avoided arousing the Crown's opposition to foreigners or the opposition of English manufacturers. He said he was trying to develop silver mines, though almost certainly he was after iron. Nine families totalling about forty Germans were imported to build a settlement above the Rappahannock falls, and Spotswood informed the Council that the Germans were a protection against Indians. By listing the emigrants as "rangers," he exempted them from taxes, and the Council followed Spotswood's proposal to build at public expense a road and a fort with two cannons and ammunition. By this time, Baron de Graffenreid gave up, returning to Europe, and Spotswood paid the balance of the Germans' passage money, £150 (sterling, not tobacco), out of his own pocket. By the summer trip of 1716, Spotswood was the owner of the enterprise at Germanna.

When Spotswood's party stopped at Germantown (as it was then called), one of the gentlemen recorded that they suffered ''bad beds and indifferent entertainment,'' and nothing good was seen in a day of looking at the mining operations. While they were there, the horses were shod for the rough country ahead, and the party moved on to the Blue Ridge. Though some controversy later arose as to precisely where the expedition crossed the mountains, it has been generally accepted as having been at Swift Run Gap, later the passageway of Stonewall Jackson's ''foot cavalry.'' They rode down to the Shenandoah River, where the great valley was divided by the Massanutten Range between the Blue Ridge and the Alleghenies. The expedition ended there, and according to the chronicler, ''we drank the King's health in champagne, the Princess' health in brandy, and all the rest of the Royal family in claret.'' To the amazement of staring Indians, after each toast the riflemen fired a volley into the air.

On their return, Spotswood sent to each of his gentlemen companions a small golden horseshoe, and because of this commemorative token the trip grew into the legend of ''the Knights of the Golden Horseshoe.''

More practically, while the souvenirs were being made, Spotswood in October had William Robertson, clerk of the Council, patent 3,200 acres, known as the Germanna tract. The following month this grant was quietly conveyed to the governor. Later Spotswood had Richard Hickman, the clerk in the office of loyal Secretary Cocke, patent (in round figures) 3,000 acres known as the Wilderness tract, which the following month was also conveyed to the governor.

At about the time of his 1719 reconciliation with the oligarchic members of the Council, the dissatisfied Germans abandoned their settlement and Spotswood openly brought in indentures and slaves to work holdings then grown (in round figures) to 8,000 acres. He also went into partnership with Thomas Jones and Robert Beverley II on another mining enterprise on a 15,000-acre grant called Mine Tract. By 1720 Spotswood owned approximately 25,000 acres, much of which was in mining property, and by this time it was becoming observed that Spotswood's partners always sold out.

William Byrd commented that Spotswood used stratagems ''to

shake off his partners, and secure all his mines to himself.'' Sensitive to this interpretation, Spotswood wrote Nathaniel Harrison that the property fell into his hands through a series of circumstances beyond his control. With the truth probably somewhere between, Spotswood, deeply involved, made an apparently spontaneous move in April, 1720, to end the stiffness between the councilors and himself and to restore the earlier warmth.

Byrd had returned to Virginia in February, having failed to win either of two heiresses he pursued in London. He brought with him two maids, and suffered the further rejection of having one of those young women refuse to become his mistress. Before presenting himself to the governor he waited at Westover until April 25, when he received from London the King's order restoring him to his seat among the councilors. In his diary, Byrd recorded that Spotswood told him he would not have admitted him to the Council without the King's order, and, according to Byrd, Spotswood ''railed at me most violently before all the people, but I answered him without any fear or any manner and came off with credit.''

It was only four days after this, on April 29, that Spotswood made a friendly gesture which included Byrd. At a meeting in the Council chamber, Ludwell and Blair were engaging in one of their harsh exchanges with the governor in which, Byrd recorded, ''an abundance of hard words'' passed. While the argument raged for two hours the other councilors, taking no sides, remained impassive spectators. Suddenly the governor turned to the other councilors with a manner of humility and, to everyone's surprise, spoke earnestly of his desire for real peace between them, and for friendship. In their surprise, the councilors ''melted.'' All of them — or, in the rush of voices, it seemed all of them — heartily joined the governor in their desire for a return to friendship.

Instantly the governor invited them to dinner at the grand new house, the Palace. When they arrived at the illuminated mansion, guns were booming in the marketplace. Spotswood greeted each man with a kiss, and ''everybody expressed great joy.'' After dinner, in one of the happiest occasions in Public Times for years, the Governor brought in musicians to play a concert, and toasts were drunk until eleven o'clock.

After the headiness of the restored goodwill wore off, in some minds a suspicion arose that Spotswood had ''dissimulated'' in his apparently sudden desire for the warmth of friendship, and had ''saluted them with a Judas's kiss.'' Whether or not Spotswood

played a part in his unexpected appeal for peace in the midst of an
argument, unquestionably he had decided it was time for him to join
the oligarchy. Politically he could not beat them, and in his personal
affairs he had reached the point in expansion of his holdings where he
needed their support. However mixed his motivations may have been,
Spotswood did restore the good feeling between himself and the
majority of the councilors.

In that way he emerged from his seven years' war against the
party with honor and — excluding the personal enmities with Ludwell
and Blair — with the respect of all his antagonists. Yet, there was no
escaping the fact that the oligarchy emerged from the struggle with
its position solidified: in London the colonial authorities were considering the possibility that Spotswood, with all his accomplishments,
had caused too much trouble to the native power bloc.

But in Virginia, only Commissary Blair, the inveterate king-
remover, seemed to want Spotswood to leave. Robert Carter wrote
nothing to indicate any dissatisfaction with the governor, and with
restored harmony quieting political activity, he and the rest of the
party gave only routine attention to government.

13

In the summer after the restoration of peace, 1720, Robert Carter
was approached by the Fairfax estate about resuming the agency for
the Proprietary. Edmund Jenings had failed as an agent, owing the
Proprietors two years' rent. Carter did not jump at returning to the
Fairfaxes' services. He considered the possibilities of the long-range
advantages of patenting land for his children, and allowed himself to
be wooed.

In that summer, the "King" began to make passing references to
gout: "Since I have been afflicted with the gout I have quite left off
drinking red wine," he wrote an English merchant. Making reference
to one of his drinking companions among ships' captains, he wrote:
"If you could send me a gross or 18 dozen of good white wines such as
Captain Russell knows I love, upon reasonable terms and in good large
bottles, 'twould be acceptable. . . ."

To another merchant he wrote: "I have ordered Mr. Perry not to
direct for any more claret for me . . . out of the belief I have it is a
great propagator to the gout."

Three months later he wrote to his son John that the gout had not
attacked him "since my first fits," but "I have had frequent fits of

that pitiless distemper, the toothache, the almost inseparable companion of old age.'' He ordered ''one dozen brushes to clean the teeth,'' and his tooth troubles apparently did not become aggravated. However, the attacks of gout were to return in severity.

In that summer also he suffered the first loss of a grandchild, the attractive and promising second son of his daughter Elizabeth and Nathaniel Burwell, his favorite son-in-law.

All of Carter's grandchildren were close in his affections, and especially after he lost his second wife their visits grew in importance to him. After Betty Landon Carter's death, the size of the family had shrunk when he sent the three oldest boys of this marriage — Robert, Charles, and Landon — to school in London, where John was preparing to pass the bar. His wife's sister, Mrs. Swan, had moved in to help look after the younger children Mary, Lucy, and George. Wanting a more permanent solution, Carter wrote asking the Perrys to try to hire for him a settled woman who would like a job in the Colony.

''In my present condition I greatly want a suitable woman for the care and education of my younger children. A grave person of about 40 years of age, that has been well bred and is of good reputation and has been used to breed up children, I would willingly entertain. If it lies in your power to send me in such a one upon reasonable wages, it will be a great obligation to me.''

He also asked John to be on the lookout for a ''school-mistress.'' ''I would willingly give reasonable yearly wages to such a person for four or five years. I know there are a great many such to be met with in London that are hardly able to maintain themselves.''

Eventually these inquiries brought to Corotoman an unobtrusive woman who appeared in Carter's records only as ''Mrs. Young.''

Though he never admitted it in words, in the emptiness left by his young wife Robert Carter began to want John, his firstborn son by his first wife, back at home. After graduating from Trinity College, Cambridge, John had been unhurriedly preparing himself for law at the Inns of Court. He had formed a deeper liking for London life than his father relished, and seemed to be experiencing difficulties in settling down to the practical course designed by his father. A young man of potentialities and of basically practical characteristics, John had — like so many other young colonials — habituated himself to an expensive style of urban life, including expensive tailoring. While John did not actually show tendencies toward becoming a dandified expatriate like William Byrd, with that example before his father, John's dawdling about passing the bar and accumulating debts aroused Carter's irritated apprehensions over his son's preparations for a return to Corotoman.

Taking him to task, King Carter wrote: " . . . you make me a great many promises to make no further use of my money beyond the allowance I have agreed to give you, and, indeed, 'tis a point of very extraordinary management in Mr. Perry to give you the opportunity of doing it. Though I have your frequent promises for a stated account of your expenses, you leave me as much in the dark as ever. You engage yourself, indeed, upon more full mouthed promises for a better regulation, a closer application to your studies, and a greater regularity for the future, but what reason have I to believe you'll be more consistent with your word, now, than you have hitherto been? However, I will once more lay somewhat upon what you say is your fixed resolution, but if you deceive me again I must be so plain to tell you I shall have little dependence upon what you say hereafter in relation to the government of yourself."

This "government of yourself" was the foundation of all the qualities of character esteemed by Robert Carter. He revealed something of his personal attitudes in replying to John's reference to a Mr. Randolph. "As for his [Randolph's] wearing finer linen or finer clothes than you, he never appeared in any such here that I have seen. My acquaintance with him is very slender — only now and then casually at a dinner. His principles and mine are of a very different nature: a rank Tory, a proud, humble parasite, a fawning sycophant to his patron, with all the other requisites of a servile courtier. These are as much reverse to my nature as black is to white. . . ."

He reproached John for not saying anything about his younger brothers (half-brothers) then in London: "Surely they are more in your cares than all this comes to."

He wrote John again: "You make me repeated promises to retrench your expenses and reduce them to the bounds I have set you — that is, to take no more from Mr. Perry than £37:10 per quarter, except the charge of calling you to the bar. You likewise promise me a strict improvement of your time that you have to spend in England, by a close application to your studies. May heaven keep you fixed on this resolution without wavering. It will prove a cordial at your heart all the days of your life. Upon these hopes I shall pass over what's past, according to your desire, and have ordered Mr. Perry to pay your tailor's bill of fifty-odd pounds. . . . Pray take a little more care of your brothers in England."

In July the welfare of the three younger boys — ranging in age from Landon's ten to Robert's fifteen — began to concern Carter even more than John's time-wasting and extravagances. When John had first been sent to London, he was placed under the general care of Micajah Perry. In exchange for Carter's looking after the Perry estates in Virginia, the elder Perry paid John's expenses out of Carter's account with him, supervised John's schooling and lodging, and sent occasional reports. Because old Micajah Perry was showing his advanced age — "Old Mr. Perry is too much a senior," Carter said — he placed Robert, Charles, and Landon under the general care of the London merchant William Dawkins, and in exchange handled the debts owed Dawkins in Virginia. Carter soon began to grow dissatisfied with Dawkins's supervision of the younger sons, particularly over costs.

On July 13, in a long business letter to the London merchant, he entered a mild complaint. "I should be obliged to you if you took more frequent opportunity to give me an account of the welfare of my sons. I have not had one line concerning them since the 'Carter.' I want very much to know what I am to trust to in relation of their maintenance. You gave me your opinion the two eldest would stand me in £40 apiece. . . . If you run me out any more money upon them, I'm upon thoughts of removing them to Manchester School, where I am well advised I can maintain them for a great deal less and education every whit as good."

Carter did seriously consider shifting the boys to the Manchester School and had written another merchant, Thomas Evans, asking him to make inquiries. However, after hearing from Evans, he wrote him: "The prices are considerably higher than I was informed, I find, but yet bear no manner of proportion to those near London. However, I cannot think of coming to any fixed resolution suddenly. Mr. Dawkins hath placed my boys to a very good man, and their improvements are as large as I could expect in the time, although they cost me abundance of money. I will struggle to keep them where they are a little longer, and yet I take it as a very particular obligation that you have been so diligent in giving me so early and full an answer to my letter upon that subject. How I shall govern myself hereafter cannot at present determine."

After abandoning the idea of shifting his sons to another school, he received a letter from Dawkins with news of the boys and a painful account of their expenses. He replied immediately. "The health of my sons and their improvement in learning and manners is one of the greatest blessings I can meet with in this world. Let others take what courses they please in the bringing up of their posterity, I resolve the

principles of our holy religion shall be instilled into mine betimes; as I
am of the Church of England way, so I desire they should be. But the
high-flown up top notions and the great stress that is laid upon ceremonies, any farther than decency and conformity, are what I cannot
come into the reason of. Practical godliness is the substance — these
are but the shell.

"I come now to their expenses. I find you have gone beyond the
bounds of your proposal. Your setting down everything in particular
is very satisfactory and what I must always desire. The character I
have of their master pleases me well enough, and their improvements I
hope answer my desire also, but their expenses stagger me very much.
Landon hath been there but half a year — I observe nothing paid for
his board. How these things comport with your proposals of 40
[pounds] per annum I can [not] reconcile, nor shall not be able to
hold out at this rate. I have good intelligence that, further from the
city, they may have as good an education for less than half the money,
and thither they must go if you can be no better husband for them.
There is several strange articles in their accounts. Mr. Harrison, the
apothecary, a person, I know very well, £7 for poor Charles's physic. I
dare say /7 would have paid for it all. The world is strangely altered,
sure, since I was young. I lived with old Mr. Baily six years. I never
stood my brother in £30 in any one year of the time. 'Tis in vain, I
know, to run into particulars. I'm unwilling to order the removal of
them at once, but to that it must come, I fear."

He had, of course, no intention of removing his sons. Recognizing
this, Dawkins evidently did not take well Carter's continual "poor-
mouth" talk, for later he wrote the master of Corotoman with a sarcastic turn that seared Carter's pride.

At the time when he was counting to the shilling the money
spent on and by his children, Carter was advising the shrewd Perry on
the investment of the sizable cash balance he always kept. Getting six
percent on the money he loaned in Virginia, he was satisfied with five
percent from sound investments Perry could make in England. He
regarded as most unsound the speculations in the South Sea Company, but even such a veteran moneyman as Perry invested some of
Carter's cash in what became that "bubble."

At the end of the summer, in September, Carter was pleased to
learn that all of his previous year's crop of tobacco had gone at elevenpence per pound. "It is a living price, and to have less will make but
poor doing with us." He looked forward to "a plentiful harvest" that
fall.

Looking after his personal needs, he ordered a suit of broadcloth "of a suitable color, to cost between 8 and 10 pounds" — a high price in his day. He also wanted "a pair of fine worsted and a pair of milled stockings" of a color to match the suit. He frequently tried different kinds of belts for the sword he wore as militia colonel, an office to which he applied himself as diligently as he did to every task he undertook.

In his social as well as his business activities at Corotoman, Carter gave no outward indication of his "mourning" for his wife, and his constant entertainment of visitors went as before. His daughter Anne, the youngest of his daughters by his first wife, was his companion at social affairs in Williamsburg and acted as hostess at the dinner table which seated at least seventeen persons. William Byrd, deepening his intimacy with Robert Carter since his return, visited Corotoman that September and found acting hostess Anne "a very agreeable girl." Byrd also made a comment on the quality of the accommodations: referring to Colonel Carter's "abundant courtesy," he spoke of being put up in a "fine room."

The next month, when the leaves were turning in late October, Byrd went with Colonel Carter from the capital on a sudden visit to Carter's daughter Judith and her husband, Mann Page, across the York River in Gloucester County. At the Pages', Byrd shared a bed with the "King," and that did not work out so well. "The Colonel," Byrd recorded, "snored and rose in the night to smoke his pipe."

Carter had become then, as he said, "a great smoker." Perhaps this gave him some comfort in his widower's estate. Sitting alone that night in the dark in the home of his daughter, not knowing he was observed, he may have let his thoughts wander into intimations of his own mortality, as his letters showed a consciousness of the mortal journey in everlasting life in God.

The reason for their trip away from the capital in Public Times was the sudden death of Secretary William Cocke. Spotswood's friend had been seized with a fit of apoplexy in the Capitol, and died immediately. The loss of this supporter in the secretary's office could have been serious for the governor had harmony not then existed with the councilors. The councilors made no demand for a new secretary, and Spotswood left the post open. Richard Hickman, his tool as clerk, continued to patent land in his own name to be conveyed to the governor.

Just before Christmas (1720) Spotswood signed an act to create a new county, Spotsylvania, which placed all his holdings in one county

— a new county in which new settlers would be free of quitrents for seven years. That night, with Ludwell and Byrd absent, Robert Carter and other councilors issued grants for more than ninety thousand acres in the new county to other petitioners. At the end of that year of restored friendship, 1720, Spotswood owned forty-five thousand acres.

Shortly afterwards John Carter completed his law studies, becoming "a barrister at law" at the Middle Temple, and Governor Spotswood appointed him solicitor for Virginia affairs in England. Within little more than a decade the governor, sometimes presented as an asserter of the Crown's threats to colonial liberties, had become one of the oligarchy himself.

14

After Spotswood became, in effect, one of them, the high tobacco prices that had brought good times in Virginia began to waver. Then money became tight again, and planters large and small were returned to the worry of making ends meet. As Spotswood had not caused the good times that came with the rise of tobacco prices, so the downward change was in no way caused by his administration. On the other hand, the improvements he had made in operational efficiency — as well as the high morale in the Colony after the *rapprochement* — cushioned the effects of the falling market, and there was no widespread feeling of acutely hard times.

Along with the drop in the price of tobacco, which Robert Carter had predicted would be the result of high production, the South Sea "bubble" burst, and shook the money speculators in England. Robert Carter accepted stoically the loss of the cash which Perry had invested for him in the South Sea stock. Against paying the same high freight charges which had prevailed when tobacco was selling for elevenpence a pound, he put up a fight. Words and feelings ran high between the plantation master and the ships' captains, and Carter broke permanently with one blustery Captain Wharton. As English merchants began keeping their ships in port to prevent flooding the market, the ships' captains (except for Wharton) in the Virginia rivers gradually lowered their freight charges.

In January, 1721, Carter felt lucky to get 10½ pence for tobacco sold at Liverpool, and in February he wrote John that the effect of the broken South Sea bubble gave the tobacco market "but a dark aspect. All that I can say is we must haul in our horns and live as we can afford." Living "as we can afford" was not the way he had gotten rich. He shopped around among English merchants in London, Liverpool, and Bristol, and dictated letters to his clerks for merchants he had previously done little or no business with.

Micajah Perry the elder, one of the founders of the firm, was nearing his end and things were not quite the same for Robert Carter with younger members of the family running the business. His vanity was hurt when he heard from William Byrd, among others, that the Perrys had sold these other planters' tobacco "in round parcels and at good rates." He wrote the Perrys: "I cannot allow myself to come behind any of these gentlemen in the planter's trade. By all the letters I have received from you [I] do not remember your mention of above seven or eight hogsheads of all my last year's tobacco sold. I will hope my reputation is not quite sinking at your house. Thank God, I can boast of as high prices from other men and as much sold as any of them."

Revealing the involvement of his self-esteem, Carter wrote Thomas Evans: "I must conclude I have lived at very little purpose if I can not get as much for my tobacco as any other man."

During the battle to get the most for his tobacco, the "King" also revealed his sensitivity over any slighting reference to its quality. He wrote Dawkins: "The worst part of your story to me is the sad account you give me of my tobacco. I am at a loss what answer to make to you. I take as vigilant care to prevent these things as any man. No one can boast of better lands or better materials to work with. My overseers are under as strict orders . . . as I can put them. The chief part of the tobaccos you had of me, both in the 'Carter' and the 'Baily,' was made at some of my best plantations. After I have done my utmost, there will be some indifferent hogsheads which must keep company with the better sort. You tell me of [Captain] Kent's stories of the damage of my tobacco in the country, which I know he had from his mate, Dove. There was indeed some hogsheads that was caught in rain — a flat load, as I take it, which did not go far in the cask — and this must be made a noise of to the discredit of my concern. If I live to see Kent he shall hear of this foolish prattling, on both sides of his ears. He was only the trumpet to sound out the information of another; he saw nothing of it himself, I dare say."

With all the fluctuations of prices, and the squabbling with ships' captains and a variety of English merchants, Robert Carter recorded the shipment of more than a thousand hogsheads of his own tobacco in the two years 1720 and 1721. On some of this he could have made no profit at all, since he urged his agents to sell quickly and not let his tobacco accumulate in hope of a better market. Here again the sheer size of his operation made it possible for King Carter, as for other large-scale merchant-planters, to keep going when small farmers went under and when overextended planters, like Edmund Jenings, ran into serious trouble.

The very enterprising, like Carter, not only kept going but, by diversification, kept growing. In early 1721 he was concluding his one venture into the slave trade. As did most of the big merchant-planters who handled imported goods for the small operators, Carter frequently sold a few slaves beyond those he placed on his own plantations. But this was the first time he acted as middleman, with a partner, Robert Tucker, for two slave merchants of Barbados. He and Tucker disposed of the slaves among Virginia planters, clearing the bills of exchange through Perry. It was a risky business, involving several thousand pounds, and complicated by the problems of currency. Carter and Tucker elected to take bonds of uncertain value rather than to hold on to the Negroes in a falling market. The price of the finest slaves dropped to £16 and £18. Carter declared he would never have anything to do with slave dealing again.

Accepting the customs of his time, Carter felt no repugnance at dealing in slaves. As a business proposition, he felt it precarious and not worth the hazards. In the steadily increasing numbers of tobacco growers turning to slave labor, and in the expanding size of slave labor forces, planters were eager to buy slaves, whether money was tight or easy. However, when the depression of tobacco prices drove down the prices of slaves and created a buyers' market, this not only threatened the speculations of the middleman, but encouraged buying among planters whose ability to pay was by no means certain. Carter was worried that many of the bills of exchange cleared through Perry would be protested.

While he was engaged in his unending stratagems for beating the fluctuations of the tobacco market, in late February Carter was stung as he rarely was by a letter from Dawkins that "carries such an air of pride and waspishness that it must not lie unanswered." Dawkins, writing primarily about Carter's three young sons, had included a personal swipe. The "King" had been affronted in his dignity of position before, but never before had his reaction broken through his controls in an intemperate torrent of rage.

"The affair of my children is handled as if they were dependent upon your charity for their maintenance; what they have I doubt not I shall pay for, even to a farthing. You may believe, when I committed them to your care, I had a respect to your friendship and an opinion of your prudence, and expected you would be so far from counting it a trouble, that you would look upon it as an obligation and a pledge of my friendship.

"Before I sent them I consulted you what their maintenance might stand me in. You tell me you believed £40 per annum apiece (?); to put you in remembrance of this, forsooth, must pass for unkindness, and wear the harsh name of bringing you under an obligation. Seeing you are a gentleman of such tender, touchy, elevated nature that cannot endure a plain style and think me so much your debtor for the oversight you have of my children, I have taken care to ease you of that burden. My son hath orders from me to remove them to another person, who will treat me and them with more civility. If you want not me, I shall let you know I want you as little. Do me but justice with the concern of mine you have in your hands and I shall not value how soon I shut up all correspondency with you.''

Then he came to the personal item, involving a Mrs. Heath and the word "muckworm," used in an earlier letter of Carter's. Evidently Mrs. Heath was the daughter of Mr. and Mrs. Baily, both then dead, with whom Robert Carter had lived when a schoolboy in London. In the earlier exchange Carter had berated Dawkins for spending more than was necessary on articles he bought for Carter in London — a tombstone and earrings — and for holding up Mrs. Heath as his "pattern" as a spender. "Had I but one daughter," Carter had written, "and she the descendant of two successive muckworms, perhaps a parallel might not be improper. . . .'' It was Dawkins's reply to this that set off the "King.''

"I shall come a little to particulars. You had laid out my money upon several things much beyond my orders. Among the rest, you had laid me out £20 extraordinary upon a pair of earrings, and tell me, in a way of banter or rather tantalizing, Mrs. Heath had a pair cost a thousand pound. This brought in the word muckworm, which is so offensive to your nice stomach. I had not the least thought of throwing any reflection upon the memory of the dead nor the living; neither doth the sentence carry any such import, to my understanding, and if you want the skill to measure the force of words you should keep a dictionary by you; but, that you may have a true idea of the scope of the word muckworm, I shall recommend to your perusal the fifth part of Doctor Scott's *Christian Life,* where he's treating of the excellency of the soul. There you'll find the signification of this word and how applicable it is to the best of us all. I knew Mr. Baily, both father and son, better than you did. I lived in the family, and have a very good respect for their memories and have been often concerned in the vindication of their characters from aspersions that have been let fly at them, and yet, after all, I think it no injury to them to say they were too much muckworms — that is, in other words, too great lovers of this world — and, by the way, I wish both you and I were more mortified to it than we are. . . .''

In his outpourings, Robert Carter gave one of his fullest, clearest statements of his philosophy of life. It was a statement which, reflecting his own times, was uniquely his — placing him uniquely at the heart of the Protestant ethic.

''The thoughts of having a little more white and yellow earth than our neighbors would not puff us up with so much vanity and insolence, nor make us so uneasy when we meet with plain dealing. I have a great value for Mrs. Heath, both for her own sake and her father's, and if it lay in my way I would requite her tenfold for any respects she has shown to my children, but let me tell you, I esteem her more for the ornaments of her mind — her humility, prudence, affability, piety, charity — than for the fine trappings of her person. These are but of short duration and will quite vanish away when a winding sheet comes to be her portion, but her virtues and graces will keep her company into the other world. We are but stewards of God's building: the more he lends us the larger accounts he expects from us, and happy they that make a right use of their Master's talents. . . .''

Having delivered himself of his thoughts upon man's place under God, he concluded with a straightforward assertion of his and Dawkins's relative positions. Dawkins's rise among London merchants had distorted his perspective on the colonial, and Carter became blunt in calling attention to the distortion. In setting Dawkins straight, Carter gave an accurate, unadorned self-evaluation of his own position in the world as he knew it, and revealed the unguarded man as clearly as anything he ever recorded.

''Now pray, upon the whole, where was your prudence, or rather manners, to use me with the language that was hardly fit for your footman, if you keep one? You might remember I was your master's equal and all along have lived in as good rank and fashion as he did, even when you were something like Graves's cabin boy, and am old enough to be your father, not to mention any more reasons that justly give me a title to your deference. I shall conclude with telling you that I resolve to live in a calm, quiet air the rest of my days, and will be treated with respect by those that do my business. If you are so overgrown and tumefied with the little success you have had in the world, I would have you vent your vanities upon those that are to be gainers by you and not upon   Your humble servant . . .''

Carter's outrage did not pass with this indulgence in insults. On the same day he wrote John, instructing him to remove his brothers from Dawkins's care. Dawkins had written ''in such a lofty, unhandsome strain that I can not tell how to brook such treatment from such an upstart that is but of yesterday's growth. He values himself mightily upon the great obligation he has laid me under by the care he has taken of my children.'' John was to place the three boys under the care of the merchant Thomas Evans.

On the same day Carter also wrote Evans, and saying that Dawkins was ''so overgrown with the conceit of his greatness that I cannot bear it,'' advised him that John would be bringing the three boys to be placed under his care.

The rankling at Dawkins's inappropriate words began to pass when a new onslaught of gout laid the proud man low. Shortly after he had given vent to his feelings in the letter to Dawkins, the gout struck him so painfully that he was confined to his chair and bed for ten days.

He immediately foreswore meat and wine. The attack became complicated by a cold that brought on a fever. Acting as his own physician, he took Anderson's pills, placed blisters above his ears to try to relieve the soreness in his head, and had his barber cup him twice. This chastening experience brought him to ''a cooler temper,'' he wrote John.

''Perhaps the little man (and such are very commonly of a waspish disposition) may upon a review of his letter condemn himself for the style of it. When you come to show him my other letter he will no doubt produce my answer, and, if he shows any uneasiness about my orders and confessions of his folly, I am not for having you put them in execution. Mr. Baily, whom he supposed I had cast reflections upon (which was very far from my thoughts — nor indeed do my words carry any such sense), was his true friend and to whom he owes his all; therefore some allowance is to be given to the zeal he justly owes to his memory. But, if his pride be so overgrown that he treats you with no better manners than he has done me, pursue my first orders and then deliver Mr. Evans's letter. After all, I can tax Mr. Dawkins with no unkindness to my children. He is a good merchant and hath done my business as much to my satisfaction as any man, and the trade is so indifferently furnished with valuable men, if I leave him I don't know where to find such another, and my concern is too large to put it all into one man's hands. Besides, Mr. Perry the elder is so very aged he must have a time to go off, which humanly speaking cannot be far off, and I'm afraid the grandson hath not a head calculated to go through such a multitude of business with that dexterity that they have hitherto done. These are weighty considerations; however, I will meet with respect from those that do my business and get my money, let the consequence be what it will. Pray God direct you in all things.''

The boys stayed under the care of Dawkins, and he and Carter went on as if nothing had happened. Perhaps the sharp reprimand did accomplish something in returning Dawkins to a sounder evaluation of his position in relation to the colonial, just as the sobering effects of time and pain gave the ''King'' a clearer estimation of Dawkins's value to him. He did not ask the services of Dawkins that he had of Perry, when the elder Micajah was still active. When he wanted new white indentures, as a clerk and a housekeeper, he turned to a merchant, John Pemberton, with whom he had done business on a small scale for many years.

''Twenty years ago you sent me by Captain Woodward two very good servants, John Babe, an extraordinary good writer, and Margaret Upton, the best woman servant I ever had in my family since I was master of one. She married very well after she was free. If you could recommend two such servants, now, it would be a very acceptable favor.''

Shortly after Carter wrote for the servants at Corotoman, he had to meet the chronic problem with overseers. Carter mostly used indentures as overseers for each of his forty-four separate and largely self-sustaining plantations. More experienced men worked as supervising overseers for several plantations, and a general overseer, Richard Meekes, was paid the good salary of £35. Of the professional overseers in general, Carter wrote: ''It's a hard case — there is not a diligent, sober man to be found for my business.''

The county officials, mindful of their own interests, always kept an eye on Carter's plantations. The sheriff of Stafford County, Captain Thomas Hooper, worked closely with him on two of his most productive plantations, Popular Quarter and the Falls Quarter. The general overseer of these Stafford County plantations, Nathaniel Hedgeman, had agreed to ''articles'' of instructions which Carter, with his familiarity with each of his properties, made specific and detailed. Carter wrote Sheriff Hooper that he had heard that Hedgeman "has been a very great delinquent from my business, and lived a loose rebelling life. . . ."

In his wildness, Hedgeman came to "a very lamentable," unnatural end, leaving his accounts with Carter in disorder. To replace him, Carter moved up one of his overseers, "unlettered" John Johnson, whom he hoped would, with the guidance of Sheriff Hooper, "prove a diligent, honest man."

After signing on Johnson in June (1721), Robert Carter showed that he could be totally unfeeling where he felt he had been wronged. Hedgeman's son Peter, whom Carter regarded as "a wild young lad" with no experience of the world, applied for the job his father had held. Carter engaged him to clear up his father's affairs, turning over the accounts to Johnson, and trusted him to weigh and mark the tobacco to load a sloop due to leave for Corotoman. But he wrote Peter Hedgeman with a candor bereft of any regard for the young man's feelings.

"The unexpected death of your father was very shocking to me. I heartily wish he had met with a more natural fate. He hath been a very great delinquent of late from my business, much contrary to the articles he was under to me. Had he been in the discharge of his duty and at the place he ought to have made his home, he might have been a living man this day. I shall be willing to do him justice for the time he was in my service. . . .

"As to your proposal of succeeding your father in my business, it appears to be a very odd thought in you. You must have some more years over your head and a greater share of experience in the world, as well as to let it be seen what courses you will fall upon in the management of yourself and your own business, before any judicious person will think you capable of such a charge as mine is. What kindness will lie in my way in respect to the long employ your father had under me I shall be ready to do you, who am   Your friend . . ."

While Carter and the other planters were working, according to the size of their involvements, against the break in good times, the English authorities decided that Spotswood's past controversies indicated the need of a change of governors. There was no immediate official announcement. Rumors of Spotswood's impending removal began to pass among the councilors in Williamsburg the next year, 1722. Robert Carter and other members of the Council, in showing their good feeling toward him, demonstrated friendship in the most practical of ways. They helped in his accumulation of land.

15

Between May and July, 1722, when they all knew Spotswood's time was running out, Robert Carter and other councilors worked with Spotswood to get 40,000 acres granted to him while issuing patents to others for 179,000 acres in new Spotsylvania County. As the Crown's representative neared the severance of his connections with the colonial service and England, he was ready to begin life as a Virginia planter with 85,000 acres. The colonial careerist could scarcely have joined the party more wholeheartedly.

Following the councilors' lead, the General Assembly supported even Spotswood's Indian policies in the friendly glow of those last two years of the administration. Earlier the governor had been forced to go it alone, when in 1715 the Yamassees and allied tribes, estimated at eight thousand braves, had declared a war of extermination on South Carolina. Spotswood had perceived the intercolonial dangers when the port of Charleston was exposed to attack from French and Spanish by South Carolina's stripping her coast to raise a force of fifteen hundred militia on the frontier. Over the opposition of the House of Burgesses, he had sent a force of three hundred volunteers to Charleston, on the understanding that Governor Craven would pay the men 22s. 6d. per month, provide clothing and food, and send on loan an equal number of slaves to work the fields left abandoned in Virginia. This move had taken a bad turn for Spotswood's position.

South Carolina, after paying the volunteers 22s. a month for nine months, broke off the payments, never provided any clothes, and issued poor rations. Worse, no slaves were sent on to make tobacco crops. This happened at the very bottom of the hard times that Virginia suffered during Spotswood's early administration, and he had been able to get the volunteers only because they went for cash wages instead of making a crop with the low tobacco prices. Some of the ragged, disheartened men returned to Williamsburg to besiege the governor and tell him — as they did not need to — they had neither tobacco crop nor cash. He had distributed £100 of his own money among them, and the General Assembly was moved to vote to reimburse him.

When more agents from South Carolina arrived in Williamsburg, seeking further help, Spotswood showed his indignation. Feeling that he had been made to appear to betray the Virginia volunteers, the

Colonel Alexander Spotswood (Courtesy of the Virginia State Library)

governor said, ''I should now be suspected of combining to kidnap its [Virginia's] inhabitants into the service of another province, upon imaginary encouragements which were never designed to be performed.''

He refused to approach the resistant House of Burgesses for more help. As it was, the Burgesses were aware that he was the only governor in North America who had responded to South Carolina's call. However, holding to his larger vision, Spotswood did what he could by winning away some of the Yamassee allies, and South Carolina finally succeeded in dispersing the Indian force.

When the last of the Virginia contingent had left Charleston, amid mutual recriminations between Spotswood and South Carolina, Spotswood had begun to comprehend the difference between ''local interests'' as they existed and his intercolonial theories. Nonetheless, he never abandoned his efforts to work with the Indians. The Iroquois, in passing the western plantations (near Spotswood's holdings) on visits to tributary tribes, casually killed and burned in passing, and in 1718 the governor tried to open negotiations with all of the Five Nations. As this happened near the climax of his oyer and terminer conflict, the Council joined the House of Burgesses in refusing any cooperation.

Then in 1722, with Spotswood's administration nearing its end, the Council and the House of Burgesses tried to reward him for all his efforts. The General Assembly voted £1,000 for the expenses of a commission, which Spotswood was to head, to work with New York's new governor, William Burnet.

As during the years of his administration the Indians had come to trust and respect Spotswood, he and Burnet were able to make a significant treaty with the Five Nations. In passing through Virginia, their parties were not to pass south of the Potomac on the east side of the Blue Ridge. This was a fine personal achievement for Spotswood, and the General Assembly, in a gesture of repentance, voted £300 to reimburse him for expenses he had incurred earlier.

With this affirmation of his policies, Colonel Alexander Spotswood completed his twelve years' administration in a climate of success. The councilors and their ladies again enjoyed the governor's private entertainments, and Mrs. Russell was again a charming hostess. William Byrd had then returned to London, resuming his quest of an heiress, and Robert Carter went with other dinner companions to the coffee house in Williamsburg. In the cool of the evening, the gentlemen strolled along Duke of Gloucester Street, their straighter-lined coats open to reveal brocaded waistcoats.

At Corotoman in 1722, Anne, the last daughter by Carter's first wife, married young Ben Harrison, the son of the "King's" dead friend Benjamin Harrison III. There were two young Carter girls left, of the second family, and Betty's last child, George. Carter was beginning to urge John to come back home, where his father's influence could help him begin his Virginia life in a position of consequence. There was, by the summer of 1722, no doubt that Colonel Carter could place his oldest son where he wanted to, for of all things in Spotswood's administration, *the oligarchy had been confirmed.*

A status quo had been established. Freed from conflict with "foreign" governors, the entrenched and expanding ruling class could devote its energies to the social aspects of life, with emphasis on the splendor and elegance which were to characterize the "golden age." Governor Spotswood, who had come to trim the oligarchy's wings while advancing his own career, would always be associated with the flowering of that age.

While the storms and the bitter personal feuds of his administration would not be forgotten, Spotswood would be remembered mostly for the age that flowered during his time. His time was colored by an aura from Spotswood personally, by the positive nature of his strengths and his accomplishments. Though the prosperity that came in his administration was caused primarily by the end of the war in Europe, and the resulting rise in tobacco prices, he was remembered for the efficiency he had imposed. The return of good times became associated with him, with his lavish entertainments and serving of fine wines. The westward expansion he encouraged, with its persuasive myth of "the Knights of the Golden Horseshoe," was climaxed by the romance of the "castle" he built at his mining colony in the Wilderness, where he brought an English bride in 1724.

Williamsburg grew to a city (it was incorporated in 1717) of two hundred houses, with a variety of public places, all manner of artisans, and a theatre. In that year Archibald Blair's mercantile establishment built a stone store on Duke of Gloucester Street. Under Spotswood's direction, Bruton Parish was rebuilt into a larger brick church in the form of a cross with a fine design which even Europeans commented upon. The high square pews, built to enclose entire families, were handsomely paneled and comfortable. In the Public Square, where fairs were held and traveling artisans displayed their wares in Public Times, Spotswood designed an octagonal powder magazine, or arsenal, built so sturdily that it endured two wars and all the mutations of time. In the expansion of the capital, also associated with Spotswood, his crowning achievement, symbol of his whole adminis- tration, was the Palace (so called without derision) to which the oligarchy gave the sincerest flattery of imitation.

Before Spotswood left Williamsburg, Robert Carter's son-in-law Mann Page began his life-long project of building his Rosewell man- sion, which would rival the Palace. Its masonry was never surpassed on the continent. Soon another of Carter's sons-in-law, Benjamin Harrison IV, began the building of a manorial seat at Berkeley, de- signed in an adaptation of the Palace with many original features of its own. Neither Rosewell nor Berkeley nor the other manor houses that began to appear from the 1720's on were in any way copies of the Palace, but most reflected its influence and fell generally in the Georgian style. As Virginia had influenced the careerist Spotswood, so Spotswood left the tangible memorials of his influence on Virginia.

For the oligarchy, it could not be said that Robert Carter and his friends were the same as if Spotswood had never happened. Their rule came to a maturation in the deadlock with Spotswood, and after he withdrew from the field, they were more assured. Robert Carter be- came bolder, both in the unprecedented scale of his land acquisitions and in his assumption of political power. For himself he had never held one of the Colony's larger lucrative posts. But when Spotswood's suc- cessor appeared, Carter had no hesitancy in recommending his son John for the office of secretary, open since the death of Spotswood's friend Dr. Cocke.

Colonel Alexander Spotswood, partly inadvertently and partly by looking to his own fortune, solidified the architects of the ''golden age'' in the seats of power.

Portrait of a Merchant-Planter as "King"

ROBERT CARTER WAS restored to the agency of the Proprietary two years before Spotswood left the governor's palace for his house in the Wilderness. It was in this second period of Carter's agency that the dimensions of his wealth and power, of his unassailable ego, placed the "King" in a class by himself. Never before in Virginia, and never again, would the climate of the environment — along with the unique opportunity of the Proprietary — favor the self-development of a single individual into the rare position of dominance combining the greatest wealth of his time with the greatest political power. He was at once an original robber baron, a very enlightened one, *and* the leader of responsible government.

His total influence extended through the lines of intermarriages among his children and in-laws, and through the lines of personal and political alliances, but King Carter stood as the trunk of a tree to its branches.

With all the tangibles and intangibles of the position he personally maintained, as a man he lived at the very heart of his day, enjoying his own time in the same ways as did his fellows. While his "haughtiness" was an outward reflection of his incorruptible sense of

self, in habits and traits Carter was very much like his peers. Nothing
in his behavior served for stories of eccentricities or variance from the
norms of the planter class. Because of the high demands he placed
upon himself, and the largest appetite for acquisition of his day,
Robert Carter was differentiated from his contemporaries by degree
and not by kind. No referencees made to him by contemporaries indicated that the solid-looking councilor was regarded as being in any
way unusual. He was simply more of everything.

Of course, Colonel Carter received great deference, by virtue of
his formidable presence as well as his influence, and he was perhaps
the only man in the Colony with the illimitable self-assurance to
expand the domain of the Proprietary in the face of every reasonable
opposition, almost even of logic. When, in all simple vanity, Carter
wrote that he believed he was the only man who could properly handle
this private dominion within the Colony, the facts bore him out.

During the years following 1712, when Lady Fairfax had sought
higher revenues by supplanting Carter as agent with Edmund Jenings, the Proprietary had at first yielded less than during Carter's
agency and then nothing at all. For the four years 1713–1716, while
Jenings had been attending to his own affairs in England, his deputy,
young Thomas Lee, had served ably as agent on the scene.

Lee met the same problems that Carter had contended with in
his first agency : rents were hard to collect, collection officers cheated,
their paper work was inefficient, and the landholders paid — when
they could get away with it — in trashy tobacco of low value. Countless occupants of land within the forests spreading over the territory
had never made compositions, and acted in effect as squatters. With
young Lee doing the work in Virginia, Jenings was able to pay only
the contractual £425 annual rent to Lady Fairfax — £59 less than
the revenue paid the Proprietors during Carter's first agency.

Thomas Lee, with the vigor of his grandfather Richard Lee I,
liked making observation trips over the whole area, familiarizing himself firsthand with the settlements and the settlers. He issued patents
on a modest scale to new settlers in the western parts of the Northern
Neck, where Indian menaces had formerly restricted the growth of the
Proprietary. Like all the agents before him, Thomas Lee patented
some land for himself. He took up sixteen thousand acres, with some
choice land on the Potomac, and a tract including the present Washington suburb of Fairfax County. He was to become the next giant in
the Lee family, building Stratford Hall and founding that distinguished line of Lees. However, while showing promise and energy as

Jenings's deputy, he was a young man overshadowed by his uncle-by-marriage.

Then Jenings returned, ill and harried by debts, and quickly entangled the affairs of the Proprietary. For two years he paid nothing on the rents owed the Proprietors. By 1719 he was nearly £1,000 in arrears to Lady Fairfax. Then, in May of 1719, Lady Fairfax died, and Thomas, the sixth Lord Fairfax, became heir to the colonial estate.

Though Lord Fairfax was then twenty-six, his mother had left the property entailed, with trustees in charge. Like his immediate forbears on both sides, Fairfax was of a class which expected to be maintained in a way of life that simply excluded the idea of gainful employment. After assaying the revenue possibilities of his various properties, Lord Fairfax concluded that the Virginia lands promised to yield the most with the least effort. Later, when Fairfax came into complete, unencumbered ownership, he grew active and showed considerable ability. Under the conditions in 1719, he merely turned for advice to William Cage, one of the trustees. Cage went to the Perrys, who naturally recommended the removal of Jenings and the return of the agency to Robert Carter.

Since the break in Carter's agency had been costly in pocket to the Proprietors, the "King" was in the position of being sought. Showing no enthusiasm for regaining the agency, during 1720 he more or less permitted himself to be persuaded by the Perrys. He wrote the Perrys: "If you transact anything on my behalf, pray remember the tobacco these rents are paid in is upon the decline. . . . Colonel Jenings has had a fine time of it. Whoever is his successor must not expect such good luck. . . ." By the end of the year Carter had allowed himself to be persuaded, but on a different arrangement from his earlier agency. He was to pay a fixed yearly rental of £450, more than Jenings though less than Carter had paid through commissions in his first agency. He probably contracted to pay additional revenues when he issued more land patents. He also agreed to collect the rental payments owed by Jenings to the Proprietary.

During his cautious correspondence with the Perrys, Carter wrote that "upon the fall of tobacco," the agency seemed "like to prove a very hard bargain to me; indeed, so it appears every day more and more." He has been accused of taking this line in order to drive a good bargain. Privately, however, he wrote his son John in London: "I am afraid, upon this fall of tobacco, it will prove a very disadvantageous bargain to me. . . . There is no repenting; I am now bound and must do the best I can with it."

It has also been pointed out that later, after a rise of tobacco prices, Carter was reputed to be taking in actually £700 a year. That was ten years later. As for 1721, he had correctly estimated that he would go to much trouble to make very little cash in the immediate years ahead.

This financial arrangement with the Perrys and Fairfax is of crucial significance to the understanding of Robert Carter's controversial exploitation of the Proprietary for the benefit of his own family. He has been accused of being a "plunderer," among other things, and much maligned for using his agency to feather his own nest. The key point of his contract with the Proprietors was that it was a business arrangement designed to benefit both parties.

Fairfax, by inheriting the colonial tract put together by his unsavory Culpeper grandfather, stood to receive the sizable sum of £459 a year for doing nothing. On the scene, Carter took on the cumbersome administrative duties of collecting rent in tobacco from recalcitrant and widely scattered landholders, of assembling and sorting and packing the tobacco, of shipping the hogsheads in a quantity to clear above all duties, shipping costs and commissions the set sum of cash for Fairfax. The bookkeeping alone was a separate operation at Corotoman. Another operation was the issuance of new patents so that Fairfax's revenues would be increased.

Obviously, with the enormous complex of Carter's own operations, and the magnitude of the wealth he was accumulating, he did not need the bothersome sideline of assuring Lord Fairfax of an income. Nor could the small and doubtful cash profit he might extract from the time-consuming enterprise have interested him too much. His sole reason for taking the agency was the opportunity to amass land on a scale, hitherto unprecedented in the Colony, which would provide dynastic estates for his children.

Robert Carter made it very plain that in exchange for providing for Lord Fairfax in a life of idleness, he expected to look after his own — with land. To the Perrys he wrote, in early January, 1721: "One great perquisite of this estate is the granting away the lands that are untaken up, of which there is a very large quantity, and I doubt not that they [Fairfax and Cage] intended me the power of doing this, and I shall proceed accordingly. However, I must entreat you not to let them rest until you have obtained from them a fuller power for all purposes. . . ."

He returned repeatedly to this point of being given the full power to issue land patents, and in this he missed the vigorous, dependable cooperation he was accustomed to receiving from Micajah Perry. The old man, one of the founders of the firm, Perry had been fading for some time, and that year he died. Before Carter received the news of his old friend's passing, he began to place on his son John the responsibilities of acting as his personal agent.

Carter still wanted his son back home. However, he made use of the situation, while continuing to berate him for staying away to enjoy the pleasures of London. Referring to a swelling in John's leg, he wrote, "When you come to live an active life in your own country, I hope that malady will wear away." Referring to the various tasks he had given John for the new Proprietary contract, he wrote: "I hope you'll apply yourself to pursue the several businesses I have put you upon, and mind less the pleasures of the town. You want a longer stay in England, but that I must not agree to — my purse won't allow it. Therefore prepare yourself accordingly. You are so taken up with your diversions you cannot find time to write your sisters nor to any of your relations. Your Uncle Armistead never had a line from you. You must expect they will treat you with the same lance. . . ."

While cuffing his son with one hand, he encouraged him with the other, and gave John his complete confidence on the project in which he was being employed.

"One great perquisite to the estate arises from the granting away the lands that are yet to take up," he wrote to his son. "I doubt not the Lord Fairfax and Colonel Cage, for their own interest as well as mine, designed me this power by their lease." He was at pains with John, who was to witness the formal contract, to make sure the full power was granted him. "I would have you be very careful of this affair and to have it executed before a sufficient number of witnesses bound to this place [Virginia]."

Until these witnesses reached Virginia with the lease granting him the full power he wished, Carter did not open the office at Corotoman for issuing new land grants. Certainly the deal was clear: in settling new lands in the Proprietary's domain, which would increase Fairfax's income, Robert Carter expected to settle some of the land in his own interests. Unquestionably the businessmen involved on behalf of Fairfax — William Cage and the Perrys — were aware that a man as rich and as busy as Carter would not take on the irksome enterprise, at which Jenings had failed, except in his own interests.

Later, Fairfax expressed some disapproval of the magnitude to which Carter's interests extended. But His Lordship never expressed any appreciation for the size to which Carter — in looking after his own — extended the domain of the Proprietary. For when all the controversial aspects of the arrangement were considered, Robert Carter extended the domain of the Proprietary beyond its bounds in the Northern Neck to encompass an area three times as large as the original grant — from 1,470,000 acres to 5,282,000 acres.

For adding 3,720,000 acres to Fairfax's holdings, Carter patented approximately 200,000 acres for his own family. He patented the 200,000 acres entirely during his second agency, when he tripled Fairfax's holdings. In his first agency Carter patented 15,000 acres for himself. In total, he took for his troubles 215,000 acres of 5,282,000 acres.

Carter's westward extension of the Proprietary was mostly fertile land, across the rolling Piedmont of Northern Virginia, over the Blue Ridge and on to the Alleghenies. Outside the Northern Neck — which comprised the intent of the original grant — Carter brought into the Proprietary the counties of Arlington and Fairfax, in the present environs of Washington, the "horse country" counties of Loudoun, Fauquier, and Culpeper in north-central Virginia, and, along with the northern counties in the Shenandoah Valley, five counties in what is now West Virginia. All together, Carter claimed land for the Proprietary in twenty-four counties.

Not only was the "King" the only man who could have accomplished this extension of the Proprietary's claims against the Colony's opposition: he was the only person with the outsized effrontery even to have conceived a scheme of such magnitude.

2

Carter's vision of expanding the Proprietary came during his first agency. The original 1649 grants of Charles II defined the Northern Neck territory as between "the heads of the rivers," the Potomac and the Rappahannock. At that time the heads of the rivers were in the distant wilderness. In 1688, when James II validated Culpeper's claim to the Proprietary, the language was changed to read: "the first heads or springs" of the rivers. By then settlements, including William Fitzhugh's large holdings, had extended northwestward to the area of the fall line of the rivers, and wherever "the first heads or springs" might be lay in the remote territory occupied by Indians. Nobody thought about the Proprietary's boundaries in the west until 1706, when Robert Carter brought the matter to the Council's attention.

Ten miles west of tidal water on the Rappahannock, the river forked into northern and southern branches. Since the northern branch ran closer to the Potomac, the Proprietary's western extension would be narrower if this fork (then called the Hedgeman River) were considered to be part of the Rappahannock. The then unnamed southern branch (called the Rapidan after Spotswood established his colony in the area) was a stream which had not even been known about when the original grant was issued. In 1706 a patent of four thousand acres north of the Rapidan — or between the forks — was presented to the Council to be ratified. Councilor Carter immediately protested the Colony's granting land in an area he *then* claimed for the Proprietary.

The Council appointed a commission with a surveyor to determine which of the rivers was veritably the Rappahannock. The commission confused matters by finding the branches to be of equal magnitude. Nothing more was done until Governor Spotswood began issuing grants in the disputed area between the two rivers. Carter recorded routine protests, but the issue would ultimately have to be decided in London. There the fifth Lord Fairfax (husband of Catherine Culpeper) showed total disinterest in anything having to do with his wife's property, except for the revenue he squandered. Then Carter was replaced by Jenings, and the controversy over the western boundaries of the Proprietary became inactive. Spotswood made no serious effort to dispute the Proprietary's claims, advanced entirely by Carter, to the land between the forks, and concentrated his own expanding holdings south of the Rapidan.

When Carter resumed his agency in 1721, he entered his protests as a matter of record against the grants that had been made. At the same time, to protect himself in the event that the final decision went against the Proprietary, he patented lands for himself through the regular colonial office. Because of this he has been criticized for covering his bets. Carter was getting no support in London. He found the sixth Lord Fairfax as indifferent as his father had been to taking any active interest in the property. Carter wrote to Perry: "I never had one line from the Proprietors about this matter, and if they do not think fit to bestir themselves in support of their own estate I shall have little reason to give myself any trouble in throwing myself into the frown of Governors. As their trustee I have done my duty in hanging out my light for them."

Carter did throw himself into the frown of governors, as well as arouse antagonism to the Proprietary and all its aspects, especially the boundaries. He gave no indication of even being aware of the growing ill feelings and protests in the General Assembly. His mind actually turned to further extension of the boundaries — the extension that was to triple Fairfax's domain.

The "first head" of the Potomac River was generally accepted as its juncture with the Shenandoah River, which ran along the western base of the Blue Ridge. Carter decided that the juncture with the Shenandoah River did not constitute the first waters of the Potomac. He introduced the contention that the Cohongarooton River, which lay north and northwest of the juncture, was the principal branch of the Potomac. As the first waters of the Cohongarooton rose in the Alleghenies (now West Virginia), Carter would claim for the Proprietary the northern end of the rich Shenandoah Valley.

Carter did not push this claim until some years after he had resumed the agency in 1721, and it was not settled until after he died, when Lord Fairfax finally bestirred himself to use influence in England. However, it was the ultimate success of Carter's grandiose claim that gave His Lordship more than 5,000,000 acres in Virginia. As King Carter's vision of the Proprietary's potential domain originated with him, as the claims were instituted by him and his protests were continually recorded without any cooperation from Fairfax, by any judgment he rendered considerable service for the 200,000 acres he exacted as a "commission" for himself in his second agency.

Nor was that the extent of his service. While patenting land for his children, he also issued grants totalling 1,300,000 acres to new settlers in the western part of the Proprietary. Despite Fairfax's later private complaint that Carter's grants to his children had kept potentially productive land idle, Robert Carter was a vigorous force in pushing back the frontier by opening the western land to new settlers. Eight years after Carter started issuing patents, including the large grants to his family, William Gooch, then governor, wrote to the Board of Trade: "Without taking up these large grants upon which great improvements were necessary to be made, these counties west of the Northern Neck would not have been settled as speedily as they have been, and much of that land which has been seated in small parcels would in all probability have remained to this day desolate."

It would be hard to evaluate his contribution to the western expansion in the movement initiated by Spotswood. When Carter had resumed the agency in 1721, Spotswood made his own contribution the following year by his treaty with the Albany Indians, which cleared the western frontier of marauding Indian tribes. Carter had by then reopened his land-grant office at Corotoman, issuing the first patent of his second agency on December 1, 1721. The next year business began to pour in.

For a time Carter experimented with a "manor" system, similar to the large landholdings in England, by which the settlers became, in effect, tenants. These settlers, mostly striking out from settled Tidewater, were products of the New World and were uninterested in any system in which they did not own their own land outright. The manor plan faded off. Many of these independent-minded customers of Carter's were Scotch-Irish indentures who had worked out their time, and they started a strain of sturdy, self-reliant farmers in Virginia's Piedmont and in the Shenandoah Valley.

Carter's claims in the Valley were challenged by Lord Baltimore from Maryland and by the executors of William Penn, as well as by Virginia, and settlers from Pennsylvania and other colonies moved in and made their arrangements directly with Williamsburg. Undisturbed by the counterclaims and the rival settlers, the "King" in 1724 began issuing patents for himself — approximately ninety thousand acres that year.

Until that move, Carter's holdings had been mostly in working plantations he had bought in Tidewater, and the manor seats that went to his children were on settled Tidewater estates. Beginning in 1724, he patented the virgin western lands, taking title ahead of the new westward movement of settlers. It was at this time that he committed himself to the dynastic ambition of founding estates for all of his sons, and for favorite grandsons.

His firstborn son John would be the primary heir, who would inherit the home estate at Corotoman, and was being trained as something like a junior partner to his father. Beyond that, Carter would not follow the primogenitary custom of preparing younger sons for professions with little or no land of their own. He took the precaution of educating his sons so that they were basically prepared for professions and, as they were growing up, pointed out that they were younger sons who must expect to make their own ways. But in 1724 he began to patent large tracts of the new land in their names.

He took out patents for his sons John, Robert, Jr., Charles, Landon, and George; for son-in-law Mann Page; for grandsons Carter Burwell, Lewis Burwell and Robert Burwell, Carter Page and Robin Page, Robert Carter Nicholas and Benjamin Harrison. In beginning the building of these separate landholdings in 1724, he wrote his most candid statement of his personal policy to a friend, John Chelton.

"Upon my first having this office, I was desirous to inform myself the best where I could find some large quantities of good land to take up for my children and grand-children. . . . I directed both Hooper [sheriff of Stafford County] and Coppedge [surveyor] to take a view of these lands. Accordingly Coppedge did, giving me a very good account of them, encouraging me to hope he could take up for me at least ten thousand acres of very good land. Accordingly I made an entry in one of my son's names and sent up a warrant for the surveying it, which was in the possession of Coppedge at his death. . . . I have since given Mr. Savage, the present surveyor, directions to lay off the best of these lands for me. Collin Mason wrote to me for a warrant to take up some lands on this Cubb run which I denied to send him for the aforesaid reason, and must be so plain to tell everybody that I will issue no warrants for any lands in those places till I am served, and I hope no body will blame me for regarding my own children in the first place. . . ."

Carter showed his awareness of possible censure of his land-grabbing when the time came for a new lease to be drawn in 1724. He wrote William Cage (October 6) : "I know the world is very censorious and 'tis impossible for men under any tolerable figure to live without enemies, and there may [be] some perhaps so busy to give you unagreeable stories of my management of your estate. All the justice I shall desire of you is that you will not receive any impressions to my prejudice until you allow me the opportunity to be heard for myself, and I am not in the least doubt to demonstrate that every step I have taken will redound to your interest and to those to whom the estate will belong."

This was neither a troubled conscience nor concern over what people were saying : in acceptance of the gossip attracted to a figure of his size, he was trying to protect himself against the effects of envious tongues where they might influence his business associates. Carter was fully aware of what he was doing for the Proprietors in settling the new counties, and of his detractors' ignorance of the multiple problems the agency put upon him.

Not all the chores Carter assumed or all the legal controversies he entered into were necessary for the management of the Proprietary. Where a shilling was concerned, however, the smallest details in which he involved himself were necessary to the "King."

By ancient English law written into the Proprietary's charter, the Proprietary was due the fines levied in its counties' courts, the forfeitures of felons' goods, deodands and other "casualties" of crime. In Carter's first tenure as agent, he had collected the forfeitures of felons in the Northern Neck. Neither Jenings nor young Lee had stood up against the collectors of revenues, and during their agency the Colony had claimed all forfeitures for the Crown. When Carter resumed the agency, he immediately returned his practice of claiming fines and forfeitures for the Proprietary. He went to the extreme of claiming the goods of a man who hanged himself, on the grounds that the suicide was a felon for committing self-murder.

Before this case the Colony's revenue collectors had given way to Carter, but on the suicide the attorney general ruled that the goods belonged to the Crown. Carter wrote Cage that he had demanded the goods, "alleging that a *felo-de-se* is the highest species of murder, that his goods are forfeitable and grantable, that the words in the grant, 'all and all manner of felons' goods whatsoever,' are both general and special, and must comprehend these goods."

Such claims as these went through all the courts up to the Attorney General and Solicitor of England, and Carter said, "I have fed the best lawyers we have in maintenance of this controversy . . ." and, if it went against him, he planned "to appeal to the King in Council."

He justified his continuous squabbling over the picayune amounts of money in another letter to Cage. "These things are not very considerable at present, but it may happen, in time to come, that they may be worth struggling for." Carter seemed not to be able to establish a legal precedent about the goods of suicides. On his major points he finally won, and evidently enjoyed the haggling.

Curiously, Lord Fairfax showed interest in using his influence with the Board of Trade over specific cases of forfeiture. Although Carter could not arouse His Lordship over the legal maneuvers he was making in Virginia to gain three million acres for the Proprietary, Fairfax stirred himself over the attempt at winning the rights to the forfeited goods of some anonymous suicide.

The "King" also managed, by his skillful control of energy, to familiarize himself in detail with the physical terrain of the Proprietary. He spent as much as twelve days at one time in riding over the lands. The purpose of this intimate knowledge was to insure that the patents taken up in his children's and grandchildren's names consisted entirely of choice lands. He refused to sell as little as half an acre of land to a man who wanted to build a mill.

Carter instructed his surveyors to exclude poor, unproductive land, and such worthless land as swamps, from the patents he was taking up. When Thomas Lee wanted a grant surveyed in the same way, Carter wrote him: "I could never agree to such a method." Holding idle the great tracts for his heirs, he insisted that all other patentees develop the land as actual settlers — in encouraging the westward development — and turned down claimants for large tracts on the grounds that the land would not be improved.

Obviously one of the reasons King Carter was called hard names over his Proprietary agency was that he had one rule for himself and another for the world. Also obviously, he was not called hard names by those whose sense of virtue had been outraged: he was resented as the man who got there first. Actually, the magnitude of his effrontery aroused more awe than envy, and more envy than reproach. Some of the resentment of him simply personalized the long, growing opposition to the Proprietary. Clearly, his imperious handling of the agency did nothing to soothe feelings.

3

There was one action for which Carter contracted — the collection of Colonel Edmund Jenings's debt to the Proprietary — that he entered into with such a grim zest as to suggest underlying personal motivations. He showed his attitude to his predecessor in a letter to the Perrys shortly after he signed the lease for his second agency. " 'Tis but a few days ago that I have got the deeds and papers from Colonel Jenings's agent. Whatever they have done with all their gains is in a great measure a secret, but they have taken care to leave the office in as much darkness as possible, so that their methods are not to be traced out. 'Twill be very well if, in a twelvemonth's time after my lease is proved out, I can bring things to a tolerable clearness."

Later he wrote Fairfax and Cage: "I shall not take upon me to descant upon Colonel Jenings's proceedings any further than to claim what is my due from the expiration of the lease, but I may be fairly justified in this general observation — that things appear to me under more confusion than when I went out of the business."

That last statement was closer to fact than his innuendo that Jenings had "taken care to leave the office in as much confusion as possible, so that their methods are not to be traced out." This was a dark interpretation to place on the records muddled by a man obvi-

Robert ("King") Carter. From a portrait in the Sabine Hall Collection,
Richmond County, Virginia, courtesy of T. Dabney Wellford
(Colonial Williamsburg photograph)

ously no longer capable of managing any of his affairs. After earlier
showing political adroitness in remaining free of factions, when he
had gotten in over his head financially Colonel Jenings lost his
political poise along with his judgment.

He had blundered with Spotswood in isolating himself from the
party when it came solidly into power. Spotswood came to feel sympathy for him, but after the governor's term ended in 1722, Jenings
was in the awkward position of being president of a Council on which
he was outside the controlling power structure. Concurrent with his
money troubles, his health failed and he began to suffer loss of his full
mental capacities. In 1723, Carter wrote of Jenings: "I take his
circumstances to be very desperate, and he is a very decayed man."

Carter's relentless determination to wring a speedy settlement
from him was not unrelated to Jenings's decay. The financial arrangements between them were extremely complicated. In July, 1720,
Carter — through six drafts drawn on merchants payable to Jenings
— had lent Jenings £1,000. This covered the amount Jenings owed the
Proprietary, and presumably Carter lent Jenings the money to retire
his Proprietary debt. Six months later Jenings had made no payment
on his debt, and in January, 1721, Carter wrote Perry: "I'm afraid
there will be a necessity for me to go into a lawsuit with him, but that
will be the last remedy."

Evidently the Perrys chided Carter for risking the £1,000 loan,
for on March 25 he wrote: "You give me several hints that you wish I
may come by my money from him as easy as I parted with it to him.
All I can say now is, it had been well these cautions had come sooner. I
should have had the wit not to let him have the fingering so much of
my money. You may believe I was not in his debt. I have both him and
his son bound to me body and bones, if that will be a sufficient security
to me."

Since it would seem most unlikely that Carter would have lent a
shilling without detailed knowledge of the borrower's circumstances,
it might be inferred that he wanted Jenings bound to him "body and
bones."

Later in 1721, during the summer, Jenings sent Carter bills of
exchange for £400 to be applied to his debt to the Proprietary. He
asked Carter to delay sending them to Fairfax, as they might not be
honored in England. Carter made no agreement not to send the bills
of exchange to England. However, in mailing them on August 1, he
did ask Fairfax to delay protesting them as long as possible. When

Fairfax presented the bills of exchange, they were not honored by the merchants on whom they were drawn.

Yet the following year, Jenings gave Carter bills of exchange drawn on Perry to the amount of £600 — £400 to make good the earlier bills of exchange, and £200 additional on his debt to the Proprietary. These went through all right.

During these exchanges, Carter was experiencing difficulty getting payments on his personal loans. A letter Carter wrote to Perry on July 4, 1723, would indicate that Jenings had gotten money to pay most of his loan to Carter by giving mortgages on his home estate to Colonel Page and Mr. Wormeley. ''I was very lucky to get that money of Colonel Jenings by a mortgage to Colonel Page and Mr. Wormeley. There is two hundred pounds more, as Colonel Jenings himself reckons it, due them, which I profess I don't know how to get a penny of.'' This suggests that his son-in-law and young friend took their mortgage claims on Jenings's property, and the cash involved went to Carter.

Carter continued to Perry: '' 'Tis reckoned he is more engaged than his state is worth. I have promises enough from him, but they come to nothing. He proposes to mortgage land and slaves; whether he will be able to meet with anybody to advance money upon such a security is a great question. I will take on the ways I possibly can for dunning. I am sure he does not want the last remedy [which] I am sure must be the law.''

On the same day, he wrote Cage, referring to the money Jenings still owed the Proprietary. ''The safest way [to collect] is to bring suit against him, which I am not very willing to do till you send me your positive orders to justify me in going into these harsh measures with him.'' Not usually troubled by the need to justify, the ''King'' possibly was aware of the personal motivations that would be involved in his ''harsh measures.''

Under the dunning and threats of lawsuits, Jenings managed to retire his Proprietary debt by 1725. By then the remainder of his personal debt to Carter was mounting, with compound interest, toward Carter's estimated figure of ''four hundred twenty-two pounds, seven shillings and three pence half-penny.'' Carter took out mortgages on Jenings's home, Ripon Hall (named after his family home in England), and by 1726 Jenings was ruined. Such was his deterioration by then that he was ready to be toppled from his post as president of the Council, and clear the way for Robert Carter to the one remaining honor that would cap his career.

4

Spotswood had been replaced as governor in 1722 by Major Hugh Drysdale, whose four-year administration was characterized chiefly by accommodation to the Virginia "custom." With Carter's party totally accepted in London as the rulers of the Colony's internal affairs, the Board of Trade had advised Drysdale: "We observe that several disputes have arisen between your predecessors and the House of Burgesses in relation to some privileges claimed by them, and must desire you to take care there be no innovations made on His Majesty's prerogative or the ancient usage of your Assemblies, and we doubt not but that by your prudent management all these animosities will cease."

Agreeable and unforceful, Drysdale conscientiously followed this advice to the letter. Two years after he had come into office, he recommended John Carter to fill the vacant secretary's office. In writing the Board of Trade that there might be an objection to young Carter because his father was already on the Council, Drysdale pointed out: "There is scarce a qualified person in the Colony unattended with some such like inconvenience, for they are all incorporated either in blood or in marriage." Soon after the return of Carter's oldest son to Virginia, John Carter also ascended to the Council, where he joined Carter's son-in-law Mann Page.

Drysdale's acceptance of this packing of the Council by the then most powerful family of the party revealed, by the completeness of the Crown's acceptance of its power, the effect of Spotswood's failure to control the oligarchy. Drysdale, in fact, began to hound the former governor over his holdings in the new Spotsylvania County. Drysdale was probably influenced by his friendship with the long-hating Blair, when he began his legal persecution of the oligarchy's former opponent for using their practices of land accumulation. Drysdale specifically charged Spotswood with irregularity in getting title to sixty thousand acres in new Spotsylvania County, and with not paying quitrents. The new settlers' seven-year exemption from paying quitrents did not apply to holders of more than one thousand acres.

Spotswood fought with great skill. He went to England to present his case, and — as had Robert Carter and other big landholders — validated his actions on the ground that he had kept the spirit of the law by opening new lands to small settlers. He gave proof of having transported families of settlers at considerable personal cost and "maintained them until the terror of Indians [was] over . . . cleared grounds, fenced fields, builded houses, made roads and bridges, set up mills" and supplied stocks of cattle. It was undeniable that he achieved the purposes of the western expansion movement, initiated while he was governor, and that his settlements served as buffers against Indians in central-western Virginia. He presented impressive figures: Brunswick County, formed the same year as Spotsylvania, had 160 tithables in 1726 as against Spotsylvania's 950. Women and children, as nontithables, would multiply the comparative number of settlers in Spotswood's growing community.

Following a tradition going back to Berkeley, Spotswood omitted mention of any items that might tend to unsettle British manufacturers — such as his experiments in iron-mining. He stressed that the land he was developing would produce naval stores for England. Spotswood won his case on all counts in an oblique triumph of those principles of the oligarchic land-accumulators which he had come to embrace. As a Virginia planter in his rustic paradise with the wife he married in 1724, the former governor established the office of postmaster general of North America and the West Indies, which he operated with his usual efficiency. A granddaughter and a great-granddaughter married grandsons of Robert Carter. Even Byrd forgot their differences, and wrote a vivid description of a visit to Spotswood in the Wilderness.

Drysdale's losing fight against Spotswood was his only significant personal involvement during the four years of his administration. He and his wife lived quietly in the magnificent mansion Spotswood had completed, and entertained with less vanity in the quality of their hospitality than had their predecessor. Colonel Carter, friendly with the governor and Mrs. Drysdale, visited them at the Palace — noting in his diary that he tipped the governor's servants.

Carter was a generous tipper. He also noted in his diary tips given to the servants at the ordinary, the coachman of his son-in-law Colonel Page, the coachman of an acquaintance, and his daughter's nurse. The only time he ever mentioned music, he referred simply to "The Concert," and noted, "I gave the singer [15] shillings and had given her a guinea before."

Carter's tavern companion Byrd did not return to Virginia until 1726, and the "King" seems not to have spent the informal hours with Drysdale in the coffeehouse and public places which he had enjoyed with Spotswood. In the aftermath of the prolonged controversy with Spotswood and the shift of feelings at the end, politics became routine

during Drysdale's colorlessly efficient administration, with its attention to details which involved no issues. As nothing critical occurred
in the Colony's destiny, Drysdale did not figure prominently in
Carter's thoughts. His notations in his diary, largely concerned with
the details of his business complex and with his family — chronicling
visits to and from his daughters — became increasingly preoccupied
with his health. His letters to personal and political friends, and to
business associates, also began to carry more references to his health.

In the year he turned sixty, Carter missed a Council meeting
early in Drysdale's administration. On February 19, 1723, he wrote:
"The gout has been an inseparable companion to me all this winter
and I have not bestry'd a horse since I left Williamsburg, nor have I
had my shoes on one whole day together nor have I escaped swollen
feet every night; indeed I have been twice or thrice at our church
with the help of my coach, taking care to wrap my feet warm."

This seemed to imply that he hobbled from his house to the coach
and from the coach to his pew with his unshod feet swathed in
wrappings. As the rest of the congregation customarily waited outside
the church until Carter's family arrived in a four-horse coach and
entered after them, the lame "King" must have required all his
imperiousness to make a dignified entrance. He also required considerable fortitude in his devotions. In the unheated brick building,
drafts circulated over the five-foot-high backs of the stall-like pews,
inside which the narrow bench seats were anything but comfortable
for a person in pain. He propped his feet on hot bricks to avoid contact
with the stone slabs of the floor.

After that attack, he was bothered occasionally by minor upsets
in which his stomach seemed affected. He recorded in his diary: "Last
night I was very uneasy." Cream of tartar "worked very well."
Another time, he noted, "I took physick." Three days later he had "a
fine night's rest," and having missed church, read Dr. Tillotson's
sermon.

During the spring of 1723, and into late summer, he was not
seriously troubled by the gout. With politics continuing to demand
only routine attention and the Proprietary agency in one compart-
ment of his mind, he was able to indulge his insatiable absorption in
the details of his planting-trading-shipping-financial operations. His
own sloops plied continually between Corotoman and his outlying
plantations. From the distant plantations, along with the tobacco to be
shipped from his wharf, his sloops brought beef, corn, wheat, butter
and tallow. He was proud of his management of these isolated opera-

tions, and in another tart exchange with Dawkins wrote: "I must take
the liberty to say I know as well how to keep overseers to their duty
and am as much master of the planting trade as any one I know."

With the constant movement of produce from the separate plantations went constant trading: nothing was too small and nothing too
large. He gave a note to Ruth Wood on W. Wood for five yards of
Virginia cloth against four dozen eggs. His awareness of every detail
extended from the breaking of a team of oxen to the sewing of bed-
clothing with labels having the names of Negroes. In keeping a personal count of hogsheads of tobacco bought from smaller planters,
numbering from two to thirty, he once noted 121 rolled into the
warehouse at the Corotoman wharf in only two days. Corn too was
bought from smaller planters.

Up sometimes at three in the morning, he rode on personal
inspections of the multiple activities at his 8,000-acre home plantation,
returning to the manor house after dark. During the lambing season,
he daily counted the new lambs and entered the number in his diary.
"I had 23 lambs . . . 29 lambs. . . ." He recorded prices, thirty-five
shillings for a fat young cow at "killing time," and fifty shillings for
a seven-year-old steer. He looked in on the distilling of cider from his
apples, for this was a staple drink with him. Watching the growth of
the tobacco plants, he gave his overseers orders "to trench their
tobacco ground and draw off all the water they possibly could."

Even with his mastery of "the planting trade," he could not
escape the usual troubles with freed workmen under contract. "The
gardener treated me very saucily," he wrote in August, "told me [he]
valued not beating, with many other important answers which too
many to repeat. . . ."

Like the humblest, he suffered reverses caused by the weather. In
July his tobacco crop, along with everyone else's, was damaged by
unusually heavy rains. On August 12 a heavy storm broke during the
night and a hard rain continued until ten o'clock. "My houses," he
noted, "all full of water, my cellar has near two feet water, my boats
all swimming in the [boat] house. . . . My cider house blew down
about 9 o'clock [A.M.], a prodigious tide. . . ." While such misfortunes were ruinous to small farmers, Carter, like his contemporary big
planters, accepted these happenings as the normal course of things and
never lingered over his losses. He did not report them in letters to his
sons in England.

Always eager to draw them back to the plantation life, which he
regarded as superior to all others, he constantly showed his fear that

his sons (like William Byrd) would stay too long in London. He wrote Charles: "You tell me some fine stories of your self that you shall make a brave fellow by that the time is out I have allotted you to stay in England. I expect this will find you at the Mathematick School where your Brother Robin has been before you [and] whom I ordered Mr. Dawkins to send in [to Virginia] last year. I am now in expectation of him every day, in the first good ship to be sure he will come away, but if any thing should happen that he should not get out before *Carter* comes away again and then if it be your inclination to come along with him I shall be glad to see you; but if you have a desire to stay till the next Spring and it will be to your advantage, I shall be contented to let you stay till then and so I have given directions to Mr. Dawkins. . . ."

Charles and Robin had stayed with Solomon Low, and young Landon was still there. After writing a letter reproaching Mr. Low for lack of news about his sons, he wrote Landon in July (1723) :

My Dear Boy Landon:

"I received your letter by the Carter *last year and you make me believe that you are a good boy and mind your book which is the only way to prevail with me to let your stay be longer in England than your brothers hath been. If I hear you are a naughty boy and do not improve your time suitable to the charge I am at upon you, you must expect I will forthwith send for you away, so that according to your behaviour you must expect to be treated. I reckon by this time your brothers hath left Mr. Low's and that you are alone, be sure don't forget to write to me per the* Carter, *I pray for your well doing and send my blessing to you who am*

Your Tender Affectionate & Loving Father.

None of his children wrote to him as often as he wanted to hear from them, and letters were the more infrequent because he corresponded with them mostly via the ship *Carter*. Other mail came in on other ships, and he was always on hand at any ship's arrival. The endless variety of the ships' cargoes made each arrival an event.

Sometimes slaves walked down the gangplank in lots of as many as twenty-five. For fifteen grown males he paid £300, a figure in itself comparable to the average higher yearly incomes in England. Four of the girls, bought at £10 per head, he gave to his granddaughters.

Frequently Carter had difficulty in getting Africans of his choice. He wrote Perry that those from Gambia "are of a larger size and have more sense and more used to work than any other . . ." and he would freely pay forty shillings more for Gambians.

Nothing engaged his attention more than the barrels of alcoholic beverages rolled from the wharf to the barred wine cellars under his house. Rum, coming in hogsheads, seems to have been used almost entirely for serving to visitors or giving away. This was not a favorite drink of his. The brandy which he loved came in by the hundreds of gallons, and was also freely served to all comers and sometimes given away in friendly exchanges. Closest of all to his heart was the wine. During the summer he wrote his agent that he liked the claret sent earlier in the year, but it "is the dearest that ever I heard of. . . . I would have this wine of the very best sort, but . . . cheaper." He sent a hogshead of the costly claret to his daughter Elizabeth Burwell — or, as he wrote, "My daughter Burwell."

When he mentioned having visited or having been visited by his married daughters, he revealed a gradation of his feelings for their husbands. He was very fond of Mann Page and Benjamin Harrison, but his favorite was Nathaniel Burwell. When he had seen the Burwells, he noted "my daughter Burwell and my son." After seeing the Pages and the Harrisons, he noted "my daughter Page and Colonel Page" and "my daughter Harrison and Mr. Harrison," or "her husband." And though he loved all his grandchildren, he never doted on a child as on his grandson Lewis Burwell.

With the visits of his daughters' families, of friends and neighbors of all degrees, with the constant coming and going of planters of smaller holdings involved in exchanges and trading, of artisans and overseers, of surveyors and patentees for the Proprietary, along with the regular activities in the outbuildings scattered from the wharf to the tobacco fields, Corotoman in the summer was like a fair. This swirl of life made a somber contrast to Carter's aloneness when he was seized in late August by a violent attack of the gout, accompanied by a generalized illness which laid him low.

5

On Friday, August 23, 1723, after a trip to the Wormeleys' with his young son George, he felt fine coming home at night, sleeping on his boat with "the awning down." Back home, on Sunday he took a walk in the cool of the evening, breathing in the breezes off the river.

The next morning, Monday the 26th, a familiar symptom returned. "I was taken a little lame in my right ankle." At noon it had grown worse, and by five he "prepared for a fit of the gout." This attack came on swiftly and savagely. "At night could hardly stir . . . went to bed half-hour after ten . . . in great pain. . . ."

He awakened on Tuesday with a violent generalized illness accompanying the intense pain. It was a time when none of his married daughters was visiting him. As his sons John and Robin had not yet left London for home, his young son George was the only boy at home. His daughters by his second wife, Mary and Lucy, were still little girls. The children were in the care of a housekeeper-governess, Mrs. Young, who worked on a straight salary. Since her name appeared only twice in Carter's diary, her duties were evidently restricted to the children and she took little or no part in running the establishment for him.

He did not send for the doctor, nor apparently did he send out any messages about the crippling attack. After suffering stoically through Tuesday, he took two Scotch pills before going to bed and had a "pretty good night, was feverish about two hours, slept well the latter part of the night . . . waked pretty easy."

He was all right until he started to rise. In his bedroom, he finished two letters on bills of exchange "in great pain." He conferred with a visitor and then was carried by servants into the parlor. There he drank three dishes of coffee and milk. Then he was carried back to his bedroom, and the pills of the night before "worked twice" during the morning.

After that he tried walking around the house with a crutch, "but the least motion of the pained ankle puts me on a rack." At four o'clock he "ate a porringer of chicken broth with bread in it," and took a glass of cider and water. The pain continuing relentlessly, he had himself moved back into the parlor at sunset. From there he could look out of the window at the dusk gathering over his dozen and more outbuildings, over the wharf and boathouse and warehouse, onto the darkening water of the river. He stayed in the parlor until ten o'clock and then went to bed.

After falling asleep briefly, he awakened "in abundance of pain . . . was very restless until about 4 o'clock . . . had a fever and mighty difficulty in breathing. . . ." He could find no restful position. He got up to drink some water. This disagreed with him, and he washed out his mouth. Around five in the morning he drifted off to sleep again. His diary made no reference to his reactions or reflections during those wakeful hours in the dead of night when at his age, just past sixty, he must have felt mortality as an uneasy burden.

As were all colonists, of high or low estate, Carter was accustomed to living in the midst of physical suffering and to the recurring cycles of birth and death. Having known more than most the visits of death as a child, having mourned the loss of two wives, shortly after he lost his second wife he experienced the first death of a grandchild, and then the death of his favorite son-in-law, Nathaniel Burwell. The specter of the end was all too familiar to Robert Carter, but to judge from his passing references in letters, he regarded his own dissolution within the comforts of his religious faith. From his stoical recording of the progress of the illness, he accepted this too without introspection and with never a plaint about the time lost from the business of life. He endured.

At eight o'clock on Wednesday morning he was up for a cup of sage tea, and then was moved into the parlor. He was shaved by his barber, a young white indenture, and ate a porringer of gruel. Throughout the day he suffered the pain, which by evening was "very racking." At ten o'clock, with his left foot growing worse, he had a tankard filled with a mixture of cider, water, and loaf sugar, and he returned to bed. He felt feverish, with a dryness in his hands and feet, and restlessly tumbled and tossed until three in the morning. Giving up trying to sleep, he had a candle lit.

He rose at eight and drank three dishes of sage tea. That morning, Thursday the 29th, a schoolteacher and Mr. Bell, the rector, came in to visit him. During the day, he stayed on his diet of a porringer of gruel. That night he began to shiver and broke into cold sweats. Around three in the morning, the fever began to decline, and at four he fell into a sound sleep.

Friday morning he rose after eight, drank three dishes of sage tea and then three dishes of coffee and milk. Though his right foot felt better, his left foot was worse. In the forenoon he sat up in his chair and read. He recorded laconically in his diary: "Grew more uneasy in the afternoon; for my dinner I ate hominy and pancake, drank cider and water. At night, was very uneasy, read now and then but with a great uneasiness; had not stool this day. Went to bed about 10, got a short nap, lay till two before got to sleep, then slept till five; a very bad night. I had take it together the left foot now the worst of the two. Am an entire cripple, have not moved a step these several days only as I am carried about in a chair between the two."

On the sixth day, Saturday the 31st, visitors came and had dinner. For the guests, the meal was probably served at the "large oval table" in the enormous dining room. In there, in addition to the dining-room furniture — seventeen black leather chairs, two black leather stools (probably for small children), a "middling" oval table, a small oval table, and a black walnut corner cupboard — Carter also kept a black walnut desk and a pair of large money scales and weights. A large looking glass hung on the wall, and in the fireplace were a poker, a pair of andirons and two pairs of tobacco tongs.

Dining with the guests, Carter managed to eat a whole squirrel, and "drank plentifully of cider and water and six glasses of wine." On that day, he made his first and only mention of a member of his family. His young son George read him four chapters in the New Testament.

On Sunday, as news of his infirmity spread abroad, more visitors came in the morning, among them the schoolteacher who contracted to teach the following year. The visitors left before noon, and Carter noted: "I had a fine stool in the afternoon while they were at church." This was followed by a refreshing nap, from which he rose and read two of Commissary Blair's sermons. At dinner he "ate a broiled pigeon that was highly seasoned with pepper, some Bermuda potatoes and apple pie; drank pint of cider in water." Another visitor came and stayed until eight o'clock. He went to bed at eleven but was awakened by a dream. When he woke up, the pain in both feet was very bad, and he felt so ill that he tried to vomit.

On Monday, September 2, the beginning of the second week since he had first been "taken a little lame," he could manage to walk around the house without a stick, though the pain came in seizures from the knee down to the ankle.

The next day the guns announced a ship's arrival, and Carter's pain decreased sufficiently to be forgotten in his absorption with a new cargo. He ate a small fish for dinner and in the evening "drank wine freely" with the ship's captain. He almost finished off a bottle of white wine. He returned to business to write a lengthy letter on pushing "Colonel Jenings' affair." In referring to Jenings's promises, he wrote: "Pray be satisfied with nothing but writing. Remember that sound maxim: *Littera Scripta Manet.* . . ."

The following day, Wednesday, September 4, though the leg continued very painful, he was caught up in the activity surrounding the arrival of one of his sloops and the sailing of another. The feverish illness had then passed and to Carter, as to a cat, once the sickness lifted it was forgotten. When an acquaintance dropped in after dinner, he played cards until three in the morning.

The next day he went off to the races with Colonel Ball. Each day the pain in his feet and ankles was lessening, though he could not yet wear a shoe on his swollen right foot. Once freed of the debilitating aspect of systemic illness, he took little notice of mere pain. He had always liked horse races, where agreeable companions gathered in an open field at the unfenced quarter-mile tracks, and shared an informal social event in the warm sunshine.

Despite his reputation for haughtiness — and unquestionably he could at times be overbearing — he was not a man to keep people socially at a distance. He enjoyed being with his fellows — drinking wine and talking, playing cards or watching horses run — without any emotional needs for friends to satisfy. His emotional needs and their gratifications were, after the death of his second wife, centered in his children. As they became adults, his daughters and their husbands had become his intimate friends, and John — with all the prodding his father gave him — was becoming a confidant.

After the horse race, Carter made no more notations about that heavy attack of gout, which lasted eleven days from the first onset to its less acute stage on September 5. Though the pain must have been slow to pass entirely, once he was fully returned to the activities of life, his mind shifted away from the infirmities of his flesh. On September 4, while still unable to put a shoe on his right foot, he sent an order to London for boots — "half Jacks for the winter and the other pair to be summer boots" — for which he would pay about fourteen shillings. By September 11, he set off on his barge for a session of the General Court, presumably wearing both shoes.

Sick or well, however, he no longer rode cross-country to Williamsburg. He had reached the age when he took the longer time to make the trip by boat.

6

During the unsettled weather of early autumn, Robert Carter turned to the chronic problem of "servant trouble." His young barber was nearing the end of his "time," and Carter wrote Perry to obtain another barber-surgeon as an indenture: he wanted one who "can shave well, dress wigs, let blood, dress sores . . . of honest character and sober principles. . . ." He also wanted a coachman, carpenter, smith, joiner, tailor and bricklayer. He reproached young Micajah Perry for his want of alacrity in supplying good workers. "Your grandfather always helped me with tradesmen [artisans]. . . ." Later he complained, "The boat-builder has been an idle rogue ever since he came here."

For the constant building on the place, with which his own brick kiln could not keep up, he gave a local independent bricklayer sixty-five hundred pounds of tobacco for bricks.

During October he recorded minor losses from the weather. The wind blew "violent here," knocking down several apple and cherry trees. Another wind, with drizzle, blew from afternoon to night, and at nine the "flood gates blew and my dam went away. . . ." Later, he went to inspect the ruins of a mill.

On October 17, he made a laconic notation of a most meaningful event: "My son Robert came home." Then eighteen, Robert showed no ill effects from his stay in London, and a spirit of independence seemed inherent in his character. As he began to work with his father in the Carter Virginia enterprises, Robert, Jr. evidently chafed somewhat in the Corotoman establishment revolving around the "King."

John had already returned home, and a personal event involving him was treated even more offhandedly. On September 30 Carter wrote a letter to Perry about his periodic attempts to recover some land from the heirs of his niece, his brother John's daughter. In a P.S. he added: "My son is entering upon this state of matrimony. The 3rd of next month is the day set. I have already said enough to you about the shortness of our crops." This was the marriage of Carter's son John, then secretary, to Elizabeth Hill of Shirley plantation. The granddaughter of Colonel Edward Hill, of Sir William Berkeley's coterie, the bride was a James River neighbor of John's sister, Anne Harrison, at Berkeley. "The web of kinship" was tightening in the new generation and establishing a Carter "row" on the James.

Colonel Carter's brevity in recording events in the lives of his children, either in his diary or in letters, reflected the attitude of his day toward revealing emotions. Only on the death of his second wife, Betty, had he expressed his emotions about another person. On the other hand, it was fit and proper to carp about expenses involving his children. To Dawkins he wrote: " 'Tis a vast charge you have put me to for my son's [Landon's] expenses this last year. . . ." In his usually impersonal business letters, he felt no restraints on giving vent to aroused feelings, even rage, when he felt ill used in commercial exchanges, when his dignity was affronted by cavalier treatment or especially when the quality of his tobacco was questioned.

He gave such personal attention to his shipped products that he called Dawkins's attention to three hogsheads (numbered 32, 33, 34) as "indifferent" and "indifferently packed." Not until the ship was ready to sail from his wharf had he discovered the work passed off under the oath of an overseer, "a notorious rogue," on one of his distant plantations.

He continued to experience small visitations of illness. In mid-October, "I was taken with a violent looseness; held me for twenty-four hours, then stopped." This looseness, evidently diarrhea, recurred at intervals and seemed unconnected with the gout. The gout did not return until early December, when Carter was in Williamsburg. After showing surface amiability to Colonel Jenings by drinking a pint of wine with him, and then eating "heartily" at Mrs. Sullivan's, he suffered the return of the pain in both legs. His feet grew swollen and he had to get about in carpet slippers.

He left town on the 12th, stopping for visits with widowed "Daughter Burwell" and the Wormeleys. From his friends' house he had to be carried to the boat. On Christmas Day, with no visitors, "I walk a little with my cane. Can endure my great slippers. My rest very much broken. My feet swell every evening, and almost in continual pain." That minor attack passed. On December 30, "Physick wrought kindly. Had an easy night."

On New Year's Day, the time for presents, he gave a shilling each to his daughters Mary and Lucy, and his son George. It was a clear day, with "wind fresh at northwest." Since Christmas, he had thought the weather was "too good for this time of year. A sourer after it is to be feared." Shortly afterwards "Daughter Burwell" came for a visit at the same time as his daughter Judith Page, with her husband and family. He gave a guinea each to his daughters "for a New Year's gift."

Sometime after his daughters' visit, Robert Carter had his first open break with a beloved child. Elizabeth Burwell was determined to marry a doctor, Robert Nicholas, against her father's opposition. He was so disturbed that he wrote to an unidentified person of his daughter's "imprudent and obstinate match with Doctor Nicholas." The doctor was not among the great landholders of the Colony, and Carter seemed suspicious of his motives. As legal guardian of the Burwell children, handling their late father's estate, Carter expected

Doctor Nicholas to involve him in lawsuits. Carter might have had other and more personal objections to Nicholas, for this was one of the periods when he referred in his diary to ''The other book.''

His daughter not only went ahead with the wedding but showed a coldness toward her father. The "King" entered one of his most poignant understatements on Monday, April 27. From Williamsburg he "went to Mr. Burwell's [as he still referred to his daughter's home]. Mrs. Nicholas did not appear.''

Three days after this, when a ship arrived, he went on a spree of buying and giving away slaves. Buying forty-one Negroes, he gave to his son-in-law Benjamin Harrison six men and four women, with whom to seat land Carter had bought from Thomas Randolph; he gave six men, four women and a girl to his granddaughter Betty Harrison; he gave four men and two women to Colonel Page, for seating some land Carter had bought; and he allotted six men and four women to ''Mr. Burwell's estate.'' Since the Burwell estate was under his management, these ten slaves would become the property of his Burwell grandchildren.

After Carter's trouble with his daughter Elizabeth, Robert, Jr. ("Robin"), whom Carter was grooming for official posts when he came of age, began to grow restive. The following year, Carter evidenced no surprise when Robin "carried away my new suit of clothes without my knowledge." Two weeks later, on June 15, 1725, "My son Robin took his leave of me." The leave-taking was apparently not unfriendly, as Carter recorded: "I gave him 5 pistoles [and] 2 doubloons.'' Wherever Robin went and whatever he did, after a short time he returned to his room at Corotoman. Then in September he went off restlessly to visit his older sister Judith and brother-in-law Colonel Page.

By then Charles had also returned from England, and the presence of the grown young men among the children unsettled the housekeeper, Mrs. Young. In mid-summer of 1725, Carter noted: "Mrs. Young acquainted me her time was up. I told her money was ready for her. [She was paid a good salary of £12 sterling and £6 current money.] She was her own woman, she was at liberty to do what she pleased. I was contented she continue here still. She answered that she would rather live with me than any other Gent. [But] the troubles of the house were so great, she could not please everybody. I told her little jars would arise in such a family. Abundant discourse we had. She agreed to stay if I was satisfied with her, so she went about her business and I to my reading."

The reconciliation was not to last. Later Carter recorded: "Mrs. Young sent me a note she would leave the house this day. I had her, Charles, Robin, before me, examined into several stories, found Mrs. Young had misrepresented several things." After that Mrs. Young evidently took her departure.

With the grown sons at home, and with periodic visits from the growing families of his daughters, Colonel Carter continued to expand his house. In July, 1725, he contracted with James Byran, the independent brickmaker, "to make me two hundred thousand bricks more. I am to give him three shillings per thousand for well making and well burning them." Earlier in the year, the Corotoman bricklayer had built a marble floor in the main house.

Robert Carter might also have been called "contractor and builder." In addition to the continual work on the village of Corotoman, he had built the Lancaster County Court House — for which he was paid in tobacco — and undertook to build a new church for the Christ Church parish, at his own expense. He might also have been called "ferry operator," as he was paid in tobacco for maintaining the Rappahannock River ferry at Corotoman. Most of all, he would have liked to be called "President" Carter, as president of the Council, and in 1726 the conditions arose which made it possible for him to move toward this culmination.

7

When the damp, still heat of summer in Tidewater Virginia returned to the capital in June, 1726, Governor Drysdale's health began to suffer and he planned to go to England on a leave. His absence would make Council President Jenings acting governor. Since the "decayed" Colonel Jenings had not attended a Council meeting in two years, an inquiry was made into Jenings's condition. Individuals reported to the Council that he was unable to give rational answers. One report stated that Colonel Jenings was not "capable of giving any directions in any business whatsoever." He appeared so broken by his debts and his efforts to borrow that his lawyer said he could get coherent answers only from Mrs. Jenings.

Jenings wrote rather piteously, "For although I have by sickness and for some time been disabled from attending the General Court and Councils, I hope I am not so much incapacitated either in body or mind as to be shut out of that post of President of Council wherein His Majesty has been pleased to place me."

When all the reports were in, the Council on June 25 petitioned Drysdale to remove Jenings. "By reason of the insanity of his mind and memory, [he] is a person altogether incapable of administering the Government of this Colony." Drysdale immediately acted on the petition and that day ordered Jenings suspended from the Council.

Robert Carter was appointed Jenings's successor to the Colony's highest office.

Before Carter assumed his office, Drysdale's health took a turn for the worse and he died on July 22. On learning the news the next day, Carter wrote Ludwell "that I am tenderly affected by the loss of so good a governor, when we were in hopes of his getting well. . . ." However, business made it impossible for him to attend the funeral.

"The 'Carter' now lies before my door, her business done, ready to depart. My letters [which would be mailed via the ship] undone, my bills of loading not taken, those things must be settled before I can leave my home. It will be impossible for me to get to town before Thursday or Friday next and the inconvenience of delaying the funeral may be so great that I do not think it proper for me to direct such a thing; therefore, let Mr. Holloway and Dr. Blair know that it is my desire the funeral may be performed on the appointed time and beg you will make my excuses where they are necessary." With Colonel Byrd, recently returned with a new wife (who was not an heiress), son John would be among the "suffering persons" to represent official Virginia at the funeral.

A week later Robert Carter called a meeting of the Council for August 1. Only six councilors were present, not including the frequently absent Byrd. Of the six, four were Robert Carter, John Carter, Mann Page, and Philip Ludwell: the other two were Cole Digges and Peter Beverley. Carter stated to his kinsmen and friends that he had called the meeting because, as he conceived it, the administration of government devolved on him by the suspension of Jenings. It was entered into the Executive Journal of the Council that he "desired to the opinion of the Council whether he is not fully authorized to act as president of Council. . . ." After reading and considering the minutes of the last meeting, the Council reached the unanimous opinion that Robert Carter became "the first named in His Majesty's instructions and is duly authorized to take upon himself the government. . . ."

On the summer day when Robert Carter took the oaths of office, he wrote in his diary, "Very uneasy. A great many gentlemen came to see me. Colonel Ludwell did not come. At 2 o'clock went to Council, took the proper oaths, ordered a proclamation to continue all in their offices. I gave the Council a dinner. After, settled the ceremony of the funeral. Sent a message by Mr. Holloway to condole Mrs. Drysdale, to know how she did and to know when she would allow herself to be visited. I would wait on her if she pleased.''

The funeral of Governor Drysdale had not gone on without Colonel Carter, as he had requested, and the new Council president described the highly formal ceremony in his diary. He and the Council then sent a message informing Mrs. Drysdale that she was welcome to occupy the governor's house as long as she desired. Richard Hickman, Spotswood's former henchman in the secretary's office, was appointed to be responsible for the care and inspection of the house and gardens after Mrs. Drysdale moved. With no other immediate business to conduct, the Council was adjourned. Acting Governor Carter took the journey to the lighter air of Corotoman, where breezes off the water lifted the August heat.

Evidently the ''King'' never occupied the governor's palace. He ran the government from the center of his empire at the home plantation. For his troubles he received roughly £1,100, a lieutenant governor's salary.

Robert Carter was sixty-three when, as president of the Council, he became acting governor of Virginia for a period that was to last more than one year. Behind him he had forty years of public life, beginning at the level of county and vestry, and including thirty-five years in the Colony's capital. Typical of the best in the tradition which he himself was forming, Robert Carter brought nothing of the acquisitive shrewdness he applied to the Proprietary's agency to his new post in the governor's office. Always highly responsible in his public offices, as acting governer he displayed scrupulous honesty, kindness in personal dealings, in fine feeling for the fitness of things, and in all matters he combined expected decisiveness with an unexpected moderation. According to the lights of his day, the ''King'' was never more the Christian gentleman than when he governed the Colony.

The Morning of the "Golden Age"

"IT IS THE PECULIAR happiness of this country that we are more than any other of the American [colonies] united in the religion of the Church of England, and our civil rights and liberties are secured to us by the same excellent laws which have been the boast of the English nation, and have made them greater than any other people."

This proud statement was addressed to King George II by Virginia's General Assembly shortly after Robert Carter's period as acting governor ended with the arrival of His Majesty's new governor in September, 1727. (The new governor, Major William Gooch, had brought the news of the death of George I and the ascension of his son.) Continuing as president of the Council, Carter remained the most powerful Virginian in the Colony when the "golden age" entered its rich maturation with Major Gooch.

As Nicholson's administration had been the fulcrum between the old order and the emergence of the oligarchy into control, and as Spotswood's administration established the new order of the oligarchy in the stable perpetuity of power — along with bringing the "golden age" into flower — Governor Gooch was identified with the full flowering of the age which continued for half a century as something

of "a life in thrall." Gooch (later, as baronet, Sir William) belonged
to the age, the time and place, as completely as the native Virginians
whose values he made his own. Nineteen years later he could say to his
brother in almost literal truth, "I have ruled without so much as a
murmur of discontent in my administration."

Gooch was the first governor since Berkeley's first term had
ended in 1649 who was *Virginia's* governor rather than His Majesty's representative in the Colony. While Spotswood became a
Virginian after his battle with the local powers, Gooch identified his
interests with Virginia's from the day he moved his charming family
into the Palace. He not only accepted the laws of custom, to which
Spotswood had had such difficulty in adjusting himself: he embraced
them. In Robert Carter's lifetime, Gooch was the first English administrator whom the people really loved. There had been much in
Spotswood which the members of the General Assembly had respected,
much they came to admire, and Robert Carter and some of the
oligarchs genuinely liked him. Gooch was loved by the colonists
generally, in a mutuality of approbation. Of the Virginians he wrote:
"The gentlemen and ladies here are perfectly well bred, not an ill
dancer in my government. . . ."

Major William Gooch was forty-six years old when he settled
among them with his wife, his children and his wife's sister. Like
Spotswood a former professional soldier, he had built a fine reputation
in service with Marlborough. Naturally affable and friendly, he
worked on the principle that "more flies are caught with honey than
with vinegar." This temperament was ideal for adaptation to the
(then) inexorable laws of custom as executed by plantation masters,
such as Robert Carter, who were habituated to the exercise of authority.

With all his social dexterity, Governor Gooch was far from being
a mere trader on personality. A cool observer, he immediately suspected insincerity behind Blair's pious courtesy. He wrote to his
brother that Commissary Blair was "a vile old fellow, but he does not
know I am sensible of it. . . . There is no perplexing device within his
reach that he does not throw my way. . . . The best policy will be to
kill him with kindness." Outplaying Blair at his own game of maintaining a surface cordiality, Gooch kept the chronic king-disposer
quiet for the last sixteen years of his life.

He looked coldly also upon Robert Carter's encroachments on the
Colony's territory for the aggrandizement of the Proprietary and the
creation of estates for his descendants. Gooch, however, did not lock

horns with the "King" or with any of the oligarchy. Since he was not committed to "the Crown's prerogatives," he used persuasion and patience in leading up to his measures to promote Virginia's interests.

Gooch began his administration with a combination of practical advantages. In England, as Parliament had established its supremacy over the Hanoverian sovereigns, a Whig oligarchy was being established with the center of power shifted to the House of Commons, where Sir Robert Walpole sat as chief minister. Walpole began to develop the responsibility of the cabinet with the supremacy of a prime minister both in the cabinet and in the House of Commons. This cabinet system, by which England was to be governed, had not been in mind when William III signed the constitutional agreement after the 1688 Revolution. It evolved, partly through the personalities of figurehead monarchs and the power-minded Walpole, whose political actions were useful in developing an efficient system among a people who were more adept as politicians than as political theorists.

In transforming the English constitution, Walpole was a strong supporter of commerce, and the laws enacted by his Whig ministry in relation to the colonies mostly promoted the interests of the merchant class represented by the Whigs. Walpole took a laissez faire attitude toward Navigation Acts and toward the details of internal government handled by the colonies' general assemblies. In all the colonies there was a drift toward a nebulous division between internal and external affairs, and Major Gooch had the good fortune to arrive in Williamsburg when Virginia's commercial prosperity was his government's chief consideration.

In the Colony, the custom of rule was firmly established and the structure of society had become stabilized around the slave-labor system on plantations. The new governor inherited the orderly methods of operation established by the efficiency-minded Spotswood and carried on by Drysdale. Gooch, no more an innovator than he was a disturber of the status quo, was interested in improving the economy generally by methods either already in use or known.

He resurrected Spotswood's hated Tobacco Act of 1713–1717 in a version more acceptable to the people and presented it in a way acceptable to the General Assembly. In restoring public warehouses and the inspections to prevent shipping of "trash" tobacco, he systematized the shipping methods to prevent frauds in customs collections, pilfering by sailors, and similar drainings of the profits. Gooch avoided stepping on the big planters' toes, as well as disrupting customary practices, by using some private warehouses as the public warehouses in the planters' districts. Corotoman's warehouse was used, and Robert Carter grudgingly accepted the change. The law, he wrote, ''caused a world of difficulty and a great deal of delay.'' Then he admitted, ''It occasions the throwing away abundance of what we used to get good money for.''

Gooch, aware of the antagonism that Spotswood had aroused by ramming his laws through the General Assembly, offered provisionally all his acts which affected the Colony's trade, and his Tobacco Act had to be reaffirmed every four years. This was a very trying business for the governor. Periodically he was forced to run the gauntlet of House of Burgesses, Council, collectors of customs, Board of Trade, merchants in England and planters in Virginia, and finally the Privy Council and the King. Considerable conflicts of interest existed among these elements, and Gooch depended on his capacity for making friends as the means to gain his ends in the Colony's interests. Since he was continually successful, the governor's harmonious relationships with all levels of the Colony brought a glow to the era. The people, delighted with their genial administrator, never suspected that he manipulated them in order to promote their economy for the good of the empire.

Gooch had to be equally adroit to avoid antagonizing the English manufacturers and the manufacturers' bloc on the Board of Trade when he encouraged a modest production of goods other than tobacco for shipping. During his administration pig iron, deer and beaver skins, pitch, tar and turpentine were shipped in small quantities to England; wheat, corn, beeswax, barrel staves, pork and beef went in small shipments to Madeira in exchange for wine; small quantities of pork and beef, barrel staves, Indian corn, candles, shingles and peas were shipped to the British West Indies in exchange for rum, sugar, molasses, coffee, cocoa, salt and some currency. Pork and beef, corn, hides, tallow, pitch and tar were traded to New England for rum, sugar, salt, cheeses, ironware and woodenware. All this trading in a circuitous exchange — via the merchant-planters — for manufactured goods amounted to little more than one-fifth of the volume of tobacco shipped to England.

While by volume the products other than tobacco scarcely constituted ''a diversified economy,'' the growth of Williamsburg and small towns, and the springing of new ''cities'' into being, offered cash wages to an expanding number of artisans. From A — actors, apothecaries, attorneys — to W — watchmakers, weavers, wheelwrights, wigmakers — the capital alone gave work to artisans in more than fifty categories. Many of these, perhaps most, were former indentures who had become acclimated at such self-sufficient private communities as Corotoman.

When Gooch arrived in Williamsburg, the flow of immigrants — both indentures and freedmen — was continually thinning, as Virginia began to solidify in its social mold. The prevalence of slave labor on plantations did more than turn planters away from indentures to the permanent labor force of Negroes. As most planters using slaves disassociated themselves from the physical work on their holdings, a stigma began to be attached to manual labor. The effect of this was both direct and indirect.

Directly, young Englishmen no longer were attracted by work which had come to be regarded as menial, fit only for black slaves. Indirectly, the planter class began to become more distinctly separated from the majority of freeholders, those working their own land. As the physical spread and political influence of the planters gave them, for practical purposes, rule of government at all levels, the old yeomanry began to dissolve as a political force. The last maneuver the non-slave-holding farmers attempted in the General Assembly was a law passed in 1723, designed — as had been the heavy duties in 1710 — to curtail the slave trade. The influence of English merchants caused the law to be repealed.

With this setting of the mold, the Virginia colony gave an impression of having a rigid social structure — with slaves the equivalent of the English peasantry — in which paths of advancement were closed to the uneducated penniless immigrant who had only his unskilled services to offer.

2

The impression of a rigid structure was largely accurate for the settled tidewater regions east of the fall line of the big rivers — the line which could be drawn due south from the present city of Washington on the Potomac to the present city of Richmond on the James. Westward, as where Robert Carter was issuing patents in the Proprietary, the way was still open for men and women of ambition, hardihood and resourcefulness.

Along with the intercolonial movement of acclimated families pushing west of the structured tidewater regions, new immigrants went to the west as freedmen. Able to patent modest holdings of land, they cleared the forests and cultivated their acres on a frontier where manual labor carried no stigma. These settlers came from Ireland and Scotland, with a strong strain of the Scotch-Irish from the North of Ireland, and there were some Pennsylvania Dutch, who moved southward up the great valley.

Slaves were carried westward, too, where successful families developed estates in a modest version of the tidewater baronies. Thomas Randolph, son of William and Mary Isham Randolph, founded an estate which he called Tuckahoe, fifteen miles west of The Falls (Richmond) in the James River.

In the same region Peter Jefferson, a physically powerful young surveyor, was developing holdings patented by his father, Thomas Jefferson. This was the second Thomas Jefferson, son of an obscure yeoman who ran afoul of William Byrd I. Accumulating land and slaves south of the James, Thomas Jefferson II had become a militia captain, a justice of the peace, and sheriff, and had assumed such perquisites of the "gentry" (planter class) as owning a racing mare. His son Peter would marry a granddaughter of William Randolph, and their son, the Thomas Jefferson known to history, would be advanced to and groomed in the General Assembly by the oligarchy.

West from Peter Jefferson's land in Orange County, at the foot of the Blue Ridge, Ambrose Madison was developing holdings of five thousand acres, worked by fifteen adult slaves. He also owned fourteen Negro children. Madison married Frances Taylor, whose father had been one of Spotswood's companions among "the Knights of the Golden Horseshoe." Taylor became the ancestor of two presidents — James Madison and Zachary Taylor — and of the first wife of the President of the Confederacy.

While the Jefferson and Madison families were rising in the planter class in the west, a hard-working yeoman named John Marshall was struggling for a livelihood on two hundred poor acres in the Northern Neck. Called John "of the forests" because of the brushy nature of his land, he would have been unknown to history except that his son advanced as a surveyor, married a granddaughter of William and Mary Isham Randolph, and had a son, another John, who would become Chief Justice of the United States.

This fluidity within the Colony showed there was still room at the top, making possible the rise of *individual* families. However, the condition of the yeomanry as a segment of the social and economic structure no longer beckoned immigrants as it had in the days before the increasing ownership of Negro slaves brought a division among the tobacco growers.

John Henry, a Scotsman who came to Virginia shortly before

Gooch, married a widow, Sarah Winston Symes, whose family was and whose late husband had been well established in the gentle, fertile land of Hanover County, north of Richmond. John Henry had been educated at college (as had his brother, a clergyman), and it was simple for him to advance to the post of presiding magistrate of the county court and to the parish vestry. His son, Patrick Henry, who had the gift of reaching the "plain people," would never have made it to the House of Burgesses if John Henry had not been sufficiently presentable to marry into a family of some substance in Hanover County.

Yet although the yeomanry as a social-economic segment was declining in political significance in the Colony's structure, there was considerable mobility among individuals in this broad level of the population. As a few families moved up into the planter class, many more dropped out of the yeomanry. Always some families had existed on the border line of subsistence, either through shiftlessness or because some honest workers were simply not cut out for farming. These became agricultural casuals.

Young men of the yeomanry found outdoor work more to their liking, in such jobs as "rangers." Back in the post-rebellion days, while waiting for Culpeper, the General Assembly had adopted a protective system which employed four Indian scouts as rangers attached to each of Berkeley's useless forts. Not a garrison at the forts, which served only as bases, these frontiersmen patroled the outlying country and sent back warnings to gather militia where the Indians were coming. "Ranger" became a regular line of work, and Thomas Marshall used it to pull his family out of the futureless drudgery of farming poor land.

Many other young men of yeoman families learned trades. Carpenters, coopers, and bricklayers were in constant demand and received very high wages. Sometimes skilled artisans used their cash to buy land and slaves and operated small plantations on the side. The use of their hands to earn cash, however, excluded them from the category of "gentry."

Among the uncounted numbers of the dispossessed yeomanry who moved out of the settled areas, some went to other colonies, to try again in an unstructured society. Failures had to move on, because there was no place for the poor in a rural society of scattered plantations and small farms. Visitors to Virginia commented on the total absence of beggars or paupers. The Virginians did not tolerate persons who did not support themselves.

When the old and disabled were taken care of by parishes, each person receiving charity was required to wear on his shoulder a colored badge naming the parish which carried him. As the unemployable had to be supported in private homes by tobacco paid by the parishioners, the tobacco growers were determined to prevent the development of a class of deadbeats who moved from county to county. Aside from those physically unable to work, the colonists made no distinction between honest failures, and misfits and triflers. All employable unemployed had to find sanctuary elsewhere.

Some of the employable unemployed among the dispossessed yeomanry had altogether abandoned efforts to support themselves. Having neither skill nor land, they joined runaway indentures and runaway slaves, mingled with the fringe of a criminal element, and as in England, roamed the countryside. Among the runaway indentures were some who had been kidnapped and others who had been induced to make the adventure by "spirits" — sinister London characters who "spirited" the susceptible, with alcohol or other blandishments of persuasion, onto ships. Naturally these victims did not take to the labor in the baking tobacco fields. Others who had come willingly, through self-delusion, turned out to be equally unfitted for the hard life.

Ten years before Gooch came, England had given the colonists the callous insult of dumping the refuse of English prisons among them. Before that, convicts had not been "cast for transportation" to Virginia since 1670, when the General Court had ordered that no person trading in Virginia was permitted to bring in "any jail birds or such others. . . ." When England resumed the transportation of convicts, over the Colony's protests, the General Assembly, in 1722, passed laws requiring ships' masters to post bond not to turn convicts loose until they had been indentured. The English government repealed this law and sent over, along with unfortunates jailed for debts or misdemeanors, an assortment of vicious, degraded criminals, and eight persons convicted of being "gypsies."

The House of Burgesses stated in a petition to the Privy Council that "many cruel murders and frequent thefts and robbings have been and still are committed . . ." that endangered "the lives and estates of His Majesty's good subjects." Arsonists were suspected of setting a night fire to Thomas Lee's house, from which Lee and his wife and children escaped through the windows in their shifts. Tobacco warehouses were burned in the Northern Neck, and a new church in Spotsylvania County. Silver plate was stolen from other churches and horse stealing became commonplace. The county courts recorded convictions for miscegenation and bastardy, and mulattoes began to appear in the records.

(Later, in 1740, the General Assembly found a rough, pragmatic solution to the problem of undesirables. "Whereas His Majesty has been pleased to send instructions to the lieutenant-governor of the Colony to raise and levy soldiers for carrying on the war against the Spaniards in America, and this present general assembly being desirous upon all occasions to testify their loyalty and duty . . . the county courts were directed to impress . . ." able-bodied persons without employment who might be classified as vagrants.)

Runaway indentures and runaway slaves and some of the dislocated yeomanry mingled with the English criminals, to form a drifting population mainly seen at cockfights and horse races. No estimate was made of their numbers. Since this floating segment was never a stable element, there was no bottom — as a peasantry or proletariat — in the white population.

The growing population of Negro slaves began to form a stable bottom in the structure, even though separated from the white population. From the earliest days the indentures working out their time had evinced a strong tendency to keep themselves free of any association with Negro field workers. In the hierarchical structure of their society, the English people never considered that a nonwhite heathen race of slave workers had any place in their scheme of things. It was in Gooch's administration, after some trouble caused by freed Negroes, that the first distinction between Negroes as individuals and white freeholders was made. The General Assembly passed a law denying the vote to any Negro. Governor Gooch wrote that this denial of the franchise. along with exclusion from serving on juries and testifying as witnesses, was intended to make clear a distinction between Africans and Englishmen "with whom they [Negroes] were never to be counted equal."

While the Virginia colony had set in its mold, with layers extending from the slave labor force to the big merchant-planters, within each level the society was anything except static. Among all those families working the land who would be lumped together as the yeomanry — the majority of the population — there was a tremendous range from the illiterate, borderline-subsistence families at the bottom to the families of relative substance. Many yeoman families were in a sounder financial position than families who were technically gentry and were in debt to English merchants for a few slaves.

Then, as in the England they had left, there was a yeasty movement among these families of non-slave-owning freeholders whose small holdings simply would not sustain the new generations. Since land was cheap, these Virginian "younger sons" continually branched out on their own, either finding some small patch in settled Tidewater or joining the movement to the west. Also, among these younger sons of solid enough families came the artisans and the odd-job workers, wolf-hunters and drovers in the Indian-trading trains, chainmen to surveyors, store clerks and jailers, and — if the head of the family enjoyed an acquaintance with a big man of the county — deputy sheriffs.

Not all who gave up farming left the land quietly. Some hard-bitten men, taking to a violent life of adventure, committed crimes before losing their individual identities in the rootless bands including the English convicts. Even among those farmers who struggled on, there was protest and resentment. Many of the small planters had paid quitrents and customs duties with trash tobacco, and they complained more bitterly than Carter over Gooch's inspection warehouses. Very probably some of the working yeomanry took part in the burning of public warehouses in the Northern Neck, for which the criminal element was given the entire blame. Certainly the small planters were open enough in their threats.

The ambitious families who acquired slaves to rise into the planter class became separated from the farmers by using, on their own scale, the same risk-taking single-purposed ruthlessness as their models among the big merchant-planters. As did the second Thomas Jefferson, a man could establish his family in the gentry in one generation, and this tangible goal aroused a tough-minded competitiveness.

The range in the gentry, from the holder of a few slaves working a few hundred acres to Robert Carter, was even wider than in the yeomanry, and the closer to the top, the fewer there were. As in England's larger and minor gentry, the planter class had its subdivision in what came to be termed the "aristocracy." In the maturing of the era during Gooch's administration, the "aristocracy" as distinguished from other "planters" would consist mostly of the families which had accumulated on a large scale early enough to have established themselves, by intermarriage, in *hereditary* political power and social prestige.

This would be similar to the classifications in late nineteenth- and early twentieth-century America, when "aristocrats" were distinguished from nouveaux almost entirely by having worn the purple a generation or more earlier — long enough to have become habituated to the effects of privilege. While the more shadowy divisions in Gooch's day were also similar, these were by no means the same. Many families of the planter class generally had been gentry just as long as the aristocrats, or longer, only they had never possessed vast riches or far-reaching political influence, and, as a result, had not married into the "web of kinship" which dominated the ruling class.

Such a family was Augustin Washington's. His grandfather, the educated son of a clergyman, was the John Washington who had come to Virginia in 1657 and, as a shrewd and industrious entrepreneur, had advanced himself to his parish's vestry, represented his county in the House of Burgesses, and served as lieutenant colonel of its militia. But Colonel Washington's oldest son, Laurence, had lacked push. Like Robert Carter's older brother John, Laurence had accepted his responsibilities by serving as a county justice and as a member of the House of Burgesses. Beyond that, he was neither politically ambitious nor acquisitive. He made a good marriage, to Mildred Warner of Gloucester County — in the heart of Tidewater — whose father was speaker of the House.

Laurence Washington died young, his widow married an Englishman, and Augustin Washington, with his brother and sister, was taken to England as a child. After their mother died, their uncle in Virginia entered into a long litigation over the children's estate with their stepfather. Augustin returned to Virginia about 1715, when he was around twenty-six, and began expanding his modest estate.

He was big for his day, a six-footer, ambitious and energetic, and having grown up amid litigations, he was contentious and aggressive. He acquired ten thousand fertile acres, with a homesite on Pope's Creek about three-fourths of a mile from where it emptied into the Potomac. He was sufficiently well placed so that one of his sons, a second Laurence, married a cousin of Lord Fairfax, and the other son, George, married the widow of Custis's son, a nephew-by-marriage of Colonel William Byrd and of a family about as old-line as they came. Yet not even retroactively, not even after George became the absolute number one citizen of Virginia and the new nation, were the Washingtons ever included in the aristocracy as it existed during the full flowering of the "golden age" in Gooch's administration. The Washingtons had not come soon enough into the dominant group within the ruling class.

While the subdistinctions might well seem to be something less than consequential, in Gooch's day every gradation in the gentry was of the greatest consequence to the planter families struggling to improve their position or even to maintain it. Falls from the top came as swiftly as the rise of Thomas Jefferson II. However, no one whose family had risen into the aristocracy ever lost his social position through poverty, ignorance, idleness, loose living, gambling debts, or any of the other handicaps to rising to that position.

The "golden age" when Gooch ruled Virginia was essentially the age of the "aristocrat," in all meanings of the word. For the tobacco growers who worked their land themselves, the artisans and clerks and the various types of frontiersmen, the lot of most was better than they could have known in England. They experienced the gratification of owning their own land, the inner security — with pride and loyal-ties — of place-identification within a confirming social order, and the personal independence peculiar to men and women living in a new country with boundless frontiers.

But life was hard and uncertain, often violent, and the struggle to make ends meet was continuous for the majority. Many of the small operators in the planter class were no better off: to keep up with the gentry could be a bitter strain bringing few real rewards. The age was "golden" chiefly for those who mastered their environment, built their private baronies, and found absolute security at the top through alliance with kindred plantation masters.

As the biggest of them all, the most complete, King Carter was not truly a representative of the age that came into full flowering with Governor Gooch. He was the arch of the merchant-planters who, as-suming personal responsibility for their government, dominated the age and gave the time of "life in thrall" its sense of permanence, its apparently changeless perpetuity.

3

When Robert Carter, at sixty-four, began to preside as president of the Council in Gooch's administration, he soon made it known to the new governor, very quietly, that he was not called "King" for nothing. During Carter's acting governorship, the naval officer of the Rappahannock district had died, and Carter had obtained the "ap-probation" of the Council to appoint his son, Robert Carter, Jr., to this modestly lucrative office of collector of Virginia duties. "Robin" was then living at Corotoman with his wife, the former Priscilla Churchill.

Young Robert was more interested in working at surveying the lands patented by his father in the Proprietary than in holding appointive offices (he did not need the cash), and he moved the naval office to Corotoman. Previously the collector's office had been situated on the south bank of the Rappahannock, at Urbanna, a port built specifically to serve the public warehouse in Middlesex County. Robin began serving his own convenience when he took office on March 1, 1727.

That autumn, when Gooch was established as governor, the shippers of Middlesex sent in a petition protesting the inconvenience caused by having the naval office across the river at a private house, and demanding its return to Urbanna. Carter's friends on the Council ignored the protest until November 1, 1729, when Robin's younger brother Charles came of age. As Robert, Jr., with his wife and child, then moved out of Corotoman to build on holdings of his own, it appeared that his father had wanted him to hold the post only until Charles was old enough to assume it. When the "King" presented Charles's name for the post, Governor Gooch turned him down.

Robert Carter held the new governor in high esteem. He had placed his grandson Lewis Burwell "under the care of Doctor Gooch, our Governor's Brother, supposing him to be endowed with the same noble qualities that our Governor is, whose temperate and gentlemanly behavior among us worthily render him a fit pattern to us all. . . ." It was beneficial to the "morale" of those "who have the honor to be frequently in his conversation. . . ."

In order to avoid clashing with a man he so respected, Carter wrote to Lord Orkney, the titular governor in England, and Charles Carter was appointed naval officer of the Rappahannock. Charles had planned to work at the post, and he moved the office back to Urbanna, quieting all objections from the Middlesex shippers. Thus, without a harsh word exchanged with the amiable governor, Carter simply went over his head, and Gooch learned that as His Majesty's representative he had less influence with his own superior than did Council President Carter.

Despite Carter's influence, Gooch aligned himself with the general sentiment against the expansion of the Proprietary. When Gooch came to Williamsburg, the popular feeling in Virginia was that the Proprietary's boundaries should halt at the Blue Ridge and should not extend south of the north fork of the Rappahannock. The General Assembly did not feel confident enough to act on this sentiment. As with the Ludwell and Byrd cases in Spotswood's administration, the oligarchy showed that it would not vote in party solidarity against the principles of the individuals — even to support its own Council president. A majority of the Council issued a grant in the disputed territory claimed by Colonel Carter for the Proprietary.

Carter entered a caveat against this grant (October 28, 1728), and demanded a suspension of the patent. At this, Gooch began to familiarize himself with the boundaries in dispute. Once he grasped the geographic details, he denounced Carter's claim for the Proprietary as a ''preposterous invasion''—which it was. Supporting the rest of the Council, he began to issue patents to any applicants who would settle the land.

Carter, stolidly continuing to enter caveats against these grants, then petitioned the Council to find a method that would quickly establish either the north or the south branch of the Rappahannock as the main stream. Carter's fellow councilors agreed to find such a method and deliver the results to the Board of Trade. At the same time, the majority decided that the governor should continue issuing patents until His Majesty's pleasure was known. Gooch said that he intended to ''refuse the suspension of patents, not withstanding the remonstrances of the Proprietor's agent [Carter], until the case should be fairly stated and determined according to the genuine construction of the Proprietor's charter.''

In taking this stand, Gooch was not acting against Carter either personally or as a representative of the oligarchy's power. He held the generally shared conviction that the land belonged to Virginia, and that the Colony's welfare would best be served by Virginians' developing the country. ''If all the [controversial] lands,'' he wrote, ''be allowed to belong to the Proprietor of the Northern Neck, as his agent pretends, the King will then have very little more land to dispose of in Virginia.''

Gooch's point was wholly sound, and was supported by the majority of the Council and populace. Only Carter's imperialistic determination kept the boundaries in dispute. In this entirely selfish cause, in the interest of his children and grandchildren, Carter was never more the ''King'' in his imperviousness to the opposition of his fellow Virginians, his fellow councilors, and the governor.

For all the agitation it caused him, Carter might have been engaged in some minor lawsuit with a merchant in London. When Lord Fairfax, after Carter's death, was able to bring influence in England to decide the dispute in the Proprietary's favor, Fairfax had a case only because of Robert Carter's long, dispassionate and skillful fight over a claim which the governor had termed ''preposterous.'' Perhaps the opposition was awed by the very preposterousness of the claim that Carter maintained, with loftily insistent logic based upon an audacious premise.

As monomaniacal as he was on subsidizing the futures of his heirs with land, Carter never acted with total indifference to his "country." With the millions of acres involved, the tracts he held idle for his family not only did nothing to deter settlement in the opening western lands but, as Gooch conceded, the patents Carter issued to small landholders in the Proprietary stimulated the opening of the western frontier. Carter actually caused a race between the governor and himself to issue patents for settling the new lands.

The major consideration to which Carter *was* indifferent was the antagonism of Virginians to the whole idea of the Proprietary, which gave the Fairfaxes instead of the Crown the quitrents on a sizable slice of the Colony. This was the consideration which concerned Gooch, this and the sheer effrontery of Carter's claims for the Proprietary.

However, the contest between the governor and the council president stayed at long range, impersonal and dignified. Gooch ordered wine through the Corotoman "importer." Gooch's strong feeling about the specific issue did not lessen Carter's respect and liking for him. Carter's own feelings seemed totally uninvolved. All during his determined fight, Carter revealed far more concern over the education of his children and grandchildren, and over new versions of his unceasing troubles with English merchants as London mercantile houses also suffered the rise and fall of fortune.

4

While Carter was still governor, on May 17, 1727, Landon, his last son then in England, had come home. A very bright boy, Landon had showed an encouraging taste for using his mind during his seven years under the care of Mr. Dawkins although, like his older brothers, he acquired expensive habits in London. In criticism of Dawkins as well as of Landon, Carter wrote the English merchant John Falconer that it was "beyond all comprehension" for a boy of sixteen "to run out" £370 in fifteen months.

Regardless of his preachments on living prudently and avoiding ostentation, his sons were too aware of the money available not to live according to their station. When Landon was in England, Carter had

£4,250 of bank stock, drawing five percent interest, handled by Dawkins and Perry, and a £1,500 bank annuity held by Perry. In Virginia he had more than £2,000 out in mortgage bonds and interest, gathering six percent. He was also surprisingly free in lending cash to his sons, other kinspeople, and even friends.

When seventeen-year-old Landon settled down at Corotoman, his father's first plan was "to breed him up as a Virginia merchant," and for some period of time he attended William and Mary College. However, while pleasing his father by his love of learning, Landon's inclinations clearly ran toward planting. "A lad of good morals and of an agreeable, obliging behavior," he soon established himself as a favorite of his father and began to work at managing some of the "King's" estates. It was an entry in Landon Carter's diary, nearly half a century after his five vivid years at Corotoman, that provided the best description of Carter's methods of planting.

"I hear abundance about plows & carts; my father never used a plow in the five years from 1727 to '32, in which he died, except one he indulged me with at home to make a little farm of turnips, cabbages & tares. And I believe, though his family was large and of course his expense of food great, no man sold more wheat and corn. I have known him year after year to load annually a large Bermudian, and many vessels from Norfolk came for his wheat; and as to his carts, he never had but old Nassau with 12 oxen for all his plantations, his home wood, which were large piles for his house and kitchen qr.; and he never carted from one of the said plantations one hogshead, either light or heavy, and never one apple or peach, though he had large crops and made abundance of cider and brandy; nor ever brought an ear of corn out of his fields with any cart, and this I can swear to; and yet who exceed him? As to wheat, each plantation aimed at 150 bushels, and this with hoes only. Besides, he built much and the same oxen brought in all his timber and boards and his planks, palings and everything."

As Landon's interest in the working of a plantation gladdened his father's heart, making him forget the boy's extravagances in London, he came in for new agitations from Lewis Burwell. Carter began to have more trouble with this favorite grandson than ever from any of his sons. On the day Landon came home, his father wrote John Pratt, in London: "I am sorry you have nothing good to say of my grandson, Lewis, but that he is well. Pray God grant him such a measure of His grace that he answer to the great design of his father in sending him for an English education."

Later in the summer he wrote directly to the son of his favorite son-in-law and the daughter who had defied him in her second marriage, to Dr. Nicholas:

Rappahannock August the 22d: 1727

Dear Lewis,

"I received your letter wherein you desire to continue at school a year longer to qualifye your self the better for the University (in which we complied), promising how good a boy you would be in following your studys. I pray God grant that you may at length leave your follys and take to your learning to better purpose then you have hitherto done. Your father was a worthy good man and sent you for England on purpose to make you a school and a gentleman. What a trouble will it be to you when you come to years of discretion to consider what little benefit you have reaped for the large expenses that have been bestowed upon you. I must tell you in all the letters I have rec'd from all your friends in England, no one speaks a word in your praise, which is a very great trouble to all your relations here. It will be a very great comfort to them to hear better things of you hereafter, and to none more than to

Your Loving Grandfather.

Two years later — incidentally showing how unaffected he was by the governor's stand against him — he removed Lewis from Mr. Pratt's and placed him under the care of Gooch's brother. At the time of that change, Carter wrote his grandson: "Your mother is a very crazy and ailing person." Obviously the breach had not healed between the "King" and his daughter Elizabeth, whom others found to be of an agreeable disposition.

Also while he was still acting governor, in May, 1727, Carter began to be disturbed by the unbusinesslike methods increasing at Perry's since the death of Micajah Perry, Sr. He wrote Dawkins: "Mr. Perry has treated me so indifferently, not to say, unjustly, that unless he will give me satisfaction in some things our future correspondence, I believe, will entirely cease." As when earlier he had been displeased with Dawkins, Carter indulged himself in the fancy of severing relations with the English merchants. He continued with Perry. (The soundness of Carter's judgment of Perry's operations since the elder Perry's death was borne out in the 1730's when the old firm went bankrupt.)

The following year, 1728, Carter showed some magnanimity when his old merchant friend Thomas Evans failed, owing him considerable money. "I heartily pity the hard fate of Mr. Evans, with whom I have had a very friendly correspondence for more than twenty years, but charity begins at home; herewith I send you my account against him as well as I can state it. . . . Mr. Evans I ever took to be an honest man, however this ruinous misfortune comes to fall upon him, and I daresay will readily own the truth of my account and will do his utmost to discharge it."

This attitude contrasted strongly with his vindictive hounding of Colonel Edmund Jenings, who ultimately paid with all his property for the imprudence of superseding Carter as the Proprietary's agent.

5

Just before Carter's term as acting governor ended, he finally consented to have his portrait painted. As he was riding with Mann Page to Corotoman for dinner, Page (Carter recorded in his diary) "in the coach urged me mightily to have my picture drawn. I denied it as strongly." During his stay, Colonel Page persisted. Having respect for his son-in-law, Carter permitted himself to be persuaded by Page's arguments. Two days later, on September 1, 1727, "I sat to the painter."

That was the unpretty, unflattering portrait of the fleshy-faced man looking straight at the world with button-bright eyes and the suggestion of a smile on his full lips. He looked stocky in his scarlet coat, open and flaring at the bottom, and he looked invulnerably self-assured with his self-contained strength of purpose inherent in his broad face. There was little to suggest the "haughtiness" which unadmiring contemporaries mentioned. In contrast to the studied pose of a portrait of Colonel William Byrd, in which a disdainful haughtiness was the dominant impression, Carter looked casual and rather cheerful, like a country squire who had never known any will except his own. He looked like what he was proud of being, a "Virginia planter" — an aristocrat in the meaning of a member of a colonial ruling class, with nothing of the elongated, dandified patrician of the usual connotation.

After his term as acting governor, in December, 1727, the "King" showed a mellowing reflected within his staunch Church of England convictions. John Falconer, the London merchant to whom he had newly given some of his business, evidently had written Carter about his attachment to one of the Protestant sects which the Virginia planter class regarded without enthusiasm. In reply, Carter wrote: "What has passed between us upon that subject shall work no alteration in my sentiments in relation to you, and although you and I go different ways to pay our worship to the Author of our beings, and that I dare say I shall never change my old road to get into yours in my way to Eternity, yet I am not so uncharitable to think but that honest is to be found in your persuasion as well as my own, and this you may believe from my entering into correspondency with you."

His own religion helped him to a calm acceptance of increasing suffering from varieties of pain. Along with the savage attacks of gout, toothaches and a generalized disturbance in his digestive system, came an inflammation of the eyes which he described to his son-in-law Mann Page as "such a defluxion on my eyes that they are almost quite glued up every morning." He wrote: "I may say with a great deal of truth the days are come upon me that I have no pleasure in."

Yet to another merchant he wrote philosophically: "Our barren wilderness affords little news. My children I thank God for what I know are all well. Colonel Page's milk diet agrees so well with him that makes me hope he will prolong his life to gray hairs. I have the blessing of seeing my children's children before me and, as far as matrimony is gone, everyone has the comforts of descendants. . . . I have lived to taste of the infirmitys of old age; every day brings its uneasinesses along with it. I am advised nothing will contribute more to a cheerfull clear temper than use of the Bristol Waters. . . ."

He asked to have two dozen flasks of the waters sent him. Around the same time, in 1728, he wrote an agent to order from Mr. Miles of Madeira "a couple pipes of the best of their wine as soon as conveniency presents. . . . I am willing to go to the highest price that I may have of the most celebrated of their wines."

Racked though he was by the physical deterioration of old age, at sixty-six he remained particular about his dress for appearing in public. While vain show in all things was personally abhorrent to him, it seems to have been a characteristic of the gentlemen in the upper strata of the Virginia planter class to avoid too much finery in dress, as unbefitting self-employed country gentry. The young sons might bedeck themselves as typical Georgian bucks while in London, but at home the silks, satins, fine linens and brightly colored hose were imported for the ladies. Carter wrote to a London clothes merchant:

"Some years ago you sent me a fine gay cloak; it lies by still and has never seen the light but to air it. It's fitter for an Alderman in London than a planter in Virginia. I love plainness and value my clothes more for their use than their finery."

Carter did not grow lax in practical economies even for the dresses of his young daughters. In a letter to Mrs. Jane Hyde, the wife of an English merchant, he revealed that assurance of position which denied any interest in competing in regality of dress. This attitude became a perpetuated tradition of the planter class as a whole.

"I received your obliging lines with my daughter's cloths," wrote Carter. "I believe your care extraordinary, and the genteelness and richness of the silk shows they were no bad pennyworth. Things that are not so dear seems much better to fit the circumstances of our country . . . from the seldom occasions we have for our gentry to appear in fine cloths. A birth night and a ball coming but once a year so that rich cloths, before they are sulleyed at all, grow to be so much out of fashion that in two or three years time even the wearers of them grow weary of them."

In the winter of 1728–1729, Robert Carter suffered a loss at Corotoman about which the details were never clear. In February, Thomas Lee's house was totally destroyed by a night fire presumably set by arsonists. Robert Carter wrote him to "condole your dismal calamity. My own suffering in the like nature I do assure you makes me sympathize the more deeply with yours, though every one that wears the compassion of a Christian can not but entertain the story with a high regret."

On February 11, the Maryland *Gazette* of Annapolis, in reporting the destruction of Lee's house, stated: "The fine, large house of Colonel Carter, on Rappahannock, was also burnt lately. The particulars of his loss we can't give you, but we are informed it is very great."

Carter's only reference to the details of his loss was a mention of the destruction of the larger part of his wine cellar.

From these three items, assumptions have been made that Corotoman was totally destroyed in 1729. It would appear incredible that no mention should be made in Virginia to the total destruction of the home of the president of the Council, the most consequential figure in the Colony, particularly as the house was the hub of the largest private commercial and shipping community in Virginia.

Robert Carter made no entry in his diary, or in his letters, about any work of rebuilding, although in the preceding decade he had continually noted the numbers of bricks he was having made and their specific purposes. His will, written in 1726, was twice revised after 1729, and in extensive alterations he made no changes relating to the vast stores of personal properties listed according to the rooms which contained the articles as of the 1726 will.

These properties included hundreds of books. "The lower chamber" must have been used as something like a library and meeting room, as it contained — in addition to the books in its closets — an armchair, twelve leather chairs, and four cane chairs. Had the house been destroyed, Carter certainly would have referred to the loss of the books in the later changes in his will. On the contrary, the books collected across the mature years of his life were claimed by his heirs.

The probability seems to be that Corotoman was not destroyed until much later — perhaps, as some believed, by the British during the Revolution. In the "King's" late years, the damage to his bolted wine cellar would have been enough of a gratuitous cruelty to the aging man enduring almost constant pain in one part of his body or another.

6

When Carter's house caught fire in 1729, he was engaged in the only major operation of his career which failed — and this was not complete failure, since his sons acquired large holdings of prime land as a by-product of the main purpose of the venture.

Robin, in his explorations of the Proprietary's grant with his brother Charles, discovered a copper deposit in a small run in the Frying Pan region in the foothills of the Blue Ridge. Through his father, Robin immediately patented twenty-seven thousand acres in the present counties of Fairfax and Loudoun, near Washington. Robin and Charles then formed a mining company with their brother-in-law Mann Page and, of course, their father. Their original plan was to cut a road to Little Falls, the head of navigation on the Potomac. Thomas Lee, hearing of their plan, quickly completed a survey which validated his claims to all navigable sites at Little Falls.

Then grown into his maturity, Lee stood up to all the anger and cajoling of the "King," who had given him such short shrift when he sought favors in patenting land in the Proprietary. Carter showed his resentment at being blocked off from the Potomac by later (June 24, 1731) writing Lee a nasty-nice letter about his accounts for land held under the Proprietary. Unlike Carter's usual direct assaults, it was one of his most circuitously phrased insults.

"It is an old proverb, and a very good one, that often reckoning makes long friends. The account of grants for the land you hold being under no right settlement according to my thoughts as yet, have I commited any errors [will] you please to make your observation." Then, referring to specific land, Carter came to the subject which to him constituted the gravest insult to a planter — the denigration of the quality of his tobacco. "In this account, I have given you credit for the three black hogsheads of tobacco . . . taken from your overseer last year — the most abused and despicable stuff ever saw in my life. But I must believe you know nothing of this and that [it was] wholly owning to the villainy of the overseer and the baseness of the receiver [collector] that you would take such tobacco. You will please to take a proper time to let me know how you reckon this matter stands between us. . . ."

This letter naturally did nothing to warm the cool civility between the old president of the Council and the power-minded young baron who would himself, in time, become the Council president. No love was ever lost between their families, even after — or especially after — Robert Carter's great-granddaughter married a collateral kinsman of Thomas Lee, and the couple produced the greatest Virginian of both families, Robert Edward Lee.

Thwarted in their plan of getting an outlet on the Potomac, the Carter company built a road to connect with the Rappahannock, via Occoquan Creek. The agony of a gout attack prevented Colonel Carter from riding the rough new road in the summer of 1729, when his presence was needed at the mining property. He and his young partners had imported some Cornish miners to direct the laborers they transported to the wilds, and as Carter was unable to give personal supervision to the mining operations, he encountered some difficulties with these Cornishmen.

They insisted on differentiating themselves from other indentures. They claimed certain holidays and took off Saturday afternoons. "I know no difference between them and other common waged servants," Carter wrote to Benjamin Grayson, at the mines. "They are employed as diggers in the mines; they can not plead custom."

When he learned that two of them had gathered two or three days at "a tippling house," he wrote directly to the men, William Haweis and Robert Brunton. Here he showed none of the oblique approach he had used with Thomas Lee: he was the plantation master, exercising his authority without gloves in a social system which demanded no humanity in dealing with recalcitrant workers.

In Robert Carter's Christian code and in the code of his class in

Virginia, it was required that kindness and courtesy be given to all those — whether Negro slaves, white indentures, or wage earners of any kind — under the protection of the planter. Plantation children were strictly trained to be considerate of servants of any color. At the same time, workers were required to do their assigned tasks as ordered and maintain the proper respect. When working laws were broken and authority defied, the offender became a miscreant at the bar where the planter was the judge, and Carter was typical of his time and place in his outrage at effrontery from inferiors.

"I have understood you have both behaved your selves in a very villanous and base manner; not like such servants as you are by your indentures, that is diggers in the mines. I have therefore thought it proper to send to Mr. Grayson copies of your indentures, that he may know that you are our servants for four years from the time of your arrival into the country; and that, if you do not know how to behave your selves as servants, that he should make you do it by correction suitable to your deserts. And to that end I do hereby let you know that I do appoint him your master in the absence of me or of my sons, giving him the same power . . . that we have. You pretend to holidayes and what not; but I forbid it you and order him to make you work dayly as the rest of my servants that are there do day by day, keeping no more holidayes on Saturdayes in the afternoon than they do. It seems one of you (Haweis) is a very profane rogue, curses his meat and us that are his masters. I order Mr. Grayson not to let you have so much meat as you have had. And, seeing you have abused the kindness you have met with, to treat you in a worse manner than you have been, and give you sound drubbings suitable to your merits. You shall know you have masters that will not be fooled by you, but will use the proper way with you to bring you to better manners."

Although he held a low opinion of the generality of what might be called the class of working people, normally Carter was not a hard taskmaster. But things were not going well with the men imported for mining. One indenture, who cost Carter £6 for his passage and another £6 advanced him, turned out to be a fake, no miner at all. Others deserted the mines, stealing off into the forests. Carter wanted them pursued with "hue and cries," and then "clapt into jail."

At the same time, the news about the copper in the ore turned sour. A local assayer had made such favorable reports that Carter wrote that it "whets up our humors to be as vigorous as we can in making search into this piece of land. . . ." Soon afterwards assayers in Bristol and London gave an unfavorable report on the copper content in the ore which the Carter company had confidently shipped to England.

Characteristically, Carter wrote off the three years of his intense interest, his plans and hopes, and immediately brought the operations to an end. Having poured large sums of his own cash into the venture, he also characteristically charged against his sons their proportionate parts of the money plus interest. In 1731 Colonel Mann Page had died, the second son-in-law whom Carter lost. John (as executor of the Page estate), Robin, Charles, and their father divided up the twenty-seven thousand acres — which their work, in the course of the unsuccessful mining venture, had done much to open for settlement.

Then sixty-eight years old, Carter called it a day on new projects. He turned down an iron-mining scheme proposed by Colonel John Tayloe, a Northern Neck friend, with the offhand explanation that he had too many irons in the fire as it was, half of which burned for want of a rigorous application.

7

For a man of his age and accumulation of infirmities, Robert Carter carried a remarkably heavy load and showed no tendency to ease off anywhere. The work done by Robin and Charles in surveying and opening up new lands in the Proprietary was in the area of expansion, in which they were incidentally looking after their own personal futures. Robin was building for himself and his son an estate northwest of Corotoman in the Northern Neck, called Nomini Hall. There the "King's" grandson, the third Robert Carter, would hold court as one of the grandees in the long "life in thrall," which extended the "golden age" to the Revolution.

Carter actually took on new chores after Colonel Page died. Already looking after the Burwell children's estate, he assumed the responsibility for the estate of Colonel Page's children. He remained close to their mother, his daughter Judith the book-lover, and he loved to have his granddaughter ("little Miss Page") spend long visits with him.

Page's sudden death had come while he was building the greatest mansion in Tidewater, Rosewell, on the northern bank of the York, and had left his affairs in the tangled state largely typical of those planters running into debt to erect baronial seats. However, with Page's overseers continuing to pack the high-quality tobacco which Page had maintained, Carter encountered no severe complications in supervising the shipping and marketing, handling the accounts, and collecting debts due the Page estate.

Where his troubles multiplied was over the Burwell estate — involving his estranged daughter Elizabeth, her second husband Dr. Nicholas, and her then grown son, Lewis Burwell. Despite Carter's distrust of his unwanted son-in-law, he advanced him "a large sum of money," against which he handled ten hogsheads of Nicholas's tobacco — "his share of Mr. Burwell's crops." Having to settle for the tobacco, Carter was also forced to ask Perry to have patience over collecting money Nicholas owed him. "I am very sorry he has been so indiscreet to plunge himself at this egregious rate; I believe it has been from his being concerned in an iron work which they now say promises wonders. . . ." From his own and others' experiences with mining, Carter obviously felt dubious about any quick riches. Probably for the sake of the family name, he assured Perry about Nicholas's debt: "I believe you may be in no danger of your money in the long run."

Evidently his daughter and Dr. Nicholas tried to use the revenue from a plantation, "Merchant's Hundred." Carter had willed this plantation to his grandson Carter Burwell, with the proviso that its profits would go to his daughter and her first husband, Nathaniel Burwell, during their lifetimes. He did not intend that, having defied him, Elizabeth and Nicholas should enjoy the profits. He wrote to Perry: "This was a voluntary purchase of mine, [I] being under no obligation to any such thing upon my daughter's [second] marriage." The estate was to remain intact as Merchant's Hundred, accountable to Robert Carter and going to Carter Burwell, as originally planned, after his mother's death. During her lifetime, she was excluded from any of its profits.

The most trouble came from the grandson Lewis Burwell. He had become a disappointment as he grew up. The same age as his uncle, Landon Carter, Lewis wanted to cut the same swath in London — only, like Byrd, he never wanted the stay in England to end. Also, while Landon had showed a real taste for learning, demonstrating a remarkable memory, all reports from London indicated that Lewis was a trifler. Then, too, Lewis Burwell did not have the money behind him that Carter's own son had. Carter wrote Perry: "Keeping that estate together and the making the most of it has cost me abundance of care and trouble, and I have a very affectionate memory for the worthiness of the dear father." He urged Perry "not to let him lavish out money that is none of his own." When Perry tightened up, Lewis tried to get money out of Dawkins. This agent had "the prudence to deny him any."

Lewis added hurt to Carter's disappointment by ignoring his grandfather, allowing as much as two years to pass without a letter. When he did write, in 1731, Carter suspected that the letter had been composed by someone else — "a frothy piece of stuff in justification of his disobedience to my order [to return to Virginia]. He talks as if he intended to stay two years at the University. It is vain for me to lay any new injunctions upon him; the only restrictions that I can impose must arise from your treatment of him by a bridging of his expenses. . . . I have done the duty of a parent by him."

Usually Carter included the most personal items in sometimes lengthy references to business matters. In that note to Perry, he revealed the effect of his grandson's letter by ending: "I shall mix nothing else here." On the same day, August 12, he wrote a somewhat resigned-sounding letter to Lewis.

"I received your letter of the 25th of January from Cains Colledge. By the difference in the style from all the rest of the epistles I have had from you I looked upon it as the effects of another's invention and not the product of your own brain, and therefore shall not run into the particulars of such a conceited piece of stuff; it tells me you are under close application after the search of knowledge. I pray God send amongst your great gettings [which] you promise yourself . . . that you may get wisdom and such that will be your guide in a Virginia life. . . . As for scholarship your head seems not to be turned to make any large improvements that way. What good the conversation of the University will do you I shall not prognosticate, but I think I may fairly suppose you will come into your own country very indifferently equipped with talents proper to govern your affairs here.

"You have broke through my orders and 'tis in vain for me to lay any more upon you. Mr. Perry tells me that . . . you talk of staying two years where you are, which will reduce to a low ebb the money that you will have to claim out of your father's estate and you will be put to the refuge of living upon the produce of your crops which, you may be informed by Mr. Perry, will do very little in these dead times. If you are capable of serious thoughts, the consideration of this melancholy cloud over us will stick close to you and put you upon thinking that money does not grow out of the tops of our trees."

At the end of the brief letter, Carter added a couple of lines which indicated that he and his daughter Elizabeth had achieved a partial reconciliation. "Your mother is here now with your sister Betty and a son by her last [present] husband." Carter's reference to Lewis's half-brother (and his own grandson) as "*a* son by her last husband" indicated that the reconciliation was only partial: no kin was claimed to the child sired by Nicholas. In this, Carter repeated his own father's disclaimer of the posthumous child borne by the wife he disliked.

Carter's reconciliation with Elizabeth may have been brought about by his sympathy for his daughter when Lewis showed her the same neglect he showed his grandfather. Carter reproached Lewis for not having written his mother for two years.

At the close of that last letter to his grandson, Carter told the whole story of his disappointment and continuing love in the signature: "I am, though disobliged, Your Loving Grandfather."

While worrying over his grandchildren's estates, he was trying various remedies for his declining physical condition. He ordered Daffy's Elixir for "windy chronic pains," Dr. Bateman's drops for "my distemper," and Dr. Stonton's drops.

He extended his personal attention to the quality of the tobacco shipped from the Ripon plantation, which he had acquired by mortgage from Colonel Jenings, and called a London merchant's attention to his own. "You must allow me to say from my own eyesight of several of the hogsheads [that] it is good tobacco . . . all stemmed and straight laid."

Nor did his interest in reading slacken. At a friend's house he saw some new books and immediately ordered some of the titles through Dawkins. He wanted the *Independent Whig; The Ecclesiasticks of All Sects and Ages,* translated from the French with a preface by the author of the *Independent Whig;* "the late Lord Shaftsbury's letters to the late Lord Molsworth, concerning the love of one's country, etc."; and a *Historical and Critical Account of the Life and Writings of Mr. William Chillingsworth, Chancellor of Sarum.* In explaining his request for Whig literature, he wrote Dawkins: "I am far from liking the liberties these free thinkers take in their writings; however, I have some inclination to read them. . . ."

As with his religion, Carter reflected the planter class of his age in his tolerance for convictions different from his own — unless money was involved. In the next year, 1732, he would even make an admission about the quality of some of his tobacco. To Dawkins he wrote that he would not complain of the poor price for thirty-nine hogsheads which the English merchant had sold for him at prices "such as you know I have not been used to receive from you for my stemmed tobacco. But I must own there were several hogsheads that were very mean tobacco. However, I must observe too that I had not shipped those hogsheads if it had not been in service to your ship, to fill her up at the importunity of [Captain] John Graves.''

That year, the last of his life, he continued to show restraint in dealing with antagonists to the yoke of the Proprietary. When the Burgesses again stirred themselves to place the Proprietary ''into the hands of the Crown,'' Carter protested mildly: ''I am [sure] the tenants in the Northern Neck are under as easy circumstances in respect to their rents, and I may say have been used with a great deal more leniency, than any other of the King's subjects — to my very great loss in the business.''

On May 12, 1732, in the middle of an unusually long business letter to Dawkins, he dropped a somber paragraph: ''Tomorrow morning, God willing, I am setting out upon the doleful occasion of my dear son Robert's funeral . . . it has pleased the Almighty to take [him] from me in the flower of his age, to my great grief and confusion. . . .''

He wrote nothing of the manner of Robin's death, in his late twenties. In another letter he wrote: ''It has pleased God in his good providence to lay his heavy hand upon me in bereaving me of my dear son Robert, who took his leave of this world by a sudden death on the 6th instant. . . .''

The ''King'' was then near the end of his own days on earth, though he gave no evidence of feeling any premonition. In July he stayed in the damp heat of Williamsburg for Council meetings, and on the 11th of July he wrote his last letter to Perry on the subject of his grandson Lewis Burwell. The day before that, he had written Perry a business letter in which he made a prophecy for the future. ''I must profess it beyond my comprehension to foresee what will be the consequence of . . . the oppression of the merchants . . . who are daily increasing their oppressions upon us. It is an old adage that oppressions make a wise man mad: what our madness will produce, I can hardly promise myself to live to see the end of.''

8

It would not have been conceivable to the stoically suffering old man that the ''madness'' produced would be a revolution against the mother country, in which leaders would be his son, ''agreeable, obliging" Landon; his then six-year-old grandson, Benjamin Harrison V; his daughter Mary's son, Carter Braxton; and his granddaughter Harrison's husband, Peyton Randolph, along with other Randolphs — Thomas Jefferson and John Marshall — and Thomas Lee's sons, along with people Carter had never heard of, such as Augustin Washington's then five-month-old son George.

But these descendants and their allies had been born in a colony which had, in its own right, become a "country" during the life-span of Robert Carter. In establishing control of their internal affairs, under the rule of a politically enlightened native oligarchy, Carter and his contemporaries had expressed their community identification by defining themselves as "Virginia planters." In this definition, Robert Carter specifically differentiated himself, his world and his status, from the England to which his "country" was attached. With this England the center of his mercantile-planting-shipping interests, the seat of learning where he, his sons and grandsons were educated, Carter's differentiation was fundamentally that of the contented provincial from the urbanite of the capital.

Since conflicts of interests, inherent in the money market and in the making of political policy, were as commonplace within the Colony as in Virginia's interaction with the capital, Carter's anticipation of reaction to the merchants' oppression was restricted to the realm of economics. As commerce meant to him an association in which the two parties each had their own rights and their duties to the other, the English merchant bloc practiced "oppression" by ignoring the human rights of the Virginia tobacco growers and by renouncing their own duties, moral and economic, to associates in trade. The merchants' "oppression" was, in Carter's view, another version of the denial of a reciprocity of rights and duties which, practiced by Berkeley's circle and Charles II, had brought on Bacon's Rebellion, initiated resistance to the Crown, and promoted the development of a native aristocracy. Though political change was remote from Carter s mind, the rule of the oligarchy had intertwined economic interests with political control in the practices and attitudes established for the next generation.

The generation following Carter's was born into, and formed by, *accepted* practices of local self-government which stressed rights in control of certain basic economic principles. As the new generation inherited — along with their positions in life — these practices of self-government, the young men accepted as *traditional* ("what hath been the ancient custom") the gains won and the conditions established by the generations encompassed in Carter's lifetime.

Landon Carter, an older member of the new generation, had been a schoolboy in London when his father and uncles and cousins and brothers-in-law fought down Spotswood, the last defender of the Crown's prerogatives. To Landon, Bacon's Rebellion belonged in ancient history. To Patrick Henry, born four years after Carter died, Spotswood was ancient history. To Thomas Jefferson, born in 1743, Council President Robert Carter himself belonged to an old order which the young Jefferson, by his time, regarded as worn-out as Carter's contemporaries had regarded vestigial Stuart attitudes to be in their early days.

Yet Carter made Jefferson possible. For when Robert Carter's generation had established the climate for succeeding generations to flourish in, the oligarchy went further in creating conditions in which their successors *would* flourish. Carter and his contemporaries established the machinery by which promising young men, with personal involvement in the Colony's wealth and welfare, were placed in positions of political influence from which the most gifted, the most energetic, the most responsible were trained for and advanced to higher office.

This is not to suggest any prescience of the future on Carter's part by his reference to the oppressions of the English merchants. Yet having been an impressionable child during the continent's first revolution, for more than four decades he had fought in establishing a personal domain and the oligarchy's control of the Colony's government, in a succession of struggles against one kind of oppressive condition or another. By his course, he was influential in forming the character of a society which had no experience in accepting oppressions of any kind. As the Colony he viewed in his last summer was a totally different structure from the colonial world he had known as a boy, he could reasonably assume that the "madness" which he expected not "to live to see the end of" would take a form of action to bring continuing change to Virginia.

9

Manifestly, the changes Robert Carter anticipated for the future were not of a revolutionary nature, nothing fundamentally disturbing to the existing social order under the direction of the aristocracy. For he had carefully prepared conditions to maintain a dynasty for his descendants — baronial seats, individual wealth, social prestige and political power. As closely as was possible in a colonial community, with frontiers facing the wilderness of an unexplored continent, King Carter had duplicated the life of the English larger gentry, with one significant difference: younger brothers and daughters' husbands would be integral parts of a spreading dynasty, interlaced with other dynastic families to form a ruling class composed of *total* families.

In Virginia, as the distinction between the appointive Council and the elective House of Burgesses was blurring to the point where, except for the prestige, no practical difference would exist in political strength between the two houses, and as the ruling class came to control the whole General Assembly, not enough families had gained an aristocratic position to make feasible a strict primogeniture in which only the oldest son inherited a place in the power structure. Carter's sons Landon and Charles served in the House of Burgesses while John, the secretary, sat on the Council.

Also, not every family in an aristocratic position produced a first-born son with both the capabilities and the inclination to assume responsibility in government. Many families of substance, some among the one hundred richest in the Colony, never entered political life beyond assuming their responsibilities at the local level. For the ruling class to exercise its control at Williamsburg, it was a necessity to advance more than one son in government as well as to recruit such obliquely connected newcomers as Thomas Jefferson — a grandson, through the female line, of a younger son of William Randolph.

Robert Carter, to judge from his comments on acquiring land for his heirs, gave no — or only incidental — thought to any effects on the oligarchy's control that might be caused by his providing for his sons the estates which assured them of position. Not trying to change the traditional English system, he was only looking after his own, to make certain that none be left outside as younger brothers.

Other families, like his Harrison kin, also tried in a less lavish way to practice what might be called modified primogeniture. They gave the firstborn the manorial seat, with enough productive land and slaves to maintain it, and divided the rest of the estate among the younger sons. Cash and personal slaves, sometimes property, always went to the daughters.

For perpetuity of a family's wealth, this provision for younger sons and daughters frequently proved to be disastrous. The younger sons did not usually have enough to maintain their estates unless they exhibited (as few did) the acquisitive force and ruthless resourcefulness of the older generations who mastered the wilderness. Often the reduction of the estate of the manorial seat made the revenues insufficient for a firstborn especially when, like Benjamin Harrison V, he devoted extensive time and energies to running the government.

On the other hand, while the deviation from the strict primogeniture of England was eventually to lose the fortunes of many families of consequence, during the "golden age" the practice kept the oligarchy vigorous and flexible in cultivating a ruling class which rewarded talent, energy and responsibility in directing the government.

The reduction of the home estate to make provisions for younger sons and daughters was not the sole, or even the chief, reason why family fortunes were lost. William Byrd II managed to maintain his estate by selling off a hilly tract of land, overlooking The Falls in the James River, as "urban" real estate.

The tobacco trade at The Falls had multiplied since Byrd's father ran his store on the edge of the frontier, as one of the public warehouses and shipping points formed there a center for planters and farmers working land to the west of tidal water in the James River. Byrd had the hilly land laid out in lots, which he sold in a public lottery. It was an opportune time for the founding of a city at The Falls, and the river trading post expanded rapidly into the city of Richmond. With such expedients, Colonel Byrd left a sizable estate almost entirely to his son. The third William Byrd ran through it in a turbulent life which he ended by suicide, and the magnificent manorial seat of Westover passed out of the Byrd family.

Robert Carter was alone in Virginia — and perhaps in the colonies — in successfully modifying primogeniture on a scale which the English did not dare attempt.

His oldest son John, inheriting the home plantation at Corotoman, added to his portion by marrying the heiress of Shirley, the riverfront plantation of the Hill family. Their son Charles, inheriting both Corotoman and Shirley, eventually abandoned Corotoman and built a charming, magnificently paneled manor house close to the James. At Shirley Charles's daughter married "Light-Horse Harry" Lee, from which unhappy union came Robert Edward Lee, a throwback in stature and in principles to his great-great-grandfather. Shirley remains today in the Carter family.

Also in the Carter family today is Sabine Hall, the broad Georgian mansion which Landon built on a rise above terraces a mile back from the Rappahannock River. Landon's manorial seat was formed by his father from several fully equipped and working plantations across from the river port of Hobbs' Hole (Tappahannock).

Charles, one of the most prominent members of the General Assembly, built a mansion called Cleve on his inherited plantations.

Berkeley Plantation (Virginia Chamber of Commerce, Photo by Phil Flournoy)

His house burned, as did grandson Robert's Nomini Hall, famed for its hospitality and style of life. Grandson Carter Burwell, from the estate the "King" so carefully husbanded for him, built his manor house, Carter's Grove, on the James River, not far from inland Williamsburg. Having passed out of the Carter-Burwell family, it is preserved by Colonial Williamsburg.

It can never be known to what extent Robert Carter financially aided his sons-in-law in building their manor houses. Colonel Mann Page, the first to build on a heroic scale, died before the completion of Rosewell. After his untimely death, the ambitious project — more spectacular than the Palace — proved to be too much for his family. Mann Page II was forced to sell off twenty-seven thousand acres to meet debts, and his son John Page struggled along in the unfinished house on a plantation running down. Eventually lost to the Page family, Rosewell passed through the hands of successive irreverent owners, and today its vine-draped ruins are a ghostly evocation of vanished grandeur.

Son-in-law Benjamin Harrison, among the earliest planters to design under the influence of Spotswood's Palace, built a handsome brick manor house at Berkeley about 1726. There were born Carter's grandson Benjamin Harrison V, a signer of the Declaration of Independence and post-Revolutionary governor of an independent Virginia, and his son William Henry Harrison, President of the United States. The manorial seat of Berkeley remained in the Harrison family nearly until the Civil War, during which the plantation (but not the house) was wrecked by McClellan's army. Berkeley is privately owned today, a working plantation in existence since 1619 and, magnificently restored, is open to the public.

Robert Carter's two youngest daughters married too late in his life for him to be intimately acquainted with their husbands or to know his grandchildren by them. He left £2,000 to Lucy, who married Henry Fitzhugh in July, 1730. They settled at Eagle's Nest, the estate Fitzhugh inherited from his grandfather — once the rival of his father-in-law for the Proprietary agency. From Lucy's marriage came the granddaughter Mary Fitzhugh, who married George Washington Parke Custis, grandson of Martha Custis Washington and adopted son of George Washington. From this marriage came Mary Custis, who reunited King Carter's lines by marrying Robert Edward Lee.

Carter left £1,800 to Mary, the last of his daughters to leave home. She married George Braxton in January, 1732, and died giving birth to a son, Carter Braxton, in 1736. He became the second of Robert Carter's grandsons to sign the Declaration of Independence.

The youngest child, George, was left Ripon Hall — the estate Carter had acquired by foreclosure from Edmund Jenings. He was the only one of Robert Carter's children who neither married nor worked a Virginia estate. After his father's death, George was sent by his brother John to study law at the Middle Temple, and he remained in London, practicing law until his death in 1743.

The building of manorial mansions by Carter's sons and sons-in-law was part of a movement, begun in the 1720's under the influence of Spotswood's Palace, to erect dynastic seats after the manner of the English larger gentry. Robert Carter and his contemporaries had built indigenous houses with comfort the major consideration, but the generation of inheritors erected mansions of careful architectural design, to stand for succeeding generations for ages to come. Most of the new dynastic seats, like the Palace, combined indigenousness with grandeur, and the center house was usually flanked by outbuildings in a formal design.

Colonel William Byrd, a decade younger than Carter, joined the new fashion and designed at Westover one of the most beautiful, graceful Georgian houses on the continent. All of Byrd's elegant tastes were reflected in the wide red-brick mansion fronting on a reposeful shaded lawn on the shore of the James River. No other manor house in Virginia so evoked the lordliness of a planter's life in the private domain where he commanded all he surveyed. For Byrd was essentially an inheritor who designed his manor seat for the cultivated enjoyment of life, and the grounds at Westover did not bustle with shipping enterprises as at neighboring Berkeley, and had none of the atmosphere of an enterprising community which characterized Corotoman.

Three children born at Westover, by Byrd's second wife (from England), were joined by marriage to Carter's family. Maria became the second wife of Landon, Anne the second wife of Charles of Cleve, and William Byrd III married Elizabeth Hill Carter, the daughter of Byrd's neighbor John. Carter's granddaughter suffered an unhappy life with Byrd, a gambling addict, and died under somewhat mysterious circumstances.

One family of consequence since Robert Carter's father's day, into which no Carter married, was the Lee family. The feeling between the "King" and the no longer young Thomas Lee influenced some of their immediate descendants. Through Thomas Lee's marriage to Hannah Harrison Ludwell, their children were cousins of Carter's Harrison grandchildren, but the younger Harrisons and the younger

Lees shared an aggressive dislike which continued even while they were working for the same ends in the Revolution. Among the new builders of dynastic seats, Thomas Lee erected at Stratford Hall a massive mansion that was unlike all others in neither reflecting the governor's Palace nor in being indigenous.

Thomas Lee was not an inheritor, except in connections. As the fourth son of the retiring, English-oriented Richard Lee II, he had received only the rudiments of education, a pittance of land and, in the English tradition, had been left to shift for himself. Of "strong natural parts," as his son said, Thomas Lee worked hard and skillfully with broad vision and almost arrogant courage to bring his Stratford Hall line back into the power his family had known in the seventeenth century. He had reached the point in 1732 where he would be appointed to the Council to succeed Robert Carter. However, the other branches of the line from Richard Lee I were in that period a colorless generation, and the Lees would not be powerfully reestablished in the oligarchy until Thomas Lee continued his rise eventually to the Council presidency.

Carter was succeeded as Council president by Commissary Blair, then aged and deaf. When Blair died, William Byrd, still wanly maneuvering for the post of colonial governor, served briefly as president until his death in 1743. With Byrd went the last of King Carter's generation. Thomas Lee was of the generation of Carter's oldest son John, a transitional generation between the founders of the oligarchy of the "golden age" and the generation of the Revolution.

Even excluding any immediate connection with the Lees through marriage, Robert Carter's dynastic lines ran like veins through the body of the ruling class at the time when his own end approached. He had fully accomplished his purpose in establishing for his descendants what he believed to be an enduring pattern fixed in time. "One generation passeth, and another generation cometh, but the land endureth forever." This saying from Ecclesiastes could be revised in his case to read: "Carter land endureth forever." Along with the land, attitudes of mind and character conforming to the pattern have endured into the present, contributing to the modeling of each generation of the land where Carter was called "King."

10

During the last two years of his life, Carter must have suffered acutely and almost continually from his physical ailments. When he changed his will in June, 1730, he wrote: "being of sound mind, memory, but in a crazy, disordered condition respecting my health. . . ." The following month, in making the final change in his will, he wrote: "being in a declining State of body, but of sound mind and memory. . . ." Judging from the medicines he ordered and his descriptions of earlier attacks of gout, he was afflicted with some of the most disagreeable symptoms of the disease. These would include windy stomach (of which he complained in his later years), tumid and flatulent belly, irregularity of bowels, falling off of appetite — all of which would give him "a crazy, disordered condition" in relation to his basic pleasures in food and drink. His sleep was affected, and he probably experienced palpitations of the heart.

In waiting for the end, Robert Carter made no change in the directions he had given for his burial in his 1726 will.

"I order my body to be laid in the yard of Christ Church near and upon the right hand of my wives, a decent funeral to be kept at my interment, a monument or tomb stone to be sent for to be erected over my grave of about the value of my last wife's tomb stone, with a proper inscription at the discretion of my son John or of my other executors in case of this mortality. . . ."

To the end he directed and paid for the building to complete Christ Church, where his father and mother, along with three others of John Carter's five wives, lay buried at the chancel. It is not without significance that while the succeeding generations built permanent dynastic seats, the man who eschewed ostentation concentrated his building for the ages in a church. He never recorded employing an architect on the building, but some high-caliber professional must have been engaged in erecting the church, which ranked architecturally with the fine English work of the period and has never been surpassed in America in its genre.

Built in the shape of a Greek cross, with red-brick walls three feet thick, Christ Church measured seventy by seventy feet outside, and inside the ceiling rose thirty-three feet above fieldstone slabs of flooring. From Corotoman a straight road, lined by high and compact rows of cedars, led directly to the double doors, five by twelve feet. The interior was lighted, and aired in the summer, by twelve windows, six by fourteen feet, and three round windows in the gable. Twenty-two of the high pews of solid black walnut held twelve communicants each, and three pews — one the Carters' — each held twenty. Reflecting Robert Carter in its atmosphere of solidity, the inside of the church was (as can be seen today) the more impressively magnificent for its solidly designed unpretentiousness.

The church represented the only goal which King Carter did not live to see entirely completed. By July, 1732, all his children were married, except for fourteen-year-old George, then a student at William and Mary. And except for George, all his children had gone from the brick house sprawling among the town of outbuildings on the tidal river. If any visitors happened to be with him at the end of July, no one left any record of his final illness.

None of his known infirmities was of a fatal nature. It can only be presumed that the attrition caused by the continual assaults on his constitution gradually eroded its vital strengths, and life gave way to "old age." He was in his sixty-ninth year. As it had never been his custom to call in family or physicians when ill, there was none to note when the end came or the time of day on August 4.

He was sufficiently well known in England for his death to be noticed in the *Gentleman's Magazine.* "Robert Carter, Esq; Aug 4, in Virginia. He was president of the Council, and left among his children above 300,000 Acres of land, about 1000 Negroes, and 1000£." The notice was a little high on the number of his slaves — he had given away countless to his children and grandchildren — and decidedly low on the cash evaluation.

In all the changes in his will he listed the £4,250 of capital stock of the Bank of England, held by Perry and Dawkins, and £1,500 of the bank annuity, which was largely divided between youngest sons Landon and George. In one version of his will, which he later changed, he left to Landon and George one-half each of £2,000 "of my best debts that are now out upon mortgage bond" in Virginia. This alone would come to £7,750. In the last revision of his will, in July, 1730, when he was alarmed by the decline in cash income from the fall of tobacco prices, he reduced numerous cash legacies — mostly to grandchildren. What remained totaled £3,280. After the estate was settled by John and Charles, the older brothers acting as executors, it was shy this £3,280. But John owed his father's estates £4,000, and with this he paid off the final cash legacies.

In addition to these cash legacies and the large landholdings left his sons and some of his grandsons, Carter distributed among his heirs slaves, land, jewelry and personal property — these beyond the gifts he had been making for years. The bulk of the personal property, which remained at Corotoman for John, was never evaluated and probably could not have been. Along with the considerable household furniture, there were goods in the brick stores and the office store and the office chambers, in the spinning house and the new dairy store, in the old dairy and the new dairy and the new dairy loft, in the still-house and in the smith's house, at the sloop landing house and in the Quarter, and in a number of chests of all sizes. Most of the goods were clothing, probably both for Carter's store trade and for the hundreds of people in his community. The rest was an assortment of tools and implements that could be, or had been, used in every aspect of operating the self-contained community. Characteristic of Carter's aversion to ostentation was the absence of silver: he remained to the end impervious to the fashion that made silver plate synonymous with ''conspicuous consumption.''

On an enormous tombstone, on which was carved the Carter coat of arms, the epitaph he had requested was composed in Latin, and its tone suggests the possibility that the rector of Christ Church was the author.

Here lies buried Robert Carter, Esq., an honorable man, who by noble endowments and pure morals gave lustre to his gentle birth.

Rector of William and Mary, he sustained that institution in its most trying times. He was Speaker of the House of Burgesses, and Treasurer under the most serene Princes, William, Anne, George I, and II.

Elected by the House its Speaker six years, and Governor of the Colony for more than a year, he upheld equally the regal dignity and the public freedom.

Possessed of ample wealth, blamelessly acquired, he built and endowed, at his own expense, this sacred edifice — a signal monument of his piety toward God. He furnished it richly.

Entertaining his friends kindly, he was neither a prodigal nor a parsimonious host.

His first wife was Judith, daughter of John Armistead, Esq.; his second, Betty, a descendant of the noble family of Landons. By these wives he had many children, on whose education he expended large sums of money.

At length, full of honors and of years, when he had well performed all the duties of an exemplary life, he departed from this world on the 4th day of August, 1732, in the 69th year of his age.

The unhappy lament their lost comforter, the widows their lost protector, and the orphans their lost father.

Westover Plantation (Virginia Chamber of Commerce, Photo by Phil Flournoy)

There was a tradition, which belongs in the Carter family legends, that an anonymous author inscribed another epitaph in chalk on the huge tombstone.

Here lies Robin, but not Robin Hood,
Here lies Robin that never was good,
Here lies Robin that God has forsaken
Here lies Robin the Devil has taken.

For some inexplicable reason, the sentiment behind this ditty entered into the half-legendary reputation that grew about King Carter. In time it became generally accepted that this dominant figure of an epochal age was merely a very rich man, with his riches tainted by shady dealings. His figure was not diminished by this reputation. If one is rich enough — in Virginia as in the nation — the aura of shadiness in the acquisition by no means detracts from the splendor of the rich man's stature, the magic and authenticity that accrue to his might. In fact, more Virginians claim descent from King Carter than from any other historic personage. But with all the size deferred to in his reputation, the nature of the man has been obscured by the emphasis on his riches, and he has become a misty figure placed timelessly "in the past," like a folk hero.

The probability is that a touch of the robber baron, as in the warlike titled robber barons of early England, was more acceptable in the prototype of "aristocratic" progenitors than was the penny pinching of a merchant-planter, a moneylender and mortgage-forecloser, a trader in all commodities from a few balls of yarn to black slaves. (Certainly, incomparably more is known of the elegance of William Byrd, an unrepresentative dilettante of the era, than of his father's store which made the elegance possible.)

That Carter's acquisitive talents aroused no pride in later generations, looking back with different values, is typical of any society's inheritors of a position which gives them a claim to aristocracy. As in the model of England, it was essential for those born into social privilege to disassociate themselves from the acquisition of money. By their superiority to money, they implied some sort of mystic anointment in which their families had been elevated by God and King to a patrician status in a time so distant as to be beyond a "beginning."

A characteristic of any aristocracy in its generalized social definition (as distinct from the specific definition of a *ruling* class) is the assumption that it has existed always. It must transcend beginnings and time and, of course, the practical means by which the position was won. In this way historically, yesterday's struggler for fortune becomes today's *nouveau* and tomorrow's aristocrat. Time has always been required for the position won by money to become "old-line."

In this suggested explanation of the historical blurring of Robert Carter, there has also inevitably been a blurring of the age he typified. In his own time, Carter was the arch of the qualities that men of his time not only respected but demanded. In meeting these demands more successfully, more completely, than anyone else then alive in his environment, King Carter was not an individual who could have been categorized by any single, uncomplicated motivation any more than his era could be defined by any single characteristic.

By modern definitions, Carter was not a complex person. This should not suggest that he, any more than any other individual, was not composed of a variety of traits and motivations which, expressed in action, could appear to be contradictory. Like any self-realized individual, Robert Carter maintained an equilibrium between his contrasts. There was nothing unique in the generous impulses of a rich man who could be ruthless when driving toward an objective. In his day, it was commonplace for a grasping man of business to enjoy literature, to engage actively in education, and it was Richard Lee II who had been unique in eschewing the earthy pleasures of eating and drinking with jovial companions.

By the nature of their age, the men and women of King Carter's day simply had more time in which to engage life with a broad range of their varied potentialities for living. By the pattern of their living, they were free of compartmentalization: they had no eight-hour days, beginning and ending at a set time, no lunch hours or coffee breaks, no weekends or holidays, and "vacation" would have been incomprehensible. Loving their work, the planters were renewed by its variety, and vacations to them meant simply changing their activities to the business of running the government in Williamsburg.

Totally responsible to themselves, their assumption of individual responsibility permitted them to follow impulses. Carter sat up half the night drinking with a companion, not because it was the weekend but because a ship's captain he liked had come ashore from another world. He took off to attend a horse race, not because it was a set event, falling on a particular Saturday, but because on that day he felt like taking off, and a horse race was available.

A dominant characteristic of the age, epitomized in Robert Carter, was this freedom from the tyranny of scheduled time. Close to the earth and its cycles, not remotely urban, the planters enjoyed a timelessness in their experience of life in the cyclic rhythms of change. Their daily lives reflected nature's rhythms in seasonal changes, with nature's unpredictability.

This relationship to nature in turn reflected their relationship to God, in which they knew the "transcendent security" of inhabiting a universe divinely ordered in the Kingdom of God.

Yet, it was as if their perfect adaptability to their time and place excluded their age from both the legends and the broad historical themes. Since their motivations were so forthrightly concerned with wealth, power and position, and since they were associated with no persuasively articulated ideals for mankind, the Virginians of Carter's era have been overshadowed by those men of the later generation who acted on a world stage.

Carter's was a seminal era. The men who came after were trained for the world stage in the Virginia General Assembly as it had been formed in Carter's time — and formed by highly responsible men whose primary concern was the reality of power.

The political leaders who, following Carter's generation, carved out a new nation dedicated to new principles of government, came into an authority which early habituated them to the reality of power. In the continuing changes which, by the time of their maturity, created new conditions, they projected their familiarity with authority beyond the sphere of the colonial capital in which they had been formed.

In extending the principles of self-government into a larger sphere, the men of the next generation did not appear full-blown, "as from the head of Jove," any more than these families, whose coagulation formed a ruling class, appeared as aristocrats as if by an act of God. The conditions under which a ruling class could cultivate and produce superior individuals for future leadership on an intercontinental scale were brought to realization by the men and women who lived during the sixty-nine-year life-span of Robert Carter. The forces in control at his death, gathered and directed since Bacon's Rebellion, made the time of his end the bright morning of the "golden age."

APPENDIX

A. *Selections from the Will of Robert "King" Carter**

In the name of God, Amen.   I, Robert Carter, of Lancaster County, in the Colony and Dominion of Virginia, Esqr., being in a sickly, declining state of Body but of sound mind and memory (to God be the praise), and being now in the sixty-third year of my age do make this my last will and Testament.

I resign my soul to God as into the hands of a Faithful Creator, and my Body (when it shall please him to take me out of this world) to the earth, trusting in and through the merits and mediation of my ever blessed Redeemer, Our great and only high priest at the right hand of the Father, to have my sins pardoned and washt away and to attain to the resurection of the Just, disclaiming any righteousness of my own and firmly believing in the ever blessed Trinity, Father, Son and holy Ghost.   Placing my only hopes in the Satisfaction and Propitiation of my dear Lord and Savior Jesus Christ.   I order my body to be laid in the yard of Christ Church near and upon the right hand of my Wives, a decent funeral to be kept at my interment, a monument or tomb stone to be sent for to be erected over my grave of about the value of my last wife's Tomb Stone, with a proper Inscription, at the discretion of my son John or of my other executors in case of this mortality; and I do dispose of that worldly estate which God hath blessed me with in manner following:

I give unto my son John Carter, esq^r. and to his heirs male all my lands, Houses and appurtenances, and all my slaves and real Estate what-soever lying and being in Lancaster County (excepting Such Land, Slaves and real estate as I shall otherwise dispose of in this my will); likewise my water mill and the lands I bought of Richard Lattimore adjoining, whether lying in Lancaster or Northumberland County.   I give unto my said son John and to the heirs male issue of his body lawfully begotten all that tract of Land I bought of Mr. John Spicer in Essex County containing seven and twenty hundred acres, with all housing members and appur^{ts} with all the Slaves and real estate thereon, excepting the Slaves in this my will hereafter excepted.

I give unto my said son John and to the heirs male issue of his Body Lawfully to be begotten my tract of Ten Thousand acres of land upon the

* Reprinted from the *Virginia Magazine of History and Biography,* V (April 1898), 408–428; VI (July 1898), 1–21.

branches of Occaquan, upon Cedar Run, Owl Run, on Licking Run, adjoining to the Germans, granted to Capt. George Turberville and by him conveyed to me, unto him my said son John and to the heirs male issue of his Body, and for want of such unto my son Charles and to the heirs male issue of his Body, and for want of such unto my son Robert and to the heirs male issue of his Body, and for want of such unto my own right heirs forever.

I give unto said son John and to the heirs male issue of his Body lawfully to be begotten, one moyety of half part of all those lands I lately bought of Robert Cary, of London, Merchant, with their and every of their appurt^s lying in Richmond & Westmoreland Counties to be equally divided as followeth: The division to begin Somewhere near the plantation of Peter Smith where the s'd Smith lives, and so to run away towards Rapp^a River in such manner as to make pretty near equal Quantities, in each part consideration being had to the conveniences of both parts of these lands and that the Fork of Totees Key come into the lower division; the lower half of this land I give unto my said son John and to the heirs male issue of his Body, and for want of such unto my son Robert and to the heirs male issue of his Body, and for want of such unto my son Charles and to the heirs male of his Body, and for want of such unto my own right heirs forever.

I give unto my said son John and to the heirs male issue of his Body that tract of land in King George County, that I bought of the said Cary, called the round hills, being esteemed to contain five hundred acres, together with the appurt^s thereunto belonging. . . .

I give and bequeath unto my son Robert and to his heirs male issue of his Body lawfully begotten all my lands, houses, slaves, appurt^s and real estate whatsoever lying and being in Westmoreland County, and likewise the mill and lands thereto adjoining in Richmond County, commonly called and known by the name of dickenson's mill; also all my lands, houses, slaves, appurtenances and real estate I have upon the branches of Wicomcoco River in Northumberland, commonly known by the name of Fielding's Plantation and necks, containing between eighteen hundred and two thousand acres or thereabouts; likewise all my tract of land I bought of Maj. John Holloway, lying upon Rappahanock in Hartford (*sic*) county, and also all my land lying upon the Branches of Attaquan in the said county and likewise the slaves y^t went from Middlesex since my wife's death up to penman's End, which I have likewise before excepted out of my gift to my said son John, I give and devise unto my son Robert and to the heirs male issue of his Body lawfully begotten as also the following negroe slaves (to wit) : my negroe George, the cooper, and his wife and Children, the two negroes I have now bound out as apprentices to Wm. Garland; also the negroe Boy that is an apprentice to George, the cooper; also my negroe boy David, Tom Gumby's Brother, and likewise my Cook wench Priss, her husband, old Robin, and her children, all that she hath or shall have. . . .

I give unto my son Robert and the heirs male issue of his Body all that other moiety and half of the lands and appurt^s that I bought of Robert Cary, lying in Richmond and Westmoreland Counties, being the upper moiety of these lands according to the division directed as aforesaid, and in case of the death of my said son Robert without issue Male then this moiety of the lands I bought of Mr. Robert Cary to go to my son John and to his issue male, and for want of issue male of the body of my son John to go to my son Charles & to the heirs male issue of his Body lawfully begotten, and for want of such to my son Landon and to the heirs male issue of his Body lawfully begotten, and if my said son Landon dye without issue male then to my son George and to the heirs male issue of his Body lawfully begotten, and if my said son George dye without issue male then my will is that this moiety of these lands and appurt[s] given to my said son Robert do go to my right heirs forever. I give unto my said son Robert that tract or parcel of land I lately bought of William rust, lying in Hartford (*sic*) County upon the branches of Bull Run to him and his heirs forever . . .

I give and bequeath unto my son Charles and to all the heirs male issue of his Body lawfully begotten all my lands, houses, plantations and appurt[s] in Lancaster and Northumberland counties, which formerly belonged to Maj. William Lesler, as also the plantation and lands I bought of Mr. Robert Jones, commonly called old plantation, and likewise the plantation and Lands I bought and purchased of John Ludley, the Father and the son, called Blough point plantation, on where Thos. West now lives, and also I give unto said son Charles and to the heirs male issue of his Body lawfully begotten all my lands in King George and Spotsylvania Counties, lying above the falls of Rappahanock River, and also my great tract of Land lying upon the Branches of Potomack River, whereon I have three plantations now seated, likewise I give unto my said son Charles all the slaves that are upon the said plantation, Lands and settlements herein given to him, and all the slaves that shall be upon the s'd plantations at the time of my death, . . .

My will is that the respective stocks of cattle, horses, sheep and hoggs that are upon my severall plantations shall go to such of my sons as the lands are given to according to my aforesaid will, and to be and be continued as an appurtenance to the several plantations to which they belong. My will is that all my lands, slaves, stocks of cattle & hoggs, houses, plantations and appurt[s] to the said lands and real estate belonging, lying upon Merchant's hundred In James river be held and enjoyed by my Daughter Elizabeth, formerly the relict of Nath[l] Burwell, Gen., dec'd, and now the wife of Doctor George Nicholas, for and during the time of her natural life, and the profits of the s'd estate to belong to her, and after her decease my will is that these lands, houses, slaves, appurt[s], stocks of cattle and hoggs do go to my grandson Carter Burwell & to the heirs male issue of his Body lawfully begotten, and for want of such unto my grandson Robt. Burwell and the heirs male issue of his Body lawfully begoten, . . . and my further will is that this estate in all times to come be called & to go by the name of Carter's Grove, provided alwaies & it is my will and meaning that the number of slaves that are now upon the s'd plantation shall always be kept up & that the mortalitys shall be still supply'd out of the profits of this estate, and that the number of cattle and other stocks shall always be kept up for the use and manure of the s'd plantation to the same number they are at my decease, and that the s'd plantation be always kept in good repair and that the contingent charges of the s'd estate be borne out of the profits,

That whereas I have bought two tracts of Land of Maj. John Holloway, lying in King & Queen County, which cost me seven hundred pounds sterling, six negroes of Mr. Augustin Moore, which cost me one hundred and twenty pounds sterling, and sundry negroes, in number twelve, of Mr. John Pratt, which cost me one hundred and eighty pounds ten shillings, which s'd two tracts of Land & Negroes are now in the possession of Mann Page, Esq., and my daughter, Judith Page, his wife, and no settlement thereof made, and having also given orders to the said Mann Page to lay out a Debt due from him to me upon an account amounting to one hundred and six pounds eighteen shillings and two pence in slaves for a further settlement upon the afores'd Lands, I do therefore give and devise the s'd Lands & slaves that shall be bought with the s'd money upon my said daughter, Judith Page, for and during the Term of her natural life, and the profits of the said land and slaves, and after the decease of my said Daughter, Judith Page, the said Lands & slaves do go to my grandson, Carter Page, & to the heirs Male issue of his Body lawfully begotten, and for want of such to my grandson, John Page, and to the heirs Male issue of his Body lawfully begotten, . . . and my will is that this estate be called and go by the name of Carter's Dale in all times to come, provided alwaies; and it is my will and meaning that the number of slaves that are now upon the s'd plantation shall always be kept up and that the mortalitys shall be still supplied out of the profits of this estate, and the number of Cattle and other stocks shall *alwaies* be kept up for the use and manner of the s'd plantation to the same number they are at, at my decease, and that the said plantation be always kept in good repair and that the contingent charges of the s'd estate be borne out of the profits.

That whereas I have bought a tract of Land of Maj. Thomas Randolph in henrico County, with the appurt[s] & stocks thereon, which cost me two hundred and fifty pounds sterling, and another Tract of Lands in Surry County, of Mr. William Macon and * * * his wife, which cost me five hundred and sixty pounds sterling, and also Ten negroes which I bought of Mr. Augustin More, which cost me Two hundred pounds sterling, and three negroes more of the said More, which cost me sixty six pounds sterling, all which lands and negroes being now in the possession of Maj[r] Benj[a] Harrison & my Daughter Anne, his wife, it is my will & I do give and bequeath all these lands & the said slaves and stocks that now are and shall be upon the said lands of my purchase unto my said Daughter, Anne, for and during her natural life, and to her second son to be christened Carter, and to the heirs male issue of his Body, . . .

And it is my further will that if my said Daughter Anne be living at the time of my decease there be five hundred pounds sterling paid to her by my ex'tors three years after my decease, and I do also give unto my said daughter Anne forty pounds sterling to be in lieu & satisfaction for her claim to my negroe wench Martha, being unwilling she shall be parted from her husband, the said forty pounds to be laid out in negroes to be intailed upon her my said Daughter Anne & upon her daughter Betty.

It is my will then when my daughter Anne's Daughter Betty shall arrive to the age of Twenty one years or to be Married, there shall be paid to her the *sume* of five hundred pounds sterling by my ex'tors, and that when my said daughter Anne's daughter Anne shall arrive at the age of Twenty one years or be married, there shall be paid to her the *sume* of five hundred pounds sterling by my ex'tors, and in case of the death of either of my said granda'ters the whole ten hundred pounds to be paid to the survivor when she arrives at the age of Twenty one years or is married, and if both of my s'd grand children should dye before they arrive at such ages or marriage then the said ten hundred pounds to be paid to such other son or Daughter as shall be born of the body of my said Daughter Anne when he or she shall arrive at the age of twenty one years or marriage. My will is that if my daughter Mary shall live to the age of twenty one years unmarried, or if she should marry before with the consent and approbation of Col. Mann Page, Maj. Benjamin Harrison, my son John & her brothers Robert & Charles, or the Major part of them or the survivors of them, that then there be paid to her by my ex'tors the sume of two thousand pounds sterling to be paid in manner following (that is to say) : at three yearly, equal, successive payments, the first payment to be made in eight months after my said Daughter's marriage with consent as aforesaid, or her coming to the age of twenty-one, and my will is that my said Daughter Mary have a genteel Maintenance out of my estate until she arrive at such age or marriage, and that she live with her sister Page or her sister Harrison as they shall agree to be best and properest for her. I do also give to my said Daughter Mary thirty five pounds sterling to be paid to my son John to be in lieu and satisfaction for her claim to my mulatto girl Molly and her child, being unwilling she should be parted from her husband; also the spinning girl Phillis and the girl Nanny, which she already calls hers, to her the said Mary and to the heirs of her Body, and if she dies without such heirs unto my daughter Harrison and the heirs of her Body forever. And I do order my executors to send for, for my said Daughter Mary, a gold watch of thirty pounds price and a pearl necklace of twenty five pounds price when she arrives at sixteen years of age, and it is my further will that if my said Daughter Mary shall marry before she attains to the age of twenty-one years without the consent and approbation of her brothers as aforesaid or the major part of the survivors of them, that in such case I do revoake & make void all the aforesaid Legacies & then order my ex'tors to pay to her my said Daughter Mary the sume of Five hundred pounds sterling and no more.

My will is that if my daughter Lucy shall live to the age of twenty one years unmarried, or if she shall marry before with the consent and approbation of Col. Mann Page, Maj. Benjamin Harrison, my son John and her brothers Robert and Charles, that then there be paid to her by my ex'tors the sume of eighteen hundred pounds sterling, to be paid in manner following (that is to say) : at three yearly, equal, successive payments, the first payment to be made in eight months after my said daughter's marriage with consent as aforesaid or her coming to the age of twenty-one years, and my will is that my said Daughter Lucy the Sume of five hundred pounds Sterling and no more. . . .

It is my will that when my son Landon shall arrive at the age of twenty-one there shall then be paid to him & delivered by my executors one moiety or half part of my said Capital Bank stocks, & one moiety of my said Bank annuity, and one moiety or half part of the said two thousand pounds to be kept out at interest as aforesaid, and likewise one half part or moiety of the interest that shall arise from the s'd Bank stocks, Bank annuity and the s'd two thousand pounds after the aforesaid two years shall be run out & expired.

It is my will that when my son George shall arrive at the age of one and twenty years the other moiety or half part of my said Capital Bank stocks, the other moiety or half part of my said Bank annuity, and the other moiety or half part of my said two thousand pounds ordered to be placed out at interest as aforesaid, together with the interest that shall arise out of the moiety of the said Capital Bank Stocks & of the said Bank annuity and of the said two thousand pounds after the s'd two years are expired and run out as aforesaid, shall be paid, delivered and assigned over by my ex'tors or the survivors of them unto my son George. . . .

Whereas that if my sons Landon & George dye before they arrive at their respective ages of one & twenty years, so that in such case my said Bank Stocks, my said Bank annuity & my said two thousand pounds with the Interest arising therefrom as aforesaid according to the intent of this my will, will go & belong unto my three elder, John, Robert and Charles, or to the survivor or survivors of them, it is in such case my will that when this contingency does happen if any of my three elder sons should be dead, John, Robert or Charles having legitimate child or children then alive, that then such child or children have and enjoy his or their Father's part.

But it is my further will that if my said three elder sons or their children as aforesaid come to have and enjoy my aforesaid Bank stocks, my aforesaid Bank annuity & my aforesaid two thousand pounds according to the intent of my will, It shall be upon this condition that they, my three elder sons, John, Robert & Charles & the Ext'rs & administrators of my said sons, if either of my said sons should dye before the time shall be answerable for & make payment of the sume of Four hundred pounds sterling to each of my daughters that shall then be alive, and if any of my daughters should dye leaving child or children the said Four hundred pounds designed for the mother shall be paid to such child or children, and this will be but an easie burthen upon my said three Elder sons when this large addition comes to their estates, provided alwaies, & it is my will & intent that my executors my sons John, Robert & Charles or the Survivors of them or the major part of them, with the consent and approbation of my trustees and more especially with the consent of Mann Page, Esq., if he shall be then alive, taking all prudent care for the security of these estate, these Bank Stocks, this Bank annuity & this two thousand pounds and the interest thereof as aforesaid, if any loss or losses do happen in any of these estates, my ex'tors shall not be answerable for any such loss or losses out of their own estates.

I give unto my son Landon and to the heirs of his body, & for want of such issue, unto my son George and the heirs of his body forever, Smith Robins girl Joan & Nansan's two eldest children (Bridget which was given away before, excepted), and my will is that Landon be kept at school in his education until he is seventeen years of age, & then be disposed of in such a manner as my ex'tor, his brother, shall judge most conducive to his future well being.

I give unto my son George and to the heirs of his body & for want of such issue unto my son Landon & the heirs of his body my negro boy Scipio & the mulatto boy Talbert & the girl Mary that is now in for a share at the old house & her children & increase, & it is my will that my son George be kept in Va. & that he be educated at the College of William & Mary so long as my sons, his brothers, shall think fit to continue him there and then to be disposed of in such Manner as my executors his brothers, shall judge most conducive to his future well being.

I give unto my said two sons, Landon & George, and to the heirs male issue of their bodies lawfully begotton, all my estate, both real & personal in Wms. Burg & if both my sons dye without issue male, then to my son John & his issue male, and if my son John dye without issue male, then to my son Robert & his issue male, & if my son Robert dye without issue male, then to my son Charles and his issue male, & in case of the death of all sons without issue male, then to go to my own right heirs forever, and I do hereby oblige my son John to keep the said estate in good repair out of the profits of the said estate. My will is that the mortgage I have of Edmund Jennings, Esq., of Rippon Hall, in York Co., the Ten following negroes be placed upon the said plantation immediately after my decease . . . & it is my will & meaning that this mortgage of Rippon Hall shall be taken & understood to be in payment of one thousand pounds. Virginia Debts, given to my sons Landon & George, and my will is that the houses upon the said Rippon Hall plantation, be well repaired and kept in good repair out of the profits of the said estate, that is, the repairs to be immediately made by my son John & he to be repaid out of the profits of the said Estate as they shall arise, and my will is that the stock that is in Mr. Dawkin's hands merch't in London, there be brought into it two hundred & fifty pounds more than now it is, by my Ex'trs in three years after my decease, to belong to my said two younger sons Landon & George in the same manner and under the same direction that my stocks given to my said two younger sons are directed to be.

It is my will that there be a true, ful & perfect inventory made of all my estates, as Slaves, Stocks, goods, Chattels, money, Debts, & both in Virginia & great Brittain, & be recorded in the General Court, & that no valuation or appraisement be made of my estates, & that my ex'trs named & appointed in this my will, be not obliged to give security for my estate when they take probate of my will.

It is my will that the tobacco now to ship & the Crops, both of corn & Tob^o, that shall be made this year shall be acounted as part of my estate & shall be ship^d to Great Britain in such probation as my Ex'trs shall think fitt, & the merchants that I at present deal with, if my Ex'trs have no reason to vary the consignment, however leaving them at liberty to whom to consign, taking care to trust substantial men, and it is my will that the aforesaid Tob^o be ship^d in the name of my Ex'tors.

And it is my will that the Crops of all my slaves, both of Tob^o & Corn that shall be made in the succeeding years, that is in 1727 & 1728, & when my son Charles will come to age, shall be held, deemed & taken as my estate, & the Crop of Tob^o to be shiped in the name of my Ex'trs as aforesaid, & the produce thereof to be accounted for to my estate for & towards the discharge of my debts, Legacies & other incumbrances of this my will, provided always, there be allowed out of the produce of the said two years' Crops, two hundred pounds sterling apiece, per anno, to each of my three eldest sons for main-tenance, likewise that the family have suitable supply for their maintenance for the said two years, & the contingent charges of the said estate to be born, & that my younger children also have a decent maintenance, and it is my will that the money that is and shall be raised in Britain by the profits of my plantations or by any other waies than what will answer my Debts, Legacies, Bequests, & orders made in this, my will, be divided into three equal parts, my two younger sons, Robert & Charles, to have a thousand pounds more apiece than my son John, towards building & settling their plantations.

And whereas several of my legacies are made payable at some distance of time & some of them upon such Contingencies which, perhaps, may never happen, it is my will that upon the division of the money that shall belong to my estate as aforesaid, that my three elder sons & ex'trs enter into reciprocal Bonds to one, and the other to be answerable in proportion for the respective Legacies and bequests in this my will when they shall become due & payable.

It is my will that the charge, maintenance & education of my two youngest sons, Landon & George, according to the direction & intention of this my will, shall be equally borne by my three eldest sons, John, Robert & Charles, out of the profits of their estate during their minority. . . .

It is my further will that if the large brick house now building by Col. Page in the room of the house that was unfortunately consumed by fire, shall be finish^t and compleated during the life time of my said Daughter Page so that she shall come to enjoy it & to have her Tithe of Dower in it, then it is my will and I do lay it as a charge upon my three eldest Sons, John, Robert and Charles, my ex'tors, out of the profit of the estates I have hereby given to them the sume of one hundred pounds, the sume of £100 apiece to be paid to my Son in Law Mann Page, Esq., if he be then alive or else to my Daughter his now wife towards furnishing the said house.

It is my will that if Daughter Elizabeth, the wife of Dr. Geo. Nicholas, shall be alive on the 10th of May, 1729, that then there be paid to my said Daughter Elizabeth the Sume of £300 by my ex'trs, and I do also give to my said Daughter a pair of Diamond Ear rings to cost £50 sterling to be bought by such person as she shall desire, the money to be paid by my Ex'trs, and it is my will that when her eldest son she hath by her said husband shall come to age of twenty-one years that there shall be paid to him by my Ex'trs £100 sterling, and when her youngest son she hath by her said husband shall come to the age of 21 years that then shall be paid to him by my ex'trs £100 Sterling and if either of them dye the whole sum to be paid to the Survivor. . . .

I give unto my son John all my furniture in the New house and half of the rest of the Furniture in my kitchen & other houses about my mansion Dwelling, the other half of my Furniture I do give unto my sons Robert & Charles to be valued by four of the most substantial of my neighbours, and my son John to pay for them to my said sons Robert & Charles according to the valuation, unless it be the desire of my sons Robert & Charles to have them in kind.

My will is that my plate both old and new be equally divided between my three elder sons John, Robert & Charles, my books to be divided into four parts, my son John to have two parts of them, my sons Robert & Charles to have the other two parts, my pictures each child to have his own picture, my son   to have my first picture and his mother's, also my gold watch and diamond ring, my son Robert have my other picture & his mother's picture, & one-half of my other rings & watch, my son Charles to have the other half, my sons Robert & Charles to have each of them a gold watch sent for at the charge of my estate to cost £30 each, all my goods that are coming in for my familys to be disposed of among the Family for their supply as they were intended all my new goods, tools, nails, utensils & not already disposed of, to belong to my said three sons, John, Robert & Charles, to be equally divided between them or appraised and the value answered to my two younger sons as my ex'trs shall agree.

My will is that thirty mourning rings be sent for, to be distributed by my Ex'trs among my friends and relations, and it is my will that all the rest of my estate, personal or real, not herein disposed of in Va., or elsewhere, do belong, & I do give it unto my said three eldest sons, John, Robert and Charles, and their heirs forever.

It is my will that in regard those negroes which went from Middlesex, are now seated and settled upon my son John's Plantation, called Penmond's End, in Essex, which slaves notwithstanding I have given unto my son Robert. It is my will and desire that my son John let my son Robert have other slaves of their value, either new or old, & that after such Change made to the satisfaction of both my said sons, such slaves be then deemed & taken to be within the purview of the intails aforesaid of my respective sons' slaves & real estates.

I give my wearing apparel & Cloth, the best of them and what are coming in for my own wearing, & my wiggs, swords, canes, pistolls, & to be divided among my three elder sons, & my other Cloths I would have some given to my good friends Capt. Thos. Carter & Mr. John Turbeville.

I give unto my son in law, Col. Mann Page, £20 sterling, to buy him mourning, also Maj. Benj. Harrison £20 for the same, and to Dr. Geo. Nicholas £10 for the same use, & do order all my Children & grand children to go into decent mourning at the charge of my estate. . . .

I do name, constitute & appoint my three eldest sons, John, Robert & Charles, to be Ex'tors of this my will and to be guardians of my younger children & their Estates, & I do request, constitute and appoint & make my hon'ble & good friends & relations, the aforesaid Mann Page, Esq., of Gloucester Co., Maj. Benj. Harrison, of Charles City County, Maj. Geo. Eskridge & Capt. Geo. Turberville, of Westmoreland County, Mr. Rich'd Lee, of Northumberland Co., & Capt. Thos. Carter, of Lancaster Co., to be assistant to my ex'tors & to be consulted and advised with upon all emergent occasions, more especially the said Mann Page, Esq.

It is my will and I do ordain that whenever the Vestry of Christ Church Parish shall undertake to build a brick church in the place where the present Church Stands, that there be paid out of my estate by my three elder sons & ex'tors the sum of £200 sterling money; one half part of this money is to be paid out of my Son John's estate, the other half is to be equally paid by my son Robert & my son Charles out of their part of my estate, this money to remain in my Ex'tors' hands until one half of the work is completed, provided alwaies the Chancel be preserved as a burial place for my family as the present chancel is, and that there be preserved to my family a commodious pew in the new chancel; & it is my further will that the bricks that are now made & burnt shall be appropriated to the building of the said Brick church or as many thereof as will perfect the building, and likewise the bricks that shall be made & be there at my decease, and if my son John shall have occasion to make use of any of the said bricks, then he be obliged to

make & burn as many more for the use aforesaid. I give twenty pounds
Sterling to be laid out in a piece of plate for the use of our church to be
sent for and engraved according to the direction of my son John.

My will is that my white Servants that are about my house that are
tradesmen be divided amongst my three Sons John, Robert & Charles, & those
that are tradesmen to belong to my Said three Sons and to be made use of as
they shall agree in their respective trades, and that the white Servants that are
abroad seated upon my plantation belong to such of my said Sons as the
plantations belong to, such of my said Sons as the plantations are given to.

I give unto my son John my Coach and four Coach horses, also my barge
& furniture. My own riding horse, my charriot & my other two Coach
horses, my will is my son Robert shall have when he removes to live on his
own Lands, my two youngest daughters to have each of them a riding horse &
side saddle provided for them out of my estate, and that my sons, Landon
& George, have found for them Constantly a good riding horse & saddle out
of my estate, until they come to their respective ages of twenty one years.

My will is that my son John have four of my best Cart horses, & y't all
the rest of my horses & mares be equally divided between my three sons,
John, Robt. & Chas. . . .

That whereas in the second item in this my will, I have directed ye Merchants hundred plantation with the slaves & stocks, to be held & enjoyed by
my daughter Elizabeth for & during the term of her natural life, my intent
& meaning is that my stocks of Cattle & hoggs & other personal goods belonging to the said plantation, be only lent to my said daughter Elizabeth
during her life and no property vested in her, & she my said daughter, to
enjoy the profits of the said stocks still keeping up the number that they shall
be at the time of my decease, and my will and meaning is the same in respect
of the other settlement I have made to my daughters Page & Harrison.

It is my will that £40 of Coarse goods be sent for and to be distributed
amongst the poor necessitous people of the parish I live, at the discretion of
my ex'tors. It is my will and I do give to Mr. John Bell our minister, £10
sterling for mourning. It is my will and I do give to my several friends my
Trustees in this my * * £10 sterling a piece, as an acknowledgement for the
trouble they will be at.

I do hereby revoke all other & former wills & testament heretofore by
me made, & do publish, utter & declare this to be my last will & testament.
In witness whereof I have hereunto set my hand & seal this 22nd day of
August, 1726.

N. B. The words in the twelfth sheet of this my will (or the Major part
of them or the survivors of them), & the words (to be paid by son John)
and in the seventeenth sheet the words (so long as my sons his Brothers shall
think fitt to continue him there), interlined before signed.

Robert Carter   (L. S.)

Signed, sealed & published in presence of us.

John Turberville, 1726,	*Alex'r Edgar,*
Rd. Lee,	*John Harvey,*
Thomas Edwards,	*Solomon Adshead.*

I the aforesaid Robert Carter being of sound mind and memory Twenty eighth sheet of my will.

I do this day make this my further addition & alteration in my aforegoing will dated the 22nd day of August last, to make my son Robert equal to his other Brothers in number of slaves. I do give unto my said son Robert & the heirs male issue of his body lawfully begotten under the same limitation as the rest of the negroes are given, the following slaves (to-wit) : all them slaves, men, women & children, that I bought and purchased of Mr. John Pratt, which were brought home to my house, also the negroe called Harry Bacon & negroe Boy called Sam, both which ran away from my nomini plantation, likewise four good negroes out of these I have given to my son Charles, two young men & two young women also as many more slaves out of these I have given to my son John, half males & half females not to be under the age of twelve years, as will make up the number I have given to him my said son Robert, one hundred working slaves above the age of twelve years.

My will and meaning is that my negroe Harry, one of George's sons shall be deemed to belong to my son Charles, he now living at my son's falls plantation.

Whereas I have ordered a Quarter to be seated upon the land I lately bought of Mr. Cary with ten or twelve slaves from my Westmoreland plantation, which Quarter will belong to my son John, by this my will. It is, notwithstanding, my will & intent that these slaves, as many of them as shall be seated on the said New plantation at the time of my Death, shall be held & taken to belong to my s'd son Robert's number of slaves.

In witness that this is a part of my will, & to be construed as such, I have hereunto set my hand and seal this eleventh day of October, 1726.

Robert Carter (*L. S.*)

Signed, sealed & published in presence of

R^d Lee,	*T. Austin,*
John Harvey,	*Solomon Ashead.*

In the name of God, Amen. I, Robert Carter, aforesaid, Since the making of my abovesaid will consisting of twenty-nine Sheets of paper, having undergone Several changes and alterations in my circumstances in relation to my temporal Estate, and forasmuch as by a late act of Assembly made Since the making of my Said will to explain & amend the act declaring the negro mulatto and Indian Slaves within this Dominion, great alterations are made in the Said act making Negroes a real estate, under the consideration of which former act of assembly I made my Said Will, being & continuing to this day thro' the mercy of God of Sound mind & memory do make the following additions, alterations, Revokations & declarations in & concerning my said will as aforesaid. Whereas I have entailed upon my three eldest Sons, John, Robert & Charles, all my Slaves belonging to my several plantations in Virginia with Several remainders over which under the former Law I had power to do, giving all my said Slaves in such words unto my said three sons as will give the property in all my said Slaves according to the Interpretation & meaning of the said late Law which was never my purpose or intent to do. I do hereby utterly revoak all those gifts to my said three Sons, John, Robert & Charles, hereby declaring it is my full intent & meaning that no property shall be vested in any of my said three Sons to any of my Said Slaves. And I do hereby declare that it is my intent & meaning that my Said three Sons shall have only the use and profits of my said Slaves & their increase for during and continuing their respective natural lives, the said Slaves and their increase however to be annexed to my respective Lands & plantations for the improvement of my said Several plantations & Lands according to the directions of my said will. . . .

That whereas I have bought Sundry tracts of Land for my three married daughters and have bought Sundry Slaves for the improving and working the said Lands which they are annexed unto, and whereas in the disposition of the said slaves I have used the words (I give the said slaves unto my said Daughters respectively for and during their natural lives or to this purpose), I do revoake the said clauses and do only give the profits of the said slaves & their increase unto my said three Daughters for and during their natural lives under the conditions aforesaid, and it is my further will that Mann Page, Esq., do enjoy the profits of the lands & negroes settled upon his wife for and during the term of his natural life according to the intention of my aforesaid will under the conditions mentioned as afores^d. And it is my further will that Maj. Benjamin Harrison do enjoy the profits of the lands & negroes settled upon his wife for and during the term of his natural life according to the intention of my aforesaid will under the Conditions mentioned as aforesaid. And I do give the property of the Said Slaves & their increase unto my said Daughters' Sons & the heirs of their Bodies, to continue annexed to the said Lands and to go and descend according to the intent of my said Will. . . .

And whereas I have given my estate in Williamsburg to my two sons Landon and George, It is now my will & I do hereby devise unto my said Son George all my said estate in W^{ms}burg to him & the heirs of his body lawfully begotten, & for want of such to my son Landon & the heirs of his body lawfully begotten, and for want of such to my son John & the heirs of his body lawfully begotten, and for want of such to my son Robert & the heirs of his body lawfully begotten, & for want of such to my Son Charles & the heirs of his body lawfully begotten, & for want of such to my right heirs forever.

And whereas in my said Will I have given to my two Sons Landon & George my bank annuity of fifteen hundred pounds, which hath since been paid into the hands of Micajah Perry, Esq., It is my will that this Fifteen hundred pounds be paid to my said son Landon when he shall come to the age of twenty-one years in three equal yearly payments in the following manner, Viz: the first payment to be made the first shipping after my said Landon arrives at his age of twenty-one, the second payment the Shipping after, and the third payment to be made the Shipping after that; & that he also have one moiety of my bank stocks in the hands of the said Perry & Mr. Wm. Dawkins, the other moiety of my said Bank Stocks to belong to my Son George according to the directions and in the manner of my said will. . . .

It is my will that this addition to my said will Contained in five sheets of paper, comprizing in the whole thirty four sheets, shall be taken as a part of my said will, & shall be interpreted as a declaration of my intent & meaning, and shall be taken as a revokation to such parts and as an addition to others and as explanatory of the whole, so that my real & true intent may be answered.

In witness whereof I have hereunto set my hand & affixed my seal this twelfth day of September, in the year of our Lord God one thousand seven hundred and twenty eight.

Robert Carter   (*L. S.*)

Signed, sealed & published in presence of

R. Lee,	*Rich'd Talent,*
John Harvey,	*John Conner,*
Barnabas Burch,	*Arthur Neale.*

In the name of God, Amen. I, Robert Carter, Esq., of Lancaster County, being of sound mind, memory, but in a crazy, disordered condition respecting my health, do make this addition, alteration & revokation to Several parts of my will which is contained in four & thirty sheets of paper, being made at three several times, the first bearing date the two & twentieth day of August, 1726, the second bearing date the eleventh day of August, 1726, the third bearing date the 12th day of October, 1728, all intended to be one entire will as far as can be made consistent, and when alterations are made the latter clauses alway to be understood to controul & revoke the former, this will under these circumstances I do now revive & republish so far as it will Stand & consist with the alterations, additions & revokations that I am now about to make.

Notwithstanding the devises in my said will I do now give unto my Son Landon all my lands and plantations in Northumberland County excepting the lands at the upper end of the said County called Fielding's, which I have given to my son Robert, to him my Son Landon & the heirs male issue of his body, & for want of such unto my Son Charles & the heirs male issue of his body, & for want of such the Tail to be continued according to the directions of my will, & I also do lend unto my Said Son Landon all the Slaves that shall belong to the said plantations now given him for and during the Term of his natural life, the property of the Slaves to remain and be in trust to my said Son Landon to and for the use of the heirs male issue of his body, and I do give unto my Said Son Landon all the Stocks of Cattle, hoggs & Sheep that are upon the said plantations.

Whereas I have been for some time upon a bargain for the whole Estate of Mr. John L. Boyd's Lands, Slaves, Stocks, &c., in Richmond County, for which I have bid in the Court of Chancery in Great Britain by the hands of alderman Perry of London the sume of £3,800, £500 of which money is already paid as a depositum into the Said Court of Chancery and the remaining £3,300 now lies in the hands of the said Alderman Perry ready to consummate the said bargain, if the said bargain be concluded then my will is and I do devise & bequeath all the Said lands, plantations, housing & appurtenances unto my said Son Landon and to the heirs male issue of his Body lawfully begotten forever. . . .

Whereas I have given unto my son Landon & my son George my bank Stock in the hands of alder Man Perry & Mr. Dawkins & also other debts, due to me in Va., & likewise the mortgage of Rippon Hall, I do revoke and alter my will in these respects & do direct as followeth:

1st. I do give & devise unto my son George all my lands & estate of Rippon Hall & the lands adjoining thereto which were mortgaged to me by Colonel Jennings & also the mill I have bought since, likewise the Lands I bought of Joseph Wade & my houses & estate in W^{ms}burg & also the Lands I lately bought of Maj^r Benj. Robinson & his Wife at Arnold's ferry lying in King & Queen Co. All these Lands, Plantations, houses & real estate I give and devise unto my s'd Son George & the heirs male issue of his Body forever, as also the Slaves that belong to & are now Seated upon Rippon plantation & in case of failure of issue male of my son George then I do give these houses, Lands & slaves unto my son Landon & the heirs male issue of his Body, & for want of such to my Son Robert & his heirs male. . . .

It is my will that my son George be kept at school at the College of Wm. & Mary two years longer & that then he be Sent to the University of Cambridge for an education, the charge of his education to be born by my ex'tors and out of the interest of my Said son George's Bank stock, & if my ex'tors his Brothers See it so fitting that he my son George may be entered first at the Inns of Court, that if his inclination & capacity Lead that way he may be bred to the Law.

It is my will and I do appoint my Son Landon to be one of the Ex'tors of this my will.

Whereas I have given to my Son Charles my negroe man. Tom Gumby, his wife and children, I revoke that part of my will & I do give them to my son Robert, Excepting the girl Mary which I leave to my Son Charles.

It is my will that some young negroes of those I have given to my son George be bred up Trades men, Carpenters & Coopers for ye use of his plantations.

It is my will that when my grandson Robert Carter Nicholas arrives to the age of ten years there be paid to his Father by my Ex-'tors the sum of £5,000 to be by him put out to interest for the use & benefit and toward the maintenance of my said grandson.

Whereas in the dispose of those slaves that are to belong to my Son Robert I have done my endeavor to annex them so to his Lands to prevent his sale and dispose of them from his posterity, however notwithstanding in Regard his present wife brought to her husband, my s'd son Robert, considerable fortune, I think it but justice to declare that it is my will that she, my s'd son Robert's wife, if she survive her s'd husband shall have her right of dower out of the s'd Slaves during her natural life. . . .

In witness whereof I have hereunto set my hand & Seal this ninth day of June in the year of our Lord 1730.

It is my earnest desire to my sons & to every one of them respectively that they always & upon all occasions behave themselves as loving brethren to one another & that upon any controversies or diferences that may arise between them they alwaies submit the determination thereof to their Friends & relations & that they do not hawl one another to the Law.

Robert Carter   L.S.

Signed, Sealed & published in presence of us, Richard Chapman, Richd Talent, John Conner, John Toulton.

4th Sheet of this addition to my will.

Rob't Carter.

In the name of God, Amen.   I, Robert Carter, of Lancaster Co., being in a declining State of Body but of sound mind & memory, Whereas I have made my last will & Testament at Sundry periods of time, to-wit: on the 22nd day of August, 1726, on the 11th day October, 1726, on the 12th day September, 1728, & on the 9th day of June, 1730, since which time by sure losses, the great fall of Tobacco & various other misfortunes, my circumstances are very much reduced at this day.   And whereas in my s'd will I have given & ordered large legacies to my children & grand children which my estates is no waies able to Support to prevent the ruin & undoing of my Sons, I do revoke & reduce the said in the following manner:

My Daughter Harrison's Legacy of £500 I reduce to £250.   Her daughter Betty's Legacy of £500 I reduce to £200.   Her daughter Ann's Legacy of £500 I reduce to £200.   My Daughter Page's Legacy of £300 I reduce to £250.   Her son Mann Page's Legacy conditionally as my will directs of £300 I reduce to £100.   My legacy of £300 to Carter Page payable as my will directs I reduce £150.   The Legacy to John Page payable as aforesaid of the £300 I reduce to £100.

My Legacy of £300 to my daughter Nicholas I reduce to £250.

Memorandum: The £50 given to my daughter Nicholas for ear rings I have already paid her in plate.   Her Son John's Legacy after the manner I have expressed in my will first mentioned £100 & then £300 I reduce to £100.

My said daughter's son George's Legacy in the manners as is Exprest altho' it's twice mentioned is to be but £100.

My Grandson Lewis Burwell's Legacy instead of £300 is to be but £100 under the condition mentioned.

Carter Burwell's Legacy under the Condition mentioned of £300 I reduce to £100.

Robert Burwell's Legacy of £300 under the condition mentioned I reduced to £100. The Legacy of £1,500 to my son Landon & the Legacy of £875 him, both these Legacies I reduce to £500, to be paid at two Successive payments after he comes of age.

The half of my Bank Stock first given to him my Son Landon I have already revoaked.

The Legacy of £300 given to my son George at his age I make payable at three yearly payments.

The Legacy of £500 to my Robert's daughter Elizabeth under the Condition mentioned I reduce to £300. The £300 Legacy to my Grandson Mathew Page I reduce to £100.

The Legacy of £300 to my grandson Robert Page I reduce to £100 under the Condition mentioned.

The Legacy of £3,000 Bank Stock to my Son George I reduce to £1,500.

The Legacy of half the remaining part of my Bank Stock to my son Landon I entirely revoke, having made other provision for him.

The Legacy of £300 to my grandson Robert Carter Nicholas under the Condition mentioned I reduce to £200.

The Legacies of £200 apiece to my Daughters Mary & Lucy payable five years after my decease I reduce to £100 to each.

And instead of my daughter Lucy receiving the portion I have given her in three yearly equal payments my will is it be paid to her in six yearly equal payments. And also my will is that my Ex'tors have five years to pay my daughter Mary's portion in, by equal payments from her age or marriage.

And whereas I have given in several parts of my will the use & profits of my Slaves only to my sons, & have endeavoured to vest the property in their Sons & heirs to prevent their Father's Selling or disposing of them, all the Clauses of this nature I do absolutely & entirely revoke & I do give my slaves to my respective sons according to my designation in my will unto my said respective Sons & to their heirs forever as a real estate & descendable according to the terms of our late negro law.

And whereas I have ordered my son George an university education, I have seen such bad effects of it that I leave the care of him to the disposal of his Brothers, particularly my son John & after a year's stay more at the College if he thinks fitt to breed him up in the Secretary's office.

My will is that if my Grandson Benj. Harrison live to the age of ten years there be paid to him by my Ex'tors the Sum of £200, to be laid out in young negroes between the ages of ten & fifteen years, one half of them to be females. My will is that if my grandson Robert Carter live to the age of ten years there be paid to him my my Ex'tors the Sume of £200, to be laid out in young negroes between the ages of ten & fifteen years, one half of them to be females.

It is my will that this writing contained in two Sheets of paper be deemed & taken to be a part of my will, & to be a revocation of my Legacies as far as it goes, as also an alteration of my will as far as it is contradictory to it.

In witness whereof I have hereunto set my hand & seal this three &

twentieth day of July in the year of our Lord one thousand seven hundred
& thirty.

Robert Carter (*L. S.*)

Signed, Sealed & published in the presence of

Rich. Chapman,	*Rich. Talent,*
John Conner,	*John Toulton.*

B. *Selections from the Inventory of the Estate of Robert "King" Carter**

AN INVENTORY OF ALL THE S * * * AND PERSONAL PROPERTY OF THE
HON'BLE ROBERT CARTER OF THE COUNTY OF LANCASTER ESQ., DECEASED,
TAKEN AS DIRECTED IN HIS LAST WILL, VIZT.

In Lancaster County at the home plantation.—In the Old house Dining Room, Vizt:

1 large looking Glass, 17 Black Leather Chairs, 2 ditto stools, 1 Large
oval Table, 1 Middling Ditto, 1 small ditto, 1 Blackwalnut Desk, 1 Ditto
Corner Cupboard, 1 pr. large money scales & w'ts, 1 pr. Hand Irons, 1 poker,
2 pr. Tobo. Tongs.

In the Dining Room Clossett.

2 chaney Basons, 1 ditto Cannister, 10 ditto Tea cups & 8 saucers, 1 Do.
small Dish, I do. Teapott with a silver spout, 2 Middling do. cupps, 1 Doz.
Earthen plates, 5 soop Do., 2 copper coffee potts, 2 do. Tea kettles, a tin
water Cistern, 2 Coffee Mills, 1 Bark Gamott Table, 1 doz. Iron candlesticks,
4 Brass do., 1 do. warming pan, 1 do. chafing Dish, a plate case, a Cupboard,
10 small water Glasses, 3 Decanters, 2 Rummer Glasses, 4 Beer Glasses, 32
Wine Glasses, 2 stone Juggs, 3 Quart Muggs, 1 Iron plate stand, 22 Black
handled Knives & Forks, 1 Secrutore, 1 I Large Floor oyl.

In the Chamber over the Dining Room.

4 Feather Beds, 4 Bolsters & 6 pillows, 4 Ruggs, 1 Quilt, 3 prs. Blankets,
I pr. blew chaney curtains vallens Teaster and head peice, 1 pr. stamped
Cotton curtains vallens Teaster & headp^s, 1 square Table, 2 high Bedsteads
and one Trundle Bedstead, 3 cane chairs, 5 Leather Ditto, 1 Dressing Glass,
12 Bed chaney chair cushings, 1 p^r Iron Doggs, 1 pr. Fire Tongs, 1 shovel.

* Reprinted from the *Virginia Magazine of History and Biography,* VI (October 1898), 145–152; VI (January 1899), 260–268; VI (April 1899), 365–370.

In the lower Chamber.

11 Leather chairs, 1 New ditto, 1 arm chair, 4 cane chairs.

In the Chamber Closett, Books Vizt:

Folios.—Howell's French Dictionary, Herman Mott's Geography. Rush-worth's Collections, Vol. 1st, Ditto collections from 1639 to 1640. Ditto Do. from 1640 to 1644. Ditto Do. from Do. to Do. Ward of Warr. Crook's Anatomix, Riverin's practice of Physick, Annotations to the first Isaiah. The Tryal of Wm. Staley &c., Plutarch's Lives. Memorials of Eng. affairs from 1625 to 1660. Brownrigg's sermons, Machiavel's Works, Holyoke's Dictionary, Collier's Dictionary, Vol. 1. Do. Do., Vol. 2. Compleat history of England, Vol. 1, do., vol. 2, Do., Vol. 3. Clarrendon History of the Civil Warrs, Vol. 1, do. do., Vol. 2, Do. Do., Vol. 3, Statutes at large.

In the lower Chamber Closets Continued.

The following Books vizt:
Dalton's Courts Justice, Croke's Reports, part the first, A large folio Bible, a Common prayer book, Selden's Tracts, Caesar's Commentaries. Modern Reports part the 1st, do. do., 2nd do. do., 3rd do. do., 4th Levring's Rep^{ts} 1st & 2nd part, do. do. 3rd part, Jones' Reports, Kirlwey, do. Ventris do. 1st & 2nd part, Keebles do. Vol. 1, do. do. Vol. 2, do. do. Vol. 3, Shovers do., Carter's do., Vaughan's do., Comberback do., Keelyng's do., Salkeel do. do., Vol. 1, do. do. Vol. 2, Dalton's office of Sheriff, Ditto Justice, Keeble's do. do. do., Statutes from 16 Car. 1st to 27, Car. 2nd Vol. * * * do. from 1st Jac., 1st to the 7th, Wm. 3rd Vol., * * do. from 7th, Wm. 3rd to the 9th & 10th, The Laws of Barbados, do. of Massachusetts Bay in New Eng^d, Danver's Abridgm^t Vol. 1, do. do. Vol. 2, Nelson's do. Vol. 1. do. do. Vol. 2, do. do. Vol. 3, Fitz Herbert's do., Brook's ditto, City of London Case, Cases in Chancery fro. 12th Car. 2d to the 31st, Hawle's Remarks, Plowden's Commentaries, Modern Cases, Historical Discourses, Laws & Governm^t in Queen Eliza., Wingate's Maxims, Manleye Interpreter, do. do. Coke's 2nd Institutes, do. 3rd do., do. 3rd & 4th do. do. 4th do., notes from 20th Augt 1702 to the 13th Mar. 1704, do. fro. 27th Oct. 1705 to the 1st April 1708, Cotton's Records, Sydney of Government, Dawson Original of Laws, Acts of Queen Ann 1705–1706, do. of do. 1707, Collier's Tryal, Waterhouse on Fortescue, Croke Eliz^a do., Carolus do., Jacob Swineburn's Last Wills & Testaments, Syntagma Theologiae, Buchaniers of America, Conimbricensis 2nd Book, ditto 3rd ditto 4th. * * * *

In the Lower Chamber Clossett, Cont.

The following Books, Viz^t:
Hugh's Abridgm^t, part the third, * * ests Presidents, Moyle's Entries, Godolphin's Legacy, Cowley's Interpreter, Prynn's power of Parliament, Attorneys' Academy, a Bible, Brownlow's Reports, How's Prescience, Wet-

wood's Memoirs, Fibmer's Treatises of Government, Hale's Contemplations, The Compleat Statesman, Brown's Clerks' guide, Essay for regulating the Law, a Treatise of the Law, Cotton's choice pieces, The Decay of Christianity, Filmer's observations of Government, * of Great Brittain * * * * 7 Grammers, 4 Cordery's Colloquies, Echard's Roman history, L. Estrange Josephus, Tillottson's sermons, Vol. 2nd, do. do. 3rd, do. do. 7th, do. do. 8th, do. do. 9th, do. do. 10th, do. do. 11th, do. do. 13th, do. do. 14th, Temple's Letters, Vol. 1st, do. do. Vol. 2nd, do. do. Vol. 3rd, Do's Introduction, Do's Miscellanea, part 3rd, Do's Memoirs from 1672 to 1679, * * survey, Lord's Psalms old Version, do. * * of the 4 last Reigns, * lish Compendium * History of Europe for 1704, do. do. 1704, do. do. 1705, do. do. 1706, do. do. 1707, do. do. 1707, do. do. 1708, do. do. 1709, Stanhope of Wisdom, first part, do. of do. 2nd & 3rd parts, Blair's Sermons, Tacitus' Works, Vol. 1st, do. do. 2nd History of Queen Ann, The Life of Queen Ann, Vol. 1st, ditto 2nd, Dr. Hick's Priesthood agst the Rights, ditto against the Rights, Dr. Turner against Ditto, Mr. Mottous' Sermons against ditto, Saml Hill's against ditto, do. do. agst do., Ludlow's Memoirs, Vol. 1st, do. do. 2nd, do. do. 3rd part, Hoadley of the Church of England 1st part, Calamy of do. 1st part, Hoadley in answer to Calamy, Calamy of the Church of England, 2nd part, Bishop Worcester's Discourse of the Trinity, Palmer's Moral Essays, Hale's Knowledge of God, &c., Tillottson's first Vol. Eikon Baptists, Terms of the Law, Abridgm^t Vir^{as} Laws, Fitz Herbert's Naturia Brevium, Robotham's gate of languages unlocked, Nelson's Reports, Wingate's Abridgm^t office of an attorney, Molloy dejure Maritimo & Navali * * Treatise of Recoverys, Terms of the Law, do. of do., Wingate's Abridg^{mt}, Selden's Judicature in Parliament, Fortescue on the Laws of Eng^d, Body of the Law, Sheppard's Offices, Perkin's do., Herne's Conveyances, Practice of Chancery, Statutes of Bankrupt, Tryals perpais, Lambert's Reports in Chancery, Abridgment of Coke's Reports, Perkins of the Law, Fynch's Law, Compleat attorney, Britton, Abridg^{mt} of Dyer's Rep^{ts}, Townsend's preparative to pleading, Mysteries of Clerkship, order of Chancery, Mantey's Clerks' Guide. A parcel of old cloths, a parcel of lumber, 1 Bason stand, 1 house lantern, 1 small square table, 9 guns, 1 Speaking Trumpett.

In the Chamber over the lower Chamber.

Close Stove, 2 feather Beds, 2 bolsters & 4 pillows, 4 quilts, 4 Blanketts and 2 Ruggs, 1 p. w^{te} Cotton Curtains Vallens headp^c and Teaster, 1 p. blew and white cotton & linen chex curt^s & Vallens and white linen headpiece & Teaster, 2 high Bedsteads, 2 p^r white cotton Window Curtains and Vallens, 1 Black Walnut oval Table, 1 small ditto, 1 Dressing Glass, 5 cane chairs, 1 arm ditto, 1 p^r Iron Doggs, 1 p^r tongs & fire Shovel.

In the Porch Chamber.

1 Feather Bed, 1 bolster & pillow, 1 Quilt, 1 Rugg, & 1 Blankett, 1 p^r norch cotton curtains and Vallens lin'd with Searsucker and a Searsucker head piece & Teaster, 6 blew Chaney chairs, 1 do. do. arm chair.

The Brick House Chamber, Vizt:

2 bolsters & 3 pillows, 2 p^r Blanketts & two quilts, 1 standing Bedstead & 1 Trundle do., a set of searsucker bed curtains, 2 p. cotton window curtains, 1 large Black Walnut Oval Table, 2 Small Oval Tables, 1 Glass Japp^d Scrutore, 1 Jappan^d Square small Table, 1 India Skreen, 1 Dressing Glass, 5 blew silk Camlet chairs, 1 Large Looking Glass, 1 chest of Drawers, 1 chair with a red leather seat, 1 p. Broken Hand Irons, 1 poker & fire shovel, 2 Brass Candlesticks.

In the lower chamber clossett.

* Brass Candlestick, * Hand Bell, * do of Leaf Gold, * Books, Viz^t:
* haramond, a Roman, Harrisse's Lexicon, Vol. 1st, do. do. Vol. 2nd, Hale's Original of Mankind, Ibrahim, Bentivolio and Urania, Lex Mercatoria, Coke on Littleton, Sylva or a Discourse of Forest Trees, Cassandra, Idea of Morall Philosophie, Glossographia, Assemblys' Catchism, Prayers for Familie, Bailey's Dictionary, Mechanical Acco^t of poisons, The Right of the Xtian Church, Wilford's Arithmetick, a Companion to the Alter, The pathway to Health, The Young Man's Monitor, Fidde's Sermons, Vol. 2nd, The life of Wm. Chillingsworth, Homer's Iliads, Controversie, &c., Curson's office of Exec^r, Puffendorf's introduction of Asia, Rassius' history of England, Vol. 10th, the New London Dispensation, Sententic pueriles, Ovid's Metamorphosis, Culpeper's practical physick, Introduction to the making of Lattin, Lattin and English Dictionary, The lives of Illustrious men, Tillottson's Sermons, Vol. 4th, do. do. Vol. 10th, Scott's Christian Life, Vol. 1st, do. do. Vol. 4th, Reformation of Manners, do. of Ditto.

In the Chamber over the lower Chamber.

1 Feather Bed, Bolster & pillow, 1 quilt and p^r of Blanketts, 1 Trundle Bedstead, 1 desk, 1 chest of Drawers, 1 Dressing Glass, 6 chairs with red leather seats, 2 stools with ditto, 1 small square Black Walnut Table, 1 small oval ditto with red velvet on the top, 1 p^r Hand Irons.

In the Brick Store.

A Black Walnut Case q^t the following Books, Viz^t: Annotations upon the Holy Bible, Usher's Body of Divinity Imperfect, Ward's Animadversions of Warr, Fuller's history of the Holy Warr, Exon's Contemplations on the history of the New Testament, Raptall's Collections of Statutes, Guicciard's aphorisms, Sedgewick's bowels of tender mercy, Mosan's general practice of Physick, Reverinse's practice of Physick, Hall Annotations Imperfect, Rushworth's historical Collections, Perkin's Golden Chain, Montgomery's Urania, Haynes' General view of the Holy Scriptures, Minohen's Spanish Dictionary, Imperfect Book of Law, West's first part of Symboliography, an Imperfect Book of Law, West's Pattern of Presidents, Bellarmini de Canone Scripturae, Cratcanthorp's defence of Constantine, Diodatis pious annotations', Echardo

Roman history, Vol. 1st, Patrick's parable of the Pilgrim, Policie unveiled, Commentariorum Colligie Conimbriscusis, Smith's Mysterie of Rhetorique, Sacheverelle Tryal, Ashe's gen¹ Table of the sev¹ books of Coke's Reports, Burgersdirius Logicam, Fennerune's Sacra Theologicca, Ursini's Corpus Doctrinae Christianae, Wendilind's Theologiae, Keckermanro's Systima Locigcae, Walker's English & Lattin Phrases, Novum Testamentum Imperfect, Scott's Christian Life part the third, Fellippe De Tractodo Dil Couscis, Aristoteles Metaphysicorum. Reports in Chancery, Vol. 2nd, Baxter's directions for Peace of Conscience, Erasmi Colloquiorum, Briggs &c., their Mathematical Tables, * Metaphisica, Nouveaw Testament, * * Historia Universsalis, * * Body of the Common Law Imperfect, * Entitled the Reformation of Manners.

7 A Chest qt.

19 yards mixed Duroys, 35 y^{ds} drugg^t, 1 p^r yellow Shalloon and some yellow Mohair, 11 yards Virg^a Cloth, 1 p^r Virg^a Cotton and linnen Cloth q^t 34 y^d, 46 y^{rds} Virg^a Cotton, 20 yards narrow Liverpool Linnen, 42 yards striped Holland, 27 yards coarse Bedtick, 2 pr. Blanketts, 1 parcell of mohair & Buttons, a Drumline, a large shuck do., a pr. of dressed sheepskins, a pound fine w^{te} bro. Thread, 1 oz. nun's Thread, 4 Livery Laced hats in a small box.

6 A chest qt.

10 p^{rs} men's French falls, 3 p^{rs} woman's do., 5 p^r boy's do., 7 p^r men's plains, 4 p^r boy's Ditto, a man's Beaver hatt, 4 monmouth caps, 6 spicketts, 2 fossetts, 2 snaffle bridles, a paper of small white nails.

A small box in which is as foll's.

32 large shoomaker's Tacks, 28 small do., 4 small round files, three square files, 2 half round files, 16 smith's files sorted, 1 p^r sheep shears.

Loose in the said chest.

2 cooper heading knives, 1 p^r Irish hose, a large parcel of mohair, a parcel of Bootwebb, a parcell of Bellandine silk.

13 A chest qt.

32 bla. silk coat Buttons, 2¾ yrd blew Broad cloth, a parcel of black, blew & yellow mohair, a parcel of black shalloon, 15 Brass coat Buttons, 3 doz. & half Breast do., 4 p^r doeskin stock^s, 5 p^r men's fine worsted hose, 6 p^r men's Rolling do., 1 p^r boy's worsted hose, 3 p^r boy's wash gloves, 2 parcels of parchment, 6y^{rds} of oyl cloth, 40^l Brown Thread, 20 gro^s horn-coat Buttons, 23 y^{rds} holland no. 19,22¾ yards bagg holland no. 1, 1 p^r fine garlix holland no. 244, 17 yards narrow garlix, 3 drum lines, 1 sheeps^d do., 3 pounds wigg powder, 17 Wash Balls, a parcel of w^{te} bro. Thread in a small trunk.

R. C. 1 a Chest qt.

A cake of Casteel soap, 48¾ y^{rds} blew broad cloth, 7 yards yellow shal-loon, 3 hanks blew silk, 7 Hanks Yellow Mohair, 4 p^r men's stockings, a large spying Glass, 5 p^{rs} boy's French Falls, 3 y^{rds} of Cambrick, 1½ y^{rds} of Flannin, 3 quilted holland caps, 2 embroidered necks in another small Band box, 2 doz. Brass Coat Buttons, 4 doz. Breast do.

A Box no. 58 In which is as follows:

4 doz. Coat Buttons, 4 doz. breast do., & 6 Hanks silk twist for trimming, 17 y^{rds} & half of Gorgoroon, 14 yards & h. of silk Taffity, 14 y^{rds} & half of Bombays, 5 yards of sear suckers, 74 y^{rds} of Ginghams, 4 cotton Hankerchiefs (Loose in the said chest), 1 gross of brass Coat Buttons, 1 gross of vest do., 5 sheapshead lines, 27 y^{rds} & h. of blew half thicks, 3½ yards of coarse garlix, 7 yards wadding, 3 silver mounted swords, 1 Gilt ditto, 2 mourning do., 9 yards broad blew Linnen, 1 whole p^r blew half thicks, a parcel of black thread Buttons & mohair, 3 p^{rs} boy's black gloves, 16 y^{rds} bla. Crape,   *   *   Buck-ram, Topps for a coach, 6 patty panns.

3d A Large Trunk qt.

9 quires & half of Large Demy Deed paper.

．　．　．　．　．

R. N. 6.   A Box abt. half full of Ditto.

A Box qt. two Coach Glasses, 1 of them broke, A small box with some Jesuits Bark in it, A Cask qt. 10 p^r wool cards, 3 Chests with Medicines in them, A Box qt. 23 Beer Glasses, A D^o kt., Some Indigo, A Do. qt., Some gun flints, 6 loafs Double Refined Sugar, 4 pound pepper, Some Cinnamon, Cloves and Mace — In a Cask.

Loose In the said Store, Vizt:

3 Butchers pads, 5 Leather Bucketts, 1 Womans pillion & cover, 8 pr. holsters and Breast plates, 1 old Embroarderd Housing pistol Caps, 1 pr. grey Cloth Laced pistol Caps, 1 pr. saddle baggs, 2 chairs with Roushia Leather Seats, 6 chince Trapps, 3 physick Sifters, A parcel of Barras, 3 Bottles Stroughtone Dropps, 1 Carpenter's adz, 1 New X Cut Saw, A pr. large Iron bolts for a Door, 2 pr. Large pott hooks, 1 brass Shovel, 2 chamber locks, 8 stone jugs, 6 large stone Bottles, 2 large earthern pans full of Turpentine, A Bottle of oyle of Turpentine, 1 Dripping pan, 3 double or flint racking Bottles, A pottle pewter pott, 9 weavers stays, 1 Cource Sifter, 2 Mopps, 4 house brooms, 3 house Lanthorns, 1 Tin Apple Roaster, A Baskett lin'd with Tin.

In the Chamber over the Brick Store.

The following Books vizt. * * Works, vol° 1st, * * 2d, Ditto, vol. 1st, * * vol. 2d, * * lgemont, vol. 1st, * * vol. 2d, Burnets history of his own time, Ditto history of the Reformacon, vol° 1st, Ditto vol. 2d, Ditto vol. 3d, Predeaux's history, vol. 1st, Ditto vol. 2d, Tillotsons 54 sermons, Cowley's Works, Wesley's life of Christ, Bracton de Legibus, Camden's Brittania, Statutes from Magna Charta to 43d of Eliz^a, Poole's annotations, vol. 1st, Colton's Concordance, Pulton's Collection of the Statutes, Tryals beginning 1681, Baker's Chronicles, Pollexfen's Reports, Bohuns Reports in parliament, the 4 last parliaments of Queen Eliz^a, Cases in Chancery from the 12th of Car: the 2d to ye 31st, Ditto from ye 30th car: 2d to ye 4th Jac: 2d, Addison's, quartos, Works, vol. 4th, Friends Acco't of Earl Peterborough's Conduct, Paschal's Thoughts, Bohuns Institut°, Temples Life, Gentlemans Calling, Cheney's Essay of health & Long Life, Dittos Essay of Ditto, Amyortor, Reports in Chancery, vol. 1st, Ditto 2d, L'Estrang's Josephus, vol. 2d, Ditto 3d, Fuller's Body of prescripts, Puffendorfer's Introduction, Poperry against Christianity, Bangor's answer to the Committee, Styles's Register.

Chamber over ye Brick Store, Contin'd.

The following Books, vizt: 8vo. Boyles on the style of the Scriptures, Defence of the Rights, Horace, Terence, Greek and Lattin Lexicon, Scotts Xtion Life, vol° 5th, Duke of Buckingham's Works, vol° 1st, Terms of the Law, Oldham's Works, A Gentleman's Religion, Of Trust in God, The Truth of the Xtian Religion, Dr. South's 12 Sermons, Fides Sermons, vol. 3d, Tillotson's Works, vol. 4th, Do. Do., vol. 5th, Rapins history of Eng^d, vol. 1st, Ditto 2d, Ditto 3d, Ditto 4th, Ditto 5th, Ditto 6th, Ditto 7th, Ditto 8th, Assemblys Catechism, Reformation of Manners, Do. of Do., Dirrections for the Study of the Laws, English examples, Tothills Chancery.

A surveying instrument, 2 cane chairs, 1 old leather Ditto, a square table, a Dressing glass, a chest of drawers, 2 high Bed steads, a pr. sear sucker Curtains, vallens & head cloths, a pr. blew & w^t Cotton chex curtains & vallens, a pr. stuff curtains and vallens, a pr. stamped cotton Curtains & vallens & head cloths, a pr. striped Cotton Curtains & vallens.

In the Brick House Loft.

7 Trunks, 7 old Cane chairs, 1 Bed stead, 1 small Oval Card Table, 1 Black Leather chair, 1 chair with a Roushia Leather Bottom, 1 napkin press, 1 chest of Draws, a parcel of Lumber, 1 Red chaney arm chair, 4 old Turkey workt chairs, 1 large oyle cloth to lay under a Table, 2 skreens.

In the Rum Cellar.

5 casks sugar, 2 hhds. of rum, 1 Teirce ditto, 2 pipes Madera wine, 1 hhd. Virginia Brandy, 4 empty hhd^s, 2 pewter gall° potts, 1 Ditto pottle Do, 1 Ditto quart Do, 1 Ditto Funnel.

In the Outward Cellar.

3 hhds. molasses, 14 Cyder Casks.

In the Kitchen.

1 Fish Kettle & cover, 5 old coppers sorted, * new copper about 40 gall°, * stewpan and cover, * pan, * kettle, * sauspan, * kettle, * covers, * ittes, * 8 old iron potts, 6 ordinary Ditto, 1 frying pan, 3 pr. pott racks, 4 pr. pott hooks, 1 pr. Tongs & shovels, 1 Dripping pan, 3 spitts, 2 Gridirons, 1 Iron bread Toaster, a pr. large hand Irones, 2 Tin pye pans, 1 Brass skillett, 1 Bell mettle Ditto, 9 old pewter Candle Moulds, 1 cold still, 21 old pewter Basons, 1 old Ditto cullendar, 1 Ditto cheese plate, 1 Ditto Magoreen Dish, 12 very old pewter Dishes, 19 pewter Dishes Sorted, 3 good Soop Dishes & one old one, 2 doz. Soop plates, 3 doz. pewter plates, 1 doz. and 10 old pewter plates, 10 earthern jarrs, 1 old Broken pestle & mortar.

In the Kitchen Loft.

A Feather Bed, Bolster and pillow, 2 blankets and a Rugg, a pr. Canvas sheets.

In the Pantry.

I Dozen casks with paint in them, no. 2 a Jarr of Linseed oyle, one Do. of Do. about half full, 4 Tob° hhds. full of allom salt, 4 casks of Ditto, 1 Ditto half full of white salt.

In the Office.

1 large Black walnut Book case, 1 smaller Ditto, 1 p. hand irons, 1 poker.

. . . . .

In the Office Chambers.

139 negroes kersey Coats, 4 pr. Irish hose, 1 wool bed, 8 negroes Bed ticks, 22 caddows, 8 yards blew Bays, 3 Feather Beds, 3 Bolsters, 1 pillow, 3 Ruggs, 4 pr. Blanketts, 2 new Baskets, 240 pound of wool, one pr. small stilliards, a Large parcel of Black walnutt in the Loft.

In the Spinning house.

I old Flock Bed, 3 small Physick sifters, 1 pr. Blanketts, 3 pr. large Taylor's shears, 1 Rug & Caddow, 1 Ballmottle mortar & Iron pestle, 1 pr. hand irons.

In ye Spinning House Chambers.

1 high Bedstead, 2 feather Bedds & 2 Bolsters, 3 pr. Blanketts and 3 Ruggs.

In the new Dairy Store.

4 p[r] Fine Damask for Table Clothes, 3 ps. ditto for Napkins, 1 ps. fine Tablem of diaper, qt. 20 yards; 1 ps. Ditto, do., 20¼ yards—40¼. 1 p[r] Course Ditto no. 1, qt. 26 yds.; 2, 20 yds.; 3, 15¼ yards—61¼ yards. 1 ps. Fine narrow hucca back, 1 pr. fine Broad ditto, 35 yards fine brown Holland, 1 ps. fine sheeting Holland 34 yds., 1 & 1 ps. Do., Do., 33½ do.—67½ yards. * * * Course Garlix, No. 20 qt., 26, Course Ditto, 11—37 ells. Garlix No. 244, 20 ells; 244, 20½ do.; 400, 19¾ do.; 4, 23½ do.; 203, 21¼ do.—105 ells. No. 400, a Remn[t] qt. 16½ yards fine garlix, 34 yds. Co. Liverpool sheeting Linen, 103 yds. brown osnabirgs, 16 yds. sacking, 9 & ½ brown and cullered thread, 23 yds. and half Durays, 5 yds. Dimothy, ½ yd. silk for puffs, 1 pr. gar[s] for Breec[s] Knees, 1 hk. of silk, Chks. Mohair, 3 doz. & 10 Ct. Buttons, 3 doz. & 6 Ct. do., 1 yd. & ½ Buckram, 1 yd. & ½ Wadding—For a suit of Cloathes. 40 Monmoth Caps, 8 doz. & 4 pr. Irish hose—In a Chest, R. No. 2. 13 ps. Ordinary Bedsack, 10 p[s] Better Ditto, 5 p[s] w[te] pladding each of 20 yds., 25 yards wadding, 7 pr. mens falls, 7 pr. womens ditto, 30 brass Dropps for Draws, 32 Do Scutchones, 5 Ditto Knob locks each 2 bolts, 19 Ditto Desk Locks and Keys, 13 Scretore Locks and Keys, 7 yards Blew half Thicks —In a Cask.

· · · · ·

R. N. 2.   A Chest qt. 30 pr. Virga. Yarn hose.

2 boxes of window glass, 2 ditto of do. lead, 4 Kirb bridles, 3 half Kirb do., 2 snaffles do., 9 leather halters, 12 ham thongs, 12 cart saddles, 10 collers and hams, 10 cart bridles, 6 Rope halters with Leather head stalls, 4 mill padds, 3 pr. mens wove worsted hose, 6 Coarce Sifters, 5 Brass Wyre wheat Ryners, 1½l. Red, blew and yellow thread, 5 pair Brooms, 3 scrubbing Brushes, A Cask of Corke, 10 Iron Shovels, 14 cart wheel boxes, 2 scyths.

A Chest qt. vizt:

9 pr. Dice, —— 2 Brass Cocks, 4 Ink glasses, —— 4 sand glasses, 1 pr. Brass scales & the following w[ts] vizt: 2, 4 pounds, 1, 2 pound, 2, ½ Pds., 1, ½ P[d], 1, ¼ P[d], 2, 2 ozs. and 2 ounce wts., ¼l. yellow mohair, 3 pr. moth Eaten yarn hose, 8 Doz. and ½ Mettle Buttons, 3 large News Ledgers, 1 large new book for Registaring Deeds.

In the new Dairy.

A broken napkin press, 1 Small Oval table, A couch and Cufbyeen, 3 Leather chairs, a safe, a Flower tray, 28 Butter potts sorted, 7 Earthern Milk pans, 6 ditto dishes, 1 Doz. Tin Patty pans, a Marble Mortar and Pestle, 1 chocolate Stone, 2 Lawn searches, 1 Course Sifter, a pr. small stilliards, 54 barrels of Pork, 7 tubs of Pork, a 14 Pound weight, a large grindstone at the Dairy Door.

In the Old Dairy.

* * * chest of Drawers, * * * sk, * * * cel of Old Lumber.

In the New Dairy Loft.

R. N: 2: A Box qt. 3 doz. Monmouth caps, 3 cloathes Brushes, 1 Copper warming pan, 9 steel cork screws, 1 Brass skillett & frame.

Loose.—1 earthen Butter pott ⅔ds full of Turpentine, 20 Ditto Butter potts sorted, 2 ditto quart muggs, 4 ditto pint ditto, 4 ditto Tea potts, 12 ditto w^te porrengers, 2 ditto gall° brown Juggs, 4 ditto white Chamber potts, 1 ditto ditto Bason, 8 doz. do. plates, 1 doz. do. soup Do., 18 ditto Dishes, 3 ditto large punch bowls, 6 water glasses, 4 ceader cans, a large Hall Lanthorn, 2 large Iron Rails, A Large parcel of Black walnutt in the cock loft, 3 doz. Jelly Glasses in a small box.

In a Chest, vizt:

2 doz. large water glasses, 7 small ditto, 9 glass Muggs, 10 large Beer glasses, 3 Doz. Smaller ditto, 8 small wine glasses, 3 Glass Rummers, 2 ditto cruits.

In the Outward Cyder house.

6 pork Barrels, 13 cyder casks, a hhd. of new sloop sails, a new covering sail, a sett of sloops old sails; sails, sculls & oars belonging to ye pinnice, yawl & flatts, 1 brass cock, 2 Barrels of finger pease, abt. 10 bushels Do. in the Loft, 1 hhd. molassus.

In the Inward Cyder house.

3 hhds. molassus, 21 cyder casks.

In the Smith's Shop.

1 Large Anvil, 1 pike do., a pr. bellows, 2 sledge hammers, 3 small Ditto, 1 large Vice, 2 small Ditto, 4 Files, sorted, 5 pr. Tongs, 1 poker & fire Shovel, 1 slice, 3 chizzels, 2 screwplates, 4 nail bores, 1 large new mill spindle, A parcel of Old Iron, 2 yokes, fitt for use, 1 ditto, unfinished, 1 Ox chain, 3 old Musquitts, 2 boxes for Coach Wheels, 2 pr. & half of H hinges.

In the Quarter.

1 old large broken pott, 1 large pott and hooks, 2 iron pestles, 1 pr. old hand Irons, 1 spade, 1 hand malt mill, 3 old Spinning Wheels, 1 wooden horse, to dry cloths on.

In the Qr. Lofts.

3 feather beds and 2 bolster, 6 ruggs, 1 pr. blankets, 3 pr. sheets, 1 bedstead, 1 spade, 7 garden Virg^a Bell glasses, 2 English Ditto, 1 old square table, 1 pr. old hand-Irons, 1 pr. Tongs, 1 good box Iron & stand, 1 old Do. and Do., 3 smoothing Irons.

In the Sloop Landing house.

Ab^t 20 bush^l of salt, a barr^l ab^t ⅔d full of Tarr, A parcel of coal, ab^t 70 bush^l, A grindstone, A parcel of inch oak planks, An old power & cable, 2 sloop anchors, ab^t 300 wt.

At the Landing.

A pinnice, a yaul, 3 good flatts ab^t 9 hhd^s burthen, a canoe, 1 new 60 hhd. sloop &c., 1 old ditto, 1 old ditto Rebuilding, a par^t of In. & h. Oak plank.

In the Still house.

4 Wyre wheat sives, 2 stills Tubbs & worms ab^t 40 and 20 Gall^o, 1 spare still and worm ab^t 30 gall^o, 6 mill Baggs, 1 old branding iron, R. 6, 1 sloops old sail, 1 Feath^rbed a chaf bolster, 2 Ruggs, a pr. blan^s & pr. sheets, 5 barrows & spayd sowe in a pen, a fattening sheep, * * * Cyder Cask in the inward still house, * * * Cart wheels in the Tob^o house.

In the old Coach House.

A charriot and four harness, a sett of old Coach wheels, 4 chain harness & Bridles, 1 phill horse, harness and bridle.

In the New Coach house.

A coach and six harness, 6 saddles and bridles, 4 old mill bridles, 1 long whip and 1 short whip, a Case of phleems & a pr. trimming sciss^{rs}, 3 curry combs and a Brush, 1 peck measure, 2 water cruits.

Horses, Mares and Colts, Vizt.

Stone horses—Pompey, Jack.

Geldens—Squirrel, howboy, Grey Diamond, Black Ditto, Smoaker, Billy, Gardener, Prince, Bod, Buckles, Conaway, Cook, Button, Willoughby, Brandey, Ball.

Dolly, a mare & a mare colt. Lydia Do & a horse colt. Margett Do & a do. colt.

Young mares—Lucy, Sary, Deborah, Dorcas.

3 horse colts, 18 mo. old. 2 mare Do. 18 mo. old. 1 ditto Do. 2 year & h. old.

In the Nail Store.

N. 7. and N. 8 a cask of neq. plains & 1 do. of Ironware.

No. 4	.	.	9 ⎫		cask ⎫	
7	.	.	10 ⎬	. . .	6 ⎬ 10 Casks.	
8	.	.	11 ⎭		⎭	
No. 2	.	.	⎫		2 ⎫ O. S.	
3	.	.	⎭	. .	⎭ Iron.	
No. 2	.	.	.	. .	1 ⎫	
12	.	.	.	. .	1 ⎬ Ware.	
					$\overline{10}$	

A. a cask of Flooring Brads. B. a ditto of Rusty nails of several sorts. . . .

A chest qt.

2 padd locks, 36 do. harps & 18 staples, 2 stock locks, 2 doz. Do. staples, 6 carpenters broad axes, 4 coopers do., 1 large mill Brass, 1 small do., 1 smoothing plain stock, 8 Do. Irons sorted, 3 jointing irons, 6 smith's files sorted, 1 screw plate & 8 screw pins, 1 —— 2 in. aug^l, 7 —— 1 in., ½ Do., 2 —— 1 in., ¼ Do., 3 —— 1 in. —— Do., —— ¾ in. Do., 5 —— ½ in. Do. * * * Borers —— cluz —— Do. —— Trowels —— Do. —— 7 boxes for coach wheels, 5 pr. claw hammer clamps, 3 iron mill wheel clamps, 1 smiths large sledge hammer, 1 Doz. ——small Do. Do., 2 gauges, 1 pr. sheep shears, a parcel small nails, 2 mill pecks.

Loose — 3 large sloop anchors, 2 long lead pipes, a Sloops new hauser, 1 mill Gudgeon and 2 Froggs, 6 doz. virg^a hilling hoes, 6 Virginia wedges, half a bagg 4^d nails, a pd. of Rosin about 12 pound, 27 Virginia Grubbing hoes, 16 ditto harrow adzes, 2 ps. pump Leather, 1 sloops new cable, 1 two in. & half augar, 1 pr. verry large stilliards to weigh 1200 wte. no pees, 17 pr. pott hooks, sorted, a large parcel of sloops old Ropes & Blocks, about ⅓ of a Coil of new inch white Rope, a new mill spindle and Frogg, 2 scyth handles, a large parcel of old Iron.

At the Nail store door.

12 Grindstones sorted, 2 pr. quern stones.

In the Nailstore Loft.

Loose — 12 white earthen chamber-pots, 3 small stone Butter potts, 4 Large Earthen milk pans, 2 papers Red Lead in a large Iron Kettle, 16 Iron potts sorted, a bagg of 8^d Bradds.

Measures — 2 Bushell, 1 half Do., 1 peck, 1 half peck, 7 steel spades. 6 Barrs of steel, 1 square barr of Iron & ½ barr Ditto, 6 flatt Barrs

Ditto, 7 new whip saws Block & Tillers, 5 new cross cut saws, a parcel of inch kotting, 4 Dead-Eye Blocks & Iron strapps, 3 Brick moulds, 1 large new Brass skill[t] and Frame, 1 large Brass pipe, 1 axle Tree for a cart, 1 old Tennant saw, half a cask of Flooring bradds, half a cask of Do. —— Do., a parcel of old Lumber on the mud Beams.

R. No. 2. A bagg of Bristol Drop shott, Do. No. 12 a parcel of Frying pans.

R. No: 2. A cask of Gunpowder.

R. No: 12. A box of Sash glass.

In a chest, viz.

10 Cross Cutt saw files, 8 whip saw wrests, 4 pr. sheep sheers, 15 hasps & 30 staples for padd locks, 1 doz. large stock lock staples, 1 doz. small Do. 2 pump boxes, 2 pump creaks.

At the home plantation — white servants, vizt.

James Robb a carpenter, John Seaton Ditto, Barnaby Burch a Ship Carpenter, John Murdough, George Brackenrigg a Glasier, John Comer—— Robert Anderson, Taylors, Wm. Judd a Gardner, Andrew Edwards Blacksmith, Thomas Stronghorme, John Banks Sailor, Lawrence Thompson—— John Palley Bricklay[s], John Foulton Cook, Rich[d] Braggley Sailor, Dorothy Stevenson, Mary Lever.

At the Home Plantation, Negroes, vizt.

Old Fortune, a woman past Labour. Butcher Robin, a man; Martha his wife. Tom Gumby a man, Kate his wife, Mary her Daught'r, a young woman, Dick a boy abt. 13 yrs. old Martha a girl abt. 1 yr. old. Criss a wom. Cook, Dorcas a girl abt. 12 yr. old. Toby a Taylor, Nanny his wife, Priscilla a young wom. his Daugh'r, Betty her Daugh'r 18 yrs. old. Mulatto Billy a Carpenter, Johnny his son abt. 8 yrs old.

Sloopers — Toney a man, Rowland Do., Scipio a young man, Talbott Do.

Joe a man, a Carter —— Man —— Ditto. Samuel Smith Do. Pratts Sary a wom., Jemmy Phills bro'r 10 yrs. old, Odo a young man, Mulatto John abt. 10 yrs. old, Will a boy abt. 12 yrs. old, Kitt a do. abt. 11 yrs. old, Whaley a boy abt. 13 ys. old, Jemmy a do. abt. 14 ys. old, Tom a do. abt. 14 ys. old, Tom a do. abt. 14 ys. old, Frank a Carpenter, Flower his wife, Duke his son abt. 13, Frank a boy abt. 9. 33 in all.

Negroes carried by Chas. Carter, Esqr. to Mid'x.

Frank a Carpenter. Homer & his Wife. Duke his Son abt. 13. Frank a boy abt. 9. —— —— 4 & 33, 37 in all.

Linnen, Vizt.

4 Byrd Eyd Diapr. Table clothes, 10 Diaper Ditto —— Do., 2 **very** fine Diaper Do., 4 fine Damask & —— Do. —— Do., 2 doz. & half Byrd

Eyd Diaper Napkins, 18 Midling Damask Do. —— Do., 18 new Diaper ——
Do., 10 old Damask — Do., 2 doz. midling Byrd Eyd Do., 1 doz. old Diaper
—— Do., 20 sco. Diaper —— Do., 2 doz. very fine Diaper —— Do., 2 setts
fine Damask —— Do., 22 Cource Towells, 6 fine new Byrd Eyd Do., 10
Diaper Do., 8 pr. fine holland sheets, 8 pr. fine do. —— Do., 2 pr. very fine
Do., —— 11 pr. servants sheets.

Old qr. George Connolly Overseer.

Negroes.

Dick, Foreman.

Abram a man, Jenny his Wife, Bridgett a girl —— ab't 1 yr. old.

Mingo a man, Long Nanny his wife, Isabel a girl —— ab't 9 yrs. old,
Betty —— Do. abt. 8 yrs. old, Wingo a Boy —— abt. 7 yr. old, Mary a girl
—— abt. 6 yr. old, Alice a Do. —— abt. 1 yr. old.

Robin a man—Sue his wife.

Snapsack a young man, Tomboy a Ditto.

Arrobella a wom.

Nassau a man, Nanny his wife, Bridgett their Daugh^r a young wom.,
Criss a Girl —— ab^t 14 yrs. old, Molly Ditto —— ab^t 11 yrs. old, Lucy Ditto
—— ab^t 7 yrs. old.

Hannah a Girl —— ab^t 9 yr. old, sloop Toney * * *

Jemmy a man, Blackwall Do., London —— Do., Tom —— Do., Dick
—— Do., Ralph —— Do., Faldo —— Do., Arthor a boy —— ab^t 19 yr old,
in all 31.

Sheep 116.

A horse called Blackbird.

Cattle.

1 Bull —— 10 yr. old, 1 Do. —— 8 yr. old, 1 Do. —— 3 yr. old, 16
Draught oxen, 2 fattening Do., 7 steers —— 7 yr. old, 16 Ditto 4 & 5 yr. old,
3 Ditto —— 2 yr. old, 12 cows, 12 yearlings, 16 Barren Cows, 17 heifers.
In all 105 head.

2 setts of wedges, 1 Iron pestle, 1 large pott & hooks, 1 small Do. & Do.

1 Caddow, 1 old Rugg & 1 old wool bed, 1 horse Cart, 1 ox Ditto & yoakes,
4 ox chains, 1 pr. Timber wheels.

Indian Town qr., Jno. Leathead.   (Overs.)

Negroes.

Sampson Foreman, Judy his wife.

Carters Will a Man, Pegg his wife.

Groshire a man.

Great Peter a man, Olive Kate his wife, Robin —— abt. 12 ys. old.
Nanny —— ab't 11 ys. old, Peter —— ab't 8 yr. old, Harry —— ab't 7 yr.
old, Margery —— ab't 3 yr. old, Betty —— ab't 6 yr. old.

Kate a woman, Hannah —— ab't 9 yr. old, Jacob —— ab't 8 yr. old.

Old Bock, Mulatto Mary a wom., Lydia Do., Rumbo a man.

Stephen a sawyer, Sarah —— ab^t 10 yrs. old, Ambrose —— ab^t 8 yr.

Appendix

old, Moll —— ab^t 5 yr. old.   *   *   *   In all.
   *   *   Hoggs in the Pen.

Cattle.

1 Bull —— 8 yr. old, 3 Do. —— 4 yr. old, 10 steers —— 3 yr. old, 12 Do. —— 4 yr. old, 2 Do. —— 8 yr. old, 1 Do. fatning 8 yr. old, 25 cows, 25 yearlings, 35 Barron Cows. 114 in all.

1 Large pott & hooks, 1 small Do., 1 Iron pestle, 4 wedges, 1 large chest, 1 old Rugg, a pr. old Blanketts.

Changelius qr., Pet^r Carter Overseer.

Negroes.

Daniel Foreman, Nell ab^t 6 yr. old, Robin —— ab^t 4 yr. old, Ben —— ab^t 2 yr. old.

Peter a man, Stephen Do.

Tom a man, Amey his wife, Billy —— ab^t 4 yr. old, Judy —— ab^t 2 yr. old.

Isaac a man.

Sue a wom., Gabriel —— ab^t 13 yr. old, Betty —— ab^t 12 yr. old, Dinah —— ab^t 9 yr. old, Manuel —— ab^t 7 yr. old, Alice —— ab^t 4 yr. old.

Sawyer Jacob, Margett his wife.

Dick a carpenter, Abram ab^t 6 yr. old his son.

Old Manuel a cooper past labour, Semendary his wife, Archibald ab^t 8 yr. old.

Acknowledgments

In the research on this book, I am particularly grateful to Mr. Francis L. Berkeley, archivist of the University of Virginia Library and currently executive assistant to the president of the university. Beyond generously making available to me the Carter letters which he had personally collected and deposited in the Library, Mr. Berkeley continuously offered collaborative details from his own background in the period. He thoughtfully mailed xeroxes of various items, and provided encouragement and guidance in the practical aspects of gathering and collating research material. I am also indebted, for supportive guidance and very real help in the practical aspects of the work itself, to Dr. Edgar F. Shannon, president of the University of Virginia; to the Honorable Colgate W. Darden, Jr.; to Congressman David E. Satterfield III; to Dr. George Modlin, president of the University of Richmond; to Mr. John M. Jennings, director of the Virginia Historical Society; and to Colonel W. H. K. Fitzroy, director of the Virginia Area University Center. I wish gratefully to acknowledge the financial assistance provided by a Senior Fellowship awarded by the National Foundation of the Arts and Humanities.

In working at the Alderman Library, I cannot sufficiently thank Mr. Edmund Berkeley, Jr., for his continually thoughtful cooperativeness in making available to me xerox copies of documents. For this kindness I also wish to thank Mr. Robert Stocking and members of the staff.

For work at the Virginia Historical Society, I am extremely grateful to Mr. William M. E. Rachal, who gave invaluable advice and suggestions for research out of his scholarship in the period. I wish to thank Mr. Howson Cole, curator of manuscripts, who deserves incomparably more than an acknowledgment for his untiring patience in producing documents from the Society's illimitable storehouse and recommending documents out of his encyclopedic knowledge of the material available. I am also grateful to Mr. John M. Jennings, the director, for his unfailing supportiveness on this book and many before; to Mr. James A. Fleming, curator of printed books; and to Mr. Virginius Cornick Hall, curator of rare books. For work at and through the Virginia State Library, I owe the deepest gratitude to Mr. Milton Russell, who through many years, and especially on this book, gave unstintingly of his time and background in guidance on research material, and who generously performed innumerable acts of thoughtfulness in getting material into my hands. I am also grateful, for continually courteous cooperativeness, to members of the staff: Miss Eudora Elizabeth Thomas, Mrs. Margaret N. Causby, Mrs. Gene H. Knoop, Mrs. Willie A. Jarrell, Mrs. Lois J. Fields, and Mrs. Francis B. Richmond.

I wish to thank Mr. and Mrs. Hill Carter, of Shirley plantation, for their encouragement on the work about Mr. Carter's ancestors, for their making available Carter material, and for their informed companionship on a research trip to Corotoman.

I am warmly grateful to Mr. McDonald Wellford, of Richmond, for his sustained encouragement, for the sharing of his family lore, and for his practical help, including a research trip to Sabine Hall, the home of Landon Carter, Mr. Wellford's ancestor, and now owned by Mr. Wellford's kinsmen. I wish to thank Miss Margaret Cook, curator of manuscripts at the Earl Gregg Swemm Library, of the College of William and Mary; Dr. Edward Riley, of the History Department of Colonial Williamsburg; and Mr. Duncan Cocke and Mr. J. Randolph Ruffin, of Colonial Williamsburg, for their friendly assistance in facilitating research work in Williamsburg. I wish to thank Mr. Malcolm Jamieson, of Berkeley plantation, for his kindness in continuously making available to me material on the Harrisons and their seat at Berkeley, and for his generous hospitality across the years.

I have a special kind of gratitude to Mrs. Louisa Fawley, of the Richmond Professional Institute, for her inestimable assistance in working critically on the various stages and drafts of the manuscripts, for her sound suggestions in recasting and revising, and for her patience in typing the various drafts, including the final version of the manuscript.

I would like to express a personal acknowledgment of gratitude to Mr. Robert Rawls, of Richmond; Dr. Edward Peple, dean of the University of Richmond Graduate School; and Mr. Joseph Heistand, rector of St. Paul's Episcopal Church.

Selected Bibliography

Note on Sources

In presenting the source material of this book without footnotes of reference in the text, I do not wish to imply a distaste for the more formal techniques of scholarship. I certainly do not "spurn" or "scorn" footnotes, as I was charged by two persons who reviewed a previous book of mine, which included an explanatory note on the absence of formal documentation. It is simply that my methods in writing narrative history grew out of my earlier work as a novelist, and as my purpose in writing about Virginia's past is essentially to sustain the continuity of narrative, I relied on the familiar methods.

I have the deepest gratitude for the formal documentation of scholars, and of course footnotes are absolutely necessary for monographs in scholarly journals on specialized aspects of history. But fundamentally I am writing a synthesis. While I hope its interpretations are sound and some of its viewpoints are fresh — I know some of its material is new — the work is not addressed to scholars. In writing a synthesis, the contribution I hope to make is a comprehensive narrative of a period for readers interested in the personalities of the past. Though there are those who regard earlier work of "the creative imagination" as a shady background for writing researched history, I have unashamedly brought to history the fiction-writer's interest in people, and I would like to think that some of a fiction-writer's training in presenting people in narrative would partially compensate, to the more generous-minded, for my failure to have been trained in the methods of formal documentation.

When I first turned to writing narrative history twenty years ago, there was not the present stress upon footnoted documentation. Now we have come upon a time when, I suppose, any unfootnoted book of history is open to attack, by those who wish to denigrate it, on the grounds of absence of "documentation."

No writer has a legitimate argument against the judgments, however unfavorable, of a review that is (as Stephen Vincent Benét once said) "fair, objective, and intelligent." Nor can he complain of factual errors being cited — except when a trivial error, of no significance to the meaning of the book, is given disproportionate emphasis. But fair objectivity makes it clear that the errors to which any writer of history is liable, regardless of methods, are not necessarily present because of lack of formal documentation, or absent because footnotes are used.

For example, in this book I am using, without a footnote, a document available but untouched for three hundred years, while historians of praised scholarship have, in books strewn with footnotes, continually inferred that John Carter came as a "cavalier" to Virginia because they did not discover the land patent he took out in Jamestown in 1642. The fact that Carter did *not* come as a "cavalier" was recently unearthed by Edmund Berkeley, Jr., in his thesis for an M.A. degree at the University of Virginia. Such items will continue to be discovered, without casting any stigma on scholars' documentation, and I mention this example merely to illustrate the point that footnotes are not a protection against inaccuracies, and certainly not against faulty (even ludicrous) interpretations of facts available.

As is known, footnotes are useful chiefly to scholars. While I am not providing scholars with this service, I think that my bibliography provides the sources to confirm the presentation of my material, and that it will also guide a general reader in further studying those aspects which might be of special interest. For scholar and general reader, I include in the text the relevant information pertaining to correspondence, which is usually placed in footnotes: for letters, the recipients and the dates are given in the narrative.

Any such explanation of working methods will apparently be found to be defensive by some. But as one of the survivors of a vanishing breed of professional writer, independent and "unaffiliated," I have believed there was still room in history for informal techniques (where adequate source material is listed), as well as for the now more generally used formal methods which fall inclusively in the category of "documentation." In this conviction of the validity of different methods *according to the intention,* I do not scorn footnotes because I do not organize documentation any more than I scorn sonnets because I write in prose.

With few exceptions, chiefly in the love letters of Governor Nicholson, the spelling and punctuation in letters have been made to conform generally with contemporary usage.

Principal Unpublished Sources

Robert Carter Letterbooks and Diary. University of Virginia Library.
Robert Carter Papers. Virginia Historical Society.
Ludwell-Lee Papers. Virginia Historical Society.
Miscellaneous Papers. Virginia Historical Society.
Berkeley, Edmund, Jr. "Robert Carter." M.A. Thesis, University of Virginia.
Cannon, Carl, Jr. "Robert ('King') Carter." M.A. Thesis, Duke University.

Primary Sources in Print

Flournoy, H. W., William P. Palmer, S. McRae, and R. Colson, eds. *Calendar of Virginia State Papers and Other Manuscripts Preserved in the Capitol in Richmond.* Richmond, 1875–1893. 11 vols.

Hening, William Waller. *The Statutes at Large, Being a Collection of All the Laws of Virginia*. Richmond, 1819–1823. 13 vols.

McIlwaine, Henry R., ed. *Executive Journals of the Council of Colonial Virginia*. Richmond, 1925–1930. 4 vols.

———, ed. *Legislative Journals of the Council of Colonial Virginia*. Richmond, 1918–1919. 3 vols.

——— and John P. Kennedy, eds. *Journals of the House of Burgesses of Virginia, 1619–1776*. Richmond, 1905–1915. 13 vols.

Extensive use was made of the 75 volumes of the *Virginia Magazine of History and Biography*, hereafter *VMHB*. Among the published sources, some specific articles from the magazine have been listed separately under the authors' names. Under *VMHB* some unsigned articles have been listed, which served as specific sources for individuals — the letters of William Byrd I, the wills of John Carter I and of Robert Carter, and material on Nicholson and Spotswood, etc.

Published Sources

Anderson, Jefferson Randolph. "Genealogy: Tuckahoe and the Tuckahoe Randolphs." *VMHB*. XLV, 55–86. Includes background of Henry Randolph and William Randolph, the emigrants, and the line from William and Mary Isham Randolph.

Andrews, Charles M. *The Colonial Period in American History*. New Haven, 1934–1938. 4 vols.

———. *Narratives of the Insurrections, 1675–1690*. New York, 1915.

Andrews, Matthew Page. *The Old Dominion*. New York, 1937.

Bailyn, Bernard. "Politics and Social Structure in Virginia." In *Seventeenth-Century America*. Ed. by James Morton Smith. Chapel Hill, 1959. Pp. 90–115.

Bassett, John S. "The Relation Between the Virginia Planter and the London Merchant." *American Historical Association Annual Report*. 1901–1902.

———. *The Writings of Colonel William Byrd*. New York, 1901.

Beatty, Richard Croom. *William Byrd of Westover*. New York, 1932.

Bemiss, Samuel M. *Ancient Adventurers*. Ed. by A. L. Jester. Richmond, 1964. Article on William Randolph, pp. 47–53.

———. "By Their Fruits." *Virginia Cavalcade*. III, no. 1, 39–42.

———. "Colonel Robert 'King' Carter." *Northern Neck of Virginia History Magazine*. III (December 1953), 239–240.

Benne, Kenneth D. "The Gentleman: Locke." In *The Educated Man*. Ed. by Paul Nash, Andrew M. Kazamier, and Henry J. Parkinson. New York, 1965. Pp. 191–224.

Beverley, Robert. *The History and Present State of Virginia*. Ed. by Louis B. Wright. Chapel Hill, 1947.

Blanton, W. B. *Medicine in Virginia in the Eighteenth Century*. Richmond, 1931.

Blount, C. A. C., J. S. Carlisle, T. K. Derry, and T. J. Jarman. *Great Britain: Its History from Earlier Times*. Oxford, 1962.

Boorstin, Daniel. *The Americans: The Colonial Experience*. New York, 1958.

Brant, Irving. *James Madison*. Indianapolis, 1941.

Bridenbaugh, Carl. *Colonial Craftsmen.* New York, 1950.
———. *Myths and Realities: Societies of the Colonial South.* Baton Rouge, 1952.
———. *Seat of Empire: The Political Role of Eighteenth Century Williamsburg.* Williamsburg, 1950.
Brock, R. A., ed. *The Official Letters of Alexander Spotswood, Lieutenant-Governor of the Colony, 1710–1722.* Richmond, 1882–1885. 2 vols.
Brown, Alexander. *The First Republic in America.* Boston and New York, 1908.
———. *The Genesis of the United States.* Boston and New York, 1890. 2 vols.
Brown, Katherine, and Robert E. Brown. *Virginia, 1705–1786: Aristocracy or Democracy.* East Lansing, Mich., 1964.
Brown, Stuart, R., Jr. *Virginia Baron: The Story of Thomas, Sixth Lord Fairfax.* Berryville, Va., 1965.
Bruce, Phillip A. *Economic History of Virginia in the Seventeenth Century.* New York, 1935. 2 vols.
———. *Institutional History of Virginia in the Seventeenth Century.* New York, 1910. 2 vols.
———. *Social Life of Virginia in the Seventeenth Century.* New York, 1907.
———. *The Virginia Plutarch.* New York, 1929.
Byrd, William. *The London Diary: 1717–1721.* Ed. by Louis B. Wright and Marion Tinling. New York, 1958.
———. *The Secret Diary: 1709–1712.* Ed. by Louis B. Wright and Marion Tinling. Richmond, 1941.
Campbell, Mildred. *The English Yeoman.* New Haven, 1942.
Carter, Robert Randolph, and Robert Isham Randolph. *The Carter Tree.* Santa Barbara, Calif., 1951.
Carter Letters. Virginia 350th Anniversary Celebration Corporation. Colonial Records. Survey Reports.
Caywood, Louis R. "Green Spring Plantation." *VMHB.* LXV (1957), 67–83.
Chinard, Gilbert, ed. *A Huguenot Exile in Virginia* (1682). New ed. New York, 1934.
Chumbley, George Lewis. *Colonial Justice in Virginia.* Richmond, 1938.
Conway, Moncure. *Barons of the Potomac and Rappahannock.* New York, 1892.
Craven, Avery O. *Soil Exhaustion as a Factor in the Agricultural History of Virginia and Maryland.* Gloucester, Mass., 1926.
Craven, Wesley F. *The Southern Colonies in the Seventeenth Century.* Baton Rouge, 1949.
Cresson, William Penn. *James Monroe.* Chapel Hill, 1946.
Dodd, W. E. "The Emergence of the First Social Order in the United States." *American Historical Review.* XL (1934–1935), 217–231.
Dodson, Leonidas. *Alexander Spotswood: Governor of Colonial Virginia, 1710–1722.* Philadelphia, 1932.
Donnon, Elizabeth. "Eighteenth Century Virginia Merchants." *Journal of Economics and Business History.* IV (November 1936), 70–98.
Downey, Fairfax. "Nicholson's Courtship." *VMHB.* LV (1947), 6–19.
Eckenrode, H. J. *The Randolphs.* Indianapolis, 1946.
Farrar, Emmie Ferguson. *Old Virginia Houses.* New York, 1955.
Fishwick, Marshall. *Gentlemen of Virginia.* New York, 1961.

Fitzhugh, William. *William Fitzhugh and His Chesapeake World, 1676–1701: The Fitzhugh Letters and Other Documents.* Ed. by Richard Beale Davis. Chapel Hill, 1963.

Flippen, Percy S. *The Financial Administration of the Colony of Virginia.* Johns Hopkins University Studies. Ser. 33, II. Baltimore, 1915.

————. *The Royal Government in Virginia, 1624–1775.* New York, 1919.

————. "William Gooch: Successful Royal Governor of Virginia." *William and Mary Quarterly.* Ser. 2, I, 1–38, and IV, 225–258.

Forman, Henry C. *The Architecture of the Old South: The Medieval Style, 1585–1850.* Cambridge, Mass., 1948.

————. *Virginia Architecture in the Seventeenth Century.* Jamestown Series Pamphlet. Williamsburg, 1957.

Freeman, Douglas S. *George Washington.* Vol. I. New York, 1948.

Glenn, Thomas Allen. *Some Colonial Mansions.* Philadelphia, 1899.

Goodwin, Rutherford. *Williamsburg in Virginia.* Richmond, 1936.

Greene, Jack P. "The Opposition to Lieutenant Colonel Alexander Spotswood." *VMHB.* LXX (January 1962), 35–48.

Groome, H. C. *Fauquier During the Proprietorship.* Richmond, 1927.

Handlin, Oscar. "The Significance of the Seventeenth Century." In *Seventeenth-Century America.* Ed. by James Morton Smith. Chapel Hill, 1959. Pp. 1–13.

Harrison, Fairfax. *The Equine F.F.V.'s.* Richmond, 1928.

————. "Henry Norwood, Treasurer of Virginia (1661–1673)." *VMHB.* XXXIII (1925), 1–10.

————. *Landmarks of Old Prince William.* Richmond, 1924. 2 vols.

————. "The Proprietors of the Northern Neck." *VMHB.* XXXIV (1926), 19–64.

————. "Robert Beverley, Historian." *VMHB.* XXXVI (1928), 333–342.

————. *Virginia Land Patents.* Richmond, 1925.

————. "When the Convicts Came." *VMHB.* XXX (1922), 251–260.

Hartwell, Henry, James Blair, and Edward Chilton. *The Present State of Virginia and the College* (1727). Ed. by Hunter D. Farish. Williamsburg, 1940.

Hendrick, Burton L. *The Lees of Virginia.* Boston, 1935.

Jefferson, Thomas. *Notes on the State of Virginia.* Ed. by William Peden. Chapel Hill, 1955.

Jones, Hugh. *The Present State of Virginia.* Ed. by Richard L. Morton. New ed. Chapel Hill, 1956.

Kammen, Michael G., ed. "Virginia at the Close of the Seventeenth Century: An Appraisal by James Blair and John Locke." *VMHB.* LXXIV (1966), 141–169. A summary of Locke's activity involving Virginia's government.

King, G. H. S. "Land Agents in Virginia of the Proprietors of the Northern Neck." *Northern Neck of Virginia History Magazine.* IV (December 1954), 291–297.

Kingsbury, Susan M., ed. *Records of the Virginia Company of London.* Washington, 1906–1935. 4 vols.

Laslett, Peter. *The World We Have Lost.* New York, 1965.

Lee, Edmund Jenings. *Lees of Virginia, 1642–1892.* Philadelphia, 1895.

Legg, Polly Cary. "The Governor's Ecstacy of Trouble." *William and Mary Quarterly.* Ser. 2, XXII (October 1942), 389–398.

Lockwood, Luke Vincent. *Colonial Furniture in America.* New York, 1901.

Main, Jackson T. "The One Hundred." *William and Mary Quarterly.* Ser. 3, XI (1904), 354–384.

Malone, Dumas. *Jefferson the Virginian.* Boston, 1948.

———. "Mr. Jefferson and the Traditions of Virginia." *VMHB.* 131–142.

Mason, George Carrington. *Colonial Churches of Tidewater Virginia.* Richmond, 1945.

Matthew, David. *The Social Structure in Caroline England.* Oxford, 1948.

Maurer, Maurer. "Edmund Jenings and Robert Carter." *VMHB.* LV (1947), 20–30.

———. "Notes on the Honorable Edmund Jenings." *VMHB.* LII (1944), 249–261.

Maury, Ann, ed. and trans. *Memoirs of a Huguenot Family.* New ed. New York, 1907.

McCullough, Samuel Clyde. "The Fight to Depose Governor Nicholson." *Journal of Southern History.* XII (1946), 403–422.

———. "James Blair's Place." *William and Mary Quarterly.* Ser. 3, IV (1947), 70–86.

McGill, John, compiler. *The Beverley Family of Virginia: A Genealogy.* Columbia, S.C., 1956.

Meade, William Bishop. *Old Churches, Ministers, and Families of Virginia.* Philadelphia, 1861. 2 vols.

Michel, Francis. "Report on a Journey from Berne, Switzerland, to Virginia, October 2, 1701–December 1, 1702." Trans. by William Hunke. *VMHB.* XXIV (1916), 1–43.

Montague, Ludwell Lee. "Richard Lee, the Emigrant: 1613(?)–1664." *VMHB.* LXII (1954), 3–49.

Morton, Louis. *Robert Carter of Nomini Hall.* Williamsburg, 1941.

Morton, R. L. "Robert Wormeley Carter of Sabine Hall." *Journal of Southern History.* XII (1946), 345–365.

Noel-Hume, Ivor. *Here Lies Virginia.* New York, 1963.

Notestein, Wallace. *The English People on the Eve of Colonization: 1603–1630.* New York, 1954.

Official Guidebook. Colonial Williamsburg. Williamsburg, 1961.

Osborne, J. A. *Williamsburg in Colonial Times.* Richmond, 1936.

Phillips, Ulrich B. *Life and Labor in the Old South.* Boston, 1929.

Rainbolt, John C. "A New Look at Stuart 'Tyranny': The Crown's Attack on the Virginia Assembly, 1676–1689." *VMHB.* LXXV (1967), 387–406.

Rawlings, James Scott. *Virginia's Colonial Churches.* Richmond, 1963.

Roberts, Clayton. *The Growth of Responsible Government in Stuart England.* Cambridge, England, 1966.

Rowland, Kate Mason. "Robert Carter of Virginia." *Magazine of American History.* XXX (September 1893), 115–136.

Rowse, A. L. *The Elizabethans and America.* New York, 1958.

———. *The England of Elizabeth.* New York, 1955.

Sale, Edith Tunis. *Interiors of Virginia Houses of Colonial Times.* Richmond, 1927.

Scarborough, Katherine. *Houses of the Cavaliers.* New York, 1930.

Scott, W. W. *History of Orange County.* Richmond, 1907. Pp. 98–113.

————. "Knights of the Golden Horseshoe." *William and Mary Quarterly.* Ser. 2, III, 145–153.

Severn, Earl G., ed. *Jamestown 350th Anniversary Historical Booklets.* Williamsburg, 1957. 23 vols.

Souissat, St. George L. "Virginia and the English Commercial System." *American Historical Association Annual Report.* 1906. Pp. 71–97.

Spruint, Julia Cherry. *Women's Life and Work in the Southern Colonies.* Chapel Hill, 1938.

Stanard, Mary Newton. *Colonial Virginia, Its People and Customs.* Philadelphia and London, 1917.

———— and William G. Stanard. *The Colonial Virginia Register.* Albany, 1907.

Stanard, William G. "Robert Beverley and His Descendants." *VMHB.* II (1894), 405–413; III (1895), 47–51.

Stone, Laurence. "The Anatomy of the Elizabethan Aristocracy." *Economic History Review.* XXIII (1948), 1–53.

————. *The Crisis of the Aristocracy, 1558–1640.* Oxford, 1965.

————. "The Elizabethan Aristocracy: A Restatement." *Economic History Review.* IV (1951–1952), 301–321.

Sydnor, Charles S. *Gentlemen Freeholders.* Chapel Hill, 1952.

Tawney, R. H. *Agrarian Problems in the Sixteenth Century.* London and New York, 1912.

————. "The Rise of the Gentry: 1558–1640." *Economic History Review.* XI (1941), 1–38.

Trevelyan, G. M. *England Under the Stuarts.* Rev. ed. London, 1949.

————. *English Revolution: 1688–1689.* New York, 1938.

Trevor-Roper, H. R. "The Elizabethan Aristocracy: An Anatomy Anatomized." *Economic History Review.* III (1950–1951), 279–298.

Tunis, Edwin. *Colonial Living.* Cleveland and New York, 1957.

Tyler, Lyon G., ed. *Narratives of Early Virginia.* New York, 1907.

VMHB. The following unsigned articles are to be found in the *Virginia Magazine of History and Biography:*

  "Carter Papers." V (1897), 408–428; VI (1898), 1–22, 145–152, 260–268, 365–370. Robert Carter's will.

  "Charges against Spotswood." IV (1896), 349–363.

  "Instructions to Francis Nicholson." IV (1896), 49–54.

  "Letters of the Byrd Family." XXXVI (1928), 36–44, 113–123.

  "Letters of William Byrd I." XXIV (1916), 228–237; 350–360; XXV (1917), 43–52, 128–138, 250–264, 352–364.

  "Papers Relating to the Administration of Governor Nicholson . . ." VIII (1899), 46–58, 126–146, 260–273, 366–385. Includes Nicholson's characterization of Robert Carter.

  Review of *The Ancestry of William Henry Harrison* by Charles F. Keith. II (1894). Includes wills of and data on John Carter I and John Carter II.

  "Some Colonial Letters . . ." III (1895), 349–359; IV (1896), 15–23; V (1897), 42–54.

Wagner, Sir Anthony. *English Genealogy.* Oxford, 1960.

Washburn, Wilcomb. *The Governor and the Rebel.* Chapel Hill, 1957.

Waterman, Thomas. *The Dwellings of Colonial America*. Chapel Hill, 1950.
––––––. *The Mansions of Virginia*. Chapel Hill, 1946.
–––––– and John A. Barrows. *Domestic Colonial Architecture of Tidewater Virginia*. New York and London, 1952.
Wedgwood, C. V. *The King's War, 1641–1647*. New York, 1959.
Wertenbaker, Thomas J. *Patrician and Plebeian in Virginia*. Charlottesville, 1910.
––––––. *The Planters of Colonial Virginia*. Princeton, 1922.
––––––. *Virginia Under the Stuarts*. Princeton, 1914.
––––––. *Torchbearer of the Revolution*. Princeton, 1940.
William and Mary Quarterly. The following articles are to be found in the *William and Mary Quarterly*:
"Libraries in Colonial Virginia." Ser. 1, XXVII, 90–106.
"Robert Carter and the Wormeley Estate." Ser. 1, XXVII, 252–264.
Williams, Lloyd Haynes. *Pirates of Colonial Virginia*. Richmond, 1937.
Wilstach, Paul. *Potomac Landing*. New York, 1937.
––––––. *Tidewater Virginia*. Indianapolis, 1929.
Wright, Louis B. *Cultural Life of the American Colonies*. New York, 1957.
––––––. *First Gentleman of Virginia*. San Marino, Calif., 1940.
––––––. " 'The Gentleman Library' in Early Virginia: The Literary Interest of the First Carters." *Huntington Library Quarterly*. I (October 1937), 3–61.
––––––, ed. *Letters of Robert Carter: 1720–1727*. San Marino, Calif., 1940.
––––––, ed. *Prose Works of William Byrd of Westover*. Cambridge, Mass., 1966.
––––––. "William Byrd's Defense . . ." *William and Mary Quarterly*. Ser. 3, II, 47–62.

INDEX

caste, 46, 47. *See also* social structure
Castiglione, *Courtier*, 118
"cavaliers," myths regarding, 16, 17
Chamberlain, Hugh: marries Mary Bacon, 91
Charles I of England, 16, 17, 24, 32, 33, 46, 65
Charles II of England: ascends throne, 34; personality, 35; relations with Parliament, 35, 42; exploitation of Virginia colonists, 35–36, 244; attempts to raise revenue, 35–36, 114–115; attitude to colonists, 36, 41, 100, 361; petitions to, 38, 41, 100; measures concerning Virginia, 38–39, 53, 158; instructions to Berkeley, 86; appoints Jeffreys acting governor, 86; conception of colonial discontent, 89, 114, 122; instructions to commissioners, 90; epitaph for Berkeley, 91; sends Culpeper to Virginia, 106; land grants of, 22, 100, 107, 160, 306; instructions to Culpeper, 114–115; recalls Culpeper, 117; appoints Effingham governor, 117; succeeded by James II, 122; mentioned, 33, 43, 44, 45, 48, 83, 91, 99, 121, 145
Charles City County, 48, 61, 69
Charleston, 242; Virginia volunteers sent to, 294
Chelton, John: letter from Robert Carter to, 310
Cherokee Indians, trade with, 56, 139, 243, 244
Chesapeake Bay, 5, 98, 188
Chicheley, Sir Henry: councilor, 45; deputy governor, 84; "cavalier," 105; stepfather of Ralph Wormeley II, 45, 105, 118; acting governor, 105, 106, 116
Chilton, Edward, 169, 170,
Chinn, Elizabeth Travers. *See* Travers, Elizabeth
Chiswell, Mrs. Charles, 258
Christ Church: construction of, 18, 99, 102, 330, 370; described, 370; mentioned, 177, 273, 371
Christ Church Parish, London, 97
Church of England, 14, 121, 148, 168, 197
Churchill, Priscilla: marries Robert Carter, Jr., 344
Churchill, Colonel William, 220
civil wars (English): causes of, 16; effect on Virginia, 32

Clayton, John, 251
Clayton, R., 236
Cleiss, Peter, 188
clergy: social position, 164, 167; conflict between Andros and Blair over, 168–169; conditions of, 197; support Nicholson, 198; support Spotswood, 272
Cocke, William, 237, 262, 285
Cohongarooton River, 308
Coke, Sir Edward, *Reports and Institutes*, 133, 155
Cole, William, 84
collation (bestowal of benefices), 272
College of William and Mary, 231 (*illus*); established, 158, 159, 168; board, 159; James Blair as president, 196; mentioned, 172, 175, 195, 348, 371. *See also* Wren Building
colonists: life in 1640's, 32–33; poverty of, 48, 92; menaced by Indians, 54; life during Robert Carter's time, 344, 376
colonization, English: reasons for, 25–26
Comenius, John, *Jannua Linguarum Trilingus*, 154
commissioners, royal: present Charles II's instructions to Berkeley, 86; defied by Green Spring faction and Berkeley, 89, 90; accomplishments, 90
Committee for Trade and Plantations, 115
Committee of Propositions and Grievances, 157, 161
Compton, Henry (Bishop of London), 164, 169, 171, 204
Constable, Anne, 28
Coppedge (surveyor), 310,
Corbin, Gawin, 237, 264
Corbin, Laetitia, 52
Corbin, Thomas, 220, 221, 236
Corotoman: John Carter settles at, 97, 98; inherited by John Carter II, 45, 96; Robert Carter works at, 113; interior of house described, 151; Robert Carter inherits, 151; activities at, 173–174, 285; Proprietary land office at, 181, 183, 236, 305, 309; mansion described, 223–224; wine cellars, 198, 223; life at, 320, 322; construction at, 330; naval office moved to, 345; loss at, 352; probable time of destruction, 353; inheritance

thets for Jeffreys, 92; removed from Council, 92, 123; opinions concerning Council, 93; marries Lady Frances Berkeley, 104, 216; deputy surveyor, 123; elected to Burgesses, 123; presents petition against Effingham, 145; refuses Proprietary agentship, 160; mentioned, 32, 84, 106, 146, 176
Ludwell, Philip, II: inherits Green Spring, 105, 157, 252; member of Council, 157, 179; family, 190, supports Blair against Nicholson, 198; entertains at Green Spring, 218, 224, 230; desires post of secretary, 230; appointed auditor, 237; dispute with Spotswood, 251, 252, 253, 254, 271, 275, 279; Green Spring land dispute, 252–254; inefficiency at post, 251, 253; removed from post as auditor, 254; letter from Robert Carter to, 331; mentioned, 217, 236, 248, 268, 269, 286, 331
Ludwell, Thomas: secretary, 70; challenged to duel, 70; opinion of Philip Ludwell, 93; member of Green Spring faction, 105; mentioned, 32, 43, 108
Ludwell brothers, 22, 46
Lynnhaven Bay, 189

Madison, Ambrose, 338
Madison (Maddison), James, 65
Madison, James (President), 338
Magna Carta, 8, 206
Manchester School, 283
Mannakin Indians, 73, 74
manor system, 309
manufacturing: urged by Charles II, 39; Nicholson's suggestions for, 158; concern of English merchants, 210; colonists turn to, 216
Markham, Gervase, *Way to get Wealth*, 154
Marshall, John, 338
Marshall, John (Chief Justice), 135, 138, 338, 361
Marshall, Thomas, 339
Mary, Queen of England, 145
Maryland: Indian campaigns, 5–6; and tobacco situation, 99
Maryland Gazette, 352
Mason, Collin, 310
Mathew, Thomas (merchant-planter), 4, 7; describes Bacon, 77; burgess, 131

Mathews, Samuel, 55
Mattaponi River, 80, 85
McCarthy, Daniel (burgess), 264
medicine, practice of, 105
Meekes, Richard, 292
Meherrin River, 244
mercantilism, 31
merchant-planters: commercial activities, 15, 37–38; 103, 132; characteristics, 15, 16, 27, 113; examples, 27, 126–127, 140; hold government posts, 38, 44; attitude to Bacon's Rebellion, 68; implications of Bacon's Rebellion to, 93; volume tobacco production, 96, 123–124; emerging as class, 103; responsible to colony, 103–104, 113, 144; shift to slave labor, 123–125; in Burgesses, 145; not affected by Tobacco Act, 246. *See also* planter class; social structure
merchants, English: position in Colony, 31; unload tobacco, 123; influence, 205, 206; dominate Board of Trade, 229; promote slave trade, 337; oppressive practices, 361. *See also* London merchants
Merchant's Plantation, 357
Middle Plantation. *See* Williamsburg
Middle Temple: Thomas Culpeper at, 22; William Byrd II at, 140, 170, 171; John Carter at, 286; George Carter at, 368
Middlesex County, 345
militia: purpose, 6; campaign against Doegs, 6; councilors as colonels, 44; ordered out by Spotswood, 243
Mine Tract, 278
mining: Spotswood promotes, 277; Carter family activities, 353–356
money: value in 1700, 182
Monroe (Munro), Andrew, 65
Monroe, William, 65
Moryson, Francis, 86, 93
Mount Pleasant, 52

Nansemond County, 97
Navigation Acts: history, 36; effect, 36, 122; mentioned, 48, 335
Negroes, status of free, 341. *See also* slaves
New Kent County, 72, 116
Nicholas, Elizabeth Carter Burwell. *See* Carter, Elizabeth
Nicholas, Robert: marries Elizabeth

Tidewater: described, 5, 98; Indians in, 5; social structure solidified, 337; mentioned, 181, 330, 343

tithables: tax on, 99; of John Carter, 99

tobacco: money crop, 15; cultivation, 36–37; types, 37; marketing, 40, 240; market glutted, 99; volume production, 103, 123, 124; duties, 115, 240, 245; attempts to control planting, 116; cuttings, 116; expanding market, 123; to be certified, 246; mentioned, 126, 149

Tobacco Act: controls shipping, 245; establishes public warehouses, 246; resented, 245, 247; repealed, 249; reintroduced by Gooch, 335, 336; mentioned, 263

tobacco prices: in 1640's, 32; effect of Navigation Acts on, 36, 122; in 1660's, 96; in 1680's, 123; in 1705, 213; reasons for drop, 239; in 1719, 111; for Robert Carter's crop (1720), 284; effect of "South Sea bubble," 286

towns, construction urged by Charles II, 39, 115; Nicholson proposes, 158

trade: transatlantic, new concept, 25; practices of merchant-planters, 132; during Gooch's administration, 336

Travers, Elizabeth: marries John Carter II, 151; marries Christopher Wormeley, 151; death, 151

Travers, Raleigh (burgess), 151

treasurer, post of: held by Henry Norwood, 43; created, 175; held by Robert Carter, 176; duties, 176

Tuckahoe, 338

Tucker, Robert (slave trader), 288

Tucker, Sarah, 128

Turkey Island, 137, 191

Tuscarora Indians: on warpath in North Carolina, 243, 244; mentioned, 56, 259, 277

unemployed: problem, 340; solution to problem, 341

Upton, Margaret, 292

Urbanna, 345

Varina Parish, 164

vestries: membership, 78; made elective by "Bacon's Assembly," 78; issue of self-perpetuating, 210–211; dispute over power, 271–273

Virginia Indian Company, 245, 249

Virginia planter. *See* merchant-planter; planter class

Virginians: characteristics, 184, 185, 377; emerge as separate people, 239; attitude to "Crown," 248

voting: "Bacon's Assembly" removes restrictions, 78; denied to Negroes, 341

Walpole, Sir Robert, 335

War of the Spanish Succession: Burgesses refuse to raise funds for, 199, 200; established monied interests, 205, 206; effect on tobacco market, 239, 245; colonial disinterest, 240; mentioned, 206, 228

War of Jenkins's Ear, 341

warehouses. *See* public warehouses

Warner, Mildred, 343

Washington, Augustin, 343, 361

Washington, George, 7, 343, 361, 367

Washington, John: career 6, 7, 84, 343; marries Anne Pope, 7

Washington, Laurence: marries Mildred Warner, 343; burgess, 343; mentioned, 7, 158

Washington, Laurence, II, 343

Washington, Martha Custis, 261, 367

Washington family, 343

"web of kinship": produces nucleus of oligarchy, 157; of Carter family, 157; of other families, 157–158; alliances of interest, 185, 186; mentioned, 250, 327, 343, 363

West Point, 85

Westmoreland County, 52, 84

Westover plantation: Bland holding, 69; Byrd home, 170, 191; Spotswood visits, 241; Byrd family loses, 364; described, 368, 373 (*illus*)

western expansion: Berkeley tries to contain, 54; threatened by France, 184; Spotswood encourages, 276; contributions of Robert Carter and Spotswood to, 308; mentioned, 318

Whaley, Thomas (leader in Bacon's army), 85

Wharton, Captain, 286

Whig Party, 206

Whole Duty of Man, 133

Wilderness Tract, 278

William III of England: recalls Effingham, 145; appoints Nicholson deputy governor, 145; supports Fairfax's

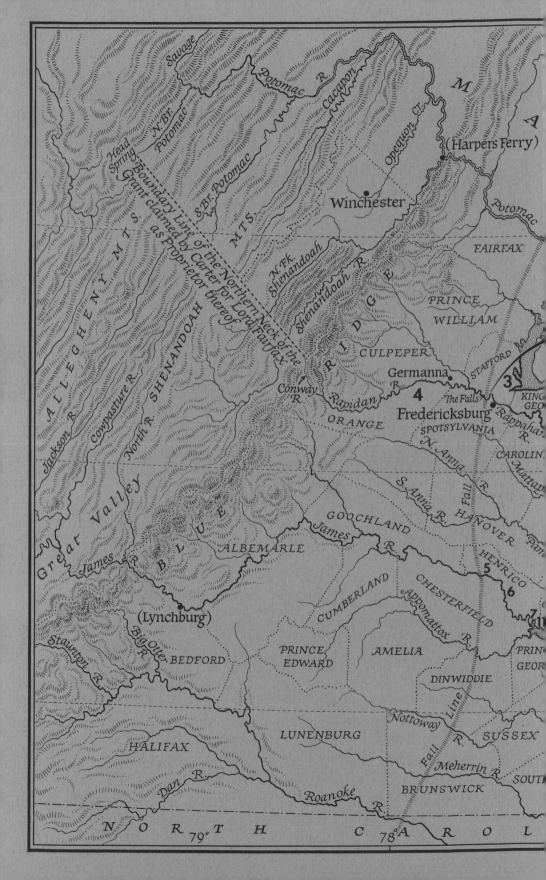

Savage

Potomac R.

Cacapon

M

A

(Harpers Ferry)

N. Br. Potomac

Head Spring

Boundary Line of the Northern Neck of the Grant claimed by Carter for Lord Fairfax as Proprietor thereof

S. Br. Potomac

Opequon Cr.

Winchester

Potomac

FAIRFAX

M T S.

N. Fk. Shenandoah

PRINCE WILLIAM

A L L E G H E N Y   M T S.

Jackson R.

Cowpasture R.

North R. SHENANDOAH

R I D G E

Shenandoah R.

CULPEPER

STAFFORD

Conway R.

Rapidan R.

Germanna

R.

4

The Falls

KING GEO.

3

Fredericksburg

Rappahan

ORANGE

SPOTSYLVANIA

CAROLIN.

B L U E

N. Anna R.

Mattap

Great Valley

GOOCHLAND

S. Anna R.

HANOVER

Pam

James R.

ALBEMARLE

James R.

HENRICO

5

James R.

CHESTERFIELD

6

7

(Lynchburg)

CUMBERLAND

Appomattox R.

Staunton R.

Big Otter R.

BEDFORD

PRINCE EDWARD

AMELIA

PRIN

GEOR

DINWIDDIE

Fall Line

HALIFAX

LUNENBURG

Nottoway R.

Fall R.

SUSSEX

Dan R.

Roanoke R.

Meherrin R.

SOUT

BRUNSWICK